SADE'S PUBLISHER

A Memoir

JEAN-JACQUES
PAUVERT

SADE'S PUBLISHER

A Memoir

JEAN-JACQUES PAUVERT

Translated from the French by Lynn Jeffress

PARIS
WRITERS
PRESS

Sade's Publisher: A Memoir
First published in France as *La traversée du livre* by Jean-Jacques Pauvert © by *Editions Viviane-Hamy*, Paris 2004

First published in the United States of America as *SADE'S PUBLISHER: A Memoir* in 2016 by Paris Writers Press.
Copyright © Paris Writers Press 2016
Translation © Lynn Jeffress 2015

The publisher wishes to thank Ian Monk for assisting with the translation and Patrick Kearney for editing the book.

This publication was granted a translation subsidy from the *Centre National du Livre, French Ministry of Culture.*

For information about this title or to order books and/or electronic media, contact the publisher:
Paris Writers Press
116 Central Park South 10 N
New York, NY 10019
www.pariswriterspress.com
pariswriterspress@gmail.com

ISBN: 978-0-9840043-6-2
ISBN: 978-0-9840043-7-9 (ebook)

Printed in The United States of America
Cover: Mara Vivat
Interior design: 1106 Design

Contents

"So, Sir,
you want to work in books."

"So, Sir, you want to work in books," Gaston Gallimard said in a paternal voice, not even in the interrogative.

A moment of silence. There was no doubt: I was the person being addressed. There were only three of us in the large director's office in what was still called, in 1941, the NRF Publishing House: my father, the publisher Gaston Gallimard and myself. I had to digest all these new things. I was fifteen years old. I was being addressed as Sir. So there was a world where one called boys of fifteen Sir. Must remember that.

And then "work in books." What did that mean? Books were a separate world, a festive world. A secret world. Everybody had his own, I supposed, just like me. What did this world have in common with the minor work experiences I had had the last few months after I had abandoned my studies definitively – or rather my studies had abandoned me? Cashier in a public bathhouse owned by one of my relatives, messenger boy in a sinister metallurgy factory, plus two or three other work attempts that I'd forgotten. So what did I know about anything?

Nothing that would impress anyone. But it was wartime. Or rather the Occupation. Money was scarce for most of the French population. When you weren't in school you had to work. Necessity makes the rules. Look for work. We looked.

Out of desperation, my father came up with an idea. Since I read a lot, why not meet with Gaston Gallimard, publisher, a lettered journalist, someone my father knew a little? And so here we were.

I nodded politely when he spoke, not knowing what else to do. Gaston Gallimard quickly moved on: as it happened, there might be a post of apprentice salesman in his bookstore on Boulevard Raspail. This was the end of 1941. You will start the beginning of 1942. Good-bye, Sir.

I

CHILDHOOD

---

*Lost in a half-conscious reverie, all my youth passed before me.
How often in the borderland of dreams, while yet the mind repels
their encroaching fancies, we are enabled to review in a few
moments the important events of a lifetime!*

— Gérard de Nerval
(Trans. by Lucie Page)

A Little History
along the way

Books. I was born inside them. You might say that. Don't imagine some sumptuous chateau library. We had been living since 1930 in a little stone suburban house in Sceaux, having moved there from Montmartre, the house built under the Loucheur law (loans made to soldiers discharged after World War I). The Sceaux line leads there. My father, a journalist with a variety of jobs, took the train home from Paris. At night, he took the Bourg-la-Reine line home. In the morning when he left, he used the Arpajonnais, a tram – with a steam engine – which transported market goods from Arpajon to Les Halles. It was around five o'clock.

In the little house there were a lot of shelves filled with books. A varied lot. My father, Marcel Pauvert, born in 1897, was the oldest son of a teacher at L'École Alsacienne, Paul Pauvert, and was destined for a university career. The war of 1914 broke out, and then Paul Pauvert, my grandfather, died suddenly in 1919. Marcel, now the head of the family (his mother, brother, and a younger sister), had to abandon the university.

He kept the Latin books (I remember the complete works of Cicero with blue covers), German books (I no longer remember the titles because of the gothic fonts), a few English. And then the classics, in cheap editions. And the rest were added little by little.

My father had to go to work at twenty-three, as soon as he was discharged. Luckily, he found work in a jewelry shop, I believe. Then in journalism – filler stories to start with.

But about the books. There were a few everywhere in the house, we never stopped buying them. More arrived every week. Frugal purchases, a few press handouts for my father. Books were too expensive to fill the whole house. But they were part of the family. There in the house books were alive. They were read, and commented on in a group. My mother, a housewife, and my brother, older than I by three years, discussed them with my father, sometimes in agreement, sometimes not. Books had their place.

Soon, I joined in the conversation. To start with, I got to know so-called children's books: old books, a little tired, the bindings coming undone. Avidly, I plunged in. Hetzel's "store of education and recreation," collections of stories, the Countess of Ségur, later Jules Verne... books which had traveled through generations, ones that dated for the most part from the post-war 1870 period, still very much part of people's memory. My parents talked of their parents who had experienced the siege of Paris and eaten rats.

During that time, my mother's father was still alive. He lived in a shack in Berneval, on the Channel coast. At his place, too, there was a library. I'll talk about it later.

I had a whole personal life that I did not share with my family. At the time, we lived in Sceaux, which was still countryside. A rather special countryside. Next to our garden, there were some fields, which the railroad ran through. The nearest neighbor was a farmer. He kept cows. But down the road there were a few houses and a grocery store.

The houses tended to get closer and closer together as you approached the station. Across from us was a modest country café, whose owner had a vegetable garden with a hen house. You rarely saw a car pass on the street, and when one stopped it was an event.

All around, there were areas of cultivated land, with broken fences, high weeds, brush, and sumptuous fruit trees, fruit that was never picked by adults because they never ventured into this paradise.

It was a children's paradise. On Thursdays, Saturdays, Sundays, I disappeared for whole days on end, alone or with a small group. A boy, some girls. The boy, Jean, was my friend. I was happy in the company of girls, and they were happy with me. We all played together, whether it was girl games or boy games. Or else I led everyone on a never-ending hunt for the source of a stream, which was sometimes underground, sometimes above ground, and which disappeared into this occasionally hard-to-penetrate jungle.

When the weather was beautiful, all of this natural area was live with noise. Birds, butterflies, flies, gnats, grasshoppers, bees and wasps made a confused din, which I listened to with an interest bordering on a passion. I observed the insects very closely. Golden beetles, which I caught in a trap of buried flow-erpots; grasshoppers, ladybugs, and cockchafers, once so common, a species that has disappeared today.

Vacations swept me still further away from the urban world of the Thirties. The biggest part of them was spent in Dordogne, six miles from the closest city (called Sainte-Foy-la-Grande, no doubt as a joke), owned by a half-ruined family. No electricity, no running water. You had to bring up jars of water from the closest source, and use acetylene lamps or gas for lighting. Two or three communities grouped together, including ours, still using a horse-drawn buggy at the time to go shopping in town.

So I escaped, alone this time, into the forests, the vineyards and the fields. Into the huge holes they called chasms, because it was a place where the earth caved in here and there. There were springs and marshlands. I observed an astonishing aquatic world: tadpoles, salamanders and, above all, water insects: nepes, water spiders, beetles, ferocious dragonfly larvæ – a world which absorbed me for hours on end as I crouched among the grasses at the water's edge, on the lookout.

And then the night, by candlelight, reading in a bed which sometimes rustled with the brief passage of a mouse under the sheets. The house was very old, sixteen-hundred and something. It creaked everywhere.

School?

Then there was school, of course... My first year, four years old, September 1930. My last at Lakanal High school, in Sceaux. A daily nightmare. Everything was black, like every Second Empire high school, the classroom, the blackboard, the enormous instructor, Mme. Ricomar, whose name has always stayed with me: a black elephant, a whale, a fat spider. Probably not mean, but brusque, awkward, severe. Not to my taste, anyway.

Then, suddenly, at the end of six months, a metamorphosis: they transferred me to a newly created kindergarten. Everything was light and pink, including, it seemed to me, the young and pretty teacher. We played in class, on new desks, with cubes and novel objects. We opened clean, new books. It was the beginning of modern education. I was happy there for the moment.

And then reading: I was among the first in my class, if not the first. I was ahead of the others. I'd learned to read very early at home with my mother. I think I can remember (I think) the first time when the lines that had before been incomprehensible signs on white paper jumped out at me as several words that meant something, metamorphosing suddenly from obscure flies' feet into meaningful terms which were readable at last. This is a lasting impression which I am still sure I experienced, even if I'm often told that such a thing is impossible.

Aside from these first years, reading and school rarely coincided. There were French lessons, of course. But in fifth grade I had a terrible teacher – in my opinion, at least. Imbecilic, arrogant, mean, disdainful. At that point I stopped listening. I just got by from class to class, ending with a last term at a well-heeled middle school run by psychiatrists near Compiègne where my parents couldn't keep me because they didn't have enough money. I was accepted at the last minute into the sixth grade at Lakanal with Paul Schricke, my friend Daniel's French and Latin teacher.

Paul Schricke worked hard to make good my examination grades so that I could pass easily. It was the first time a teacher had really taken an interest in me. He was intelligent, a good instructor, and, as I later learned, the author of an excellent grammar book. I respected him and I listened. Suddenly, I got a second place in French, which that year earned me a "Saint Charlemagne" dinner. A second place in natural sciences, too, but there was no follow up. The young teacher claimed, for example, that green grasshoppers were herbivores, although they were eating each other with great alacrity in the box I kept them in. Therefore, he was an ignoramus. I gave up in a fresh divorce from official knowledge. And then there was math: a catastrophe. I started playing truant. And spoken languages? They made me begin German: I was put off by the gothic letters.

My break with education was nearing when the war broke out September 1939, which temporarily made it easier for me to stay in school. However, I had to do my sixth grade over with Paul Schricke. Meanwhile, everything else was falling apart. They replaced German with English. I resisted the absurd phonetic characters, which supposedly stood for the pronunciation. I didn't see the point of this complication. My truancy got worse. I sloppily forged letters of excuse on my father's visiting cards. All hell broke loose.

But I still read a lot. At thirteen, what was I reading? Anything I could find. *Les Hommes de bonne volonté* by Jules Romains and the *Chronique des Pasquier* by Duhamel, the successive volumes of which were read by my family, along with everything and anything else. For example, there was *Locus Solas* (by a certain Roussel, an unknown author), which I read in short spurts, while feeling very uneasy. There was Jarry: *Ubu roi* of course, but also *Le Surmâle*, which fascinated me. And doctor *Faustroll*. As well as the *Minutes de sable mémoria*, which impressed me by creating a funereal ambiance that I couldn't explain. Victor Hugo, and Dumas: with mixed feelings. And so many other books.

My father, who followed my reading, began by giving me his favorite books of poetry: *Les Trophées*, by Heredia, and *La Négresse blonde*, by Georges Fourest. My father was a great lover of spoonerisms and Rabelais. Puns attracted me. I started to make a few – not always very good ones.

There were also, mixed in with the rest, some mediocre books devoured along with the others which raised questions: how was it, for example, that their writing bothered me at times, while certain other passages kept my interest?

And then Littré's *Dictionnaire de la langue française*, an object of paternal veneration. I consulted it often after the age of twelve. At the same time I began to read it systematically, page by page, which took a long time. I didn't abandon this project until I was nearly twenty, and I was still only mid-way though the letter "D."

I have to say that when I was about thirteen to fourteen years old, I rather often read and reread books that raised my parents' eyebrows (especially my mother's) when they found them in my hand. *Aphrodite* and Pierre Louÿs: a great discovery. The historical novels of Maurice Maindron, so long (and unjustly) forgotten: *Saint-Cendre, Monsieur de Clerambon, Le Tournoi de Vauplassans.* And titles which are even less well-known and more obscure than ever, for ever so, one might say; for example, *Monseigneur voyage*, by Gaston Chereau, certain passages of which plunged me into a delicious queasiness last time I reread them.

And Colette, whose every move was an exquisite mix of literary and sensual emotion. Every Colette that I could find...

Sometimes there were family discussions – should he be allowed to read such and such – which always ended in the same way: anyway, how can we stop him? My father was infinitely indulgent. My mother loved me too much to hold me back. So I snooped among books.

Note: there was no secret, genuine "erotica" in our house. Not a hint of Sade.

But there was *Les Liaisons dangereuses* which I grabbed without delay after only a quick glance and took to my room. I now had my own room in the loft and my own bookcase. *Les Liaisons dangereuses* would hold sway for a long time.

When I was around thirteen, I also enthusiastically discovered at my grandfather's his Arsène Lupin in illustrated editions by Pierre Laffitte, and Rosny aîné (Joseph Henri Honoré Boex), with his *La Guerre du feu, Vamireh* and *Félin géant.* Vacations at Berneval would now be bathed in the strange light from the dizzying spiral through which I fell into long-gone days, thousands of years before.

Reading Arsène Lupin made me drift off into a dream because of the enormous distance he stood from society. Alone against the establishment, he tricked everybody. *L'Aiguille creuse, Le Bouchon de cristal.* Not to forget Jules Verne, who went everywhere with me in the old Hetzel edition. But at Berneval there was also Octave Mirbeau and Jules Renard, among others, in great illustrated (but cheap) editions, from before 1914. So many discoveries.

There were no complete works by any author in these actually quite modest bookcases, so I made requests. When I liked an author, I wanted to read everything. And my parents bought them for me – little by little – in small modern editions. It was a collision course with the Green collection for Jules Verne or the Pink one for the Comtesse de Ségur, or the Question Mark for Arsène Lupin, which meant that they lost some of their magic. I then had to learn to separate the text – which kept its prestige, more or less – from the period wrapping it was put in. There were two things that went their separate ways, though not entirely. This was an abrupt (but profitable) lesson in reality, which worked its way through the basement of my mind – only to resurface later.

A Little More History...

I followed the news, thanks to my father. Thanks to him, I learned not to believe journalists, nor the radio, which was more and more widespread. February 6, 1934, and the days that followed, the stories we heard on the radio, for example, often contradicted those we read in the press. Short news items took on another color. The death of Stavisky and the assassination of the magistrate Albert Prince opened up a whirl of thoughts for me. The Spanish Civil War became less black and white with its controversies. My grandfather, an anarchist, Freemason, and veteran of the disciplinary battalions during the Tonkin War (as it was called before 1914), added his personal insights into the unfolding of events. I listened.

Events speeded up, accelerating at the same fiery rate as my apprenticeship. From September 1939 to September 1940, we were thrown into another space-time continuum, without at first even realizing it. Especially me. I was at an age when you ride with the flow of time at the same speed as it goes by, straddling epochs as though riding on a flying carpet, with the unstated understanding that there will later be a taking of stock.

Let's return to the beginning of 1939. Politics were being discussed by my father and grandfather. They talked about Hitler, about England, the camps in Russia (they didn't yet say "concentration camps," or "gulag"). I was unclear about who was fighting whom. The war reminded me of the one in 1870, not so far back in my family's memory, and that of 1914–18, which was closer. It broke out just before the new school year and was unlike anything I'd experienced before, thus making me feel even more that all of this, even if it interested me, concerned me very little. I was in the front row, watching a series of rapidly changing scenes.

For the moment, there were nothing but words and images. My father, with two children, was now too old to be drafted, and my brother was sixteen. The front lines were not moving, except in Poland. It was the "phony war." We read the communiqués in the papers. We – I – understood very little.

At the high school, all was calm. Except me. I was getting good marks for essay writing and textual analysis. The rest seemed increasingly distant, lost in a fog. What difference did it all make! My discipline broke down. I became more and more footloose. That winter was harsh but beautiful. The electric cables in the streets were covered with transparent ice, which looked lovely. The snow held up for three months in the fields around Sceaux.

The spring of 1940 was superb. I remember radiant weather starting in May, when the French front snapped under a single blow: 1870 and 1914–18 were suddenly light-years away. A new war had begun. There was a rush of armored vehicles and diving fighter planes. Suddenly it was a debacle.

Before long there was an exodus, which came to a head in June. My brother had just got his driver's license, in time for my mother and me (my father stayed in Paris) to get into an old Renault KZ, the same model as the Marne taxis, bought from an aunt of my mother's. Stuffed with mattresses, suitcases and bikes, our KZ got in line with the other vehicles (gas or horse-driven, along with tanks, and some armored cars) all heading south. One half of France was folded over the other. It took us three days to arrive on the old family property in Dordogne, after various incidents.

And a surprise was waiting for us! The city hall of this tiny town had requisitioned our old house to lodge some refugees from the north who had arrived before us. We in turn requisitioned the modern part of the adjacent building (dating from around 1800). It belonged to some cousins who had left it abandoned since 1918. It was much bigger, even though half of it had been demolished. The roof was in tatters and the woodwork rotten in places. But we would have enough room. And then a few years later it became ours.

Meanwhile, the building filled up. A few days later my father arrived shaken, his feet bleeding, with a week-long beard. Before long my Uncle Jacques (my father's brother) turned up in uniform in an army car, but with his nine-year-old son Christian, my first cousin. Uncle Jacques gave me a brand-new police rifle. We listened to the radio, we talked, I heard the voice of an old man bleating from the radio:

"I make a gift of myself to France." My father didn't seem to agree with this. Everybody discussed it. The Germans cut France in half with a demarcation line. We were in the non-occupied zone along with Vichy and Pétain.

I was fourteen, and freer than ever: the woods, springs and marshes belonged to me. The adult world was falling apart, apparently, but not mine.

I explored the huge house. I rummaged through the attics.

It was there that I made some amazing discoveries in publications from before 1914: the *Journal de l'Université des Annales*, illustrated reviews, some incomplete volumes of works dating from the 18th century, in period editions, some Erckmann-Chatrian, with illustrations from the late 19th century Hetzel edition.

Above all there were copies of the *Journal de l'Université des Annales* from before the previous war, along with some literary reviews from the same period. Thanks to this journal I discovered literature which was forward looking, often a little academic obviously, but singularly alive. Even more so, because the *Journal de l'Université des Annales* consisted in large part of lectures and literary investigations, it was illustrated with numerous photos of writers.

I came upon, in particular, a series of lectures on poetry by Auguste Dorchain (1857–1930, "a poet with a delicate imagination," according to the old *Larousse*). I remember a lecture in which Dorchain, daringly for the period, brought together Victor Hugo, Verlaine and Rimbaud under what pretext I have now forgotten but which was far from being inept. This was the Victor Hugo of:

> In the setting sun
> you who look for
> gold,
> watch you don't fall,
> the evening earth is
> brown.
> ("La Chanson du Fou" *Trans. by Robert Cole*)

Alongside the Verlaine of:

> Your soul is as a moonlit landscape fair,
> Peopled with maskers delicate and dim,
> That play on lutes and dance and have an air
> Of being sad in their fantastic trim.
> ("Claire de Lune" – Fêtes Galantes. *Trans. by Gertrude Hall*)

And the Rimbaud of:

> It is found again.
> What? Eternity.
> It is the sea
> Gone with the sun.
> ("L'Éternité" *Trans. by Louise Varese*)

All at once, I had arrived at a higher level than Heredia or Sully Prudhomme, and Victor Hugo had been elevated above the little I knew of him before.

I had discovered unknown but intuited territory, something I had been blindly groping for.

What state was I in when we returned to Paris in September 1940, to my mother's uncle's house, in rue Notre-Dame-des-Champs? I no longer know. We didn't see my uncle often. His name was André Salmon. He was a friend, if that were possible, of Max Jacob's. He was above all a friend of Apollinaire's. On July 13, 1909, André Salmon married a model who posed for artists in Montparnasse. We called her Jannot and still do. Apollinaire wrote a poem about the marriage. It's in *Alcools*:

> They've adorned Paris with flags because my friend André Salmon is getting married...
> ...love determines that today my friend André Salmon is getting married.
> ("Poème lu au mariage d'André Salmon" *Trans. by Anne Hyde Greet*)

By 1940, beautiful Jannot had become a fat gossip, filthy and cantankerous, always in the same slippers, with the heels trodden down. André Salmon patiently put up with her, then used to explode. He welcomed me warmly, loaned me books: Cocteau, Cendrars, Apollinaire, Max Jacob.

With Apollinaire and *Alcools* I discovered a whole world I had not known before. The years 1940–41 broadened my field of vision enormously, widened my horizons, opened up borders that revealed vistas little known to me up till then, which I felt my way around slowly but surely.

Apollinaire! I kept *Alcools* for a long time, as it was unavailable from bookstores. André Salmon's copy, like all his books, had a plate with a sumptuous dedication, which I've forgotten, alas! André Salmon was born the same year as Apollinaire. I held onto *Alcools* for several months. Before giving it back, I copied out parts of it.

In the library in Sceaux, I was now reading Céline. *Mort à crédit* which astounded me (not to mention the passages that were half censored and left blank): it was a new language. A new language? How is this possible?

> Towards the end, my old concierge was unable to speak. She was suffocating, she clung to my hand...The postman came in. He saw her die. A little hiccup. That's all. In the old days, lots of people used to knock on her door and ask for me. Now they're gone, far away

into forgetfulness, trying to find souls for themselves. The postman took off his cap. Me, I could have vented all my hatred. I know. I'll do that later on if they don't come back. I'd rather tell stories. I'll tell stories that will make them come back just to kill me, from the ends of the world. Then it will be over and that will be all right with me. *(Translated by Ralph Manheim).*

This added to the rest, without replacing anything. It simply occupied a corner of my mind, at a slight remove.

I was also reading *Bagatelles pour un massacre*, which seemed extraordinarily funny to me; with its attitudes and injustice, it was difficult to take seriously. Besides, I read in *La Nouvelle Revue Française* (NRF) (my father also got the NRF) an article by André Gide (I read a lot of André Gide, especially *Les Faux Monnayeurs*, *Paludes*, and all of *Prétextes*) with which I rather agreed:

> It seems to me that the criticism, in general, has gone a bit astray in terms of *Bagatelles pour un massacre*. How could it be so mistaken is what surprises me. In fact, Céline is gambling for high stakes. The highest stakes possible; as he always does. He doesn't mince words. He does his best to say that none of it was any more serious than Don Quixote's ride in midair.
>
> You remember the fuss that was made about his two first books. Then when Céline talks about a sort of conspiracy of silence, a coalition to stop the sale of his books, it's clear he's being funny. And when he makes the Jew responsible for his lack of sales, it's obvious that it's a joke. If it's not a joke, Céline would be completely crazy. The same thing holds true when he pell-mell throws Cezanne, Picasso, Maupassant, Racine, Stendhal and Zola into his massacre along with the Jews...This isn't reality that Céline is describing; it's an hallucination which reality provokes; and this is what interests me. Who would dream of seeing in the following lines the innocent Tuileries Gardens on a feast day?
>
> It was more than an enormous delirium, this crater two miles wide, rumbling of the abyss and of drunks.
>
> It spewed forth cuts of meat, pieces of ass, kidneys thrown far and wide, beyond rue Royale and into the clouds... There was an implacable odor, innards in urine and whiffs of corpses, *foie gras* cut up very small...You ate it in the atmosphere...There was no escape. Three stunning embankments the entire length of the terraces made

it impossible... Baby carriages stacked six stories high... (André Gide
La Nouvelle Revue Française, April 1938.)

This same thing goes on throughout *Bagatelles pour un Massacre*. Céline
piles "six stories high" pathetic, useless jokes like the ones we hope he will
continue to make in his following books... As for the question of "semiticism,"
it is not even touched upon. If there was anything else in *Bagatelles pour un
Massacre* except a game, Céline, in spite of all his genius, would have no excuse
for stirring up banal passions with this kind of cynicism and casual frivolity.

The question of "semiticism," at the time, went over my head. But I got
to the end of *Mort à Crédit*, (*Voyage* also, but less so) as though ending an
explosive expedition in which everything, language, the hopeless vision of
the universe, seemed to be happening in a new world. My father didn't share
my enthusiasm. We began to have intense discussions. He tried to trap me by
citing verse: "Who is this? Mallarmé?" Not at all: it's Heredia. I knew Mallarmé
well by then, which left him quite indifferent. I learned that intelligence was
only one approach to things, and sometimes divisions existed.

On November 30, 1941, André Salmon inscribed his *Saint-André* to me:

> To my handsome nephew
> Jean-Jacques Pauvert
> Whose clear eye pierced so soon
> The screen
> Of the world of appearances and
> poetic prestige
> his old uncle
> André Salmon

I read all the books that André Salmon inscribed for my mother, his niece. In spite of an honest effort, I can remember only the epic pulse of his poem "Prikaz," and the disturbingly hermetic nature of his novel *Archives du club des onze*. Something disembodied lay at the bottom of most of his writing, it seemed to me. The importance of the flesh was beginning to show itself to me. I reread the preface to *Aphrodite:*

> "Sensuality is the mysterious but necessary and creative condition for intellectual development. Those who have not felt either through loving or damning the demands of the flesh are not capable of understanding the sweeping demands of the mind."

My Education,
The End

The end of school for me was bumpy, like all things when they are in their last moments. At the beginning of school, in 1940, Lakanal High School was requisitioned by the Germans and moved in its entirety to the girls' high school Marie-Curie, a little bit higher up the hill in Sceaux. As a miracle under the Occupation, I was able to enter high school, thanks to some underhanded trickery. It all ended well, as it turned out. I skated through my courses, more and more absent.

I still remember two teachers: one was a man named Baudoin who taught natural science, because of a talk he gave during our first class. His throat tight, he announced that it was necessary to work because our old France no longer existed. "That France is dead," he told us, his eyes misting over (we could clearly see this behind his glasses, even me, and I was in the last row). All this was moving, in spite of his overblown rhetoric. But we found him ridiculous as he rose up vainly on his little heels to give more weight to his words.

Our French teacher was much more interesting. José Lupin. I'm giving his real name. There is no reason not to, on the contrary. He is dead now. And besides, he has a certain importance in my story.

José Lupin was young in 1940. About thirty, I suppose. Short hair, glasses, he used familiar but authoritative language to announce his project to us at the outset: he detested over-sized classes, and as he had to start the year with more than forty students, he intended to end it with fewer than thirty.

I already felt that this didn't really concern me. I was a long way from being part of this world. But even so, Lupin's lessons interested me. They were far livelier than Paul Schricke's, and at last they dealt with authors who were familiar to me, who were discussed with feeling. It was through him – let's say rather with him – that Chateaubriand entered my collection, firstly in an imaginary work. José Lupin read out the first chapters of *Mémoires d'outre-tombe* well:

Supper finished and the four guests having returned from the table to the fireplace, my mother threw herself, sighing, onto an old cotton and silk day bed; we put a pedestal in front of her with a candle on it. I sat near the fire with Lucile; the servants cleared away the supper things and withdrew. My father then began to walk up and down which didn't stop until he went to bed. He was dressed in a white terry cloth robe, or rather, a kind of coat that I had never seen anyone but him wear. His head, semi-bald, was covered with a large white bonnet which stood straight up. When he had walked a long way down the hall we couldn't see him anymore the enormous room was so badly lit by a single candle; we only heard him walking in the shadows; then he slowly returned toward the light and little by little emerged from obscurity, like a ghost, in his white robe and his white bonnet, a tall, pale figure. Lucile and I exchanged a few words in low voices when he was at the other end of the room; we were silent when he came back towards us. As he passed by he said: 'What were you talking about?' Terrified, we said nothing; he continued walking. The rest of the evening we heard only the noise of his footsteps, the sighs of my mother and the murmur of the wind.

He also read us *Les Fleurs du mal* advising us to buy it – which I instantly did in the little Payot edition, nicely printed on beautiful paper, illustrated with drawings by Baudelaire:

The kind-hearted servant of whom you were jealous…
(Trans. by William Aggeler)

There are perfumes fresh as children's flesh,
Soft as oboes, green as meadows…
(Trans. by Geoffrey Wagner)

The violin quivers like a tormented heart,
A tender heart, that hates the vast, black void!
The sky is sad and beautiful like an immense altar;
The sun has drowned in its blood which congeals…
(Trans. by William Aggeler)
I soon knew the rest by heart:

We shall have beds full of subtle perfumes,
Divans as deep as graves…

My darling was naked, and knowing my heart well,
She was wearing only her sonorous jewels...
And her arm and her leg, and her thigh and her loins,
Shiny as oil, sinuous as a swan,
Passed in front of my eyes, clear-sighted and serene;
And her belly, her breasts, grapes of my vine...
(Trans. by William Aggeler)

And Nerval:

A pure spirit grows under the bark of stones...
Sighs of the saint and the cries of the fairy...

And *Le Bateau ivre:*

Eternal spinner of blue stillness
I miss Europe with its ancient parapets!

I had just been introduced to the highest level of language. Infinite, new vistas were opening up.

I no longer know if all the authors he told us about were on the program (I hope they weren't). I remember having been literally hypnotized by José Lupin's presentation of certain pages by La Bruyère (I still am). Yes, La Bruyère was probably on the program. But the others?

Words. The art of words. Sentences that we use every day could break up into a shower of sparkling lights.

Timidly, I started to make tentative constructions using these materials both common and brand new.

One day, when José Lupin was set to talk to us about Villon, I came to class with an edition of Villon illustrated by Dubout. He bent over my book and we talked. The course was often interrupted by brief conversations between the two of us. I had surprised him, I think, on another occasion by successfully (!?) writing a set poem using the end rhymes of some verses by Verhaeren. I only remember the first alexandrine, whose final word (the only one imposed) was "air." I wrote:

Unexpectedly, in the night, a breath of air...

Then, apparently inspired by the other end rhymes, I produced a dozen verses which seemed to me (and I was the first one to be surprised) rather good – for French homework.

José Lupin stopped stopped and read it, murmuring distinctly, "Not bad, not bad at all." After that, he made fun, pretty harshly, of the poor attempts by the best students in the class in other subjects, like mathematics. I was thrilled. I should point out that we were all in a sort of rivalry, and their good grades irritated me sometimes, just as my rare unforeseen successes disturbed them.

José Lupin read the newspaper *Je suis partout* (as everybody did). He even published a short story in it (not very good; I was disappointed). He was a supporter of the "National Revolution" and youth government. I must say that his ideas, which we guessed rather easily (because we could make out – even distantly – the different lines of political thought which were beginning to form) were only conveyed to us through quotes from Montherlant or Corneille, with discreetly veiled allusions to the advanced age of certain heads of State, and by referring repeatedly to historical heroes who were eighteen or twenty years old and had done particularly well in antiquity or under Henri IV. We noted all of this – at least I did – with interest and not being particularly troubled, except for a few rare diehards with other opinions.

Before the end of the second trimester, José Lupin showed his hand by reading out a list of the names of those students he wanted to see expelled. There were a dozen. He gave his reasons. Briefly for some, generally because of their poor marks. But with more personal reasons for others, including me.

Pauvert, to sum up his words, had better – or other – things to do than study, so he showed little inclination for it. Certain studies seemed especially alien to him. An education, no matter which direction it took, had to be a vocation. I was certainly gifted for something, but he didn't know what. Then he wished me good luck, sincerely, I think.

It was awhile before my parents saw what was happening. My father tried a last recourse. Being the son of a teacher at L'École Alsacienne and a former student himself, he saw to it that I did my last trimester there, rue Notre-Dame-des Champs, by the metro station Port Royal, on the Sceaux line.

I was interested, as much as I could be, by L'École Alsacienne. First of all because it was mixed; a new society could be found there, one in which I felt more balanced. And then because the classes were of a quality (to my modest knowledge) unrivaled in state high schools. And finally because some students were at an unusually high level, and I, oddly enough, felt at home there. I bonded with them. I even made some progress. Too late, however. In July '41, my parents were informed that it was useless for me to go back to rue Notre-Dame-des-Champs in October.

I had learned a great deal in three months. I had realized that while I was learning with other people, I too had something to offer. For example, I remember arriving in class with some books by Valéry in the NRF collection, lavishly printed on *alfa* paper. I was the only one who had read Valéry. I was very drawn to another student, Deschamps, who had read, in turn, philosophers whom I didn't know. He was upset that I was leaving L'École Alsacienne. He could already picture me at "Normale Sup" where he was headed. But it was a world that already had no meaning for me.

I also learned certain other little things. In the end, it was my first contact with the very heart of society. I realized that I didn't know anything about certain customs. For example, another student offered me a glimpse of how some members of the upper middle-class modeled their offspring. This student, although modest-looking, apparently came from an industrial family which was very rich, and he loaned me five francs (at the time, actually very little: about seven francs fifty in 2000). I was late returning it to him. When I did, at the end of a month, I think, he told me, apparently offhand, that I owed him interest on top. I think this ended up being five per cent, a lesson that stayed with me. Money in a certain milieu is not important, but it is taken very seriously.

No more École Alsacienne. A definitive break. Seven or eight of us found ourselves in July 1941 at a certain Magali's, a girl we were all in love with. There were other girls there I hardly looked at. It was a fairly joyful get-together. I observed their manners, which were unknown to me: for instance, how to greet the parents who met us at the door before we discreetly retired to another room. I didn't know any of this.

We talked very freely. The conversation centered on the future for those of us who had been failed (I wasn't the only one, far from it). Some talked about their private coaching, always with the idea of continuing their education, more or less. I didn't see myself in that position. Two other students expressed rather different opinions. The first I'll call Ballorey (I remember his name perfectly well). He was sixteen, a year older than most of us, because he had had to repeat classes several times, being a little slow. He rather vehemently gave a speech that we had already heard, but about which he appeared to be convinced: he had had enough of school, these were serious times, and the war was in fact between the West and the East, represented by Soviet Russia (which Germany had suddenly attacked a few days before). So he was going to sign up for the newly created LVF (French Volunteer Legion). We were rather impressed by his self-assurance. Nothing else.

Someone else amicably suggested that he had misunderstood the situation: General de Gaulle (whom we were vaguely beginning to talk about) was, he said, Marshal Pétain's representative in England. Absolutely certain. The two of them were preparing for an important war later aimed at defending the West against the USSR, but they didn't want to support Germany too much, which held excessive, hegemonic views. He leaned toward de Gaulle. There was a general discussion, a rather short one. We realized we were exchanging adult opinions – which were pretty confused. We quickly went on to other things that were more entertaining.

Ballorey did in fact join the LVF a little later (I knew because he stayed in contact with some of the students from L'École Alsacienne whom I also saw for a while). I don't know what became of him.

Also in July 1941 – was it before or after the afternoon at Magali's? – a number of us (from Lakanal this time) ended up at José Lupin's, a visit initiated by my friend Jean-Pierre Castelnau who had also found him interesting. José Lupin cordially gave us something to drink, offered up some general, relatively well-thought-out ideas, and once again wished me good luck.

Then it was over. My parents were dumbstruck, never having envisaged anything else for their two sons other than education, as they had always supposed us to be brilliant. My brother, who was very serious and focused, satisfied them. But what to do with me? Put me to work? Given my age, I could only be an apprentice. That, in principle, demanded a certificate of education, which I didn't have. What was worse, I categorically refused to get one. After several fruitless tries at answering Help Wanted ads, then two attempts, on Sundays, at working the cash register in a bath house in the suburbs for Uncle Jacques, my father had what he thought was a good idea...

II

EVENTS

—————

Events are the spume of things.

— Paul Valéry

A Flower Shop

As for me, I wasn't at all so sure. I found myself a little in the situation of an adolescent in love with flowers who, from one day to the next, is made a delivery boy for Interflora. But be that as it may.

At the end of 1941, life began to get hard in France. The winter of 1940–41 was relatively calm, but from the spring on, food became scarce and prices started to climb at a dizzying rate. Restrictions were talked about, as well as the "black market." Coupons were king on the official market. You had to survive and get along by any means possible. As I was not in school, this meant I was a child to be taken care of with no state aid. Everybody in the family had to do their part. In the end, *everybody* meant me when it came down to it.

From the end of June to December, in this world at war, forces attacked and counter-attacked. I remember Germany turning against her ally of the day before: without warning, the Wehrmacht attacked the USSR. In October it had almost reached Moscow. On December 7 it was Pearl Harbor: Japan attacking America.

About that time, an imperceptible event occurred: I was in the office of Gaston Gallimard. A few days afterwards, at the beginning of 1942, I was in the Gallimard Bookstore, at 15 boulevard Raspail.

The Gallimard Bookstore –
The Left Bank In 1942

The Gallimard Bookstore, boulevard Raspail, a stone's throw from the rue du Bac (it's still there), is rather large. The Gallimard brothers started it right after WWI. In 1942 it consisted of three distinct divisions: the reading room, directed by Madame Van der Pere, a very dignified woman with white hair, a corsage made of lace and a lorgnette; the rare editions, kept under glass, to the left of the entrance door, and separated from the store by a partition of shelves containing bound books; and finally, the bookstore proper with M. Watin, the first clerk, officiating, and the second clerk, Maria, a small brown-haired mother, who was an Italian Catholic (was she from Italy?), lively and talkative.

At the either end of the bookstore, the two heads, relatively speaking, of the enterprise could be found. At the back was the director M. Saucier who was to play a certain role in my existence; a tall man in his forties, with a neat, discreet elegance, most of the time residing in a closed office which he left only on important occasions. Near the entrance door, by the cash register, was Mlle. Sigle, a dried-up spinster with a chignon, a typical cashier, who surveyed everything from her observatory. She was keeper of the keys to the bookstore which she opened each morning, always on time, and closed at night, the last one to leave unless M. Saucier stayed late in his office, for mysterious reasons, with important clients from other large bookstores, selling rare editions.

Finally there was the messenger boy, the owner of a bicycle he polished twenty times a day (when he was there), aged about thirty, a classic Parisian look, and always in golf pants (this detail will have its importance later).

I modestly took the place assigned me, at the bottom of the list. Everyone was basically welcoming. I rather took an interest in M. Watin, who was touched. He was a bachelor, in his thirties, already balding, a bit stooped, with an extraordinary archive of the bookstore in his mind. Not very intelligent (to my mind), but gifted with the mechanical memory of a chess player, he could answer anything concerning the bookstore as it was then. That is, he not only always knew the exact title and author, but also the publisher, the precise year of publication, if there had been other editions, which were different or not, with whom and when, and of course the complete biography of the author. What was more, he was in on all the rumors about the world of publishing and the whole history of its milieu. I was to learn a lot from him.

He immediately pointed out a sensational first novel, which had appeared at the end of 1941: *Les Coups,* by Jean Meckert. Soon an article, by Gide, appeared in *Le Figaro.* I was convinced. I immediately put *Les Coups* among my bedside books.

During 1942, the world at war was on fire. In Russia, in Africa, in Asia. The Battle of Stalingrad began in September. The Japanese occupied China and Indochina.

France started to come out of its stupor, but survived in isolation, as though living under a lid. The most surprising rumors circulated, being confirmed or denied by carefully filtered or biased news in the papers. We were equally suspicious of British radio, which we listened to uneasily, despite the interference. My father, now at the press bureau housed in the *Préfecture de police* (tel. # ODE 22 20, I still remember), on boulevard du Palais, completed and corrected the news when he could.

I find in a book by Jean Grenier, written day by day, during the Occupation (which is its title: *Sous l'Occupation*), but published by Claire Paulhan in 1997, notes which give a good idea of the climate in the 6th arrondissement in '41–'42. In particular, this book strikes me by the calm objectivity with which it presents the question of collaboration by intellectuals in 1942, from an unexpected angle, far from all the comic book reconstitutions to which young (and not so young) people willingly surrender themselves today:

> One can be in fact part of the Collaboration for many different reasons, because one thinks that the future of France has always been in an alliance with Germany, because one judges the pact to be preferable to resistance, or finally because it is in one's personal interest to be on this side. This last case is that of almost all the collaborationist writers but not all. They do however have excuses, the condition of a writer, as an artist, is the least independent of all: a writer is subjected to all sorts of capricious opinions, depends on the rich, on administrators, on governments. In their youth, writers wanted to escape from social constraints, those which weigh on businessmen, functionaries, craftsmen, workers, and ends by

falling under a tighter yoke, which is that of money or the State. He sells his pen, as they say.

Further on, this little picture of Saint-Germain-des-Prés in 1942:

> ...Two cafés in Saint-Germain-des-Prés share collaborationist customers: Le Flore, cradle of Action française, and where one finds writers like Chateaubriant and Grasset, and above all the Brasserie Lipp where you run into, aside from Picasso who takes almost no interest in politics, writers like Fargue, Fernandez, Thierry Maulnier, etc.
>
> The Brasserie Lipp is also the gathering place of the rich from the Saint-Germain neighborhood, particularly Sunday evenings, when they come to eat sauerkraut because the help at home is gone for the weekend.

In 1942, Jean Grenier didn't talk a lot about writers who were "resistants," as we still called them then. First of all because there were hardly any, at least not openly stated, and then because they were closely mixed in with the collaborationists, often sharing the same table, rather peacefully discussing everything. It was only later they began to form opposing groups.

For the moment, the lid hadn't come off the pot.

I got to know the city a little better. The École Alsacienne had taken me into Paris on the Sceaux line, right to Port-Royal, and now I pushed on further to the next station, Luxembourg, the end of the line at the time, antechamber to Saint-Germain-des-Près.

Around 1938, steam engines were replaced by electric tracks. Rail crossings with marked stops were replaced with cement guard rails. A great rail line going into Paris now crossed the fields and orchards that I knew as a child. A small six-story building, a new thing, had been built across from the station at Sceaux.

Either I took the train to the Luxembourg station and then took the 84 bus to boulevard Raspail, or I changed at Denfert-Rochereau and after another change arrived at the Rue-du-Bac station. The time these took were about the same, except for the unforeseen circumstances of the era: electrical outages, bus lines being canceled.... The 84 buses, which now ran on gas, had an enormous white shell on top of them which, I imagine, contained the gas. At every station, there was a number dispenser; you were jostled about when trying to get on in turn. There were still open-air platforms at the rear of the bus which the conductor closed with a leather-covered chain, and then signaled the driver via a series of steel wires. The regulars on the bus had the right to lift up the chain and pull it. The conductor wore a belt with a machine that gave you your tickets (one to six, according to the distance), which he punched at the same time.

I earned eight hundred francs a month, or about nine hundred francs in 2000. It was not much, but I was only an apprentice and very young. I was doing well enough in my position. I knew more about the authors than most of the customers.

I often talked with some of the regular clients. For example, there was a man about thirty whom I chatted with freely. Rather small, with the physique of a boxer, and a broken nose, he didn't go anywhere without a briefcase made of ersatz leather. He had a kind of education, but cobbled together and with big basic gaps. I taught him quite a few things and felt just a bit superior to him, but benevolently so. I didn't ask him any questions and he told me nothing about his work, but I felt like his instructor. We would often see one another for many years afterwards.

A fair number of authors came by, above all those from the NRF which was nearby: Jean Paulhan, Raymond Queneau, Marcel Aymé, Audiberti, Montherlant, or Sartre, who appeared from time to time. Others less well known were not so interesting to me.

There weren't many books in bookstores then. Interesting books, I mean. New works came out one by one, and sold out immediately, their runs being limited by a lack of paper. All the books on the infamous Otto list, created by the occupiers, were seized by the Germans (or rather handed over by the French publishers): anti-Hitler books, Jewish books, Anglophile books. For English-language books there were some strange exceptions: for example, *Moby Dick* by Melville, translated by Giono for Gallimard and commended by a very favorable article in *Je suis partout* by Georges Blond.

In general, customers didn't dare ask for what they wanted but instead took whatever they found. A form of underground began. Some felt convinced that publishers kept hidden stocks. I remember once having a lot of trouble getting rid of a fat dairy maid who wanted, in exchange for a pound of butter, and then two, *Gone with the Wind* (highly sought after during the Occupation and published just before the war by Gallimard).

There was also a market for rare books, on a large scale. From current books sought after for one reason or another to an original edition of *Les Fleurs du Mal or Les Liaisons dangereuses,* speculation grew and prospered: for example in so-called "semi-luxury books" of more or less limited editions, most of which were illustrated, with prices going up as rapidly as genuine rarities.

I followed all of this with curiosity. Soon Roland Saucier started to confide in me his semi-secrets (but never completely, given his taste for mystery). On another occasion, I was to slip up by showing him that I had cracked the (rather childish) code which he used to mark the purchase prices of rare books below their sales prices. I was to get to know a few booksellers who specialized in highly sought-after books, as well as the book-brokers who frequented the store. I also extended my knowledge of Paris to include the bookstalls on the quays. I already knew some of them; I now explored them systematically on both sides of the Seine, and I was soon familiar with many bookstores.

To my appetite for reading was now joined, more distinctly, my taste for actual books.

Among the customers for rare books, I got to know one who intrigued me. He was not interested in the shelves of current books; he just flicked through two or three new publications before entering Saucier's office rather quickly. He apparently noticed me, and little by little started to speak to me, and then conversed freely. He was about forty. Well-dressed. Let's call him Boris, because of something foreign about him that was hard to pinpoint. He spoke perfect, even refined French, but with a slight accent that I could not distinguish.

We talked about books, of course. Rare editions. I was beginning to have some opinions of my own. As for general culture, I was starting to get an idea.

I soon noticed that he broached political questions more and more, in a very general way without taking sides, and quite formally. I answered in the same tone, not really having any cut-and-dried opinions. I have to say that no one seemed to have any, aside from superficial reactions. For example, Mers el-Kébir in July 1940 (the English bombing of the French fleet: 1,200 French killed), or various events in Syria and the surrounding area in 1941, during which the French were pushed by the British into attacking other French citizens, were widely commented on, often violently, but with more emotion than reasoned words. Such was my opinion, and I shared it with him. What about the collaboration? The famous battle for the West against barbarism? Maybe. But I was suspicious of the excesses that went with it. As for the yellow star for the Jews, and the Gestapo which was beginning to take up too much room... Yes... there was mistrust... And then there were the collaborators, some of whom were sincere and others too aggressive. How about taking sides against the Germans? I thought the student protest on November 11, 1940, in front of the Arc de Triomphe against the Germans to be childish. I was not the only one. I claimed to be cautious, when in fact I hardly had any clear ideas.

Boris was very much of my opinion. I slowly become aware that he was making me take a sort of exam. He asked me to have a glass of wine with him one day after closing at the Deux-Magots, where I had never been before. Of course I said yes.

Boris was nice, he had a good sense of humor, and he seemed to be interested in me. I ordered a cocktail (at least something going by that name) and I felt good. Boris asked about my salary. I had no reason to hide anything from him. He thought I was worth more. Would I be willing to do him some favors from time to time? For money, of course. I said okay. He became serious and told me I couldn't tell anyone. I felt fine about that. He said that we'd see each other again.

So it started. From time to time I took thick envelopes of different sizes to various addresses in Paris. I handed them to people I hardly saw, who very quickly closed their doors. My mission was to avoid doormen as much as possible. There was nothing written on the envelopes. I had been given the floor number beforehand, and which side of the elevator.

Boris gave me ten or twenty francs each time, depending, apparently, on the distance I had to go. He was always charming, full of good humor, a bit protective of me, and we continued to talk in the different cafés we went to. I was very happy with this relationship.

The War Comes Back To France –
The "Jewish Question" – Moving And Staying Still

As the months went by, 1942 took on a new, more disjointed rhythm. We began to talk a little, here and there, of the "Resistance," a word spoken favorably by older, somewhat reactionary people, and sometimes with suspicion when it got mixed up with communism. Violent actions by communists against the occupiers were generally disapproved of, because they could bring about reprisals. But they had their followers. The tone of café conversations got louder.

However, on the Left Bank the daily contacts between "resisters," "collaborators," and those in-between, remained mostly, shall we say, courteous. Often there were differences of opinions among old friends, rather than real conflict.

Even so the war was reaching us, little by little. The British had started bombing France. There were alerts and sirens. I was caught short one day by an alert in the street in Sceaux. Fed by air defense fire, a few shells burst nearby. Planes passed overhead, very high in the sky. I took cover under the branches of a tree overhanging an enclosure, with no illusions. Two or three pieces of paper floated down to the ground. They were tracts. I picked one up. In broken French, England (de Gaulle was very probably behind this) was entreating occupied France, very awkwardly, to remember who were the wicked collaborators in order to take revenge after the war. For example, "Henri de Montherland" [sic]. Contemporary documents, literary documents. I admired Montherlant for his Maurice-Barrésian tone in *Aux fontaines du désir*, for example, which I thought was the equal of *Le Jardin de Bérénice*. I folded the tract and put it in my wallet, hidden awkwardly in a flap. I would soon forget about it.

Then there was the "Jewish question," as they called it. It lingered at the edge of general opinion, but was relatively disturbing. Since 1942 there had been yellow stars among the crowds. There were some at the high school, where I recognized some old friends on their way home. We joked with those who were wearing stars. One day we even sewed on fake ones, just to be provocative, though this didn't seem to provoke anyone. There were also some in the book trade. Simon Kra, for example, the former publisher whose tall figure strode about Paris, a large leather briefcase in his hand, full of books. He ran a clandestine bookstore for people in the book business on rue Gozlin in Saint-Germain-des-Prés, which was reached through a corridor. We got along well together. I had a little group of customers to myself, mostly regulars from the Gallimard bookstore, who couldn't find everything they were looking for on boulevard Raspail. This was wrong of me, apparently, but that didn't matter.

In April 1942, I turned sixteen. I was constantly hungry in spite of the heroic efforts of my mother, who had twenty ways to prepare rutabagas and to make pâté from fish bones. Food restrictions were more and more severe. The climate stayed the same: winters were icy cold, with very little heating, and summers very hot. Prices climbed every day on the black market, and the stores grew more and more empty. What I made in a month, including from Boris and the resale of various books, was not enough to pay for a meal in the secret restaurants I heard about.

Suddenly, one night in July my father came home bearing very bad news: the French police, with the help of German soldiers, were going to round up a huge number of Jews in the Paris region. So my brother and I had to warn all the Jews we knew. I knew two who lived in Bourg-la-Reine; they had been in the same class with me in Lakanal, and I still saw them from time to time. I went to see them, and each time got the same suspicious and incredulous reception from their parents: "We've been in France for the last twenty years, this doesn't concern us." The father of the one I knew best, a rich dentist, argued by repeating again and again the same thing: the round-up was certainly justified for all the foreigners who had just arrived, particularly from Poland (he didn't like them at all). As for the Jews who were established and made a good living like him, they certainly didn't have anything to fear.

After an hour talking with him, his wife backing me up, I should add, as well as my father's professional prestige, I left feeling somewhat reassured. I heard a few days later that I had convinced him. They had left. The other family seemed to have disappeared, too. Kra was arrested, denounced, it seems, by a neighboring bookstore. We never saw him again.

Also in July, a tidal wave submerged the French bookstores: *Les Décombres*, by Lucien Rebatet, published by Denoël, was published. Stores were overrun like never before. Denoël had to get more paper because *Décombres* was everywhere.

There was a crush at the Franco-German bookstore on boulevard Saint-Michel the day that Rebatet signed his book. I went; the crowd was blocking the sidewalks. Almost in unison, the critics, though not always in agreement about the essentials, hailed the liveliness, the talent, of Rebatet. You can find in *Mon journal pendant l'Occupation,* by Galtier-Boissière, these lines about August 15, 1942, which reflect the general opinion:

> Have read *Les Décombres.* I hate Lucien Rebatet, "the cream of the *Sturmabteilung,"* and his ideas, but I recognize he has written an extraordinarily lively pamphlet.
>
> Some quotes were then appended.

In 1946, Pierre Audiat was still thrilled by the book four years later, and in his *Paris pendant la Guerre,* which cannot be suspected of underhand collaborationism, produced a more critical analysis:

> The work, which has no fewer than 665 tightly printed pages – an unlimited amount of paper seems to have been allowed the publisher by the German authorities, under the circumstances – appears to be a documentation of the events which the author personally lived through after 1938. With Rabelasian verve and a verbal virulance which he seems to have borrowed from the best of Daudet, this light horseman of Nazism in France recounts the founding of the *Je suis partout* team, the battles it fought before and after Munich, its spats with the nationalists whose political in-fighting didn't allow them to join with Hitler, then the tragic-comic adventures which he experienced during the so-called "phony war"; and finally it exposes and tries to justify the attitude that his friends and himself adopted during the Occupation: rallying totally to Nazism, condemning any wait-and-see policy of whatever kind or any repudiation of Vichy of its doctrines, its paternalism, or its influence, while outlining – and this is the weakest and most disappointing part of the book – what could have and should have been Hitlerian politics with regard to France. Full of anecdotes, satirical, contemptuous and cynical, joyful or ferocious portraits, *Les Décombres* added a certain spice to malice, answering a need common to a great many French and an even greater number of Parisians, to topple statues, even those that they had erected with their own hands. The pages dealing with the milieu of Action Française, and the old nationalism that

it had collaborated with for so long, are particularly welcome: this disciple turned his sharpest blades against his master, after stealing them from his arsenal.

My vacation approached. I was given a month off in August (or three weeks, I can't remember which). I had a secret project, which I only talked about with two friends my own age, Daniel Schricke and X (I forget his name, I'll call him Maxime): to leave on a bicycle, on the pretext of an excursion, and secretly cross the demarcation line. They had family on the other side. I was aiming for Dordogne.

Ah, yes, I also mentioned this to Boris, who seemed interested. Once in the "free" zone, why not push on to Bordeaux? Why not, indeed? It was a matter this time of taking a small package to a certain address. What was more, Boris knew a way to cross the demarcation line by using country roads around La Haie-Descartes in Touraine.

I soon got the detailed address in Bordeaux which I had to learn by heart, as always. The roads looked like unintelligible drawings to the uninitiated and were hidden in a sketchbook. Finally, I had a French road map, which was not at all compromising. No address was written on the package.

We took off early in August. It was a beautiful day. Everything went well. But the first night Maxime started whining around the campfire and suddenly declared he was not going any further. It was too dangerous. He left the next morning. It was all the same to me.

Daniel seemed pensive. At our next stop, he told me that he had carefully weighed the pros and cons (as usual), and he preferred not to go on, either. I sincerely agreed. The thought of Boris's package, well protected in my tent in my saddlebags, was becoming more and more painful. Thinking about it (a little late), I hardly had the right to involve Daniel in this adventure without warning him. We hugged, our eyes moist, then we separated. I liked him a lot.

That night, I stopped in a field on the side of the road. It was still beautiful. In the fading light, I read *Les Amours de Psyche et de Cupidon* by Jean de La Fontaine, forcing myself to be enthusiastic about the beauty pointed out by Valéry. Certainly, beauty was there:

...Days became moments, moments spun with silk...

Nonetheless, I didn't lose myself as I usually did in my favorite books.

By cycling all the next day I now got fairly close to La Haie-Descartes by the back roads. I checked my sketches more and more often, which now seemed so incomprehensible. Suddenly, three hundred feet ahead I saw two German soldiers sleeping under a tree by the side of the road. It felt as if they'd seen me. What was more, they had big dogs which could catch me very fast. In a half second, I decided what to do. Hidden by a bush, I rummaged in my saddle bags, brought out the package that was in the tent and threw it into the underbrush. I thought fast. What should I do? I continued on, innocently.

They stopped me, more or less politely, questioned me in pidgin French and asked me for my papers. I gave them my wallet. After all, I hadn't done anything wrong yet. Nothing allowed them to establish any relationship whatsoever between me and the package, if they found it.

They led me away to a bigger road. A German bus, already half-full, came by two or three hours later to get me. They gave my wallet to the officer who appeared to be commanding operations.

We were almost in Tours when I remembered the tract.

A German Prison –
Jules Verne

I was to spend almost three months in prison, in Tours, in L'École Michelet (it still existed twenty years ago, I went back to see it), which had been turned into a detention center. Strictly German and military in its organization and its personnel, it was, now that I think about it, pretty much a sorting center for all those who were arrested at the demarcation line. So there was a permanent coming and going in each room.

The old classrooms had been transformed accordingly. They included, if I remember right, about forty bunk beds. As for toilets, the necessary was done outside, aside from two hygiene buckets for emergencies.

Two or three of us arrived that night in the room that was going to be my residence. They assigned us our beds. We fell asleep in a silence that I would soon find unusual.

The next day, so as to size up the new arrivals, questions began, at first cautiously. We only answered if we wanted to. Everybody was suspicious of everybody else.

I didn't see any problem about coming forth with some information. I lived near Paris, my name was Pauvert Jean-Jacques, yes, I wanted to cross the demarcation line to visit my family, yes, I had been arrested near La Haie-Descartes. They informed me that the area, once so safe, had become dangerous. It was better to head towards... I forget the name.

I inspired confidence. It was easy for me to talk to people. They forgot my age because of my height (I was close to the six feet which I would soon reach) and my relaxed elocution. They readily call me "big boy." "Hey, big boy, explain this to me." I cagily invented a profession for myself: a journalist, like my father. The fact that this was unbelievable apparently went by unnoticed. I seemed to know more than I was letting on. I got good marks. They adopted me. Moreover, I was soon to be one of the oldest prisoners.

As soon as men are locked up, codes are established. First of all, space. The best beds were those next to the corridor, by a window covered with paint, but with a little corner scratched clean so you could peek down the corridor. I got this privileged place after three weeks because of my seniority.

During the day, there was so much coming and going that we could only exchange a few words with each other. It was at night, after curfew, that we talked, or sang softly. Before my arrival, a song relating to our circumstances had been made up, and the prisoners sang it endlessly, adding couplets day by day. Here is the refrain, sung to a tune we all knew at the time:

Ah, what a great invention
The line of demarcation
They couldn't have done better
As a way to provoke
The happy people
Who are returning home...

We sang all the words we could remember. Some thought they had a good voice (they were rare) and added certain effects to sentimental songs. I was a hit with the songs of Charles Trenet, discovered in 1938, and whom I liked a lot. I sang more or less in tune. The audience particularly liked "Le Soleil a rendezvous avec la lune." As a result, some of them started calling me "All-the-cats," because of a song that particularly struck them:

What are they saying on the roofs
What are the voices of these cats repeating?
These cats who are bored to death

****
All the cats, all the cats, all the cats...

Some said nothing. Some cried as quietly as possible, but we heard them. Some showed their neighbors photos that they looked at by the light of matches.

Everybody came through l'École Michelet. Escaped prisoners who were picked up again, even Germans who had fled Germany. There was an old American who had been living in France for years. There was a black man, about 25, French, who couldn't read. I started to teach him. His name was something like Menouar. He stayed nearly three weeks, then disappeared suddenly, like others. He had made some progress.

I shared with him the few packages I received. Some letters got through to us, and we were allowed to answer, briefly.

My mother was horrified. My father tried to resign himself, from what I understood in the cryptic letters that I got.

Oddly enough, I hardly worried. Things are the way they are. What can you do?

After a few days, I was interrogated by a young lieutenant, I think, who spoke fairly good French and who prided himself on his cultural knowledge. Everything revolved around that tract. The package had obviously not been found, or someone else had picked it up.

So it was all about this wretched tract. Ah! So you distribute tracts in English, do you? No, not at all, I picked this up in the street. I kept it because it was about writers. I work in the Gallimard bookstore. Ach! Gallimard! The *Nouvelle Revue Française!* No, the bookstore. I emphasized "bookstore," not knowing if Gallimard was a good thing in Germany. Yes, yes, the bookstore. I have French books in my house. So what were you doing at the demarcation line?

I hesitated slightly. But then, so what if I told the truth or part of it? Yes, I wanted to cross the line during my vacation. I have family in Dordogne. You meant to hand out your tracts! – Not at all, I only have one. It was out of curiosity: because of the writers, the bookstore. He summed the situation up in his own way: "It's about Jules Verne!" I will never know exactly why he said that.

Up until then, there didn't seem to be anything to worry about. Sometimes he spoke roughly, then he calmed down. I had the impression that he didn't really know for sure why he was there.

So why this same interrogation again and again for three months? I began to fall apart. The wooden beds were full of fleas and bedbugs. It was too hot; I'd had enough.

And then one day, suddenly, they summoned me, for a trial, evidently. What trial? Now I was beginning to worry.

The trip from the École Michelet was made in a military car, driven by a soldier. I was all alone in the back, except for another soldier. Being all alone worried me even more.

We stopped rather suddenly in the courtyard of a large building. Still alone, I was led by two other soldiers through what seemed to me long, interminable, and deserted corridors.

Then all at once I was pushed through a little door into a large solemn room. I was to learn later that it was the Tours courthouse. I felt cramped in the dock, alone and guarded by two soldiers. The room was empty. Soon a man in civilian clothes entered and introduced himself: he was my interpreter, he said. He happened to be a distant cousin of my mother's, and he had been in contact with my parents. He offered a few words of encouragement. This didn't comfort me. Anyway, I could hardly hear him.

Finally, three officers in splendid uniforms entered through a door at the end of the room, took their places at the top of a high platform and put their hats in front of them. Then some underlings sat down in a row beneath them. Two of them opened large notebooks. The three officers looked at me and exchanged words in low voices. They did not seem to be joking.

After a little while, which seemed extremely long, the officer in the center of the trio started to speak. His tone was very serious. My interpreter translated softly: I should know that all propaganda coming out of England was punishable by death. Possessing propaganda material was punishable by death. The fact that I was sympathetic to subversive English ideas, or acts of sabotage by the Resistance, was punishable by death...

Everything was punishable by death. Death could be extended to the rest of the family. I listened standing up, my head bowed. I was now very conscious that this was no longer a game. I couldn't hear anything else. The interpreter touched my arm. The officer stopped speaking. What did I have to say in my defense?

I came down to earth. In a choking voice, I repeated what I had already said twenty times. I had picked up the tract out of curiosity. I mentioned literature, the bookstore. The interpreter translated. I stopped talking. Heavy silence. The officers consulted one another in low voices. The one who had spoken before started talking again. Very seriously. Finally it dawned on me: German is by nature a language that sounds severe. The interpreter translated: I had been imprudent. But I was young. In the future, I should remember that the Great Reich could be indulgent. I was free to go. The military tribunal left the room.

But in the end, it had been a game. They had put on an impressive show for me, a play by a repertory company. What it all meant, I would never know. I asked lots of people who had found themselves in similar situations at the time; no other denouement was ever quite like what I had been through. A great show. By Jules Verne, the lieutenant would have added.

I went back to the École Michelet. I had five minutes to gather up my things. When they heard the news, the others hurriedly wrote a few letters for Paris, which they gave me. I hid them away any old how.

One final interrogation and a final cold sweat: "Has anybody given you any letters? – No, no." And that was that. They didn't insist. They pushed me outside. They gave me back my bike. The interpreter waited for me at the gate to take me to his place. He didn't understand the show they had put on for me, either.

First a bath, to get rid of the lice. I changed clothes. I would spend the night there. The next day, I took the train to Paris, with my bicycle duly registered. That night, I was back with my parents. Happiness all around.

La *NRF* –
Albert Camus

October 1942, I was rehired by Gallimard without any problem, for reasons I didn't understand and which didn't interest me. I was surrounded by people who treated me with a kind of consideration. They hardly dared question me, aside from Maria, who was as nosy as could be. I had nothing against recounting what had happened, although in a shortened version, as befitted someone who knew more than they were letting on. The scene in the large room of the courthouse in Tours hardly seemed real; it impressed everybody. Had I been tortured? No. Even so, a German prison was no small thing. I was apparently the only person anyone knew who had been through such a close shave with the occupiers.

My friends felt the same way about me: in short, I was a part of history as it was happening. I had experienced a tiny part of the events that were happening and causing such a stir around the world, and which seemed to be speeding up – in principle, this was true.

Before the end of the year, the Germans began in their turn to be encircled at Stalingrad. The British landed in North Africa on November 11; then the Germans crossed the demarcation line to attack the French fleet in Toulon on November 27. The fleet was sunk. Everything was in confusion.

In my little world, there was something new. Watin told me that during that summer a new author he had told me about in July had come on board: Albert Camus. He really mattered, he said. He'd just published a short novel, *L'Étranger*, followed almost immediately by a philosophical essay, *Le Mythe de Sisphe*. I read them at once. They were electric. I think that I found in the absurdity of Camus an expression of the uneasiness I was feeling. I rushed over to the *Nouvelle Revue Française* (NRF) where Camus apparently had a little office in the attic. He was serious, but young. About my age (actually, he was twenty-nine) with the handsome face of a Mediterranean philosopher.

He seemed flattered, signed my copy of *Le Mythe de Sisphe:* "To Jean-Jacques Pauvert, may this Myth of Sisyphus take him further." But I didn't want to go further. Not yet. A relationship began which was a little distant but was to last until his death.

At the time, Gallimard publications were very much involved with the *Nouvelle Revue Française*. They were housed in a little building on the rue Sebastien-Bottin, which had not yet grown into the Bottin building at the corner of the street. The entrance was like going into a windmill. I girded myself, then abruptly pushed open the doors on which were written the names that interested me: Raymond Queneau, Jean Paulhan... "Am I disturbing you?" I asked. "Well...!" At the time, you didn't see that many sixteen-year-olds show their enthusiasm with such familiarity. What was more, I knew what they had written. My questions weren't totally inane. Altogether, I came in for a good reception.

From One Book To The Next

I read with equal curiosity a book recommended by Watin, *Cadavre exquis*, a novel written by Louis Carette, published September 20, 1942, by Les Editions du Houblon in Bruxelles. It had nothing in common with *L'Étranger* or *Les Coups*, but it was a pleasant sign of the times, an agreeable shock. After the war, Louis Carette was to become Félicien Marceau, and refused to let a second edition of his book be published.

By the end of 1942, I was sixteen, and yet I wasn't sixteen. A bit more, or a bit less, depending on circumstances. Less, because not having had the training, I didn't always know how to conduct myself in public. A bit more, because professionally, if I may say so, I knew more, much more than the other apprentice clerks in the bookstore. And I didn't know anyone else as young as I was. I was a little out of step everywhere.

Even with friends my own age, outside the bookstore, I was not at ease. I played tennis with them (balls were rare and rackets expensive), I joked with them, I had friends, but I didn't have a real confidante. I was invited to parties which were very conventional. I began to know something about jazz, I played the piano a little, I got along pretty well with girls; but there was something awkward about our relationships. I had fed too much on *Les Liaisons dangereuses* not to seek complications in something, which was, in the end, simple. Too simple perhaps.

At any rate, I was making huge strides in my knowledge of rare books, which had become one of the principle areas of general speculation. The prices climbed every day, some more than others. One part of the game consisted in knowing how to anticipate the books which would have the most cachet the next day. I was fairly good at this game. There were even bookstores which asked my advice. My customer base was growing. I was starting to make money by reselling books to booksellers who were less knowledgeable than I was about market fluctuations.

I learned about "erotica": clandestine books – deluxe editions which were the only ones I knew at the time – that certain bookstores really wanted to have in stock and which others refused. There were, however, degrees of refusal. Saucier, for example, never accepted expensive erotic books, which were vulgar according to him, but had no trouble accepting, if not in the window at least in his office, original editions (at the time the only ones) of the *Livre blanc,* which was very rare and which everyone knew was by Cocteau. I had already noticed that Saucier seemed to have a weakness for homosexuality – at any rate of the literary kind.

I was interested in this "erotica" which sometimes turned up in certain bookstores. And I had special talks with Watin during which he advised me about some official reads, which were a bit "olé olé," or "saucy," as he put it. For example *Puberté,* published anonymously before the war by Saillard. Or *Trique et Nénesse* by Alfred Machard. What about Jules Renard? I already knew *L'Écornifleur,* which was very different from *Poil de Carotte.* In his Journal, Jules Renard wrote at the end of his life, "There's pornography in *L'Écornifleur;* I'm not going to start that over again."

I continued to read Simenon, which I had started in Sceaux. Literary controversy surrounded it. Gide supported Simenon, who was currently published by Gallimard. He also supported Dashiell Hammett, now banned but whom I found in the stalls along the quay, *The Maltese Falcon* and *The Glass Key,* published before the war in a collection of police novels by Gallimard with photographic covers. *The Glass Key* now found a place among my favorite books.

During the winter of 1942–43 I was in for a shock, a major shake-up in my young literary existence. A book-broker with whom I'd already made a few deals discreetly offered to sell me a little pile of books in a corner of the Gallimard bookstore. He undid the paper a bit to show me the covers: there was *Le Con d'Irène,* and *Histoire de l'œil* – in the original clandestine editions – and three out-of-print volumes published by Stendhal and Co. (1931–1935) of *Les Cent Vingt Journées de Sodome.* He wanted a little money, but not too much; *Les Cent Vingt Journées* had been remaindered towards the end of the Thirties, and the two others were in little demand. I bought them.

Back at my place, I began reading *Le Con d'Irène.* It was brilliant:

> Whatever I think naturally expresses itself. Each man's language varies with each man. I, for example, do not think without writing, I mean that writing is my method of thinking. The rest of the time, not writing I have only a reflection of thought, a kind of grimace of myself, like a memory of what it is. Others rely on different procedures. Thus I greatly envy erotics, whose eroticism is their expression. A magnificent language. It really is not mine....

The kitchen servants looked at each other. A great wind that blew in out of a black, hollow sea, that came out of the sea full of naked drowned bodies, a great wind lifted, billowed the percale curtains with the sound of a sudden reef in the topsail. Bad looks had been seen on the road: faces of dust, irascible.
– [*Trans. by Lowell Bair.*]

Histoire de l'œil left me perplexed. I didn't have anything in principle against this exasperating, sickly look into abjection. I sensed the necessity that was being expressed. But it wasn't really my language, in the words of the author of *Le Con d'Irène*, whom I knew to be Aragon, just as I knew that the author of *Histoire de l'œil* was a certain Georges Bataille about whom I knew very little.

What remained was *Les Cent Vingt Journées de Sodome*.

It took me a while to read the three volumes of Sade, in more or less closely spaced periods of time, according to my mood.

This was something I didn't understand. I didn't understand what I was reading, how I was reading it, or how it should be read. That resonating voice, now like bursting thunder, now sweet, often with an enormous comic undercurrent, was unlike anything I had read up till then. Was this really reading? There were no other examples, to my knowledge, of such huge indecencies, such outrageous obscenities, or such atrocious details, methodically multiplied.

What was more, no one I knew actually considered the books of Sade as being part of the world of literature. Sade was a name that came up from time to time in conversation, usually as a brief allusion, a momentary detour outside of one's usual reading. Nothing had prepared me for such a meeting. And it so happened that I started with *Les Cent Vingt Journées*, Donatien de Sade's most revolting work.

This meteorite which had fallen into my hands raised essential questions prior to any questions about it as literature. Was this really reading material? Was this book a book? Was this text part of something I had never questioned before: literature? Yes? No? The answers that I got from my literary friends showed that they didn't accept the book as a real read, but instead as a kind of outline for a work. But had they READ it? It hardly seemed so.

I had to wait forty-five years to read Annie Le Brun's extremely concise definition of what it means to read *Les Cent Vingts Journées* (in *Soudain un bloc d'abime, Sade*, chapter 1), which is also the best account of how I had felt in 1942:

How can one explain the physical upheaval which accompanies an actual reading of this text? There was a time at the beginning of my rediscovery of Sade when I was like an obsessed person. I couldn't stay away from it. Maybe because I had leaned so far over the abyss, I had the overwhelming impression that my life was going to slide into it. What disturbed me the most was that this impression went along with a stronger and stronger desire to lose myself in some sort of indeterminate confusion. I was the prey of a desire which apparently had no object but which stripped me of everything, even my nudity. For the first time, deprived of the mirrors of pleasure, I was caught up in an erotic turbulence inside of which I could not see nor even conceive of the end. Even to the point that one night in April, after one of those sudden storms which empty the quays of the Seine like a tidal wave, I discovered myself completely alone in the reflective cage of a sulfurous and metallic sky which shook the horizon under my feet. It was doubtless the most concrete way I had of representing to myself the erotic reverberation of which I was a prisoner, with all the incandescence of being, all the rustling of ideas, the dazzle of emotions, the glimmer of memory, the persistence of perspectives, obeying this invisible glow of the organic which had made of me its theater.

I now knew Jean Paulhan and about the important role he had at Gallimard (though I didn't understand very well what it was), and we had exchanged a few words. I hesitated a long time before talking to him about Sade, although I knew he was interested in him. It just happened gradually.

I had seen Boris again, who was perfectly aware of what I had gone through, probably thanks to Saucier. He put me at ease right away. I had the vague impression that he didn't attach much importance to what had happened to the package. Had it been another test?

He was, however, very interested in the episode at the courthouse in Tours, which I had to tell him about in great detail. He confirmed that as far as he knew, this was a rather rare case. In his opinion a play, in fact, and pretty much in line with the German soul. What was the reason for it exactly? Our conjectures multiplied. He remained rather pensive. I got the impression that I had lived through something exceptional. An impression I forgot quickly – although it came back to me much later.

We took up our old habits again. Boris used the informal *tu* form with me (I always used the formal *vous* with him). He spoke openly about London and about missions. The Tours affair seemed to have clarified things between the two of us. Once I was invited to his place; his prudence seemed to have relaxed a bit. I remember an armoire in a room we passed in front of, its door open, and I thought I saw enormous piles of bank bills (of what denominations?).

When precisely did this business end? I can't really remember. Possibly in the first months of 1943. It was a harsh winter. Undernourished in spite of a good salary, I now had very painful chilblains.

The German demands for compulsory laborers grew stronger, and would soon provoke the creation of the underground (or "maquis"). Paulus had capitulated in Stalingrad (end of January). In Africa, the first German defeats occurred. There were savage American battles with the Japanese in the Philippines; we only heard distant echoes. In July, the Americans landed in Sicily.

I noticed that my mother was now sometimes involved in bizarre activities. She entertained people I didn't know. Their conversations sometimes lasted a long time. Some of these people more or less hid their faces.

One day Boris announced with his usual jocularity that I was now part of a "network." He pronounced the name BCRA. "You have been officially signed up as of...in the BCRA network." (I don't remember anything else). "Mine," he added. The BCRA? The Bureau Central de Renseignements et d'Action, he explained. Oh? I soon forgot about it. He saw that I was not very interested in the news, and added (this I remember very well): "You'll see; this will be of use to you later."

And then he disappeared.

No one saw him again in the bookstore, or anywhere else. He simply vanished. I risked alluding to him one day to Saucier, who said briefly that Boris, as far as he knew, "had had to leave." I didn't ask where, naturally. He had left, that's all. I didn't go to his place. Besides, he had always advised me against trying to contact him. I never heard of "Boris" again.

As for the BCRA, I only made contact with this mysterious agency again after the Liberation, in a totally different way, as will be seen, and it had nothing to do with my becoming a member in 1943, a fact that was lost forever, assuming that it had ever really been made formal.

Speculations, Malpractice, Bans

I n *Mon journal pendant l'Occupation* by Galtier-Boissière, two notes from 1942 clearly paint a picture of the rare book situation and the production of art in general during those years. Speculation, malpractice, shady transactions with or without the occupiers, things cost what anyone was willing to pay:

> June 2. In Drouot, end of the sensational Louis Brun library sale, the commercial director of the Bernard Grasset firm, assassinated by his wife just before the war started.
>
> The sales have been prodigious. One of the five copies printed on Japon paper of *Du côté de chez Swann*, full of signed letters, brought 185,000 francs; a restored version of the complete series of Proust: 105,000; a drawing by Seonzac: 30,500.
>
> Manuscripts brought unheard of prices: a typed copy of *La Musique interieure*, by Maurras, sold for 20,000!
>
> And the same for everything else.

****

> December 8: It's a great period for painters, art dealers, antique sellers and publishers of deluxe edition books. The newly rich hurry to buy whatever at whatever price in order to invest their piles of cash.
>
> Someone gives me the name of an art dealer who made more than a hundred million in sales this year either to the newly rich or to German collectors.

1943: I was still working as a bookseller. I'd had a raise twice at Gallimard; I was up to ninety francs a month, then a hundred. These raises were underlined by Miss Sigle each time she handed me my monthly envelope. I said thank you, but I was now earning twice or three times that each week in personal business. I was to leave Gallimard in the first half of 1943.

Before leaving Gallimard, I played hooky successfully two or three times. My business affairs occupied me more and more. Each time I missed a day,

I confided mysteriously in Miss Sigle; I always had a good reason. One day, it had been an underground copy machine that had to be immediately dismantled; another day, clandestine people had to be taken to safety.

Each time Miss Sigle shook her head with a deep, worried look. She then talked to M. Saucier. Later in the day, the response was announced by her thin lips; we won't mention it again, but be careful. In a certain way, these fictions were about to become reality.

The beginning of 1943, *Pilote de guerre* by Saint-Exupery was banned, or rather withdrawn from sales by Gallimard, as soon as it came out. *Je suis partout*, the newspaper, spoke out against it (a piece signed by Cousteau). The book was:

> The apotheosis of Judeo-warmongering, which illustrates all the stupidities and dirty tricks which are currently killing us.

There were some strange aspects to these German bans, or sometimes Vichy bans – they were not the same thing. For example, Elsa Triolet, who was thought to have disappeared into the underground, had had two books published by Denoël since the beginning of the Occupation: *Mille Regrets* and *Le Cheval blanc*. Aragon, too, a notable communist, had a big book published at the beginning of 1943 by Gallimard, *Les Voyageurs de l'impériale*. There, again, screams from *Je suis partout*; Gallimard prudently pulled the book from circulation.

But it was Vichy that banned Céline's *Les Beaux Draps* in 1941. The book remained available in the occupied zone. And if you searched a little you could also find it in the "free" zone.

Given these various factors, French publishing in general hesitated and squirmed. I was not very well informed about what was happening between the big publishing houses and the occupiers; the most varied rumors circulated. Grasset openly manifested its good feelings toward the Germans. Denoël also, but it published Elsa Triolet and Aragon at the same time as *Les Décombres*. Flammarion reissued *La France juive*, by Drumont, an anti-Semite from before 1914. Gallimard sheltered Jean Paulhan, known to be helping the Resistance and who would be arrested for a while by the German Police. But there were also rumors that Gaston had written a compromising letter to the authorities so as to buy up Calman-Levy, which had become Editions Balzac (he underscored the fact he was "a good Aryan"). Was he playing both sides? Of course, as was usual with Gaston.

It was an interlude of knavery, a sign of the era. Since the beginning of the Occupation, volumes in the *Pléiade* collection had had a sure speculative value. Even new and reprinted books, which often had ersatz bindings instead of plain leather, garnered a good price (six or seven times the official amount). For some time now, one noticed at the Gallimard bookstore that the *Pléiade* editions were missing. Thanks to the attentive surveillance of Miss Sigle, it was discovered one day that it was the messenger boy who was occasionally making off with the odd title in his golf pants.

What I Will Never Be

Something ended in 1943. Or did it begin? As usual, I was not very clear about things. It was all the same to me, in the end, except that I was being sucked into whatever was happening. I was still at a loose end.

It was difficult to divide up the coming year into twelve months. From the first months of 1943 there would be, for me and the world around me, a series of events, or transformations, let's say, a series of successive metamorphoses. I would go from seventeen to twenty in accelerated stages, mostly without realizing it at the time. A little text that I wrote when I was twenty, of which I have found only the beginning, really shows, I think, and curiously so, in what way I lived those years – and even the years that came after:

> And so the days passed and in the end I was twenty. It seems that you're only twenty once. That's possible. I hope so, anyway. No, I don't regret anything, but I'd like to know what's going to happen. Wrong or right, this story interests me...

One thing is certain, I would no longer follow the path of rare books or bibliophiles, the one that leads to great bookstores such as Blaizot, Saucier, Lardanchet (in Lyon), or later Bères (which had not yet been admitted into this exclusive seraglio). It was a path I had now been right down and which only led me to an impasse. I grew older day by day while learning the tiny refinements of the trade: the original edition of such and such a text has on page 276 a printing error which needs to be corrected during the next printing; or to measure to the nearest millimeter the margins of an ancient text; to recognize at a glance unsigned bound books. I was beginning to know about these things, but more and more I realized that this was not my vocation.

But what then was my vocation? I didn't know and it wasn't my problem. I just wanted to know what was going to happen. I soon would.

The Demons And Marvels Of The Occupation

1943. My seventeen years turned out to be free of all constraints. I continued to learn about Paris. I fleshed out my personal library in the farthest neighborhoods of the city, which I also explored at the same time. Old houses, deserted passageways, bizarre monuments, statues with hollow columns, the bronze having been requisitioned. All that remained were the inscriptions, which often didn't mean anything to anybody.

The price of books climbed so fast all you had to do sometimes was buy and wait – for a few weeks. However, the really rare books disappeared more and more, scooped up by speculators. I kept some of them, for as long as possible.

Many shelves in the bookstores were empty, new books and everyday reading matter were lacking. There were very few bookstores. The new corporatist laws of Petain stopped new ones from being set up. And anyway, why do it?

The numbers I'm giving you weren't known at the time; I got them from archived statistics. During the Occupation there were fewer than fifteen hundred new bookstores in France, and fewer than three hundred "real" bookstores, meaning those which only sold books, and not just whatever (knickknacks, etc.) Out of these three hundred bookstores "worthy of their name," only a little over half were registered with the *Bibliographie de la France*, which announces new editions. Once again, why do it? Rumors announced publications a long time in advance, and the large bookstores had already reserved their copies.

Over these years, the best readers had a passion for *Quand le temps travaillait pour nous* by Paul Mousset, *Travelingue*, by Marcel Aymé, *Premier de cordée*, by Frison-Roche, *Le Solstice de juin*, by Montherlant, *L'ancre de Misericorde*, by Mac Orlan, *Lunegarde*, by Pierre Benoit, *Le Journal de la France*, by Fabre-Luce, *Le Mort saisit le vif*, by Henri Troyat, *La Grande meute*, by Vialar, *Corps et ames*, by Van der Meersh, *Le pain des rêves*, by Louis Guilloux, *Gigi*, by Colette. And Péguy, who Gallimard, through arm-twisting, reprinted. Who remembers the enormous success (even though there were very few copies available, as they were all loaned) of *La Quête de joie*, by Patrice de la Tour du Pin, a thin little book (published by Gallimard, too)?

All countries that have no legends
Will die from the cold...
Far away in the soul solitude spreads out
Under the sun dead from its love of self.

And Céline? In truth, something remarkable happened to him. Denoël had very quickly published a thin volume by Céline in 1941 (under their Nouvelles Editions françaises imprint): *Les Beaux Draps*. I thumbed through it with consternation. The magic wasn't there anymore. Those who read very carefully, word for word, might have thought that when reality joined with the dreams of Céline, he would have been in his element. It was the opposite; Céline wrote in a vacuum. Gide was right; Céline wasn't painting reality, it was an hallucination of reality. When reality was suddenly right in front of him, at hand, it horribly disturbed him, it seems. He just got stuck.

Though to tell the truth, contrary to the era, I was experiencing a golden age of books where my tastes were concerned. If the usual customers for new books were disheartened by the penury they found, I was going into small used bookstores which were springing up a little bit everywhere, and making discovery after discovery. Along the quays there were still lots of books from the massive sales during the Thirties, a result of the Depression.

To think that in the basement of the Gallimard bookstore, we were literally walking on copies of *La Conquête de l'irrationnel* by Dali (published around 1930, unsaleable) which had fallen out of a broken box of books! In the little stores I'm talking about, you could find cheap pre-war first editions of Michaux (still not much sought after in spite of Gide's banned defense, *Découvrons Henri Michaux*, published as a booklet by Gallimard): *Qui je fus, Un certain Plume*.

I no longer know if it was under the Occupation or a little afterwards that the whole stock of Fourcade publications went on sale. They didn't interest anybody, and for weeks, for months, the first edition of *Mes propriétés* (Michaux) could be found in the stalls on the quays, copies printed on *Hollande*, mixed in with copies of the trade edition at the same price. The Breton of *Manifestes du surréalism*, Aragon of *Paysan de Paris* or *Traité du style* were a bit more popular, but they were far from the price that people were paying elsewhere for copies of *La Mousson* by Louis Bromfield – when you could find it – or *Via Mala* by John Knittel. At the same time, along the quays or in the little bookstores I'm talking about, the whole avant-garde of the Thirties could be found. In fact, between 1942 and 1944 I built up my first surrealist collection, which I sold, like the others. But I had smelled them, touched them, read them.

It was during the Occupation, I think, that I cut a great deal, wrenching as it was. A dealer on the quays that I knew well, we called him Old Joseph, quay des Grands Augustins, one day asked me if I knew much about surrealism and if I'd be interested in a batch he had just acquired for nothing, at the end of a sale, in a "toilet" (that's what for a long time we called the black canvas-curtained area behind which we pitched books, one at a time, at Drouot, when nothing else of interest was being sold).

Yes, I was beginning to know about surrealism, and yes, I was interested. He took me to his loft on rue Guénégaud and undid his toilet. He had nosed out a really good deal, without evaluating its true worth. I was amazed; all the big surrealists from before the war were there, not only in first editions, but on the most sought-after rare paper: heliotrope vellum for Breton, *Japon* or *Hollande* for Eluard and Aragon, etc.

That wasn't all: each copy was wrapped and had a detailed address written on it, often with letters addressed to the same person. Old Joseph had acquired the library, dispersed through an anonymous sale, of Maurice Heine, a member of the group and the first real specialist of Sade, who had died in Verouillet May 26, 1940.

By what strange paths had this unique library found its way to a black market sale in 1943 or 1944, Old Joseph evidently had no idea, and I never learned, either. Maurice Heine had left no inheritors.

Old Joseph trusted me like most of the booksellers, for that matter. I'd try to get ten thousand francs for the lot of them, I promised (about ten or eleven thousand francs in 2000), and I took these treasures home in several loads.

I spent days thumbing through them, reading several of them two or three times. I impregnated myself with these marvels, some of them relatively new to me. Getting to know them in this wondrous environment augmented their prestige. *Nadja*, by Breton, on a pale violet paper, I think; *Une vague de reves*, by Aragon, in a small, separate printing by the review; *Commerce, La Femme visible* by Dali, enhanced by one or two original drawings. *Le Con d'Irène* on Japon paper with a very long inscription by Aragon – the entire lot in perfect condition.

Was it then or a little afterwards that I had yet another shock, at Jeanne Bucher's place in her gallery? I had gotten in the habit of going there to just look around (it was on boulevard Montparnasse which made things easy for me, as I was used to the Left Bank, having become a regular). I rifled through some cartons of drawings which they were selling as defective illustrations from certain surrealist books. I picked up, for example, some pages of *Chants de Maldoror* with illustrations by Dali.

Whatever the fascination that Dali exercised over me, nothing could match the incredible impression I had on seeing pages of *Histoire naturelle* by Max Ernst rising up out of a box like a revelation. I stood there frozen, and I didn't decide right away to take the drawings, tempted by some unknown superstition to leave them there, in their present state, as a treasure. I had to come back several days in a row before I ended by buying them one by one from Jeanne Bucher, a charming little old lady. The series, of course, wasn't complete. I carried them away enveloped in large sheets of paper. I still have them. Every time I look at them I'm carried away to another planet.

I afterwards met Max Ernst, and I spent a lot of time with him. I enormously like certain of his paintings. But the *Histoire naturelle* always transports me.

To finish the story about the surrealist library of Maurice Heine, I resold the whole lot for twenty thousand francs to Jean-Pierre Mauclaire, owner of Cinémonde, formerly the famous Studio 28 where *L'Age d'or* by Bunuel and Dali was shown for the first time (among other films). I'd gotten a really good deal for those days. Mauclaire, or his heirs, an even better one. The contents of Old Joseph's "toilet" today would be worth a hundred or two hundred times more. What has become of it all?

It was about this time that I was invited twice by rich clients to the famous black market restaurants that I mentioned. These were in very large apartments in beautiful parts of Paris. The food was served at little tables in the sitting room. The customers were varied: German officers – always accompanied by charming women – well-known actors and actresses, profiteers and businessmen of the moment, all endeavoring to behave themselves and usually not alone. The service was very stylish. Sometimes the mistress of the house came and sat at a table. The price, so far as I could make out, was four to six hundred francs – per person, of course. Certainly, too expensive for me. As a guest, I ate well, trying my best not to gulp down all that food which I hadn't tasted in years.

I was known now in the business. I had solid connections. Many were astounded by my young age, which I made them forget fast, by my knowledge and my literary friendships. I went regularly to the NRF where Jean Paulhan held meetings on certain days and to which a variety of people showed up. I mixed very easily with them.

Portrait Of Marie-Claude At Fourteen

Among my business connections, I knew a rare book dealer who had a bookstore on rue de Seine. He was a quaint little guy, young, gifted with a knowledge of Parisian slang, full of raw expressions. He was called Richard Anacréon and he's still alive, it seems, very old and living in La Rochelle.

I was fairly close to him; sometimes he asked me to watch his store. There I met writers: Colette came in two or three times; Paul Valéry, who had his rituals, came in now and then. He arrived, sat down at Anacréon's desk, which on one side had a pile of books, on the other a pile of cigarette packages. Valéry signed his books, one by one, passed them to Anacréon, who then slipped him a package of cigarettes.

They had short little conversations in slang, generally obscene. I watched Valéry with fascination, not daring to join in (besides, I didn't have the style, not yet choosing to use slang, although I understood it very well). Valéry had great fun with these conversations.

I remember one particular time like it was yesterday. They had a particular exchange about the Zazous style then in fashion. Suddenly I risked a remark; it was a question about dandyism. Valéry looked at me and I instantly froze; I had caught the attention of Monsieur Teste.

I found a quote by Albert Béguin recently in an excellent biography by Denis Berthollet, which exactly caught the impression engraved in my memory that day, by the look Valéry gave me, what Marie de Regnier called "the little dry monsieur."

> Everyone remembered his eyes, lit up by an incredible light I had never seen before, the instant they landed on an exterior object. Almost vapid the moment before, they looked at a form with such precision one thought the object was going to enter and stay in his memory forever.

I think Anacréon appreciated me – certainly my healthy look. He got it in his head that he would "place" me, as he called it. He introduced me one day to a woman of a certain age with whom I had a lively exchange. She looked me up and down with her shiny, brilliant eyes, stared at my suit, my tie, my scarf, and repeated over and over again, "We can find him something better than that!"

I wasn't tempted, as I later told Anacréon. He was irritated. Pandering was a vocation for him. He made several other attempts of the same kind, without success. He even presented me to a homosexual, about my same age, who very much liked me. It wasn't reciprocal. Relationships with Anacréon almost always had a certain kind of gaminess about them which I didn't like at all. "Listen," he said, "a little fuck here and there, it costs almost nothing and brings in a great deal. And you really don't risk anything! Anyway, think about it."

I reflected a lot about these things, in fact more and more, and issues around them. But my thoughts were elsewhere. For some time I had noticed the little sister of a classmate I had been friends with in the high school, Pierre X. His family had been fairly rich at the beginning of our friendship, but their situation seemed to have devolved rapidly over time. Marie-Claude was younger than we were by eighteen months. She seemed wild and ran away the minute I arrived. At this point, she was dressed like all other young girls of fifteen from a good family, sensibly like an adult. The fashion in 1943 was short skirts, at least to the knees, and proper middle-class young women wore nylons fairly early, to which I was always attracted. Marie-Claude had long legs, beautiful dark eyes, and a tight bodice stretched over promising breasts. Always literary, I thought that she represented the *Portrait d'Eliane à quatorze ans* by Valéry Larbaud. (I hadn't yet read this short story; it was the title that charmed me. When I did read it, I saw that there really wasn't much relationship.)

Little by little, I began to have a few words with her each visit if she was there. She was rather shy, but smiled sometimes at my jokes, as though in spite of herself. Then she pulled back and left the room soon after. I fell in love.

Since secrets must be told, I was still a virgin, and besides that, rather ignorant in spite of my detailed readings about sexual practices. In fact, I really didn't want to know the theory without the practice, which I suspected of being a much bigger world and more complex than a dry anatomical description.

An occasion for practice presented itself. Sometimes we had parties at one house or another – oh, very innocent in spite of all the little flirtations that went on. At one of these, Pierre decided to bring his sister. They arrived and Marie-Claude immediately sat down on a sofa with her pouty expression. I had greeted them, waiting for the right moment. When it seemed right, or rather it seemed that it would never be right, I asked Marie-Claude to dance. She said no curtly. I don't know what came over me, but I gave her a little lesson in manners, explaining that she exhibited a really difficult character, she was isolating herself stupidly, and that no one would want to be around her. Then I turned my back on her and walked away.

I'd just taken a few steps when someone took me by the arm. It was Marie-Claude, her head bowed. She wanted to say she was sorry. We danced a very welcome slow number, holding each other tightly, then I took her outside where we stayed, kissing like quite a few other couples. Awkwardly, she made up for her inexperience by a childlike ardor that was very moving. I was touched. But oddly I had suddenly become the leader, a man of experience – which I wasn't. But I hid it well.

Then it was time to go back inside, to our separate corners. I had found the person I had been looking for.

Everything went very fast. The X's had to sell their house. Sometime later, after the party and one or two meetings in the Parc de Sceaux, Marie-Claude miraculously had to stay home alone one night to watch the house. It was being emptied little by little of furniture but wasn't completely empty yet, during the period that her parents and brother were moving into their new place. She deliberately invited me to spend the night with her.

It was May. The weather was lovely. We were soon on the bed naked. I started to explore her body, which all this freedom allowed. Marie-Claude was ready for anything, even taking some initiative. But above all, she was waiting to be taught, and I played my role of teacher with a lot of outward authority while trembling with emotion inside.

In spite of everything, when we fell asleep in each other's arms as the sun was coming up, I was still a virgin – she was too – but both of us knew what we wanted to know. I did, anyway.

A little while after this my friends wanted to organize an expedition to a famous whorehouse, Le Sphynx in Montparnasse. Their aim was to clarify the whole sexual issue, which preoccupied them. I followed, although I was more advanced in this area than most of them.

I still have a very precise memory of this adventure. We had no trouble getting into the large room in the Sphynx, paying the asking price and then ending up, each of us, in a little room with the creature of our choice – or rather the one who had chosen us. Neither really beautiful nor too ugly, what really bothered me was how terribly average they were. A half hour or an hour later, I was back in the big room where I had started. In spite of the rather kindly efforts of the creature, nothing had happened; I was somewhere else. The situation didn't seem to have any relationship with – with what, in fact? I really didn't know. Let's just say it wasn't my cup of tea. I would not repeat the experience.

It's odd. We hardly talked on our way back, and I suppose that certain of them had left there feeling the same way I did, but something strange happened. My friends who, up until the Sphynx business, showed a lively curiosity about sex and were given to books (that I often got for them) dealing with medical issues, even underwear catalogs, seemed no longer interested in these things. When they talked about sex now it was with derision and vulgarity. The expression that occurred a lot in their conversations was "a fuck" or "get fucked." Women had now lost all their mystery and were most often classified as "sluts" (except their mothers, and sometimes – not always – their sisters).

I made note of this metamorphosis, which confirmed in me the idea that I didn't have a great deal in common with the kinds of human beings which revealed themselves in all this: men, in fact.

But we stayed good friends.

The Theater

My activities widened. For one, I had been appointed on the recommendation of Frédéric Loliée, the nephew of the famous bookseller Marc Loliée, rue des Saints-Pères, to stand in for him at the bookstall in the Saint-Georges Theater, where two plays by Montherlant were on, when there weren't too many alerts and electrical stoppages. *Fils de personnne*, with Suzanne Dantes and Marcel André as principle actors, and a little curtain raiser, *Un incompris,* whose star was a young ingénue, beautiful and lively, about whom everyone was already talking: Sophie Desmarets.

The bookstall in the hall, owned by the Rombaldi store, was open a quarter hour before the plays started, then at the intermission and before closing. It was a rather pleasant job, and I was on good terms with the battalion of women who worked there, almost all of them charming and who replaced me when I was absent or helped me out when there was too much of a crowd. Business was good. Besides, I'd found a way to augment my income by mixing Rombaldi's stock with mine. It seems – I learned at the end – that I wasn't allowed to do this. Couldn't they have told me? I wasn't used to this kind of thing.

I must have seen the plays twenty times, sitting at the back of the room while the women workers watched my inventory: *Fils de personne* and *Un incompris*. And then a play by Balzac, a dark melodrama whose title I can't remember.

As is well known, the Occupation was rich in creativity, in the theater as well in the movies. In 1942, there was *La Reine morte*, by Montherlant, a huge success at the Comédie-Française, and *Jeanne avec nous*, by Claude Vermorel, in which collaborators could see an anti-British theme, while a second meaning was implied: resistance to invaders.

In 1943, there was *Les Mouches* by Sartre, published immediately by Gallimard (I found the text verbose and repetitive); *Le Soulier de satin* by Claudel in December at the Comédie-Française; I would go with Marie-Claude in the spring of 1944. In February 1944 *Antigone* by Anouilh, a huge success for this tragedy in suits and evening dresses, which really struck me.

At the movies in 1943 and 1944, *Les Anges du péché* by Bresson and Giraudoux, *Goupi mains rouges*, by Jacques Becker, *Les Enfants du paradis* and *Les Visiteurs du soir*, by Carné, *Le Corbeau*, by Clouzot, *L'Eternel Retour*, by Cocteau, *Lumière d'été*, by Jean Gremillon, *La Nuit fantastique*, by Marcel L'Herbier...

Of course I'm forgetting some great works. It doesn't matter. I only wanted to make clear, imperfectly, what readers and audiences now can only understand with difficulty, even those who have seen, since then, some of these entertainments – the importance each scene had, each piece of dialogue, each kind of lighting, often interrupted by alerts or lack of electricity, playing in badly or unheated rooms. The words and the stage sets had, as with books, an importance, a resonance, they will never have again. But that's the way it goes, of course. None of this has any importance today. Neither the scenes nor the books, for the most part.

An excitement was building in France, especially among the students who had heard talk of the "maquis," or underground, without knowing what it was or where it could be found. Through Jean-Pierre Castenau, I was involved with a small group from the École Alsacienne including the charming Xavier Schlumberger, a nephew I believe of Jean Schlumberger. The obsession with these young people, about my age, was to get hold of guns in order to take action. No matter how. I let myself be roped into a crazy expedition, mostly out of curiosity. It took place in a tea room called Penny, on Place de la Madeleine, where we were to wait until some German soldiers were seated, having hung up their belts with guns in the cloakroom, as they often did. Then the conspirators were to put their raincoats over the soldiers' belts and carry them away after a reasonable period of time. Hours went by, but the right moment never came. I remarked that the plan was not very logical, and we all went home.

I never had any more news from the Xavier Schlumberger group. I learned later that at the moment of the Liberation, all these young men, those who had gathered in the Bois de Boulogne (had they finally found some weapons?) were discovered by the Germans and all of them shot. What a senseless waste.

Various Business Affairs

Not long after the landing in June 1944, I was again involved in a surprisingly good deal. I was summoned by Saucier who entrusted me with a mission, under sworn secrecy, to hide some cash – well, let's say about two hundred thousand francs at the time – for the acquisition of some rare books. Beautiful books were hard to find just then, since a lot of people were thinking the same way with the approach of victory, which was more and more certain.

I was lucky enough to uncover, among the ancient books at the old Rossignol house, rue des Saint-Pères, a La Fontaine illustrated by Oudry, and a Molière by Bret (experts will know what this means). I began by settling on a price. Then by a succession of clever (and not so difficult) maneuvers, with an increase here, a reduction there, I managed to obtain a commission of twenty thousand francs, which corresponded to around twenty months' worth of salary for a qualified employee, or about two hundred thousand francs in 2000.

The Rossignols entrusted their books to me (not without trembling). I gave them to Saucier, who took a long time inventorying them, then paid me, and I took the money to rue des Saints-Pères. Minus my commission, of course.

It was good timing. For reasons I'll explain later, I had to leave.

Detentions And Liberations

At the beginning of 1944, the clandestine activities of my mother were becoming far more manifest. Even stranger people passed through our house in little groups and shared our meager meals, especially at night, and sometimes they slept in the living room on the sofa, or on the floor. They had bushy or carefully cut beards and were relatively well dressed. Some spoke French badly and expressed themselves awkwardly, others spoke correctly but with a pronounced English accent, still others were clearly French and evidently came from diverse social origins. I listened without ever asking questions. They spoke openly.

I have a relatively clear memory of a dinner in 1944. Was it in April? I think it was after the fall of the Glières underground, in March. Three men were there with a military air, and I learned later they were in the Secret Army. One of them was obviously the superior of the other two who called him captain. His arm was wounded, tightly bandaged, and he ate with one hand.

My mother, after a short pause, questioned him directly, as she was used to doing. He choked with rage: yes, the maquis of the Secret Army had been betrayed. By whom? The English, of course, as usual. He described the inexorable advance of the German troops, the machine-gunning by the stukas, the SS parachuting in, insufficient weapons, the dead, and more dead. He was going to London. He calmed down. In fact, it was just a diversion. The real war would soon start. He talked about a landing in Normandy which would clarify things.

Germany would capitulate very fast when confronted by the Anglo-Saxons. It was expected that Hitler would be eliminated and that the German Army would join up with the Americans. The last battle to be fought would be against the Russians, of course. Naturally, Pétain and de Gaulle were in agreement. So, weapons would be pulled out of the secret places in France, and we would arrive in Moscow along with our allies, in three weeks. The other two approved.

All three soon disappeared into the night. My mother was thoughtful. Where was my father? As I remember, he wasn't at dinner that night.

I had the impression that I'd learned a bit more, but indirectly. I felt, in the end, that none of these rumors, no matter how high up the people who spread them, had any real importance. In fact, I accepted some and rejected others, just as with everything that I heard. There was so much being said.

June 6, the landings, and almost at once, in spite of the pitched battle in Normandy, there were the first signs of a German debacle. Behind the Madeleine, as usual, I was in a crowd surrounding the German tank units coming back from the front. They were selling butter, cheese, or cuts of lamb. They were scruffy, jocular, openly fraternizing, slightly or totally drunk. Agents watched the scene without moving. A German officer tried to involve himself. He loudly questioned the tank drivers. The tone rose. He was snubbed summarily. He went away. I never returned to that place behind the Madeleine, the competition was too great, the quantities too small and the goods too greatly coveted.

I confuse April and July because it was in July, one night returning from Paris, I was stopped at the station by a young neighbor: I shouldn't go back to the house because my mother had just been arrested – by the French police.

I have only vague memories of the days that followed. My father was arrested for twenty-four hours, then quickly released. I learned later that he had played an important role in the Resistance in league with the police department. The Germans – some parts of the army, at any rate – were already in talks with the police resistance. It was a matter of getting out of Paris without too great a military loss, in exchange for which the city would not be destroyed. However, there were heated negotiations going on in a variety of different sectors. At the time, I didn't know anything about the important diplomatic maneuvers made by the Swedish consul Raoul Nordling with the German general in Paris, Von Choltitz, whom Hitler had personally charged with destroying Paris, top to bottom, and who had refused this order.

I still have an eight-day hole in my memory, a block, until my mother's return, freed, no doubt, thanks to my father. She had been at the Petite-Roquette. She did not have good things to say about the nuns who took care of the detainees.

But where had I been? Not at home, at any rate. I remember one night going by a house next to ours (imprudently) and ringing the bell where my mother's aunt lived, an old woman with her husband who was even older. After a long time (I saw the curtains move) my great-aunt cracked open the door and whispered, "We're too old, you know, to get involved in all this." Then she shut it again. Really, they weren't wrong. I left the way I had come.

What exactly had happened? No doubt my mother had been denounced by a neighbor. Did my father know about her involvement? How could he not, at least to a degree? But wasn't my mother going too far, endangering the role of my father, as far as I could tell important in its own right, just to take in Resistant fighters and English aviators momentarily?

Oddly, we never talked openly in the family about this, not then or afterwards. I was able to discuss these things years later with other members of Resistance families. Several of them reported the same singularity: in general, they could never really talk about it, except by allusion. Odd.

Where had I been during these eight days? Obviously, at the homes of different friends, but which ones? What about my older brother? Did he have a role of some kind in all this? He and I never talked about it either, as strange as that might seem.

When we were all finally reunited at the house, my father told my brother and me that it would be best if the two of us went away for a while. As for him, he had to stay; it was July, everything was being decided in Paris. Serious things were in the works.

But, I had other ideas. Hadn't everything turned out well – as usual? In the end, it was the vacation season. Wasn't I still young enough to take one? I seriously asked myself this question.

———

Vacation

I t was an accumulation of disparate factors. Pierre X, far away from all these adventures, had to leave with his sister for the Haute-Marne on vacation. We agreed, along with Jean-Pierre Castelnau, to meet at the end of August, or the first of September, in the Herault, where the Castelnaus had a family estate. We made a date for a particular day and time. For us, this meeting was the beginning of a mysterious expedition whose precise goal was as yet undetermined, so far as I can recall. Above all, the point was to leave.

State transportation was completely disorganized. But Pierre X, his sister and I got to Bourbonne-les-Bains, then on into the surrounding area. I spent a part of July in a sort of paradise. There was a gathering of young cousins or friends of Pierre X, of both sexes, of whom Pierre and I were the oldest. The parents of these cousins were hardly part of our world. There was a big family house in a little town. I stayed close by in a hotel surrounded by greenery. Marie-Claude, glowing, fresh in a summer dress, came and joined me sometimes in my room. It was then that we consummated our frolics. She was seventeen, and I would be eighteen in three months.

I have a strangely vivid impression of this short period of time. It can't have lasted any longer than two weeks, but in my memory, it was a sort of eternity. Time was suspended. The weather was always beautiful. We listened to the news on the radio, then we each organized, separately, little group outings into nature.

One day, we had to leave for that preordained meeting in the Herault. And things were heating up in France, in a confused sort of way. I wanted to be part of what was happening, but I didn't know how to go about it.

I got back to the town and its train station, after I bribed the postman and climbed into his miniature car. At the station, I had to wait several hours for a train that was having problems. Finally, it arrived and I left for the south. I had all my things in one suitcase, my money in my pocket.

Wanderings

Chaotic travel, unlikely or unexpected, was the rule. Overcrowded trains, eight people to a toilet (with all the necessary consequences). Steam engines broken down, or were machine-gunned sometimes by British planes (scattering passengers into the countryside, like flocks of sparrows). Pregnant woman on the point of giving birth, babies in tears, camp escapees (from where?), old people dying...And then, suddenly, the silence of a luxury train with an electric engine, practically empty (only a few German officers; where were they going? To Spain?) which sometimes ran along the Côte d'Azur.

Finally I arrived in Lunel, and in the Castelnau family. Jean-Pierre had left a few days earlier for Paris, and I was unable to reach him. Unpredictable Jean-Pierre.

Solitary wanderings. A trip to Albi (why not?). Was it in Albi, or in Montauban, that this minor episode took place? There were no more trains. The evening was wonderful. I was sitting at the terrace of a café, my suitcase, as always, next to me. I was looking at the girls, all in a group, sometimes with young men.

A young man, also by himself, not far away, watched me for a while, discreetly, timidly. He was twenty-five or thirty, modest-looking, but extremely well groomed. After a while he got up and politely approached me. He saw that I was not from the area. A traveler? Yes. I didn't seem to know where I was going. Right, but I'd find my way. If I wouldn't mind... he would like to extend his hospitality. He didn't live far away, he was alone. If I wouldn't mind, we could have dinner at his place. I didn't say yes or no. I asked if he'd like a lemonade. He didn't drink alcohol. He insisted on offering me one, too.

He had a strong Portuguese or Spanish accent. He spoke the same way he was dressed: simply, but in a formal way. He said ordinary, but true things. He was nice, even handsome, above all, he had lovely eyes, very soft. He offered his hospitality again. I accepted, making it clear that I would pay him. He made a negative gesture and looked shocked.

We left together. He lived farther away than he had said. A little house that was a bit like him: modest, but very neat. I sensed something in the air, indefinable. I didn't know what, and I didn't care. Everything was neutral, as if on hold.

It was hot outside, but less so at his place. I was in shirt-sleeves, he was also. He said he was going to make dinner. He brought in a bottle of wine. He didn't drink alcohol, except for wine with meals. That suited me fine; I felt like drinking. We drank a little, and pretty soon we ate. It was an excellent dish, spicy Spanish cooking. Now I knew he was Spanish. We drank some more.

I felt very good. Everything was perfect. No lack of taste. José (he had mentioned his name right at the beginning) changed plates without any noise. Dessert? Some excellent fruit. If I wouldn't mind, he'd like to propose some liquor from his country. Why not?

I was tired. I needed to sleep. José apologized again: he only had one, double bed. All right. I plummeted into sleep, out like a light, prudently wrapped in a sheet which was the only thing covering us.

In the middle of the night, I was awakened by furtive caresses, which became more insistent. I woke up slowly. The light was on. On his knees on the bed, Jose was looking at me in astonishment. He had pulled back the sheet without waking me. He was caressing me everywhere, his skin was soft. I instinctively returned his caresses, my eyes closed. Furtively, I glanced at his erection, stupefied by its enormity. "A cock like a stallion" is the conventional expression and the only one that came to mind. He caught me looking at him. He shook his head, a bit irritated. We spent part of the night caressing each other, nothing more. I was happy like I was with Marie-Claude (not totally though), satisfied with the contact of his perfect skin. I don't know when I fell asleep.

In the morning, waking late, I found food prepared and everything I needed to make coffee. But I drank tea. It didn't matter. He must have gone out early to get jam and croissants. Oh! He had left a message. Awkward handwriting, too many words: he had never experienced before what he had with me. A divine night, unforgettable, a revelation. I was the love of his life. He had to go to work, but please let him find me on his return.

I had no intention of being there. I dressed, gathered up my ever-present suitcase, and asked directions to the station which was full of travelers who had been waiting all night. No train in sight.

Around noon José arrived, distraught. How could this be! The love of his life had left without even leaving a note. He got down on his knees in front of me, crying. Now he was really irritating me. He kissed my hands. I spoke to him gently. It had certainly been fun, but our paths led in different directions. Okay? He balked a bit: but we weren't just animals, were we? I thought vaguely that, yes, we were, but I didn't say so. I made up some muttered commitments. Yes, yes, I'd come back. He resigned himself. Besides, the train was coming, I had to get on. I only just had time to climb aboard. He sent me kisses as he sobbed. In fact, where was the train going? To Toulouse? Okay, let's go to Toulouse.

The Return

Toulouse the last days of the Liberation. I checked into a hotel, but soon joined a motley military group based in a police station not far from Matabiau Station. There were a number of uniformed policemen with us. Food: mainly sardines in oil and tubs of jam. Sometimes I slept in the police station on a mattress on the ground, sometimes at the hotel (a modest one) where I put the huge Lebel rifle they'd given me in the hall, in front of the admiring looks of the owners, before returning again to the latest skirmishes.

Bursts of gunfire. We shot at anything, to tell the truth. The Germans got out of there as fast as possible. Corpses of German soldiers in front of the Matabiau Station. The last burst of heavy machine-gun fire into the wall which I had climbed up on. Sudden fear. Then a parade of women with shaven heads – horrible. Chaplin movies brought up out of basements were playing in the movie houses (such was the overall impression). A huge crowd in front of the Capitol to welcome the governmental commissioner. Very well-built barricades had been set up in each of the streets leading to the central plaza. There, soldiers or others wearing armbands, gently disarmed those who had come with their weapons (I was one of them). Good-bye gun. End of the liberation of Toulouse.

How did I join a little convoy of military vehicles heading to Paris? It just happened by chance, I think. I make friends easily. I'm quickly accepted. There were a number of cars preceded by a front-wheel drive convertible at the back of which was welded a heavy machine gun on its tripod. Most of the cars were full of officers in uniform. I was in a 201 Peugeot with three young soldiers and managed to get hold of a Sten gun (I bought it, in fact). Along the way, I also bought an automatic pistol with a broken part from a soldier and a working Beretta 9 millimeter with some ammunition.

We were well armed; but it would be to no avail. The trip was long because we carefully avoided the retreating German troops and the last pockets of resistance. The officers were in a hurry to return to Paris, which had just been liberated. When we camped, they talked above all about years of service and promotions.

We went through Berry. One day, to our astonishment, the mistress of an enormous farm with lots of buildings had set up by the side of the road some trestle tables on which her valets and servants, along with her grandchildren, had placed all sorts of food I hadn't seen in four years – and I was not the only one. There were pats of butter, fat cheeses, lamb, hams, and sausages. The entire military convoy was invited! The woman farmer, fifty years old, was in charge of everything, an eye on everything (reminiscent of the *Con d'Irène*). The food kept coming, non-stop. The wine ran. A dream. It was the end of the war, no doubt about it. Just in case, I grabbed a sausage and two or three cheeses, like my comrades, though it was not really necessary; everyone was swimming in abundance. The memory of those giant pats of butter offered by the farmwoman from Berry would haunt me for a long time.

The next day they left me in Sceaux with promises to see each other again. Exchange of addresses. My mother was full of joy. My father was happy. He hugged me tightly in his arms. What did my brother say? I don't remember at all.

Other Times

Return to Paris. I'd hardly got there before I noticed, in the window of the Gallimard bookstore, a brand-new volume printed in crown quarto with cream wrappers. The title was printed in black, *Notre-Dame-des-Fleurs*. The author's name, Jean Genet, vaguely meant something to me. He'd been freed from prison the year before, but could be sent back. He had been defended by Jean Cocteau, who told the jury, "You're going to condemn the greatest poet of the century." I thought: the usual thing, of no consequence. Once freed, he had published his first novel "paid for by an admirer from Monte Carlo... for subscribers only" in a limited edition of 350 copies.

While I was mechanically examining the book through the window, Roland Saucier showed up. "That's an extraordinary text," he said. A revelation. Cocteau was right. There's been nothing like it since Proust. Saucier was really excited.

And all at once a person arrived whom I recognized immediately. It was the "teacher" from before I'd left Gallimard. Introductions: "Jean-Jacques Pauvert, Jean Genet." Cordial remembrances from earlier times. Genet hesitated between the persona of the great writer he wanted to show himself to be, his natural amiability, and a touch of boastfulness. He was talkative, off and on. He told us how he used to steal books from the store with his briefcase that had a false bottom, into which he used to stuff books without being seen. Saucier was fascinated. He smothered Genet with his eyes. He was this century's genius. Genet and I made plans to see each other again.

The bookstore business was changing. In the new stores, books on the Otto list were being replaced by new banned titles: now it was Céline who was being sold on the black market. For *Décombres*, the asking price was five thousand francs. All the illustrated semi-luxury publications, which had appeared during the Occupation and were the preferred reading matter of the dairymaids, were to vanish. The prices of real books (large illustrated ones, first editions) never stopped going up.

Everything was changing. My mother was soon to be triumphantly elected to the city council in Sceaux. My father had been promoted to a higher position, still at the press office in the police department.

We had visits from new (or old, from the time of the Occupation?) acquaintances of my parents. A few women rather intrigued me. They were clearly – openly – communists. This was now all right, not like in 1939–40. They were about forty. I well remember the name of the woman who appeared to be in charge. She was Monique Brun, a little chubby, with dark brown hair, very intelligent, almost mannish.

She seemed interested in me. We talked a lot together. She presented Marxism in a very clear way. She had an answer for everything, for the positions taken by the USSR in 1939–44: the German-Soviet pact being made in order to gain time, then on to a leading role during the war.

She didn't dwell too much on the role of the French communists during the Occupation, which had been vital, as we now know. The courageous acts of the communists, once they had been forced to take sides, were numerous. I suppose they would also have been just as courageous allied with the Germans under an American occupation. But never mind....

The return of Thorez (and his departure) was the subject of a short, rousing exegesis which left me a bit skeptical.

I found Monique interesting. I vaguely sensed why I would never adhere totally to her system: just because it was a system. I didn't clearly know it yet, but any system aimed at perfectly explaining the world offended me a little, because of something I couldn't as yet define. (In 2004, close on to my eighty-fifth birthday, I still don't know exactly why.) In spite of everything, I was often forced to yield ground to her dialectic.

We got along well together, very freely and openly. She was naturally aware, through my parents, of my adventure in 1942, though without knowing the details (I never told anyone about certain things). She now drew me into private conversations in Paris cafés.

And then one day, quite quickly, she showed her hand: the French Communist Party needed to keep the advantages it had gained during the war and, if possible, expand them. Her principle goal was to reinforce the position held by the Party during the Occupation. In 1944, given all the various events, enormous holes had been left in the network's organization. These holes needed to be filled as quickly as possible by active participants. But, don't worry! There was no need to join the Party. I would simply be introduced, if I agreed, as the surviving member of a network, though not a communist one, the BCRA. So there we were. Afterwards, she was rather vague: We'll see, she said. Do you agree to be introduced?

Since there were no conditions (I in no way wanted to be a member of the Party), and the adventure attracted me, I made my mind up. Okay. I soon found myself in a bigger group, with Monique's partner (I suspected them of being lesbians) and an unknown person, who was bossy but warm-hearted. So here was the situation: from January 1, 1944, I had been a member of the Velite-Thermopyles network. I was handed a couple of papers. I now had to show up at headquarters of the BCRA on boulevard Suchet, as soon as possible. I needed to be vague about what I had been doing during the Occupation: liaison work, that was all. This was perfect, as I clearly remembered my missions for Boris (but I kept all that to myself).

I headed over to boulevard Suchet. The BCRA building was a buzzing beehive, full of hectic uniforms. I thought again about the little troop that had headed back up to Paris; positions in the system were being rapidly snatched up. After a long wait, I was received by an officer. I told my story. I was making contact again, having been on the run for a while. My parents' arrest in July made a good impression, but the officer remained reserved. I was given another appointment, so they had time to look into things, I suppose.

I had another meeting. The atmosphere was more relaxed. Information about my parents probably helped. Fine, so I had been in the Vélite-Thermopyles network, as of January 1 (oh, somewhere about then). This would be noted down in my military papers. Meanwhile, I was given some attestation papers enjoining the police to give me a helping hand if I ever needed it (what could I need?).

Another meeting with people from the Party (at least, I think so), who were fairly enthusiastic. I assumed it was a done deal. We were going to see each other again. If I understood rightly, this retroactive repopulation of their decimated network was coming along fine. And there would be other examples.

I had no news for some time. We no longer saw people from the group at our house during 1946. After a long delay, I finally asked my father some questions, and he seemed a little disturbed. Monique Brun had left, called to other duties (we never learned what exactly). My father, who had never been a member of the Party, no longer seemed to be in agreement, in front of me, with Monique Brun and her friend. The same went for Madeleine Jacob, a friend during the Occupation, but whose blood-curdling articles in the *Franc-Tireur* (death for all those who had had anything to do with the Germans) ended up incensing my father.

Okay. For the moment, enough about the Vélite-Thermopyles network.

In fact, I have never talked to anyone about this except one person (Christiane). And I owe my apologies to the survivors of the Vélite-Thermopyles network, some of whom have contacted me from time to time, over the past sixty years. I am just a minor player in memories which are, for some, still far too vivid.

I have always remained rather vague with these network survivors. One day, in a telephone conversation, I made a mistake: I alluded to a pseudonym, "Jean-Jacques." But that's your first name, the person said, suddenly. Luckily, in fact, I was not officially called Jean-Jacques, following some mysterious complications, invented by my parents. I told him this and everything then appeared to be all right.

I have to say, if I need to justify myself, that I have never asked for any of the advantages which would have resulted from this fictitious role: a war combatant card, certainly, maybe a little pension, who knows? The only thing I got out of it was an exemption from doing military service.

And then, after all, perhaps I officially was a part of the BCRA in 1942–43. At any rate, I should have been.

A Special Liberation

I saw Patrick L. again several times. He was one of the three companions who took me back to Paris. The smartest of the three, he had a Parisian sense of humor of a special kind, which I liked. We became friends. One day I introduced him to Marie-Claude. I was trying with my father's help to normalize his official situation, which seemed a bit complicated.

How did he live? I didn't know if he was still in the army, if he had been demobilized (in fact, had he even been in the army?) or was a deserter. He was twenty-three and no longer wore a uniform. I soon understood that he was part of a gigantic black market network which had been set up in France between Mafioso G.I.'s and local thugs.

One day Patrick asked if he could borrow my Sten gun. When I hesitated, he suggested buying it from me. I like weapons, but I didn't really need a machine gun. In the back of my mind, I could remember walking around with it for a long time, stripping it down, then putting it in a bike bag, in the BCRA building.

We concluded the deal quickly. I wouldn't take anything in exchange for the gun. Patrick simply promised me "a part of the deal he was working on now." Okay.

Several days passed without news. One night my father returned home worried. Patrick had been arrested. A serious armed robbery (a currency exchange bureau? I don't remember) on rue Saint Denis, which involved G.I. deserters. The military police had intervened, along with the French police. People had been wounded. Each police force had arrested its own people. The G.I. deserters were in the hands of the Americans, the French thugs in those of the Paris police. My father gently warned me about the people with whom I was associating. He, too, had found Patrick likeable.

I panicked a little. No more information was forthcoming. Patrick apparently had kept his mouth shut; he could have compromised my father, as well as myself. I would never hear from him again. He was no doubt sent to prison during the next months, never to reappear again. I didn't try to find out what had happened to him, but I missed his sparkling smile, which had also won over my father. One more person lost.

I took up my previous activities again, somehow. Books reappeared little by little, but the semi-clandestine market had almost completely ceased, except for the *Pléiade* volumes, NRF hardbacks, first editions and the oversized illustrated books, whose prices continued to rise, as well as some other trifles. Rare works owned by bibliophiles, more and more sought after, were back in the hands of the large bookstores. The beautiful surrealist editions barely interested anyone and were remaindered everywhere. However, there would soon be a bookstore depression, part of the great 1945–52 recession, which everyone has forgotten about today.

Occupation,
Which Occupation?

I'm now grouping together one or two years of memories. For me, these particular years are a sort of dark hole in which a lot of things got mixed up; it doesn't seem useful to make a detailed list day-by-day of this period, and besides, I'd have a hard time doing it. Up until December 1945, what we call the Liberation had just been a lot of despair and exaltation. It was that way with a lot of people my age, I think, except we didn't talk much about it. Sixty years later, we've replaced a lot of these facts – which often went unmentioned at the time – by romantic images: a resistant France triumphantly welcoming American troops. Pétain forgotten. Prisoners returned. Everything's okay.

This is only one side of the story, in my opinion. My memories are more jumbled. About the business with Patrick, for example: I'd like to correct a certain side of the situation, but just one for the moment, which will help explain the rest to those French today, who for the most part never experienced this period. I refer to an aspect of it that was carefully covered-up at the time, according to some witnesses, including my father, though even he didn't tell me the whole story.

I'm borrowing numbers and citations from a well-documented source which, it seems to me, did not get the attention it deserved at the time of its publication. *Vie et Moeurs des G.I's en Europe* by Marc Hillel was published in 1981 by Balland. It's a picture that is certainly biased (as the author admits), but one that is real, concerning the situation in France during the years 1944 and 1945. I quote:

> The inoffensive traffic of ammunition, cigarettes, or bars of chocolate in exchange for a bottle of alcohol or a meeting with a woman, to which, instinctively, the liberator and the liberated freely agreed, suddenly transformed into a vast illicit traffic fed by raids on military supply centers. The golden age of big-time dealers and pimps began at

the same moment as an incredible climate of violence and debauchery spread throughout France. Paris and some large provincial towns, near large military camps, intermittently lived through terrifying times. People were killed by stray bullets in the course of fistfights in bars or in dance halls, in the street or in the central squares of small villages. Also, lots of victims were crushed by jeeps going at top speed. Aided by the French police, the Military Police hunted down fugitives, combed Paris day and night, trying by every means to stem the traffickers and the prostitution rings that the pimps had set up around the camps. Alone or in groups, the deserters pillaged banks or stores, and raped women, these crimes, for the most part, following upon unimaginable binge drinking... (Hillel, pp. 147–148).

At the same time, there was a silence in the French press about the number of crimes. Only my father told us about it. Hillel explains it this way:

... However, the French press kept quiet and continued to portray the American G.I. as a smiling soldier, chomping on his chewing-gum and without whom the 'Krauts' would still be there. Same thing for the radio. Not the least disparaging commentary was heard which could have, with British press integrity, helped the French better to understand the negative aspects that come with such an enormous massing of men in a country largely lacking its own...

(Here Hillel inserts a note observing that in April 1945, two million Frenchmen, prisoners and workers who had been requisitioned, were still in Germany.)

Some invoked the lack of paper – newspapers, in fact, were only one or two pages long – or the fear, according to others, of publishing articles which could be seen as 'collaborationist' (the newspapers would remain very pro-American until 1946, even including newspapers on the left) plus the fact that the rearguard soldiers, bivouacked in cities or concentrated along the supply lines, were still living in the same closed universe that they had known for the last thirty months, in the British Isles... (Hillel, pp. 152–153).

I'll end by citing two more American articles reproduced by Hillel, an editorial in *Time Magazine* from November 19, 1945, entitled "The Wrong Ambassadors":

It was a difficult thing for U.S. correspondents to write about, but in intermittent dispatches they were sending back a disturbing story. The behavior of U.S. soldiers abroad, particularly in the liberated countries of Europe, has left a bad taste in the mouths of all concerned. Relations between the G.I.s and the civilian populations have been strained to the utmost. This was especially true in France. There were things to be said on both sides; there were excuses and rationalizations. But the ugly fact was that the behavior of many G.I.s in Europe was disgraceful. It's not just the fights in Place Pigalle, or the fights on the docks in Le Havre. It's not just the hold-ups and the drunkenness and the vandalism. It's above all the way that a lot of GIs conduct themselves as conquerors to whom everything is due. A lot of French are saying: 'Americans are the new Germans.'

And an article by James Finucane, special envoy for *The American Mercury*:

They whistle at the girls, drive their jeeps too fast, loot in conquered countries, 'borrow' in liberated ones, cheat on the black market, think any girl is willing to discuss 'how much?' [...] A GI jeeping along the Rue Paradis in Marseille after dark leans out of the back seat to inquire of each girl passed on the sidewalk: 'How much, baby?' And the Rue Paradis is not in the red-light district. [...] The Yank who steers his jeep at a civilian is probably one of those zombies who has been overseas too long. [...] Mentally, he never left home. [...] French, German, Czech, Belgian or Dutch – they all speak a silly mumbo-jumbo; they're all foreigners, and, as foreigners, are inferior, suspect and repulsively un-American."

Palimugre –
Do Whatever You Like

Most of my rare book customers came back, and they'd certainly heard (who from? Sometimes from me) about my role in the "Resistance." Some of them fawned on me a bit, like one film producer who did his best to offer me proof that another producer was an active collaborationist – a competitor, no doubt. I found it hard, actually, to correct them about the importance and the exact goal (which I didn't know) of my role. They held fast to any little thing in order to denounce, and denounce again... like under the Occupation.

Besides, I was soon going to leave official circles. In October 1944 I got an urgent summons from boulevard Suchet. A newly commissioned officer grilled me, and ended up telling me that he was not convinced about my work as an informant, and I'd be demobilized in September. All right. I didn't feel like looking for the precise reasons for this sudden firing. At any rate, they were probably as opaque as they were complicated.

I wandered around Paris, occupied from time to time by the book business, which interested me less and less. The situation was somber. Battles for political influence were at fever pitch, over and above the internal social situation. It seemed to me that the overriding question, the one which dominated the others, was the ferocious struggle of communism to assure its power in France. Was it justified? I thought about this sometimes, but the communist dialectic was strong, and they controlled a part of the press. My father seemed to have broken all ties with the communists, whom he referred to in rather harsh terms.

I found Marie-Claude again at the end of September, when she returned from Bourbonnais with her brother. Her family situation had worsened. She finally admitted, at least to me, that her mother was a drug addict, that she always had been, and that she was now more addicted than ever. She used to send her daughter to seduce pharmacists in order to get what she needed. Laudanum? I think that's what it was.

We rekindled our old relationship. I felt responsible for her. At the same time, I was getting involved in new interests. For example, I was taking magic lessons from Professor Alma in a little street by Montagne Sainte-Geneviève. I was gifted. Apparently, I had the right kind of hands to "palm" cards. Professor Alma had a whole collection of objects used in the trade, for example Robert Houdin's pendulum in which you see the hands turning, but without seeing any mechanism at work.

At the same time I'd taken an interest in graphology. I soon had an entire collection on the subject, the same way I did for palmistry. I often visited an arcane bookstore on boulevard Saint-Germain, run by a curious, rather corpulent guy, about forty, with a short, black beard, who leaned over to look with great curiosity at my handwriting. I soon learned that he was what they called a Satanist. I felt uncomfortable around him.

I was also learning to shoot at Gastine-Reinette, the famous gunsmith's on avenue Victor-Emmanuel-III, to whom I'd given my Colt single action handgun for repair. He fixed it. Soon I was the best shot in the group. I met other gun enthusiasts, officers from the French army, Americans passionate about "Lugers" (the name they gave my handgun). They congratulated me. I was a little bit the king of the shooting range. But ammunition was expensive.

I was working during the day, and sometimes at night, for two newspaper agencies, on the recommendation of my father, who was worried about me and thought I was feeling rather lost. In fact, I was.

At the same time, I got caught up in a well-known tendency of the human race after catastrophes: the need to have children. It's a curious reflex which produces thousands of more or less banal or improvised marriages. There would soon be a "baby-boom." Marie-Claude was there. I stopped using condoms when we had sex. I waited, eyes wide open, for what would surely happen, and it did during the first month of 1945: Marie-Claude was pregnant.

A family war council; did I want her to have an abortion (dangerous in every way, at that time)? My parents even suggested that I take a little trip. I remained stubborn; I wanted to get married.

LA PRESSE POPULAIRE
Agence de Presse — 5, Rue Saint-Augustin - PARIS-2ᵉ
N° 6

CARTE DE PRESSE

M onsieur PAUVERT Jean Jacques   Rédacteur

Demeurant à SCEAUX (Seine),39 Rue des Coudraies

I wanted to have a child. Perhaps, for me, it was an antidote to all the threats that I felt hovering over the world. So why not go for Marie-Claude? In some

ways, we got along very well. In other ways, I was beginning to sense in her certain limits, but what? We got married in May, and Marie-Claude gave birth in December.

At the same time, I felt suffocated by the situation in my country. Ration cards were still needed. (I got involved in a fake card operation, the work of a printer. Of course fake worker cards were very expensive.) Bread rations had even been reduced. Ridiculous political games started up again. And purges were in full swing, amid great chaos. Dances were outlawed everywhere, as a sign of mourning (for what?) The death knell tolled in every town, and in Paris. The radio commemorated endlessly "our dead," "our victims," Oradour-sur-Glane, etc., and concentration camp images were shown ceaselessly. Besides, the war wasn't even over. Everywhere, boys about my age joined the army, like my friend Daniel. It was a matter of "participating." At last. No one talked any more about *littérature engagée* – committed literature. Committed to what?

I'd had enough. At nineteen, I rebelled, but against what I wasn't exactly sure. How could I express myself?

The idea for a publication, or a review, took hold in my mind. To say what? One day, in 1945, I wrote a sort of manifesto, which I began to send to various writers I knew. To make this easier, I mimeographed off several copies. Marcel Aymé answered me and I went to see him. I liked what he wrote. He inscribed for me my favorite book, *Le Chemin des ecoliers*, to my mind the best novel written under the Occupation, with *La Neige etait sale*, by Simenon (which didn't come out until 1948). And perhaps, *Les Forêts de la nuit* (Julliard, Prix Goncourt, 1947) by Jean-Louis Curtis.

Andre Salmon (he had some trouble at the time of the Liberation, having written some anti-English articles) had already put his name down for the second issue. I took a chance, sometimes with a timidity that I can't explain very well, with other literary stars. So what should I call this review? Any title that sounded too explicit about its purpose (and what was its purpose?) seemed unacceptable to me.

An obscure word sprang to mind, one which had arisen awhile before, in a state of confusion, between two dreams: "PALIMUGRE." The word had then stuck after I had awoken. I pronounced it several times, perplexed, and looked for it in dictionaries; the only word which came close to it meant a kind of sea shell. No relationship. This arcane word soon seemed to impose itself as a title (why?) So I told the people around me that my review would be called *Palimugre*; they heard the news with a certain astonishment. But Marcel Aymé liked the name.

In August 1945, American planes dropped atomic bombs on the Japanese cities of Hiroshima and Nagasaki. I learned about this while I was standing in for the old bookseller on the quay where I used to leave my books to be sold on commission; he'd broken his arm. My anguish grew. "This end of the world is not ours," André Breton was to say later.

I will always remember a letter from Jean-Pierre Castelhau, a short time later (he was then working in the provinces). It said: "The hole I'm living in just got deeper since the atomic bombs..."

In the fall of 1945 I read an article by Sartre in *Cahiers du Sud* and it stuck with me: "Explication de *L'Étranger*." It was evidently about Camus, whom I still saw from time to time, and I continued to gravitate to his books. I also knew Sartre (and Simone de Beauvoir). Sartre never recognized me, but when I said my name, he used to say, "Of course, of course." And he was very nice in the NRF offices. I found Simone de Beauvoir to be pretty but very much "a teacher" in what she said and wrote.

In short, I sent Sartre a short handwritten letter. The text has disappeared (they didn't yet save all the texts by authors as soon as they were written). Why didn't he write a little book?

Why not a little book, indeed, but why write one at all? At the time I didn't think about it much, and sixty years later, after instinctively reacting this way, I still haven't actually found the reason. Wasn't it really so I could understand something that I wanted out in the open, something I could read?

Sartre certainly had some flaws (I was to discover more and more of them), but he had a rare fount of generosity, and a huge indifference to material things. Instead of saying to me, "You know, I already have publishers and contracts, so what can you offer me, what do you want to do exactly?" he simply sent me a short letter, handwritten too, which is one of the few things that I regret someone stole from me. It said, "What a good idea, so do whatever you like."

III

PATHWAYS

Men travel by many different paths. Whoever tracks and compares their ways will see wonderful figures arising; figures that seem to belong to the great Manuscript of Design which we encounter everywhere, on wings of birds, on the shells of eggs, in clouds, in snow, in crystals, in rock formations, in frozen water, within and upon mountains, in plants, in beasts, in men, in the light of day, in slabs of pitch and glass when they are jarred or struck, in filings around a magnet, and in the singular Coincidences of Chance.

— Novalis

(Trans. by M. T. and U. C. B.)

How Do You Make A Book?

The end of 1945 was extremely busy; we were having a baby. I was rewriting press dispatches and writing occasional reports. I still did a little business in books, half-heartedly. Nothing much was happening with my project for the review. And I had a book in the works, or at least a project for a book. And how do you make a book out of an article by Sartre? I knew enough to know that in order to make a book, you had to have a printer. That was the most essential point.

As I walked along the Left Bank (of course), I saw a sign on rue de Seine: "HENRI DIÉVAL, printer."

I went in. They were friendly, but a bit astonished. I wanted to make a book? All right. Was I an author? No. A publisher, then? No, no. Well. But what kind of book? Oh! A little book. Did I have a mock-up? Well, no. Right then, the people at Diéval's just shrugged, helplessly. I had to have a mock-up. They showed me their slim catalog of typefaces. For the first time, I designed a cover. Ah! Who was going to pay? I was, of course. How should I pay you? Ah! Let's say a third when the order is taken, a third when the proofs are ready (they explained to me what that meant), and a third on delivery. What about the paper? Did I have any? No? We can take care of that. Do I have a bookbinder? No. We can arrange that, too. There's Wendling's, next door, just down the street. And how much is that?

It wasn't too expensive. Deal done. Well, not exactly, there was one last detail: there must absolutely be a publisher's imprint. Are you the publisher? Well, yes, in fact I am, but I'm not putting my name on it. Why not?

I didn't really know why not. A taste for secrecy, a distrust of being too easily identified. I was no more a publisher than I was anything else, I thought. So what mark will you use? I gave them the name of my future review: you can put "Palimugre éditeur."

The little book came out at the end of December 1945. I got the calibration wrong; the volume was a little thin, and the pages too crowded. Even so, the cream colored, tucked-in wrappers weren't bad. I took the entire print run to Sceaux in a taxi. Damn, I had forgotten the print limitation; some of the copies were on ersatz *Japon* paper. My mother, who had very clear handwriting, inscribed by hand a sort of numbering on the copies printed on *Japon*.

Here's What Happened

M y review project got started again. Nearly sixty years later, I'm copying out the words of Paul Léautaud in his daily notes, his *Journal littéraires* concerning what my approach to him inspired in his. Our first meeting was not friendly. Luckily, I couldn't read the following words over his shoulder:

> Wednesday December 5, 1945 – This morning received a letter from M. Jean-Jacques Pauvert; it seems I've heard of him before" [*Really?*], "living in Sceaux, and has created a review 'to defend the rights of artists and freedom of the mind.' He thought it necessary to do something 'for freedom, the joy of being alive, and the love of art' and he has asked if he can count on me for something for his first issue, not hiding the fact that there might not be a second.
>
> The "joy of being alive!' Apart from the fact that this expression is terribly crass, the idea is all right with me...

Okay, but then I showed up at his place!

> "Tuesday December 11 – M. Jean-Jacques Pauvert will soon be here to pay a visit, the man starting a review to proclaim the return of freedom to write what one wants. I haven't answered his letter yet: one less letter to write – assuming I had decided to answer him. Nineteen years old! He makes a living by doing little jobs at newspapers."

"He makes a living doing little jobs at newspapers." Yes, in the office that my father helped me get into. Rewriting telegram dispatches at night on the last floor of a building on faubourg Montmartre. From time to time, I had a drink (without alcohol, I wasn't drinking much then) at the all-night café. There were tired prostitutes, some very young, some not bad at all. We became comrades, like all nighttime people. They were friendly. I was young and funny. I looked at them with curiosity, but without any desire. I had another idea of what one calls love, physical or not. What idea? I don't know. In any case, "a fast fuck" never meant anything at all to me.

The continuation of Léautaud's journal, still December 11, 1945:

> The cost for his first issue, just the printing, 75,000 francs. When I told him that I'd never spend 75,000 francs on this kind of thing, he said there were certain people who were interested in his project, and who wanted to help make it happen. He has his paper. He is authorized to print his review according to the terms he repeated to me: on the condition that the review is not sold and that it is sent out as sealed copies. He saw Salmon who has signed up for the second issue. He's going to bring me the program article that he's written for the first issue. He wants me to be in this first one. If his text excites me a little, we'll see.
>
> [...] He appears to be pretty knowledgeable about what I write...

The technical details are now meaningless to me. It seems strange this idea of mailing the review as sealed copies. But sometimes Léautaud just said any old thing. I remember once stopping him from writing in his Journal that they had cut off Arletty's breasts after the liberation of France. He really thought it was true.

It must have been in December that I gave him my famous manifesto, which was dated October 1945. I found it, and here are some extracts – no, all of it; in the end, a memoir has to be a tell-all.

> Here is what happened. We fought for the freedom of expression, and then when we had it, we did not take advantage of it. That's okay. We just forgot, that's all. Some thought we had just forgotten to think. That is impossible. Tons of printed material flood us every month, every week, every day, in the world of letters. If there is not a gram of thinking in all that, we would know it. That isn't the case. These people are full of intelligence. They are overflowing with it. The world of letters is suffocating under its intelligence. It is in the hands of the professors. The time has come when, far from countering stupidities, it is a matter of countering intelligence. It is Jean Cocteau who says this. And he is right. Professors have a lot of ideas. But literature is created with words. This is why, in spite of appearances, there is so little real literature now in the French literary world. There is a gap in that area.

And if I say there is a gap, of course I think we are going to fill that gap. And we are going to repair the forgetfulness I mentioned. Because we don't take very good care of art when our minds are not free.

Do not think that freedom of mind supposes apathy or detachment. We have convictions. One, at any rate. We do not think it is necessary to be 'committed' in order to be involved in art. Let us be clear. We do not mean that an artist should not be 'committed'. We mean that his commitment does not matter to us, and we do not take it into account when we are judging a work. Of course politics are important. But we are dealing with art. There is no relationship, obviously.

I am going to talk about politics, even so. Not at great length, though. We are not indifferent to the art of governing people. I am going to tell you what we think.

This war began in 1917. It is still going on. It will last for a long time. It is a war to the bitter end between two ideologies. The Russian ideology and the Anglo-Saxon one. These five years of war were only an intermission. There are, in fact, only two sides participating in this. A compromise may not be impossible, in the long run. But it would take too long. So, it does not interest us. Even so, our sympathies are with the Bolchevik system. Given that the capitalist system has been in existence for some time and isn't working, it is logical and necessary to try something else. We will do what we can to help the Marxist revolution. But not everything. We will not give our lives, for example. We are very attached to our lives. There would be nothing left to give afterwards. That is the way it is.

In Russia, two generations in a row sacrificed themselves for the happiness of future generations. A generation of workers and a generation of soldiers. They were taught that death ends everything and that this life is irreplaceable. They gave their lives anyway. It was beautiful. It is beyond our capabilities. The welfare of human beings leaves us indifferent. It is too far away. We have had enough of waiting. We know that nothing will be settled for at least ten years. Everything will be perfect then, maybe. We do not care. We do not want to be committed. We do not have the sacrificing spirit. We do not have the spirit of duty. We have no respect for cadavers. We want to live. Is that so difficult? The world will soon be in the hands of the secret police and the directors of conscience. Everybody will be committed. Everybody will serve. But us? We do not want to serve anything. We do not want to be used. A rain of ash is slowly burying the earth under boredom and constraints. Men, one by one, are getting involved in group missions. We are the village idiots. We play with girls, the sun, or with books. We play with our lives, sometimes, too. We will do anything to keep our lives away from the big machines that would exploit them, for whatever reason. It is dangerous to steal the sunshine from idiots.

You thought that men were only good for choosing their side of the barricade – if that. You thought that everything was in place and we could get started. Look again. Do you not feel that there are still human beings for whom happiness is not a matter of servitude, for whom poetry is not yet a weapon, for whom magic has not yet deserted the earth? We feel the days of our lives as they pass. Hour by hour. On and on. The days of our lives will not serve you. Did you really think that everything had been taken care of? Did you really believe that you could rely on everything? There are some of us who still know the cost of a threatened, dead-end life. Life is too precious to be taken advantage of by anyone.

I am sorry. I have gone off on a tangent. But it is never useless to say what one thinks. And do not suppose that I have just defined the attitude of an entire group. I have profoundly shocked several of my comrades. They will tell you just that a few pages further on. If I have a belief, it is not so I can impose it on people. Right now, with two camps issuing their call to arms behind the walls, I wanted to welcome the deserters. I wanted to welcome the free spirits. Are there still newspapers that do not issue orders? Can we still find artists who do not hate, who are not submissive? Independent creators, poets who take no sides? These artists have to be given refuge somewhere.

Let us open a haven for uncommon spirits.

Well, it wasn't too bad after all. A manifesto written at nineteen years old is quite likely to contain terrible stupidities. Altogether, sixty years later, despite a few rather exaggerated flights of fancy (that said...), or flippancies that sometimes fall flat, I really don't have anything to feel ashamed of. What's more, I am pretty much of the same opinion today as I was sixty years ago. Except for Marxism. I have taken a step back from that.

Besides, Paul Léautaud – and that really means something – was touched by it. At the beginning of the year, he signed a copy of his booklet *Notes retrouvées*:

To Jean-Jacques Pauvert
Whose turn of spirit and style of
Writing enchant me, may he
keep them, as long as possible.

> — Paul Léautaud.
> January 1946

The Purging Of Books?

Paul Léautaud's *Journal littéraire* continued:

> Monday December 9, 1946 – Tonight, visit from young Jean-Jacques Pauvert. A good six months since I've seen him.
>
> He's become a publisher. I got a copy of the first little volume that he published. He asked Montherlant for a text. Montherlant said he had one all ready for him, but he has just been given a cease and desist order: publish nothing for a year, as of last October. The jury chosen to examine his case was composed of six writers. Four deserted. Two stayed to decide his fate. One of them was R. Good to know…

I think that this first small volume, really the second or the third, was *Prière sur l'Acropole*, by Renan (being prudent, I did not want to give Léautaud *Explication de "L'Étranger"*; Sartre and Camus were not his cup of tea).

Actually, I had seen Montherlant several times at his place, quai Voltaire. It was there, on my first visit, that I learned a very good lesson about publishing: he had welcomed me quite amicably, though with a little distrust. We talked; he seemed thoughtful. Suddenly, he had some very precise questions: what was my project, how was I managing the financing, on what basis were we going to draw up a contract? I hemmed and hawed, and he said calmly, "Listen, I can tell you don't know anything about this business. You're going to go down to the Voltaire tabac at the corner of the street, and you're going to come back with two pieces of stamped paper costing …francs. Here's a typewriter (I don't have a secretary today). I'll dictate the contract."

And he did. I am sorry that I no longer have that contract – my first one. It was short, and rigorous: a print run limited to a thousand copies, a royalty payment in advance, 50 percent on signing, 50 percent when the proofs were ready, no ancillary rights, a guaranteed exclusivity for only a few years.

I was charmed. A first contract with an author aware of his own interests and who protected them extremely well. It was true that I knew very little about this new business. I'd learned a good lesson. This was around June or July 1946; I'd just turned twenty.

I've forgotten to say which text we were talking about. It was *Sur les femmes*, which had appeared several years earlier published by Sagittaire, with illustrations by Henri Matisse.

Why Montherlant? I'd admired his writing for a long time, a certain freedom of spirit which allowed him to alternate between moral writings (*La Vie en forme de proue, Service inutile...*) and writings that might be called Dionysian, like *Aux fontaines du désir*. His point of view – or rather his points of view – about women interested me without always convincing me, but he said things that you were not used to reading on the subject.

And besides, I wanted to redress (all by myself!) the injustice that, it seemed to me, had been committed in regards to Montherlant, the whipping boy of the French literary world, without special reason save his literary success during the Occupation.

There was a lot of confusion about the purification of literature, for both authors and publishers. This little world fell under different and contradictory authorities, both ignorant of each other. For example, there were different courts of justice on one hand, and on another a Comité national d'épuration des Gens de Lettres, while a third consisted of the regional professional committees for the cleansing of business; in general, it was considered that these last committees were not competent to judge men of letters.

As for publishers, Bernard Grasset, for instance, had been an active participant in the collaboration during the Occupation, both in his actions and in his writings, and was not condemned by the National Commission of Professionals, except for a three-month suspension of his business (because, it seems, the members of the Commission "all knew the psychological state of the accused"). The law court, which also followed the case, decided otherwise in June 1948, so that Grasset's firm would be dissolved and 99 percent of its holdings confiscated. In the end, however, the dissolution measure was replaced by a fine, and the company was practically pardoned.

As for Denoël, things would be even more spectacular: on December 2, 1945, Robert Denoël was mysteriously murdered. What remained of the company was the publishing house office building, which became the object of a lawsuit. On April 30, 1948, the Seine Court of Law rendered a staggering verdict. These are the main points

... First question:

Was the publishing company of Denoël, the corporation represented by the person of Monsieur Weil, the legal administrator (representing the said corporation, appointed by Monsieur the President of the Seine Tribunal, dating from February 23, 1948) ex officio, guilty, in Paris, of having between June 16, 1940, and the Liberation, during a time of war, printed and published brochures and books in favor of the enemy, of collaboration with the enemy, of racism and totalitarian doctrines?

Answer: No, by a majority...

"It was unbelievable," wrote Frédéric Vitoux in his very well-documented biography, *La Vie de Céline*. "What about its subsidiary, the Nouvelles Editions Françaises? Or its series *Les juifs en France*? Its works by Doctor Montandon, Rebatet and others?"

Answer: You are dreaming, just fiction.

On the side of men of letters, the National Committee of Writers had already published lists at the beginning of 1944, in the clandestine *Lettres françaises*. After the Liberation, these lists were expanded several times until the number reached one hundred and fifty-eight names. Sadly, a lot of the names were of people who had simply denounced the obviously suspect conduct of the Communist Party in 1939–40. One remembers, for example, the violent attacks by Aragon in the *Lettres françaises* against André Gide, on the sole (unacknowledged) pretext of Gide's reticence about the Soviet regime, before the war, in his *Retour de l'URSS*, and *Retouches à mon retour de l'URSS*.

As for Paul Morand, about whom there was a lot to say, if one chose to, the National Committee of Writers exonerated him "because those writings by Paul Morand which have been criticized have a purely literary character," a judgment that could have applied to a lot of other writers, too. To Céline, in particular, who struggled in Denmark, first in a hospital prison and then in a residence which was watched over by the police. It's true that Sartre had written on December 1, 1945, in *Les Temps modernes* : "If Céline upheld the socialist theories of the Nazis (!?), then he was being paid." What a joke!

I found, I'm not sure how, another printer, Van Daele, in the 11th *arrondissement*. For paper, which was still cruelly lacking in France, I had come up with a deal: Sennelier, the paper merchant on the quai Voltaire, had *Ingres* drawing paper. *Sur des femmes* was not a big book, and I had bought enough paper for my print run. Of assorted shades, admittedly.

Only I'd forgotten to warn the printer. And this meant that of the two thousand copies, a certain number were printed on different kinds of paper. Just a few people noticed. Or else they thought it was meant to be like that. The book came out in December 1946.

The publication was held up for several months. Montherlant, the second time I visited him, was trembling with fright (he was losing his prestige): everything has to stop, I have been forbidden to publish anything. The third time, I'd found the truth and told him that, yes, he had certainly been forbidden to publish for two years, but retroactively, as of October 31, 1944. So he was now perfectly within his rights. Sadly, the bookshops, being prudent, had almost totally scratched him off their lists.

Shortly thereafter, I discovered another facet of the publishing world: distribution. Who says publication, also says distribution. A certain number of new publishing houses had been started. Charlot, the first publisher of Camus in Algiers, had moved to Paris, hungry for business. Nagel, the Swiss publisher, had signed contracts with Sartre. Some new distributors had also been born. I went to see one of the new companies, though I can't remember how I arranged this. It was the Book Cooperative, on rue de Grenelle, I think. The Cooperative encouraged me warmly to carry on what I was doing. They needed new books. This wasn't the best time. And I was busy elsewhere.

And besides, my centers of interest weren't always theirs. I wanted to publish, at the very least, Sade's *Les Crimes de l'Amour*, which to my mind was entirely acceptable to moralizers. The Cooperative only accepted the preface, *Idée sur les romans*, which seemed very interesting. I have discovered a very curious little letter by Jean Paulhan, dated July 24, 1946. He had just received the book and I had raised the idea of a preface by him for *Les Cent Vingt Journées de Sodome* :

> Thank you for your words, and for the little book. But why didn't you follow up *L'Idée* with *Les Crimes de l'Amour*, which one can't find anywhere today and for which *L'Idée* is just the preface? This would seem to be a hundred times more urgent than *Les 120 Journées* that can be found just about everywhere. [...] and the *Marquise de Ganges*! And why not *Justine* and *Juliette*?
>
> P.S. I wouldn't be able to say anything about *120 J*. About *Crimes*, happily."

Actually, you couldn't find *Les Cent Vingt Journées de Sodome*. As for *Justine* (*La Nouvelle Justine*) and *Juliette,* no distributor would have anything to do with them. But something was pushing me on beyond all reason.

Jean Paulhan (who was hardly ever at a loss) would soon have plenty of time to change his mind.

nrf

Paris, le 24 Juillet 1946

Monsieur,

    Merci de votre mot, et du petit livre. Mais pourquoi n'avoir pas donné à là suite de l'Idée les Crimes de l'Amour introuvables aujourd'hui et dont l'Idée n'est que la pré-face? Voilà qui serait cent fois plus urgent que les 120 journées, que l'on trouve un peu partout.

    Recevez, Monsieur, l'assurance de mes meilleurs sentiments.

Jean Paulhan.

* et la marquise de Ganges ! Et, pourquoi pas, Justine et Juliette.

Je ne saurais que dire des 120 d: des crimes, trè volontiers.

Paris, 43, rue de Beaune — 5, rue Sébastien-Bottin (VII*)

A Fleeting Friendship –
Other Dramas

Continuing on with the *Journal littéraire* by Léautaud, which certainly had to do with me (and vice versa, I must say; I have always had a weakness for his non-conformity and his writing). It was still December 9, 1946:

> Jean-Jacques Pauvert has become the representative, the deputy, the salesman of sorts, for a group of film making bibliophiles who are colossally rich – which is not said to astound – and who have had published, in editions of about 50 copies, texts which they like, and which are not for sale. Absolutely private editions. One of these enthusiasts (I am well known among the members of this group) is apparently dying to come see me, but hesitant, not sure how he will be received (my reputation for being unapproachable is exaggerated), to ask for authorization to publish a copy of my *Journal* according to the conditions mentioned above, talking about a million francs for me...
>
> This charming young man already has lots of connections in the literary world. Cocteau[...] Albert Camus[...] the literary critic Maurice Nadeau[...] Saillet, the young clerk at the Monnier bookstore...
>
> And now he is the representative for this group of multi-millionaire film-making book lovers. The young make their way very fast today...
>
> Each time Jean-Jacques Pauvert comes to see me, he brings a packet of tobacco as a present. That's something!

Well, I was about ready to abandon newspaper work. In fact, my literary connections had grown considerably. I often saw Paulhan, Dominique Aury, Queneau and their entourage, in meetings (did the Wednesday nights at Paulhan's already exist?).

Publishing? Let's say I had become a "publisher," rather in spite of myself – with distrust. Was I really a publisher? When I was introduced, people often said JJP publisher. I tried to correct this, but what could I say? Who was I? There was a very small catalog, with the Palimugre imprint: Alphonse Allais (*Le Pauvre Bougre et le bon génie*), Montherlant, Renan... a half-dozen titles plus some "off-prints of Palimugre" (I'll talk about these later).

I saw a lot of Genet, with whom I'd established very friendly relations. He came to dinner in Sceaux; he appreciated my family life, at least what he saw of it when he was there. He was very friendly with Marie-Claude, whom he seemed to consider a curiosity. For someone who was almost a celebrity, we had an incredible relationship: I was a bit superior with him, but with lots of friendliness. He called me "my little Pauvert," to take back the advantage – also with lots of friendliness. I knew worlds of which he was ignorant. He knew about prison, but I was more familiar than he was, in a way, with the world of real thugs, which he had never really inhabited.

One particular time we arranged to meet in a café on the Champs-Elysees. I'd just been to Gastine-Reinette's. We started to talk. I had my Colt 45, now repaired, in my briefcase. He wanted to see it, he pleaded with me. He was entranced. I slid it carefully out of my briefcase so he could see it. He wanted to touch it. He begged me. I gave it to him, telling him to turn around facing away from me. He didn't want to let go of it. It was the first one he'd seen. I guessed from his awkwardness that it was the first firearm he had ever had in his hands. I had a hard time getting it back from him. He was trembling.

February 1947 was the time of a little revolution: the new Christian Dior look, a good international idea. Skirts had become shorter during the war, now let's lengthen them down to the ankles. A jolt for the Americans, who loved it. France regained its prestige in the world of frivolity. In Paris, I was there during the riots on rue de Buci when hungry housewives violently attacked the Dior models who were, preposterously, being photographed amid the crowd.

I was with Genet during the first months of 1947 for the rehearsals of *Les Bonnes* at Jouvet's theater, L'Athenée (Monique Mélinand and Yvette Étiévant played the Papin sisters). The atmosphere between Jouvet and Genet was one of exaggerated, icy politeness. They used the formal "vous" form. This is how it went:

> Jouvet (from the pit) – There you go, Jean: we've changed the stage sets a little. We haven't touched the decor. You know, it's what we decided on in the beginning. I hope you're satisfied?

Genet (from the balcony) – Yes, yes, Louis. Perfect, perfect. Now we're in the middle of a catastrophe, right? My text has been completely misrepresented. But that's okay, just the way you wanted it, so don't touch anything. Right. Anyway, I'm not interested in it anymore, not at all."

And he proved it. No dialogue was possible. I greatly admired Jouvet. I saw *Knock ou le Triomphe de la médicine* before the war, with my parents. I was also thrilled by *L'École des femmes*, with the marvelous sets by Christian Bérard. Jouvet was sublime in it. As he was in *Dom Juan* by Molière. But I vaguely felt that Genet was already involved in another form of theater, which I didn't yet understand, which was totally new and which would gradually establish itself.

The way *Les Bonnes* ended up was bizarre: Genet decided not to go to the full dress rehearsal, on April 19 (I've looked it up), 1947. He sent me instead. A little thoughtlessly, Marie-Claude and I were put in the author's box, in the middle of the theater, and I sent the actresses their flowers (red roses, some mistake, surely?). In short, I was a stand-in for Genet, in front of an amazed audience that was, I guess, trying to play along with me – but sometimes failing. I was personally rather pleased to transgress a certain number of codes which I didn't even know existed.

For some time, in fact since the autumn of 1946, I'd been involved in the creation of the *Cinéastes bibliophiles* private club, started by Charles Spaak. It meant a lot to him. He was one of my oldest customers and had become a friend. There was also Georges Van Parys, Noël-Noël, the producers Pierre O'Connell and Arys Nissotti (completely illiterate but full of good will), Pierre Fresnay, Fernand Ledoux, Jouvet obviously, Henri Jeanson, Max Douy, Bernard Blier, Jean Boyer, Pierre Cheret, Raoul Ploquin; I've forgotten some and added others maybe... It was a long time ago... Spaak organized little banquets. I participated, the target of everyone's curiosity because of my young age.

The aim of the club was to publish, in editions of sixty copies, new works by important living writers. Spaak had followed my arrival (through the back door) into the world of publishing. He was aware that I knew Genet, and we talked about this more and more. He asked me to approach Genet; he wanted a text. Genet gave me a play, *Haute surveillance*. I signed a contract with him on January 27, 1947.

I have found the contract. It was a simple (but formal) letter, typed on a portable typewriter, which Erika Neumann had bought just awhile before for twenty-five thousand francs on the black market (typewriters were impossible to find in 1947):

> January 27, 1947
> Monsieur,
>
> I agree concerning the various points in your letter of January 26, 1947, as follows:
> I give you the right to publish my play entitled *Haute surveillance*, sixty copies, not to be sold in bookstores.
> The copy I am giving you is a typed copy of the play and does not include any other publishing rights beyond those mentioned here.
> For this ceding of my rights, I will be paid 130,000 Fr of which 30 (thirty) will be received on handing over the manuscript, and 100 (one hundred), on March 15, 1947.
> PARIS, January 27, 1947
> Jean GENET

I was very, very busy at the beginning of 1947: February 3, the *Cinéastes bibliophiles* Club was formed. On February 5, Paul Léautaud signed (for me, not the filmmakers) the contract that he had being refusing to sign his whole life: a contract for his entire *Journal littéraire* – a limited-print run, it's true, but even so. I am recopying the contract here because it's never appeared anywhere else, and a photocopy of Léautaud's handwriting is hardly readable:

> Between,
> 1° Monsieur Paul Léautaud, who resides at 24 rue Guérard at Fontenay-aux-Roses (Seine),
> And 2° Monsieur Jean-Jacques Pauvert, living at 39, rue des Coudrais, in Sceaux (Seine),
> The parties agree to and set forth the following:
> Monsieur Paul Léautaud authorizes Monsieur Jean-Jacques Pauvert to publish his *Journal litteraire*, said publication absolutely not to be sold, reserved for sixty subscribers and limited to sixty copies.
> It being expressly understood, that the ownership of the furnished texts by Monsieur Paul Léautaud for this publication remains fully and entirely his.

Monsieur Paul Léautaud will receive from Monsieur Jean-Jacques
Pauvert, as royalties for each volume, the sum of a hundred thousand
francs, payable on delivery of each volume.

Fontenay-aux-Roses, Wednesday February fifth, one thousand
nine-hundred and forty-seven.

Read and approved,
P. Léautaud,
Read and approved
Jean-Jacques Pauvert

Toward the month of April (I don't have even one copy in order to verify
the exact date) *Haute surveillance* came off the press. I remember it as being a
mildly successful book, a crown octavo, sewn... I was too busy to watch over
the details of the printing...

So, a semi-failure.

I've unearthed a letter written by Genet on May 20, 1947, which gives a
good idea – and rather an unusual one for him – of our relationship. He must
have once again come to dinner at my parents' place awhile before:

My dear little Jean-Jacques,

Above all, please ask your parents to excuse me and tell them how
much I was touched by their great kindness. Everyone was so good
to me, and if I dare, please give your wife a kiss for me.
****

I am your friend and I shake your hand.

environ le 70 ...
'12

Mon petit Jean-Jacques

Avant toutes choses voulez-vous m'excuser auprès
de vos parents et leur dire à quel point j'ai
été touché par leur gentillesse. Tous ont été
si gentil pour moi, et si j'osais je vous
prierais d'embrasser votre femme pour moi.
Que devient votre travail? Êtes-vous au courant
de la sortie de Pompes Funèbres? Et
des Mystères de Brest? Auriez-vous la possibilité
de vous renseigner et de faire que tout cela
s'active. J'ancien vous avais dit que je lui
ai demandé 5.000 fr. Vous voudrez-bien les
compter sur ma note déjà terrible. Enfin,
Écrivez-moi, je serai content.

Je suis votre ami et je vous
serre la main

Jean Genet

Financial Depression

B ut what about publishing? Well, French publishing in general was not doing well at all. There were no really successful books in the stores, except for the "new authors," meaning above all the "existentialists" as we had begun to call them. And even then, sales weren't spectacular.

It was the beginning of a black year generally; De Gaulle left power in January 1946. Felix Gouin, a socialist (who remembers Felix Gouin?) was elected president of the provisional government: a tripartite government with the MRP (who remembers the MRP?) and the PS-PC (Socialist Party – Communist Party). The communists had pushed their way forward in order to seize power. The National Assembly election of November 1946 resulted in the communists and allies,182 seats; MRP and allies, 172; SFIO, 101; MTLD (Algerians), 5; radical and diverse Leftists; 77; moderates, 82; non-affiliated, 13. Abstentions, only 21.9 percent. The print-runs of the main newspapers showed *L'Humanité* to be in the lead.

Rationing tightened even more: there would be ration cards until 1949 (who remembers this?). In August 1947, bread rations fell to their lowest point since 1940: 200 grams.

The bookstores, which were filling up with books, were progressively losing customers. When *Explication de "L'Etranger"* came out, I sold my entire stock at one go, to a cartel of Parisian booksellers. This would have been impossible in 1947. One example of the financial crisis: at the end of 1946, Jean-Pierre Mauclaire, the owner of Cinémonde, was enthusiastic about the small book by Sartre and wanted to go into publishing with me. He promised to order books from me, a million francs worth. He even set me up in an office at Cinémonde. In the spring of 1947 he backed out of the deal.

Adding to this publishing gloom, French books were generally very ugly. The paper certainly was horrible and yellowed very fast (too much wood pulp), while the layouts were terrifyingly ugly, even those of the NRF, with covers of quite incredible vulgarity. In a book of memoirs (rather dull) called *Les Auteurs de ma vie*, published by Buchet (of Buchet-Chastel, ex-Correa), I came upon this note dated February 8, 1947:

> The sales crisis is putting publishers in a difficult situation. We have all brought out far too many books and still have schedules that are crammed. The publishing houses born during the war are the ones above all responsible for this inflation.

Oh, of course! The older publishers too.

Declarations

Straddling two important activities which were very different (very small print-runs and everyday volumes), I was not sure how to handle everything (although that hardly bothered me). But I couldn't completely neglect my daily duties.

Since I'd started dabbling in publishing, I now had administrative concerns: I'd founded a company with a business office, and I had been given vouchers for paper (which I sold right away, preferring to make use of better quality paper from the black market). I visited paper-makers and printers (not too many, I'm pretty faithful). I inquired about the responsibilities of a businessman: he had to have (or did, at the time) an apparatus called a "letter copier." I bought one, which I never used. He also had to have an account book: I stuck to the little notebooks with Debit and Credit columns, which seemed essential.

One day in my mail at Sceaux, I got a very nice letter from an inspector in the region, who was worried about my taxes, or at least about my returns.

(I forgot to say that as soon as I turned eighteen, my parents signed off on any responsibility for me, fearing – rightly – that they might be dragged into business complications. I had been using their garage for my commercial activities.)

My idea was to never pay taxes except on those books that made money. To tell the truth, I did make money, but never enough to my mind. In the end, I telephoned the tax agent quite innocently and assured him that my business wasn't worth declaring, nor any kind of payment, for that matter, to the State; the publishing business wasn't doing well. He agreed with me, upset on my behalf, and wished me better luck. The era could be like that as well.

It wasn't until much later that I realized what I had avoided.

In fact, I had convinced him that I didn't consider myself, in the deepest sense, a PUBLISHER. I was just playing a little role, that's all. PUBLISHING was another world, made up of big companies very far away, each one entrenched in the closed universe of their enormous buildings, everyone jealous of every-body else – even more so since the end of the war.

Far from the front lines, I was playing a small marginal role, barely attached to a world almost unknown to the literary fringe of the NRF. I realized that the game was being played somewhere else – and I didn't see myself getting more involved with it.

Besides, I didn't attach a great deal of importance to my little book productions. I was vaguely waiting for something else. I had had some man-uscript proposals, all rather pallid ones. The times were dire, and, it seemed to me, its means of expression as well. Nothing seemed to be coming my way in this morass.

———

Madame Lou (De Coligny-Chatillon)

It was during 1947 that I would at last really get to know Gaston Gallimard. One summer day, Roland Saucier telephoned me in great excitement; he had to see me right away, just like in a detective story, hurry, hurry.

I got to boulevard Raspail an hour later. I now had an almost friendly relationship with Saucier. That day, he was in a dither and almost beside himself. He kept saying: a detective story, this is just like a detective story. Then he corrected himself: no, a spy story.

He calmed down finally and explained: Gaston Gallimard had been paying attention to my activities, from afar, but closely. (Oh? Is that right?). He had a mission he wanted me to undertake: it was a matter of going to a place near Grasse to visit the Countess Louise de Coligy-Chataillon, Apollinaire's Lou, who, from 1914 to 1916, had been sent a long series of letters and poems by him, which had remained unpublished and were of great literary value. Of course, I'd be happy to make the visit. A meeting was then arranged with Gaston Gallimard.

Gaston (as everyone called him) received me with kindness, in the large office which I already knew. This time we were alone. He seemed to be vaguely aware of my activities. He was noticeably intrigued by me. I could see him more clearly this time: rather small, round, intelligent, and cunning – extremely so. Everything about him suggested an impenitent hedonist. He fished about, pushing me to confide in him my secrets (which I did with caution).

Clearly, he liked me. Or seemed to. He got around to talking about my mission. He briefly recounted the story (I already knew a bit about it) of Apollinaire and Lou. He added that he would, of course, pay for the entire cost of the trip. There would even be something for myself if I succeeded. Good-bye and see you soon. This time there was no "Monsieur" in the air.

Soon Saucier and I took a sleeper car to Cannes. We had two rooms reserved in a hotel at the end of a jetty, to the west of Cannes. I soon understand why. Genet was not far away, next door to his current lover, a young fisherman from

Cannes, "the Suquet fisherman." Genet was protecting and financing him. This was quite a job, as the Suquet fisherman was married and the father of several children. Saucier insisted that all three of us be photographed on the shore, Genet, Saucier, and I.

The adventure lasted several days. Saucier and I took little trips to Nice. One night I saw him a long way off, in a working class area. For his part, he was also hunting male game. Several times, I approached girls of my age, always, as luck would have it, in groups of two or three. We had drinks together on the terrace of cafes, but nothing more. Their level of stupidity was off-putting. When one among them was rather seductive, and vaguely susceptible to my charms, she was dragged off by her friends.

The rest of the time, we tried to accomplish our mission. We had the telephone number of Mme. de Coligny-Chatillon. I telephoned: her servant handed me over to her, and she answered willingly, even amicably. No, no, she didn't want to see me. We rang at the door: her servant told us that she did not want to see us. I was constantly troubled by the presence of Roland Saucier. I felt that I could do a lot better without him.

But maybe I was wrong, after all. On the second or third day, I realized that I had made a mistake on the phone. Louise de Coligny suddenly asked my age. And I stupidly told her the truth: twenty-one. Even though she seemed better disposed towards me that day, she suddenly shut down. I pressed the point. She ended by softly telling me the truth: she was alive and young in the poems of Guillaume Apollinaire, and in his letters; she did not want a young man of twenty-one to compare this image with the old woman she had become.

I realized that our mission was over. Saucier wanted to push it (I understood that above all he wanted to continue making the most of this surprise vacation). But it was over. Lou would no longer take my phone calls. We returned to Paris. Saucier was given the job of announcing the bad news to Gaston.

I would soon see Gaston Gallimard again.

IV

INVESTIGATIONS

There is no explosion like a book.

— Stéphane Mallarmé

Sade Among Us?

In one part of my mind, half hidden, was something I had not yet sorted out: Sade.

But in this matter I was advancing a little. Without realizing it I had accumulated elements that were allowing me to put together the pieces of a sort of sculpture.

First of all, I pushed myself to get hold of texts. Texts of every sort about Sade – rare books, almost unknown apart from some titles that were rather inoffensive: *Historiettes, Contes et Fabliaux, Les Infortunes de la Vertu* (let's not forget that I had started with *Les Cent Vingt Journées de Sodome*), which were still to be found in bookstalls on the quays. Then biographies, those that one found everywhere, including along the Seine: Jean Desbordes, Cabanès, d'Alméras, and Ginisty. And most of all, the monumental *Correspondance inédite du marquis de Sade et de ses familiers*, by the notary Paul Bourdin, on sale before the war and in which I discovered a living Sade, close-up. I also had Eugen Dühren, *Le Marquis de Sade et son temps* (1901) ["It was June 2, 1740, when one of the most remarkable of men of the 18th century was born, one could even say of modern humanity in general"], the Œuvres choisies et pages magistrales (very mild, but what a preface!) by Maurice Heine, whose one and only volume appeared before the war, without success.

As Baudelaire put it: "One always has to return to Sade, which is to say to natural man, in order to explain evil."

And, above all, I had Apollinaire's *Œuvres du marquis de Sade, pages choisies* (1909) which had been excessively expurgated by the censorship of Briffaut, his publisher, but his preface was amazing; it inaugurated, forty years in advance, a new era which had been late to get started:

> It appears that the time has come for those ideas that have matured in the infamous atmosphere of the *enfers* of libraries, and that this man who appears to have counted for nothing during the entire 19th century, should now dominate the 20th.

The Marquis de Sade, this freest of all spirits who have ever existed, also had particular ideas about women and wanted to see them as free as men [...] Justine is the woman of the past, subservient, miserable and less than human; Juliette, to the contrary, represents the new woman he envisioned for the future, a being one cannot yet imagine, who will have wings and who will renew the universe.

All this was rounded out by the surrealist explosion of Breton/Eluard in *La Revolution surrealiste* of 1926, and the *Anthologie de l'humour noir*.

Little by little, the pieces of a portrait came together, not yet by any means complete, but all of its collected features had a place in my mind.

The intellectual era was now dealing a lot with Sade, more and more openly. Everybody, or almost everybody, was in agreement about his "importance." He is very important, they said gravely. "A great novelist," one said; "a great moralist," said another. Camus and Queneau had serious reservations (as later Michel Foucault would have). "The charnel house is the end game of philosophy," wrote Queneau severely in 1945 (in *Les Lettres françaises*, I think) in reference to the concentration camps. Was there really any relationship?

I began to ask openly: why not publish him?

People shrugged: the time wasn't right yet. Communists, socialists and MRP (Popular Republican Movement) were still strictly watching over morality, protecting the weak spirited (women and adolescents, and other mental defectives). In September 1946, the Cartel d'Action Morale – run by M. Daniel Parker – had just filed a demand for a judicial investigation into the publication of *Tropic of Cancer* and *Tropic of Capricorn* by Henry Miller. The hair-raising law of 1949 was being prepared.

In November 1946, René Eertelé, whose publishing house Editions le Point du jour had just been bought up by Gallimard, displayed unimaginable audacity. He republished in the collection called "Incidences" an entire text by Sade, *Les Infortunes de la Vertu*, with a long preface by Paulhan: "The dubious Justine, or the revenge of modesty." It was a pallid kind of temerity, really, but revelatory of a trend.

Personally, I felt an urge to bring everything out in the open. At my suggestion about publishing the entire work of Sade, timidly broached to my distributor of current books, the Coopérative du Livre, I was gently rebuffed with a smile: Don't think about banned books right now; it really isn't the time.

At the beginning of 1947, I took a timid first step: I officially printed (keeping Palimugre as the publisher) Sade's preface to his *Crimes de l'Amour* : *Idée sur les romans*, which the Coopérative du Livre had agreed to distribute, "with the caveat of not placing it everywhere."

However, in the meantime, Pierre Klossowski's *Sade, mon prochain*, had been published by Seuil. A bit of a scandal. Some months later, Maurice Blanchot published in *Critique* some "remarks about Sade." Toward the end of the year, the publishers *La Table Ronde* announced a *Morceaux choisis* by Sade for January 1948, with a preface by Maurice Nadeau. In March, another *Morceaux choisis* was published by Seghers, prefaced by Gilbert Lély, whom I only knew by name (I was a little suspicious).

So many commentaries on select pieces of an œuvre that couldn't be found! You couldn't read Sade, but you could talk about him, and partially cite him, guardedly!

I had already begun, over the last several months, to announce firmly at Paulhan's (and Nadeau's, at *Combat*, and at Adrienne Monnier's) that I was going to publish the whole of Sade, to great incredulity and concerned warnings: he's crazy, he's young, Jean-Jacques may end up in prison, etc.

I was obstinate, and, at the end of December 1947, my printer (who did not wish to be named; I understood that) delivered the first two volumes of a complete edition of *Histoire de Juliette*.

With hindsight, I understand that I instinctively did just what was appropriate concerning a vague feeling. As usual, I had acted before understanding.

No preface. No living person, in fact, seemed to have felt as profoundly as Apollinaire (and I still only vaguely glimpsed that fact) about what was at stake here. Eluard had dishonored himself during the Moscow trials. Breton had just returned from America: I didn't know him yet. I didn't know where he stood on this.

This was no luxury edition; the volumes were very commonplace, on ordinary paper (the kind that could be found then), with a very sober white cover, at a standard price.

But above all, something I did not realize until much later, for the first time I had put out into the world a publisher's name on the cover of a full version of a "forbidden" Sade, above the address of my parents' garage: "Sceaux | Jean-Jacques Pauvert |39 rue des Coudrais, 39 | 47." The copyright registration was also there, which I had scrupulously taken care of (I hadn't done that very often in the past).

In the spring of 1948, I became clandestine again; I didn't have enough money to support Genet. I joined with Paul Morihien, Cocteau's secretary, to print Genet's novel *Pompes funebres* without a named publisher (cover by Pierre Jahan). At the same time – a little earlier, actually – Gaston Gallimard secretly printed, using the same printer we used ("Gaston Coquette," a pseudonym, rue de la Glacière, an old habitué of the underground), the original luxury edition of *Pompes funebres*, which he asked me to sell to special customers.

This really upset Noël-Noël, who sent me an incendiary letter asking that I never again recommend books to him, having discovered "this pig filth" called *Pompes funebres*. He had a right to his opinion, of course.

Also in the spring of 1948, I was resigned – for the first and last time – to print a clandestine edition in Brussels of Sade's *Les Cent Vingt Journées de Sodome*, with a little "Note about the *Cent Vingt Journées*" at the end of the fourth and last volume.

There were several reasons for this step backwards: first, of course, the refusal of the distributors. I continued to publish *Juliette*, volume by volume, but the police searches had begun, and summons from the vice squad sapped my morale a bit. The refusal of the bookstores, with rare exceptions, also troubled me: weren't those who accused me of destroying morality by publishing Sade right to an extent?

But wasn't Sade, for a lot of intellectuals, "a great moralist"?

Les Cent Vingt Journées de Sodome was the real key to the problem: never, at any time in history, in any literature, had anyone written so scandalously, so repulsively, so intolerably. And the same question returned over and over again: was it, or was it not, literature? If yes, no matter to what degree, wasn't it imperative that one should be able to read these texts, outlawed for such a long time, but to which more and more poets – especially poets – ever since Baudelaire, were attached?

But *Les Cent Vingt Journées de Sodome* was the summit of scandal! A touchstone of the forbidden! It seemed to me that with the publication of this text

I had profoundly taken responsibility for my commitment, considering the atrocious consequences that people never stopped making me aware of.

The idea of *Les Cent Vingt Journées de Sodome* in the public eye, officially and fully, made me hesitate for another five years.

But the competition was in no hurry to take over...

None Of That Kind Of Literature Here! –
So Where Then?

I had abandoned the *Palimugre* review. You can't run a review all alone. Marcel Aymé had given me an excellent text, others had promised the same. However, something didn't add up: I only had contributors from the preceding generation – or further back. My manifesto was supposed to express a collective discontent. But I was the only one in my age group: I had to realize that. I had affirmed, loud and clear, that "I had profoundly shocked several of my comrades." I had no comrades with ideas similar to mine.

And I didn't feel like looking for any.

I wrote to Marcel Aymé that *Palimugre* had lived before being born, then I carefully published his text, by itself, under the company name of "Off-Prints from *Palimugre*" (he had titled the work: *Le Trou de la serrure*; a very good text, which would not be published again for fifty-five years). *Palimugre* was a company that would serve me two or three more times in the future.

My marriage was in trouble. Marie-Claude did her best to keep up with me. It was just that my interests didn't really match hers. I was surrounded by kindness, in case I needed it; but it was a tenderness that was totally lacking in understanding. My parents, too, did what they could when I saw them. They were worried about me. In the end, I was all alone with my periodic rages, which went nowhere. I did have a daughter, it was true, but she didn't yet add up to much for me. It wasn't a fun time.

I published another book for the *Cinéastes bibliophiles* : *La Marguerite*, a play by Jean Anouilh. Then they published a book without me, after which the group broke up. I had decided to do Léautaud's *Journal* by myself, but suddenly, after having signed the contract, he began to quibble: was word not going to get around about the whole thing?

It was true. I couldn't be responsible for the discretion of fifty people. Were little indiscretions, unavoidable really, all that serious? We were supposed to start at the beginning of the *Journal* : would gossip dating from 1910, from 1920 or even from 1930, really be of any consequence today?

Apparently so. Léautaud wrote me a letter one day, in rather bad faith. Instead of waiting him out, I got angry, obtained the first legal advice I could find and sent him a harsh letter – it was stupid, really. I did the wrong thing. I regret it now. Old men have a right to their whims.

In the *Mercure de France* edition of his *Journal*, he made no mention of me whatsoever, as far as I can see, except once, on June 26, 1947: "He only has himself to blame," he wrote mysteriously. For what? End of my relationship with Léautaud.

The Coopérative du Livre did not want *Juliette*, and my other books were selling badly – the same as those by other publishers. Here are some crybaby remarks from Buchet's Journal (*Les Auteurs de ma vie*), written in September and October 1948:

> September 5, 1948: Situation difficult. During the whole month of August we didn't sell any more books than in a normal week [...] If things don't get better, we will temporarily stop any further production starting the first of January.
>
> October 15: Things are going from bad to worse: factories are on strike, as well as printers, social agitation keeps growing at the same rate as the cost of living. [...] The fact is we're at an impasse. Quality and sales oppose each other more and more. In order to attract the public, one has to put oneself at its level, which is deplorably low. This is the drama facing serious publishers, as well as good theater directors or good fi lm producers. Our production no longer corre-sponds to current tastes, which are, alas, those of *France-Dimanche* or of *Confidences* [...] Closed up in my offi ce, surrounded by men of letters and by critics, I no longer have an accurate idea of the book market. In the last few months, I visited several bookstores in Paris and in the provinces, visits both instructive and disappointing. The bookstores, overloaded with books they had to take because of contracts, lack money and are demoralized. 'Publish as little as possible,' they advise.

I still published a little, however. For example, in 1947, the year of Gide's Nobel Prize, I published a little text by him, *LÁrbitraire*, a very short piece that appeared in *Combat* under the title "L'Art bitraire." My visit to his place went very well, he was curious to see the thin volume when it came out. He was crafty, suspicious, trying to appear confident, and cautious. Wrapped up in a scarf, hidden behind his glasses.

As the production advanced, he began to change his mind every morning: wouldn't it be better to simply use the title *L'Arbitraire*? Won't people think this a rather elaborate pun? No? The next day: Oh! In the end, I rather like *Art bitraire*, which is intriguing, don't you think?

Finally, I sent him packing, and I published the text with the title *L'Arbitraire* (although I preferred the other), because from his last telephone call it seemed to me this was his final choice. Maybe it hadn't been, in fact. I felt irritable, and what's more I had forgotten to have his dedication to Pierre Herbart printed. I was annoyed.

Gide just let it go by sending me a letter and a copy of his book, which he signed: "With my cordial regrets."

Disappointments everywhere: *Histoire de Juliette* that I'd been counting on wasn't selling well. Lacking a distributor, snubbed by the few bookstores I visited personally, I was forced to go back to the booksellers on the quay, or shady stalls around Saint-Denis, where they were quick to tell me that the book wasn't very entertaining and the customers didn't like it. Sade – he's too serious, too bloody. I had even had two or three phone calls from deluxe book publishers who accused me of ruining their business: it was so simple to produce deluxe, illustrated books – clandestinely!

To top it all off, I constantly had the police on my back. To start with, they waited several months: I don't think they believed it was a real name and a real address when they discovered the first volumes by Jean-Jacques Pauvert, 39 rue des Coudrais, Sceaux. And in addition with a real date. "Jean-Jacques Pauvert," and in Sceaux! Right, just another joke.

Probably it was the specialized bookstores that informed them. Yes, yes, Jean-Jacques Pauvert exists; I've met him. They had shown up one day in Sceaux; but this visit to my garage was not very productive for them. My mother, indignant because of their manners (luckily my father, warned by telephone, had someone in the police pull rank), told me what had happened and I naturally presented myself to the vice squad. Was I really the one who had published the first volumes (they now numbered six or seven: I didn't have enough money to bring out the ten planned volumes all at once)? Yes, I was the one. We have to arrest you; it's forbidden to publish these books. Forbidden by whom? I intend to continue publishing them. But what's wrong with you? (The officer who was questioning me seemed very close to advising me to use the much more expensive illustrated books, just like the clandestine publishers). And why Sade? Just between us, he's no fun to read. Does he sell? No, not a lot. Well then? I couldn't explain it. The officer, who wasn't a bad man, didn't understand.

In the bookstores, the normal market place, the Sade books weren't having much success either. I was particularly struck by the welcome I had from José Corti, an old-school bookseller, on rue de Medicis, a publisher of respectable authors and someone I was really counting on. I had vaguely hoped to have a sort of commercial base in his bookstore, as he had provided in the heyday of surrealism. I got along fairly well with Corti. Couldn't he take one or two copies of *Juliette*?

He listened to me, pulling on his eternal pipe, and then calmly, categorically stated: "None of that kind of literature here."

Violette Leduc – More Genet, And Orsay Perfumes – *Portrait Of JJP At Twenty*

J ean Genet wanted to help me. He had just published *Querelle de Brest* clandestinely (it was Paul Morihien, Cocteau's secretary, and first-time publisher, manager of the bookstore on rue de Beaujolais belonging to Cocteau, who was responsible for the publication, evidently illustrated with expensive drawings by Cocteau). So he had me sign a contract (so long as a check was forthcoming, which was normal) for a big manuscript that he had me read, *Pompes funebres*, which I had published, as I said, with Paul Morihien.

At the same time he introduced me to Jacques Guerin, the rich owner of Orsay perfumes, who had a publishing project.

It was a very simple project, but one which created complicated relationships between three people: Genet, Jacques Guerin, and Violette Leduc, who had just been published by Gallimard. Genet wanted to help Violette Leduc, who had fallen hopelessly in love with Jacques Guerin, and admired – also hopelessly – Genet. Jacques Guerin, a homosexual and admirer of Genet, had agreed to finance a deluxe edition of a new novel by Violette Leduc, *L'Affamée*, and to give her a hundred thousand francs in royalties.

Violette Leduc recounted some of the twists and turns of the Guerin affair in *La Folie en tête* (Gallimard, 1970). Jacques Guerin greeted us in his immense and sumptuous apartment, which looked directly out on Park Monceau.

(It's a strange thing to see oneself young through the eyes of a writer, a long time afterwards):

> Jacques, always glacial on the phone, had invited me to lunch at his place on Thursday. Jean-Jacques Pauvert, recommended by Genet for the deluxe edition of *L'Affamée*, would be there. I would have preferred a jewel from the Place Vendôme, a fur from the faubourg Saint-Honoré, a ticket from Cook's for a trip to Mexico, which would have been a homage to my femininity and my leisure. You

are never happy, you will never be happy, I heard a voice say to me, that of Hermine, no doubt. His plan for the edition confused me. I listened to him on the phone, I hung up: a bit of white chalk was crushed at the end of my fingers – it was me, discouraged each time by his curtness. I left the Aveyronais café...the earth was spinning, the sun shone brilliantly.

Jacques was in heaven the following Thursday; his plan was taking shape; Jean-Jacques Pauvert said nothing, he was doing business, he wasn't going to interrupt a customer. He was, at that time, a cold, very cold young man, distant, very distant, a sort of icy work of art, with a friendly face and an Asian-like contemptuous smile. He wore glasses and a tight suit. Timid. A presence in retreat. He was just starting out, he was finding his way. Heartened by the absence of Denis (Jacques Guerin's boyfriend) and the good humor of Jacques, I played a fabulously well-kept hooker, a mistress of the house very sure of herself. Pauvert, sitting across from me, avoided my gaze, which was understandable. My suit, an old present from Jacques Fath, all unstitched, then re-stitched, dyed once, twice, and a rabbit Russian-like hat encouraged me to eye scornfully the debutant publisher, and to pretend that the furniture, the paintings, the books were mine, those of a connoisseur. Like a pampered fool, off I went to smell a rose in the lounge, as though at home. Jacques emphasized the uniqueness of the selections made; Pauvert, polite and attentive, seemed completely uninterested in what I had written. The rising price of each copy frightened me, the enormous reach of a bibliophile distressed me. Pauvert took everything in without reacting. Was this out of disdain?

We sat down for lunch; I made myself very small. There was lots of room for Jacques's good mood. They talked about rare books. Sometimes a human being splits himself in two; he simply gives you a child by being near you. They talked about the number of copies. On Place de l'Opéra, I had on my arm an intellectual retard, an idiot, a fool. He never let go of my arm. Jacques shone brilliantly, Pauvert had a hearty appetite.

The deal was concluded, but not without difficulty. I didn't much like Violette Leduc's writing. As a protégée of Simone de Beauvoir, she irritated me. It all seemed contrived. It was my first – and one of my only – vanity accounts. I wanted to handle it through the Palimugre label which I had pretty much abandoned. Jacques Guérin was counting a great deal on my name being on the book. I believe (I don't have any more copies) that this is what transpired: Palimugre and Jean-Jacques Pauvert both figured on the cover, or on the title page.[1]

L'Affamée came out towards the month of June. I would sometime later be obligated to see Violette Leduc again.

———

1   "Sceaux : J.-J. Pauvert, 1948" appears on the title page, "Palimugre éditeurs" on the wrapper. – Editor's note.

The Forbidden And The Unspeakable

I thus became, somewhat in spite of myself, a "publisher." I wasn't really comfortable with this; I think it was because of my wish not to be labeled, to remain, in some way, open to whatever might happen.

At any rate, I noticed a curious twist in my adventures as a publisher. During the time I was doing everything I could to publish *Juliette*, volume by volume, under my own name, I continued to use the Palimugre imprint for books distributed by the Coopérative du Livre. For example, I used it in 1948, for a volume of *Lettres inédites* by Gustave Flaubert. In this way, I came up against a form of censorship different from the one I had experienced before.

In fact, I wanted to use the Palimugre imprint for books that were designated as "unspeakable." More and more, in the last fifty years, the term had been used in a sense that verged on the metaphysical: Bataille, Blanchot... I wanted to bring it back into the concrete: what cannot be said, because it must not be said.

What one cannot, what one must not say. One assumes the right to suppress something when there is little chance that it will ever see the light of day. While at the same time, where *Juliette* was concerned, I was struggling with the "forbidden" pure and simple (at least that's what they told me). With the letters of Flaubert, I discovered the "unspeakable." One had to suppress that which is "not decent," that which is impossible to be said in the way it has been said.

This was about a little cache of letters, either unpublished, or notably different from the text which had been included in the already published *Correspondance*, which was one of my favorite books. A nosy, patient guy by the name of Auriant had found them, brought them to me, and I published them with enthusiasm in 1948.

In the end, with these *Lettres*, I made two mistakes, the first of their kind (and I'm afraid not the last): First of all Flaubert at the time interested almost no one; people were only talking about American novels. The second mistake was that the publication of a genuine text appeared to oddly unhinge a certain number of people, starting with the publisher of the "complete" correspondence of Flaubert, in the collection of his *Oeuvres complètes*.

He made a furious phone call to me, during the course of which I was accused of "dishonesty." "The people who amended" (he said amended!) "these texts knew what they were doing," it seems. It was easy for me to answer that the dishonesty seemed rather to be in the publication of tampered texts, and the conversation ended there.

Thus, I entered into a dream world, which I have never altogether left. If Flaubert wrote to Maxime Du Camp, in 1851: "It bores me to eat, to get dressed, to stand up," why make him say: "It's a torture to eat," etc. If he wrote: "Don't you think I get an erection like anybody else?" why replace this sentence with: "Do you think I lack stamina?" Why completely suppress: "I'm afraid for you when I perceive you as a serious love: the pox is less fearful than passion. You can cauterize canker sores but not those of the heart?"

Flaubert's case wasn't the only one, nor the publisher Conard's. (I can't do anything about that; it's his real name).[2] At the end of the 19th century, Arthur Meyer, the manager of *Le Gaulois*, offered a large reward to anyone who could find the famous letter from Vigny to Marie Dorval, full of obscenities and sperm stains, "so that he could destroy it." This showed a will to censorship so savage, lasting more than a hundred years, that one wonders where it derived its incredibly strong rationale?

For myself, why was it that these passages were the very ones which interested me, and which cried out to me to be discovered and then published? It was my job, that's all. I felt it; that was good enough.

I met some strange people. The publication of *Histoire de Juliette*, snubbed by most "honest" bookshops, meant that I had to enter, little by little, as I said, into the world of those shops the police were keeping an eye on, most of which were run by criminals and occasional informers. They viewed me with suspicion. I didn't fit into any of their categories. I acted openly and wasn't interested in the shadier side of their business, the dildos and the whips, and they looked at me askance or stopped talking whenever I walked in the door. They didn't understand why I was publishing these "filthy books," yet refusing all the lovely accessories that were on offer, sometimes for an exchange. But generally, I wasn't offended by their behavior.

---

2   Pauvert's reference here is to a play on the French slang expression "Connard" which may variously mean a 'jerk' or 'idiot' at one extreme, or 'motherfucker' at the other, depending on the robustness of one's source of information. – Editor's note.

There was another side to this more or less secret world: the individual customers, who were a mixed bag. There were those who had vaguely heard of Sade as a "spicy" author, who ordered volumes and who showed their disappointment. And there were buyers who covered Sade with a whole philosophical/esoteric sauce, and wrote me long letters which I never answered.

Then there were even more special customers, who wanted to meet me, hoping, no doubt, for something to spice up their unhappy existence. To the few meetings I agreed to, they sometimes came as couples, which was even more annoying. They also explained to me that Sade was disappointing, by contrast with a so-called secret world that they described to me mysteriously and timidly. And how did I, the publisher of Sade, see life; had I never been tempted to play out fantasies like they did? After all...

I remember being dragged into the Cercle ésoterique on rue Bleue, just a short time before this estimable meeting place had trouble with the police. Nothing of interest: just fakery.

What would have happened if in such circumstances I had met, even once, some pleasant people? Well, I suppose I would have followed them, wherever it led. I was ready for anything.

But never, absolutely never, did I meet the least interesting or human specimen, who was tempting physically or even mentally.

As for the world of the imagination, let's not talk about it. What they described – and in what terms! – in order to tempt me was all false fantasy, bad theater, just that and nothing more. I was confirmed in this impression on the rare occasions I ventured into places like the Cercle ésoterique with its particularly grotesque attempts at flights of the imagination.

A Little Soviet Parenthesis

The year 1948 still saw me in a double bind: clandestine publisher of "erotica" and official publisher – under two different imprints. Several works were distributed officially, and then there was a large work by Sade that I was forced to sell on the black market. I published, "under the counter," works by Apollinaire: *Les Exploits d'un jeune don juan, Poésies libres*, and above all the important (his major work, Picasso said) *Les Onze Mille Verges*.

Continuing to push my luck, I officially published in 1948 *Oxtiern*, the play Sade had staged furtively in Paris after the Revolution, which is very moral but which the Cooperative du Livre did not accept without hesitation.

It was in 1949 that an event of considerable importance took place from 24 January to 22 March, and which shook up the intellectual world: the trial of Kravchenko. Thanks to my father, I was able to be present as a privileged spectator at two or three court sessions.

There are numerous historical reports about this trial, which raised wild passions. Kravchenko, a high-ranking Russian engineer, sent to the United States on some sort of mission, had chosen to stay in the West and to testify about the hidden face of the USSR: concentration and extermination camps in Siberia, summary executions, police presence everywhere, the total muzzling of all opposition, Stalinist cruelties and dictatorship.

His enormous book, *J'ai choisi la liberté*, filled with testimonies, came out in 1948 in the United States and in Western Europe, especially in France. *Les Lettres françaises*, a communist weekly, attacked him, saying that it had proof that Kravchenko was a double agent, paid by the United States, expelled from the USSR where he had been discredited, and that his book had been written entirely by the American propaganda machine, etc. Kravchenko fought back, charging *Les Lettres françaises* with defamation of character.

I think the Kravchenko trial marked the first big split in the minds of people about the real nature of the USSR and the relationship between Stalin's communism and that of Marxism. It was often a crafty, hypocritical split, a distancing then a dissimulation. But just as often an explosion, proclaimed out loud to the whole world, a definitive separation.

In fact, the basics of the trial were very quickly clear: Kravchenko was in the main right, the USSR was a savage dictatorship, forcibly repressive, and of an innate hypocrisy.

The testimony of Marguerite Buber-Neumann was particularly damaging. Together with her husband she had been part of the German Resistance to the Nazis, and she had been interned in a Russian camp in 1938, without news of her husband since 1937. She was handed over to the Nazis at the moment of the German-Soviet Pact, and did not leave Ravensbruck until 1945. With great dignity and poise, she reduced to relative silence little by little the lawyers for *Lettres françaises*. In her memoirs (*La Force de l'âge*, Gallimard, 1960), Simone de Beauvoir admitted that she had been shaken, and Sartre too, by this testimony. I don't remember if she said anything about it at the time.

With the energy of desperation, the witnesses from the newspaper, Joliot-Curie, André Wurmser, Claude Morgan, d'Astier de la Vigerie, Vladimir Pozner, Albert Bayet, Louis Martin-Chauffier, Pierre Debray, Pierre Courtade, Vercors, Roger Garaudy, etc., tried not to deny things, but rather to give their point of view, which fell apart each time, given their weak arguments. Perhaps this was right, but you couldn't hope for a better tomorrow if you didn't accept some distortions of the truth. The excesses of the police, the camps (they didn't yet say gulags), the millions of deaths and the starvation, were all necessary for the USSR to make the communist ideal a triumph.

In other words, the end justifies the means. Without thinking it through clearly, I was against it. Viscerally.

The judicial epilogue to this affair was characteristic of that period in France: *Les Lettres françaises* was found guilty on April 4 and fined five thousand francs, plus fifty thousand francs in damages and interest.

But it was all reduced on appeal to one symbolic franc.

This was the time when Aragon was writing articles explaining that Lysenko, in the USSR, had just demonstrated the inherited aspect of acquired characteristics and the failure of bourgeois genetics. Lysenko was supported by Stalin (who had awarded him the famous Stalin Prize) and he was doing his duty as a good communist, demonstrating the superiority of discoveries made by proletarian science as opposed to capitalist science. Today Lysenko is forgotten.

Aragon also wrote numerous articles exalting the great art work produced by Soviet artists: *L'entrée du tracteur au village, Le camarade Dimitrienko contemple la cent millième faucille sortie de sa machine-outil (record), Le Camarade Staline félicite la camarade Ilena, mère de famille nombreuse (onze enfants) et ouvrière metallurgist diplomée.* But he made certain that reprints of these masterpieces never got published.

The sinister erasure of a man, Victor Hugo would have said.

André Breton would masterfully crush this fraud in *Pourquoi nous cache-t-on la peinture russe contemporaine?*

Sade With Me

The ten volumes of *Histoire de Juliette* were finally finished printing in July 1949. Still, no real movement in literary circles. No press, certainly. They explained to me for the twentieth time that they approved of me, but one couldn't talk openly about "banned books." We will come back to this expression, shortly. Paulhan showed interest, without going further for the moment.

That same month, on July 16, 1949, the infamous "Law on publications intended for youth" was passed, which permitted the repression of any publication of any kind. In June, the Minister of the Interior, using a law covering foreign books, banned the sale of *J'irai cracher sur vos tombes* published by Scorpion and *Elles ne sont pas toutes comme ça* published by Fleuve Noir.

And the Coalition for Moral Action went on the attack again against Girodias for the publication of Miller's *Tropic of Capricorn*.

As for me, I was in for a series of searches and meetings with the vice squad. To be honest, this was all rather random, depending on changes in the leadership of the vice squad, or the whim of a magistrate, or possibly the bad mood of the infamous Book Commission. Such searches were totally useless; they never found anywhere the slightest copy of anything. I got a kick out of handing over to the vice squad a copy of each volume as it was published (which, by the way, mysteriously disappeared during the trial).

I have to say that certain members of this commission distinguished themselves by their severity: a) the communists, who were the most virulent, and generally demanded the destruction of the books; b) the socialists and the MRP. The representatives of the Société des Gens de Lettres also voted in general for prosecution, but with degrees of variance. We'll come back to that very soon.

The leaden yoke of morality that prevailed in France at that time was frightening. A little later, we would see the founders of Family Planning harshly attacked by *Humanité*, with sharply critical articles by Jeannette Vermeersch, the wife of Maurice Thorez. For example: "We don't need to have working-class women being contaminated by the vices of the bourgeoisie." As in the Soviet Union, they were there to bear children, like it or not.

André Thirion, in his excellent book *Révolutionnaires sans révolution*, perfectly summarized the moral climate of the period:

> What was occurring in the State, in 1946, didn't just have all the characteristics of fragility; it was also ripe with civil war. A monstrous advantage was given to the enterprise of ignorance and subservience, which spread its audacity and its stupidity everywhere. Three parties, which worked well together in their exploitation of the nation, colonized the State. The Communists ruled through terror, in their domain. The democratic Christians from the MRP rivaled their partners with their own demagogy, not in order to maintain freedom, but to defend the old Catholic privileges; they got along with the Communists on the issue of a nauseous morality and also, which was much more serious, in the glorification of a sort of working class mediocrity.

As for the Socialists, the third party in power, they were as moralizing as the other two:

> ...In 1946, the apparatus reconstituted by Daniel Mayer and directed by Guy Mollet protected itself with sectarianism and bitterness against all intruders

What struck me at the time was the silence of the press about this business of an "outrage to good morals through books." Such a total silence was either due to the indifference of the journalists, or else to their lack of seriousness, which allowed them to be too easily discouraged from plunging into the legal twists and turns of censorship. It must be admitted that the laws being passed were intentionally complicated, and the press, by not paying close enough attention, couldn't find their way through them.

Hence all the lewd jokes in the newspapers about the "publicity" that the so-called banned books benefited from – while, in fact, the books had promptly been removed, for all practical purposes, from circulation.

It must be admitted that the entire earth was subjected to the same regime. For the first time perhaps, in 1947, our international civilization of words found itself entirely being ruled by the same ethic. Islam was what it had been for centuries: a world ranging from a low level of liberalism – as we shall see later – to none at all.

China, in the grip of a complete change after hundreds of years of authoritarian puritanism, saw fit to submit itself to a regime, one of whose first concerns was to continue to ban any even slightly frivolous work, and especially any that alluded to human love, physical or not. Japan was conscientiously broadening the American sort of puritanism it had been imposing on itself for some time. Russia had been crushed since the Twenties under enforced conformity, which rivaled the German puritanism inherited from Hitler and William II. Italy for the last one hundred and fifty years had had no moral freedom. In Spain, Franco continued the attitudes of the previous rigorous regimes. The Anglo-Saxon world remained the same as the one in which two friends who loaned each other the *Dialogues des courtisanes* by Lucian (c. AD 125–190) were in danger of going to prison, where licentious booksellers and publishers were threatened with jail, where the translations of Proust, Zola, and Colette were expurgated, where Faulkner (even in Philadelphia, in 1949) was impounded. A world, in fact, where citizens who wanted to read Lawrence, Miller and Joyce had to come to Paris to buy them, and that was becoming risky.

To return to France, there was sometimes (though, rarely!) a rather juicy revenge. I'm going to mix up the chronology here with a little story which I think is very significant.

It has been noted that the Cartel d'action morale was in the forefront of prosecutions, seizures, and censorship. It turns out that the secretary general of this Cartel was an apparently highly respectable person, but of a savage moral vigor. This association quickly obtained the censorship of books, authors, publishers and bookstores, and the said secretary general was soon greatly feared by the members of different corporations. I will call him Monsieur X, for reasons that will soon become apparent.

Remember that the Cartel d'action morale had attacked Henry Miller, published at the time in French translation by Gallimard, Denoël, and Girodias. At the time, Gallimard and Denoël were one company, Gaston Gallimard having bought up the shares held by Madame Jean Voillier after the murder of Robert Denoël.

The prospect of finding himself in jail several times over was not a pleasant idea for Gaston Gallimard. Nor did he like interviews, press conferences, or petitions.

He preferred to hire a private detective and have him keep a file on Monsieur X. Who was this paragon of Christian virtue?

The file was soon full. Monsieur X, of course, had a highly specialized past, full of moral corruption of minors (preferably males) through the abuse of his authority, and other such things. It was thanks to his privileged relationship with senior members of the church that he was not in prison but instead ensuring the well-being of the souls of his contemporaries.

I don't know precisely how Gaston Gallimard made it known to Monsieur X that he had firm evidence against him, and that it would be in his interest if he vanished quietly. But in the space of a day people stopped talking about Monsieur X, and his association quite clearly changed its objectives – at least for the moment.

In the following years, I often gave talks about the problems involved in publishing, especially in the provinces. About censorship, I would recount the story of Monsieur X for the enjoyment of the audience, and I always gave his name. That invariably ended the talk on a high note – to my mind.

One day in Toulouse, I think, during the Sixties, I stayed after the talk to converse with some of the audience. I saw an older woman, very dignified, with a sad look, who remained sitting in the first row, evidently waiting. When everyone had left she stood up, came towards me, excusing herself for keeping me even longer, and courteously and humbly made a request of me. The "Monsieur" whom I had just spoken of had been struck dumb when his faults were discovered, as by the hand of God. He had withdrawn into a religious community where for the past fifteen years he had lived in penitence and maceration. Didn't I think that he had paid enough? Besides, his name had been handed down to his children – who were now grown up... She was counting on me.

Honestly, without knowing exactly why, I promised this woman to no longer give the name of Monsieur X. I have, however, learned of his death since then, through a surprising channel which has nothing to do with the story.

As for his children, perhaps, in the end, they became good people, in spite of his depraved example.

A Woman

The period between the ages of twenty-two and twenty-five was a very curious time in my life, which I would have a hard time describing exactly. In a way, I had been rejected as a publisher by society – with a few niceties, but even so. What I wanted essentially to accomplish (though admittedly rather blindly) was the publication of the complete works of Sade, and this was thwarted by seemingly insurmountable barriers. I was rejected by the clandestine press because of other publications that were important to me. Nor was anything working in the realm of contemporary works, even less so in the few manuscripts others offered me. I was getting nowhere.

Marcel Aymé steered me away from a project, which would have been close to my heart. Céline was in Denmark, without much money, and seemed to be looking for a publisher. I had very little money; but I could perhaps have found some if a cause was worth the effort, as this one would have been had it presented itself. Marcel Aymé recommended that I do nothing for the moment; Céline was fighting juridical and publishing problems in which it was best not to intervene. Marcel Aymé stayed in contact with him.

My private life was coming apart. Marie-Claude and I were pretty much in agreement for a divorce, but divorces were very complicated around 1950, especially if the spouses were in agreement.

Our daughter had already turned four, and little by little my parents had taken charge of her. Marie-Claude had found a job as a secretary in a ministry. She lived in the 20th *arrondissement* in a little studio.

I continued to live a disjointed life. Conformist overall, the literary world wasn't really propitious for intimate relationships. I still had friends from high school, both men and women, I was close to. Those who weren't married organized parties from time to time where I tentatively flirted around without anything coming of it.

I maintained, of course, good relations with a lot of writers, who were generally quite a bit older. They looked upon my youth with astonishment, sometimes with a certain suspicion: who was I exactly? As far as being a publisher, my situation wasn't clear. Nor was I any longer a distributor, as the Coopérative du Livre had filed for bankruptcy.

For my part, I had soon done the rounds of those writers who were available (the big publishers took better care of them in terms of a contract). There was still Paulhan, and his entourage... Dominique Aury intrigued me and, I have to say, attracted me. She always stayed very courteous, but distant. I knew very few writers my age, and I judged them to be insignificant.

In 1949, I took a break from my publishing work. I merely had the copies of *Histoire de Juliette*, which were still selling poorly, put in cardboard cases designed by Mario Prassinos.

In 1949, I made the acquaintance of a small group of literary "gatekeepers," so to speak. They had a little office on rue du Dragon and were all about my age, in particular the head of this little enterprise, Bernard Amouroux. They did a little distribution, above all of books by K Editeur, newly founded by, among others, Bernard Gheerbrandt, a bookseller from La Hune, who had just moved from rue Monsieur-le-Prince to boulevard Saint-Germain. Pierre Faucheux was the designer for K Editeur. We were all pretty much of the same generation. At last, I was vaguely associated professionally with people of about my own age. We were on the fringes, really, apart from Gheerbrandt, who already seemed to be on the way to his future brilliant career as a bookseller, but who also remained quite a close friend.

There was also a young woman, Christiane Sauviat, who was courted by most of the young men in this little group on rue du Dragon. She was blonde, charming, lived with her parents, and had done theater. She worked now at the new Hune and often came by rue du Dragon. Cultivated and with a rare maturity, she soon attracted me. I started making advances.

And then an unexpected opportunity presented itself: the poet Robert Ganzo (*Orenoque, Lespugue, Domaine,*) was selling his bookstore, 10, rue de Vaugirard. It was a narrow tunnel-like space, badly laid out, and not well kept up. He couldn't be asking a lot for it. I formed a partnership with a curious friend of Bernard Amouroux called Michel Roethel, a chess champion (of France in the 2ᵉ category, he had just moved up to the first category) who was also a good and aspiring bookseller, and my age. We bought the Ganzo bookstore and immediately baptized it the Librairie du Palimugre.

The bookstore didn't do too much business. We scoured about everywhere to find batches of books; I brought in a good part of my collection, but customers were scarce.

I turned twenty-four that year, on April 8th as usual. My relationship with Christiane Sauviat had become more intimate. I had finally found someone of the opposite sex I could talk to. And she was decidedly ravishing. Of course we were not always in agreement: let's say she had principles about life, which I sometimes did not.

We kissed for the first time on boulevard Saint-Germain in a café, the Old Navy, I think.

Christiane had spent countless Sundays during her youth in the forest of Fontainebleau with older friends. She wanted to show me the forest which I didn't know. We took off on 8th of April, on a motorbike (a Guzzi 250) that I had managed to keep intact. It was in Fontainebleau, in her sleeping bag, that we made love for the first time.

Intermission

I t was a confusing time, a period of my existence which I would have wondered a lot about if I had been in the habit of thinking about such things. Going back over it again, the happy times prevail, alternating with inexplicable passages of what – numbness, emptiness?

First, the happiness. Soon Christiane and I had an urge, more and more irrepressible, to be gone, to be alone, to look at each other at last in peace.

On checking an old bank account, I discovered the sum of twenty-seven thousand francs (old francs, of course, in 1950) which had been sleeping there without my knowing it. Where did they come from? The only logical explanation is that they resulted from simple oversight, or forgetfulness. It had been some time since I'd looked at my bank statements.

Summer was approaching. Twenty-seven thousand francs was a fortune! About five thousand francs in 2000, or seven or eight hundred euros today. In any case, we had enough to leave.

To leave for where? Far away. Christiane remembered a place where she had camped the year before, in the Var, about eighteen miles from Saint-Tropez. I'll call it Le Rayol to keep the peace. We headed first to Saint-Tropez. Michel Roethel could take care of the bookstore. I bought Christiane a beautiful blue swimming suit.

We took the train, second-class, to Toulon, then to Saint-Tropez by bus. Like the rich, we rented a room on the port in the Hotel Sube Continental, just for one night, we thought.

Saint-Tropez at the time was a quiet little port town, which had only recently begun to get lively at night. There were only a few nightclubs, which we found the first evening. At the Ponche, Don Byas and his saxophone and the singer Marcel Mouloudji ran a modest little place. The drinks weren't expensive, there weren't many people: mostly the usual suspects from Saint-Germain-des-Pres. The weather was beautiful, it was summer.

Almost without thinking, we stayed on at the Hotel Sube and got into the habit, after swimming, of spending most evenings at the Ponche. Time didn't exist anymore. We were having a wonderful time.

Obviously, we eventually had to check our pockets to see what was left. We hardly had enough francs to rent two bicycles. There was no way we could leave right then. So we headed over to Le Rayol, a little town on the coast that Christiane knew about.

Le Rayol at that time – I mention this for those who know the area – had only been a town for a few years. During the Thirties, a real estate agency for millionaires tried to make it into a luxury resort, before going bankrupt. The stairways were still there which wound down to the sea, two or three sumptuous houses, like that of Mr. Royce (of Rolls-Royce) or the house of Potez (the airplane manufacturer), and a few villas, plus some hotels, some of which were closed.

I'll end this episode quickly, because it can only be of interest to a few friends. In Le Rayol, Christiane had given lessons the year before to the children of the bakers, M. and Mme. Ferragu. The Ferragus welcomed us and put out two or three tables and some chairs under an enormous pine tree near their bakery, next to a cement tennis court, which had been abandoned for some time. They fed us on credit until the end of vacation. Were they the ones who also found a charming lady on the hill to rent us, on credit, a marvelous room?

Everybody extended us credit. The Ferragus even found us a truck which kindly took us to Toulon when we headed back to Paris. Luckily, we had return tickets.

The Bishop's Move

As I remember, there followed a very long period like an endless tunnel lit only by the presence of Christiane. Sadly, it was hard for her to leave her parents. Why was this? Because I was living in a little room next to the Porte de Vincennes, which was not very comfortable and where we stayed only once in a while.

French books still weren't doing very well. Most of the publishing houses or distribution agencies created since 1945 had gone bankrupt, or were in great difficulty. Some perhaps remember the poster campaigns from November 1950 to November 1952, put out by the publishers' union, as well as the book union: "Better than a gift, a book." The posters showed Gérard Philipe with printed pages in his mouth: "I devour books." Timid book lovers began to follow suit, but they were still rare.

As far as the censorship issue went, a general amnesty in 1947 wiped out the little infractions committed during the Liberation, including "outrages to good behavior through books." Not long afterwards, organized groups "in defense of the family and French morality" took up their campaign again. On March 2, 1950, the first meeting of the Commission for the Control of Publications for Children and Youth was held, a group which could ban posters, advertisements and sales to minors.

On the sixth day of the same month, *Sexus* by Miller was outlawed, published by Editions de la Terre de Feu (Girodias).[3] On the 17th, the trial of *J'irai cracher sur vos tombes* began, with the prosecution of Jean d'Halluin, the publisher of Scorpion, and Boris Vian, the so-called translator of the book, now known to be the author.

---

3   Editions de la Terre de Feu (18 rue Guénégaud, Paris VIe) was created on a one-off basis by Maurice Girodias specifically to publish Jean-Claude Lefaure's translation of Miller's *Sexus*; it was issued expurgated in an "ordinary" edition, and complete in a deluxe, limited edition. – Editor's note.

On May 9, Isidore Isou was found guilty for *La Mécanique des femmes* and given a two hundred thousand franc fine, and eight months in prison deferred!

The 13th, Boris Vian and his publisher d'Halluin were found guilty and made to pay a hundred thousand francs each.

December 12, a total ban of any editions in French or any foreign language of *Sexus* by Miller.

March 3, 1951, the publisher Edmond Buchet notes in his diary: "Worried about paper which has gone from 21 to 57 francs a pound. And you can't find any anymore."

I witnessed all this as if it didn't concern me. The *Amouroux* enterprise turned out to be a business selling half-price books rather than acting as a distributor, and it had swallowed up my final cache of books with almost no return. I discovered in myself, thanks to the obsessive activities of Michel Roethel, a pronounced taste for chess, which practically absorbed all the meager resources of my gray matter.

What's more, a whole world of chess players had invaded the bookstore. Almost like bums, with absent looks, their brains completely occupied by sixty-four squares. There were two exceptions: the young Hubert Monteilhet, the son of a good family with an excellent education; and on the other side, so to speak, Alphonse Boudard, newly released from prison, who greatly irritated me at this point, though I didn't know exactly why.

Boudard, though, didn't give a damn about chess, and he was right. He seemed only to be thinking about getting rid of the stuff he could steal. I think he already had something else in mind, but we didn't know it yet.

Roethel and I went so far as to found a chess club in order to participate in the interclub championships. One or two of the meetings took place in the bookstore. I took part in one of the tournaments. I dreamed of King's Indian Defense, an ultra-modern opening.

Then I realized that chess champions have minds that are fundamentally different, rather like those of great mathematicians, or of those geniuses who can recite the telephone book from memory, forwards and backwards. I managed to rank at the bottom of the Federation's list and had fun from time to time reading chess reviews. But I abandoned my chess pretentions a long time ago.

I also sometimes wrote to Julien Gracq about a preface he was going to write for me for the reedition of a book by Philidor. He never wrote the preface. Luckily, we had other things to talk about.

All of this had to come to an end. We started by selling the bookstore to the Monteilhet family, then it passed to another hopeful. Christiane and I found ourselves in the middle of Saint-Germain-des-Pres, on rue des Ciseaux, in a miniscule one-room book-rental shop that I immediately baptized Palimugre.

Essentially, we were starting over from zero. But there were two of us. Christiane ended by coming to live with me. She often ran the shop while I was out drumming up business. We still have memories of this period, such as the week when a box of noodles fed us for two days.

I went looking for a job outside of books. For example, I spent a few days as a salesman for a home credit agency. Also, tempted by a delightful ad, I applied to the headquarters of the French Workers Party which was looking for a canvasser to deal with generous donors (so to speak). They did indeed have some, but the president (I never saw anyone else in the office) could hardly pay his canvasser.

We made friends. Or rather, through Christiane, I met people our own age. She had met Maria Pacôme in the theater, when she had been starting out as an actress. And then, Maurice Ronet, an up-and-coming actor and very handsome leading man. They would very soon be married. We organized wild poker parties at our house with frightening sums in the pot – purely fictitious ones, luckily. We had nothing to pay each other with. This was genuine Bohemianism, with all of its crazy laughter and its misery.

My relationship with the French Book Club was more serious. Its founder, who liked to be called Lhopital, was looking for a director. He decided to organize a competition in which each candidate had to offer suggestions for publishing projects (a clever idea for acquiring ideas for free). There were twenty of us, I think. He chose five or six serious candidates. The first, Jean Rousselot, a poet, was chosen and lasted two days. The second was Claude Gregory, who stayed the course. The third, who did not have the opportunity to be tested (but I don't think he would have lasted very long) was me.

I did get something out of it though: the relationships I picked up again with people from the literary world showed me that not only had I not been forgotten after my eclipse, but a sort of legend had even formed around my name.

The second benefit that I got was a solid order from the Club Français du Livre for a preface to a Sade text. Oh! It was only for the 1791 version of *Justine*. But at least it was Sade, and the months of 1952 during which I spent my free time putting together this text of seventy-five pages, *Le Marquis de Sade, l'histoire de la littérature* – in fact a short biography, plus an analysis of Sade's place in French letters – allowed me to form a clearer idea of what I thought myself about Sade.

I was now absolutely convinced. Yes, Donatien de Sade filled a unique, enormous place not only in French, but in world literature. He had to be given back his rightful position, or rather just given it, because it had never been publicly proclaimed before.

Here and there, a real interest in Sade began to manifest itself, but peripherally, one could say. Gilbert Lely, the writer who was continuing the work of Maurice Heine, had managed to get in touch with the Sade family. In 1949, he had acquired some material, for a volume of magnificent unpublished letters, which he had published with Éditions Georges Artigues, under the title *L'Aigle, mademoiselle*, a quote from one of the Sade letters. His presentation was a bit grandiloquent, and I was always vaguely suspicious of him. Otherwise, his work was fascinating, and he had managed to crack the fortress the family had built around the name of its cursed ancestor since 1814.

In 1949, too, Maurice Blanchot published *Lautréamont et Sade* :

We have here the most scandalous book that was ever written. Isn't this a reason to be interested in it? We have the opportunity to know a work beyond which no other writer, at any time, has dared go: we have in our hands, in this relative world of literature, a veritable absolute, and we aren't asking questions about it? We're not asking why it is unequaled, what there is in it that is so excessive, why it is consummately too much for people? What strange negligence.

Strange indeed. Not a word about the publication of *Histoire de Juliette*, which had just come out to a huge silence, as I said. Yet, Maurice Blanchot was in fact alluding to *Histoire de Juliette*, even though his analysis would have applied better to the *Cent Vingt Journées de Sodome*. Hadn't he read it?

In 1951, Simone de Beauvoir published "Faut-il brûler Sade?" in *Les Temps modernes*, an honest piece of work, a little laborious, but fairly objective: "Sade created an ethical night analogous to the intellectual night that enveloped Descartes; he didn't set forth a clear rationale: but at least he opposed every easy answer."

But how and where did he oppose them? In his books that no one could find anywhere, with the exception now of *Histoire de Juliette*, about which there was not a word.

Sade seemed destined to be banned, by principle, or by fact.

The searches and the interrogations became less frequent. There was no trial in the works. It's true that I never missed the chance when confronted by the police or a judge to reaffirm that *Histoire de Juliette* was only the beginning of a publication of the *Œuvres complètes* by the Marquis de Sade. I suppose that the courts were waiting for the other works to be printed before acting. Besides, I probably wasn't an interesting case; the police never found any books, apart from those that I generously gave them, and my official address remained the garage in Sceaux, a place they had given up on some time earlier.

Real Gold

The world of books in France began to move, along with the general situation, which was clearing up slightly. Gallimard started a new collection for the general public called *L'Air du temps* (*La Réalite dépasse la fiction*, by Albert Aicard and Jacqueline Franck, *Le Tout-Paris* as seen by a young journalist with lots of ambition, Françoise Giroud). A little earlier, to general disapproval, Gaston Gallimard had signed a very advantageous contract, at last, with Céline, on July 18, 1951, for all his works, past and future.

In October 1951, the Éditions du Seuil, flush from the enormous success of the *Petit Monde de don Camillo*, began a collection called Écrivains de toujours. In December (who remembers now?), Gracq refused the Prix Goncourt for *Le Rivage des Syrtes*, and made a fortune for the man he paid to publish his books, José Corti. In February 1952, Paul Léautaud, on the radio, made it possible for all of France to hear his sardonic laughter and his uncompromising personality. Paulhan, co-founder of *Lettres Françaises*, dropped a bombshell: his *Lettre aux directeurs de la Résistance*. In August, Gallimard started its *Club du Meilleur Livre*.

We were now printing on acceptable paper. The new lay-out designers, Pierre Faucheux, Massin and Jacques Darche, put together new and imaginative books (sometimes excessively so), which had never been seen before. The printers once again started looking for customers. Some buyers found their way into the bookstores again. Trains were running a little more. Bridges were being built. Food stocks were more normal. A little economic renaissance was in progress, timidly. In February 1953, Hachette brought out the *Livre de Poche* collection, with its terribly ugly covers.

I got a shock when Paulhan gave his *Lettres aux directeurs de la Résistance* to the new Éditions de Minuit. I felt I had a right to this book. But why would he have given it to me, who hardly existed anymore? In what way could I claim it? I was slowly becoming less numb.

Sade. I had now completely made up my mind. Bataille had just written a preface for the umpteenth edition of the 1791 version of *Justine*. During the summer of 1952, a clandestine edition of *La Philosophie dans le boudoir* was printed by my neighbor on rue Gozlin, Marcel Zerbib, but of course without his name on it. It was impounded, and there were, finally, a few protests in the press.

Outraged, I launched my own edition of *La Philosophie dans le boudoir*, with my name on it (and still using the Sceaux address). It came out at the end of the year printed by the Nesle printers, on rue de Nesle, although they didn't sign it, either. But that didn't matter; they had taken the risk – or sort of. So now I existed again.

Still no distributer for Sade. And very few bookstores that dared to sell him. But at the same time Gallimard brought out Volume I of *La Vie du marquis de Sade*, by Gilbert Lely, who seemed a fairly interesting person. I was soon going to meet him.

Okay, no distribution. But there were some new agents, like Jules Vernier, a former courier I'd done business with in the past, and who had an office on rue Madame. The international market was once again opening up. I now had customers in Lebanon. A clever bookseller on the quays, a Belgian called Thiellemans, who moved to a posh area, in the passage du Retiro which opened onto the faubourg Saint-Honoré. He bought fifty copies of *Philosophie dans le boudoir*. In the foreign books section at Hachette, there was a director who really did his job. He called me up whenever he saw one of my announcements in the *Bibliographie de la France* for a book which seemed interesting to him, and he would order it in relatively large numbers, sometimes two or three hundred copies. And he would pay the bill in ninety days. I sold Sade to Jean Galtier-Boissière, director of *Le Crapouillot* and *Le Petit Crapouillot*, which sold books by mail.

Full of fresh optimism, I started production of the four volumes of *La Nouvelle Justine*, to appear in May 1953, and *Les Cent Vingt Journées de Sodome*, to appear in December. My "Bruxelles edition" had used standardized spelling for the first time. But this had been done very quickly.

This time I wanted an impeccable text. So Christiane and I undertook a revision of the edition printed in the Thirties by Maurice Heine. To be quite honest, this work on the Sade texts made us profoundly uneasy for several weeks, the atmosphere broken by outbursts of unexpected, truly crazed laughter. It took us a long time to find our balance again.

The format for the three volumes was the one I had always used for Sade: in-16 *raisin*. But for the printing I invented something very simple and pretty extravagant at the same time. The covers were made of black Ingres paper decorated with a few words stamped in real gold: on the spine it simply said

Sade*, Sade**, Sade***. On the front wrappers, *Les 120 Journées de Sodome*. I have only one copy of these *Cent Vingt Journées* left. Everything considered, with fifty years of hindsight, it was a success.

This time, I deepened my research. I had consulted psychologists, one of whom now worked with me: René Diatkine, a specialist in teenage delinquency. He did not quibble: for one thing, young delinquents read very little, and when they did it was usually ersatz detective novels; for another thing, the specialists in question had a tendency to orient young delinquents toward entertaining books to help them let off steam. The magistrates, those specialists in "outrage against morality through books," were all wrong.

Naturally, the police showed up as soon as *La Philosophie dans le boudoir* came out. Once again, I announced to the vice squad and to the judges that this time I would see it through to the end. I had begun the first official edition of Sade's *Œuvres complètes*, with my name as the publisher, and nothing was going to stop me now.

Once again, there were useless searches and interrogations, which went nowhere. The police were sometimes indulgent, like officer Fernet, and sometimes severe. But never understanding. They'd say: in the end, Sade is boring. Can't you do something else? Or, others would say: but do you realize you are perverting all of France? Think about the women, the teenagers, all those weak minds who will be driven into debauchery!

Well, I had thought about it, and we'd talk about it again later. Only, it seemed to me that as long as there had never been a real discussion about the books' morality, with the books on the table so that they could be looked at, nothing was ever really going to get done.

By chance, between March and June 1952, I happened to hear on the radio, in snatches, some André Breton interviews with the journalist André Parinaud. I had a mixed impression. I remember being disappointed by a program where Breton praised "the beautiful poems of Francis Vielé-Griffin," which certainly weren't lacking in interest, but which were now obviously dated, like the shipwrecked vestiges of a past time.

On the other hand, I was literally stunned by another program. Breton was answering questions from Parinaud. I transcribe here what I heard (I can cite Breton almost perfectly from memory):

> Parinaud: However, there exists an apparent contradiction between your conception of free love and the admiration of the surrealists for someone like Sade, for example?...

Breton: If surrealism set this idea of 'courtly love' at the zenith, a
tradition usually associated with the Cathars, it has also with anguish
leaned over its nadir and it is this dialectic approach which has shone
light on the resplendent genius of Sade, like a black sun. Wasn't it Valéry
who said that 'eroticism is never far from the truth'? By maintaining
itself in the immense stratosphere where poems such as *Hymne* by
Baudelaire, *Aimez* by Germain Nouveau, or *Amoureuses* by Eluard are
situated, as well as almost all the collection of *Je sublime* by Benjamin
Péret, this love carried to incandescence tends to quickly become
disembodied. The admirable, dazzling light of the flame must not
hide from us what it is made of, or steal from us the profound depths
of its mines, often blown through with mephitic blasts of air, which
have nonetheless allowed for the extraction of their substance, a substance which must be maintained if one doesn't want such love to be
extinguished. It is by starting from this point of view that surrealism
has done everything to lift the taboos that stop people from freely
dealing with the sexual world and all the sexual states, perversions
included – a world about which I have been led to state that 'in spite
of the memorable probings carried out by Sade and Freud,' surrealism,
so far as I know, has 'never ceased except against our will to penetrate
the universe, its own indestructible core of night.'

This time I was transported. A great voice, picking up from the likes of
Baudelaire and Apollinaire, seemed to have come to my support at just the
moment I was doing battle again.

True, I still had in my library the *Manifestes du Surréalism, Point du jour,* and
Nadja. However, *Arcane 17* left something to be desired. And I had never read
La Lampe dans l'horloge; clearly, Breton seemed sometimes to drift into the past.

And suddenly, he came back, born again, as alive as ever. His trajectory,
at the time, did not appear totally clear. I saw him sometimes as being bur-
dened by rather useless polemics, and then suddenly picking up from where
he had left off, on high, with a dazzling intensity never seen before. And that's
the way it was also in 1949, with the *La Chasse spirituelle* affair. Does anyone
remember it now?

In the spring of 1949, in the month of May, on the 19th to be exact, in
the literary pages of the newspaper *Combat,* Maurice Nadeau announced with
feigned modesty some sensational news: they had just found the most celebrated manuscript of the lost works of Rimbaud, *La Chasse spirituelle.* Nadeau

let Pascal Pia have the glory which was due him: "This discovery belongs to M. Pascal Pia, the first publisher of Rimbaud's *Œuvres complètes*, whose erudite discoveries have been numerous, and is here to tell the public about the existence of this new manuscript which was given to him following a series of lucky breaks." At the same time, the *Mercure de France* put into circulation a sensational brochure entitled *Arthur Rimbaud, La Chasse spirituelle*.

Everything unwound in a few days. The literary world rebelled. On May 21, a radio panel was formed with André Chamson, Stanislas Fumet, André Maurois, Claude Mauriac and Pascal Pia. Chamson affirmed the authenticity of the text. Maurois and Stanslas Fumet expressed vague doubts. There were two camps: one for authenticity, and the other of doubters, for whom the argument sadly lacked any basis. "The Battle of Rimbaud," announced *Le Figaro*, and *Carrefour* : "For or against *La Chasse spirituelle*."

Then, very quickly, there was André Breton. On May 19, after merely being presented with the text, he denounced this fake in a letter to *Combat*. No, this *Chasse spirituelle* could not be by Rimbaud. Why? All you had to do was read it. In just a few lines, André Breton ripped the text apart, irrefutably destroying the whole affair:

> ...The extreme mediocrity of the phrasing, which fails to mask a laborious work of pastiche, leaves in its wake the most unfavorable impression concerning the authenticity of this document.
>
> [...] Just from the use of epithets and images, who – with just a little sensitivity and scholarship – would believe that Rimbaud could succumb to associations such as cat claws, hypocritical brides, furious mammoths, or be so lacking in analogies that he resorted to a sonorous head like a giant shell, or hot earth like a bird? [...] It is hardly worth pointing out that Rimbaud in 1872 – at the height of his powers – could not have known such serious and continual failure without rejecting the whole principle of identity..."

And in a brochure published almost at once, *Flagrant délit*, he sent all these critics back to rethink their theories, or to put it bluntly, back to their insincerities and their incompetence.

Besides, two young actors, Mlle. Akakia Viala and M. Nicolas Bataille, with all the necessary proof, soon declared themselves to be the authors of this rather clumsy pastiche. Once the affair had died down, the *Mercure* donated the royalties ("a rather considerable sum," said M. Hartmann, director of *Mercure*) to the Rimbaud Museum in Charleville. In *Combat*, Maurice Nadeau and his accomplice Maurice Saillet, after spitting their venom at André Breton, insults included, soon lost heart. Pascal Pia escaped rather cleverly. Breton, the king, had crushed them: "All (Maurice Nadeau) could now do was to retrieve his venomous work from where he left it – under my foot."

It was in this way that André Breton, in one blow, distinguished himself from the crowd of "critics," and took up his unique, indisputable position once again, as Grand Master of the spiritual world, far above the literary masses and their in-fighting.

Maurice Girodias –
I Try To Toe The Line A Little

In April 1953, a certain Maurice Girodias started the Olympia Press, and our paths crossed soon afterwards for the first time. I want to say a few words about Maurice Girodias, who was to play a role for a while in my existence.

Maurice Kahane-Girodias was the son of Jack Kahane, pre-war founder of the Obelisk Press, which first published Henry Miller, in English and in Paris, and other books that were unauthorized in the Anglo-Saxon world. Girodias had had a kind of Boy Scout childhood and a theosophical one, which led him to be a virgin and a vegetarian at twenty, probably in opposition to his alcoholic, womanizing father. He was twenty-two when his father was found dead at his office headquarters in 1940. It was Girodias himself who told the story, writhing about with a sinister laugh when he was in, let's say, a farcical mood.

What I am now going to recount, I did not witness. I heard it from various sources, several of whom were friends of his whom I met after 1950, and who were my friends until their deaths.

Playing on his two names, he slipped through the Occupation. In order not to be classified as a Jew like his father, he adopted, I don't know by what sleight of hand, the name of his mother, Girodias. Towards 1942, Girodias inherited a large sum of money. He immediately founded an art publishing house, Le Chêne. I recently discovered some strange information that no one had ever given me before, about the Éditions du Chêne and about its owner under the Occupation, at the home of the American Herbert Lottman (I only read his book last year!). I quote:

> We had a wonderful surprise with the Éditions du Chêne which, under the Occupation, had published works in German for the occupying forces, notably tourist guide books aimed at German soldiers, and even an album on French race horses confiscated by the German army. We guessed that the owner of this publishing house must have kept up

good relations with the occupier to the detriment of certain colleagues less well connected, to the point that the Purification Commission erupted in protest when the American magazine *Life* described Girodias as a hero. One assumes that it was a matter of self-protection that he so assiduously frequented notable collaborators such as Lucien Combelle. [*A friendship which Girodias later accepted responsibility for.*] Once the Purification was in effect, he found a much more efficient disguise; at the moment the Purification Commission was to hear his case, they received a letter from Éditions du Chêne informing them that the owner was deceased. [*A maneuver which probably came from Hachette, who, at the time, was very close to Girodias.*] Sometime later, the publisher came back to life in order to start another publishing house. (Herbert Lottman, *L'Épuration*, Fayard, 1986)

I imagine that these revelations in 1986 surprised a lot of people, just as much as they had me. Girodias' memoirs, *Une journée sur la terre* (Paris: La Difference, 1990), dictated in a hurry into a microphone and full of errors (intentional or otherwise), do not allude to this at all.

If I had known about this in 1953, I would probably not have attached much importance to it. That a half-Jew does whatever he must do to escape the occupier, then, after some compromises, escapes from a purge which is just as incoherent, would have struck me, no doubt, as a case of all being fair in love and war – literally.

Girodias was, according to his own admission, rather against the kind of production his father was involved in. He made a lot of money from Le Chêne, and during the Occupation made numerous friends, some of them girls, who, he claims, granted him no favors, or just the strict minimum. In his memoirs, there is a sentence in which he evokes "the life of a young publisher on whom everything smiles. Except love, of course."

He went camping in the forest of Fontainebleau, deserted at the time, and there happened to be among the entourage a mystic named Vivian. Vivian was the guru of the very young Laurette, who Girodias had been in love with for a long time, without success (during this time she was sleeping with his friend Chavarche, it seems), before finally marrying him immediately after the war and having two daughters.

Vivian was surrounded by a group of women and other disciples, a sort of new European sect. I offer these details so that the complex personality of Maurice Girodias can be understood. Up until the death of his father, he was, according to his friends, a vegetarian, a virgin, and a non-drinker, until the day when these very friends (including the one called Chavarche in his memoirs) got him dead drunk and pushed him into bed with the first available girl.

From that day forward, Maurice Girodias was a complete alcoholic, as I knew him in 1952. But he held his drink remarkably well, remaining very dignified and very straight when he was drunk which, in the end, caused him to pass out standing up, in one fell swoop. Then, and only then, would he be sick as a dog. And that's what he wanted: "I don't get drunk for the pleasure of drinking," he used to say. "I get drunk to be sick."

At the end of a lot of messy financial complications, whose outcome I never heard about, he said he was (at least this is what he says in his memoirs) divested in a rather disgusting way of the Éditions du Chêne by Hachette. In 1953, almost without any money, he founded the Olympia Press in Paris in order to exploit, as his father had before him with Obelisk Press, licentious books in English. He also published – still in English – Jean Genet, Beckett, *l'Histoire de l'œil*...

We became fast friends. We had interests in common, comparable financial means, in other words very limited, and a similar sense of humor (Christiane, Maurice and I). I was very suspicious of Maurice (rightfully so, as you will see), but he was often an agreeable companion, with a great sense of black humor, and a total absence of scruples. I also discovered little by little that he had a totally suicidal temperament.

At the time, there were still a certain number of American bases in France, and English-speaking tourists were numerous. Girodias' business affairs slowly began to prosper, at any rate as long as he was able to employ American and British expatriates living in Paris, who were bohemians for the most part, some of them very talented. Girodias had sublet a boutique on rue Jacob with Amouroux; Christiane and I were still on rue des Ciseaux.

We had some customers in common – with more business for him than for me. We had lunch or dinner together in modest restaurants whenever we had a big sale.

In the spring of 1953, I think, an important step in the career of my publishing house took place: with Christiane, I started a SARL[4] called the Librairie Jean-Jacques Pauvert, just as the publishing house Hachette had its bookstore as its official name, and the Éditions de la NRF had the Gallimard Bookstore. This is a tradition which has since vanished, having lost its meaning. The word "librairie" has not been part of the names of the Éditions Gallimard or the Hachette group for a long time.

---

4   SARL – "société à responsabilité limitée"; a limited liability company. – Translator's note.

It was, indeed, an important step, and an acceptance of my status as a publisher, which up until then I had more or less avoided. It was my entrance into a line of business. And now it was done.

I took advantage of it to do something rather naïve. If you're going to sort things out, you might as well sort them out properly. So I put forth my candidacy to be a member of the publishers' union. After a while, I got an embarrassed phone call from the secretary saying that there were some obstacles to my candidacy (he didn't say what they were, but I guessed). Besides, the candidacy had to be sponsored by two representatives. I could have found them, I think. But I answered that a professional union shouldn't copy the ways of the Jockey Club, and I swore never to be part of the publishers' union. I've kept my word.

Apart from the union deal, starting to toe the line again was no small deal. First of all, we had an accountant, thanks to the bookstall seller Thiellemans, whose wife zealously kept the books and to all appearances respected the rules.

I first had a long meeting with this remarkably professional bookkeeper, who asked right away to see my accounts, that is to say, the real ones.

I didn't have any. For the last eight years, I had deliberately avoided anything that might seem official. There had been no declaration of my business dealings, or trace of any commercial activity, no legal presence, in fact. But that period was now over. I had to keep accounts, which I did in a little notebook: Expenses, Receipts, Money Owed. From time to time, with a bit too much optimism, I added a column for Future Earnings, which always turned out to be in excess of what we actually made, while the expenses were undervalued.

This accountant, an excellent man whose name I've forgotten, mentioned all the legal papers that he said were missing, then he drew a deep breath, and made a decision:

"Okay," he said. "Let's not talk about this anymore. What happened happened. Let's say that you didn't exist before 1953."

Funny as it seems, nothing at all happened. The times were like that: things weren't always bright, but the situation did have its advantages; the administrative straitjacket wasn't completely buckled up the way it is today.

And then, during the winter of 1953–54, Jean Paulhan gave me a lovely surprise.

V

A ROCKET BARRAGE

A banned book is a fire that one wants to stomp out,
and which shoots sparks into one's nostrils.

— Voltaire

The Unpredictable Jean Paulhan

I often saw Jean Paulhan. I had seriously started to work on my *Œuvres complètes* of Sade, which interested him a lot. I went pretty regularly to the Wednesday meetings at Gallimard. Paulhan and I sometimes had lunch together. He even invited me to rue des Arènes. He apparently liked my article in the stillborn *Palumugre* review, which I finally showed to him, along with my preface to *Justine* for the Club Français du Livre.

We got along well. I liked the seemingly naïve humor of this tall, thick-set man, his head resembling an owl a bit, his hair shooting out every which way, and who talked in a thin little voice. His *Fleurs de Tarbes* and his *Clef de la poésie* had left me at the edge of an impenetrable underworld, but his *Guide d'un petit voyage en Suisse* had thrilled me. And besides, he had shown himself to be courageous under the Occupation. There was his *Lettre aux directeurs de la résistance*.

But during the winter of 1953–54, to be honest, he began to irritate me. For some months, each time we met, he talked about a mysterious manuscript that seemed to be taking a lot of his time; he spoke in a way that seemed more and more urgent. You're the only one who could publish it, he said. Really, you're the only one I see doing it. No one else would dare.

After telling him endlessly that I would certainly read the manuscript, with pleasure, but without seeing anything concrete, I got fed up. Besides, he more or less stopped mentioning it.

One night in December, or January, during a freezing rain, I ran into him on rue Jacob. We exchanged a few words, and suddenly he said to me: you remember the manuscript I told you about? Well, as it happens, I have it with me.

He showed me an envelope that he had in his hand. Feeling spiteful, I showed very little enthusiasm. Then he almost shoved the envelope at me. Yes, yes, you'll see. Besides, you're the only one... etc.

I returned home soaked and in a rather bad mood. After dinner, I took a quick look at the manuscript, which was machine-typed, very clean, with just two or three corrections. Title: *Histoire d'O*. A little message from Paulhan at the beginning (addressed to me? To whom?):

> I would like you to read this. Either I am very much mistaken, or else this book one day will have its place in the history of literature.
> (Do I need to add that it is in no way – in spite of the little corrections – mine).

Intrigued, I started to read.

It was one in the morning when I finished it, stunned. I said to Christiane: this is my book. Paulhan was right. It was the book I'd been seeking for years. Okay, I was the publisher of Sade, but with *Histoire d'O*, I would change the era. It was true: I was the dream publisher for *Histoire d'O*, just as the *Histoire d'O* was the dream book for me. There couldn't be two encounters like that in fifty years... I felt delirious.

The next morning, very early, too early to be social, I called Paulhan: I woke you? Yes, a little – Listen, you're right. It is my book. Introduce me to the author; I'll have him/her sign a contract right away.

Here, Paulhan coughed several times. He said in a high-pitched voice: Okay, very well. Hmm, um... But I have to tell you there's a little problem. Oh! You'll see, it's almost nothing, a trifle. The author has already signed a contract with another publisher.

I hardly heard this. Nobody could publish my book instead of me. I felt violent. I trembled with a cold, savage resolve; I thought of knives, pistols, poison, a man-to-man combat resonating through the night at this competitor's house, then knifing him and snatching the contract.

Confronted with what he felt to be criminal resolve in me, and also, I guess, because of the sleep he was still full of, Paulhan quickly threw out the name of the publisher in question: M. René Defez, Éditions des Deux Rives. He barely had time to say, "Anyway, he's having some trouble at the moment and perhaps you can make an arrangement..." before I had already hung up.

Thirty-six hours later, I left the office of René Defez. In my pocket was the contract for *Histoire d'O* with the Éditions des Deux Rives. In his pocket was a check for a hundred thousand old francs (about ten thousand in 2000, or one thousand five hundred euros). It had all gone very well.

Sure enough, Les Deux Rives was having big problems. The publication some time before of a book by René Despuech, *Le Trafic des piastres*, had raised an enormous scandal, and above all a police raid and a determined magistrate. A good many of the high-ranking military in the Indochinese government had been compromised, as well as a certain number of parliament members and, they said, even the immediate entourage of the President. Not only had they searched the domicile of René Defez, but they had tried a number of times to break in. Several lawsuits had been brought against him.

René Defez was a middle-aged man, courteous, and gifted with a cool reserve. However, he wasn't facing the storm without a certain worry. He revealed his concerns to me, then: "Ah! Yes. Madame d'O, the little pornographic piece that Paulhan foisted off on me! It's really not the moment. You're really interested in it? I gave him a hundred thousand francs. If I can get that back, the contract is yours."

Just in case, I'd brought my checkbook with me, ready to do battle with this individual who had stolen my book. Not necessary: if I had insisted a little, I think he would have paid me to take it off his hands.

I had no idea what I would do to cover the check, which, for the moment, of course, was going to bounce.

It didn't matter. Leaving René Defez, I literally flew above the sidewalk. A great adventure was beginning. I found the hundred thousand francs just in time.

Who Is This Woman?

One question raced through my mind. Who was this woman? I was immediately sure that the author of *Histoire d'O* was a woman, Christiane was, too. But who was it? I was struck by the precise writing, clean in all the details of this implacable dream world. I could swear I had already read texts written by the same person. A woman, and one I had read! Les Deux Rives contract was signed only by PAULINE RÉAGE, with no address. A few possible names crossed my mind, only to be immediately rejected. I knew I was getting close; I had the name on the tip of my tongue, but it wouldn't come. It became an obsession.

Luckily, my obsession came to an end fairly quickly. A few days later, Jean Paulhan, in the bar at Pont-Royal, introduced me to Pauline Réage. It was, of course, Dominique Aury.

We knew each other well. And not only that, I had read her with delight. Prefaces, yes, and articles, but above all short texts – why hadn't I made the association immediately! – in the *Cahiers de la Pléiade* issue number 12 (no longer in print), Spring-Summer 1951: "Le Révolte de Madame de Merteuil."

She stayed there, in her chair, as always modest, almost invisible. And seductive (she was 47 in 1954). Discreetly coiffed, discreetly dressed, discreetly seated like a well brought-up young woman, her voice soft and sweet.

I carried on wildly about her novel: a masterpiece, but above all a revolution. No one had written anything like it, and we were going to change the world, because no one had ever officially put a work like this into circulation. She spoke very little, finding me, no doubt, excessive. I came back to earth. I was going to bring out the book right away. I had prepared a contract.

It was reduced to the essentials: the only demand was for a preface by Paulhan, "Le Bonheur dans l'esclavage." The fifteen percent royalties would be shared thus: twelve for Dominique Aury, and three for the preface by Paulhan. I obviously had all the copyright for all countries, the cinema rights, etc. I felt fabulously rich.

How did the *Histoire d'O* come to be written? I didn't worry much about it at the time. The book was there, that was all. It was only little by little, over the years, that the details came together. For example, in 1969 I learned about the birth of the novel, when Dominique Aury put together for me the story of this adventure in a heart-rending text, *Une fille amoureuse* :

A girl in love one day said to the man she loved: I could write these stories that you like…You think so? he said. […] One night, after this 'You think so,' and without the slightest idea that one day she would find in a registry book the name Réage which would permit her to borrow her pseudonym name from two famous Jezebels, Pauline Borghese and Pauline Roland. One night, this girl, instead of picking up a book before going to sleep, lying stretched out on her left side, curled up like a hunting dog, held a big black pencil in her right hand, and she began to write the story she had promised. […] Working in the light of the little lamp near her bed, the hand holding the pencil scurried back and forth over the paper without any worries about the time or about how much sense she was making. The girl wrote like one talks in the night to someone one loves, when words of love have been held in too long and are now tumbling out. For the first time in her life, she wrote without hesitation, without letup, without erasing, without rejecting any-thing; she wrote like one breathes, like a dream. […] Tomorrow, no, the day after tomorrow, she will present him with the notebook. […] And what if the fantasies that are revealed in the notebook outrage her lover, or worse, bore him, or worse yet, seem ridiculous? Not for what they are, of course, but because they come from her, and one rarely pardons the loved one that freedom which is readily accorded others. She was wrong to be afraid: Ah, keep going, he says. What happens next? Do you know? She knew. She revealed it to him slowly. Through the whole of summer's end, through all of autumn, from beaches aflame in little towns near the water, and the return to Paris, red and burned, she wrote what she knew. Ten pages, five pages, chapters or parts of chapters, she put it in an envelope addressed to a *poste restante*, these pages with the same format as the original notebook, sometimes written with pencil, sometimes with ink, a kind of Bic or a good pen. No copies, no drafts, she kept nothing. But the post office is faithful…

Everything is exactly as she wrote it. The only text I had to print from, in the beginning, was a typed copy with two or three spelling corrections. Sometime later (I'll talk about this, too), I happened to have in my hand the first, authentic manuscript. It was in little notebooks (six in all) with handwritten pages, all in the same format, in pencil, for the most part, or sometimes with a Bic or a good pen. The lover and the girl (I'd rather refer to them this way than as Jean Paulhan and Dominique Aury) had at last ended their life together – I mean with the death of the lover, who was older – with this manuscript.

I also had with me some correspondence between the two of them, written in rather short notes. They were the observations of Jean Paulhan about the text (which he had absolutely not written, contrary to certain legends), and the answers, sometimes not in agreement, of Dominique.

> I don't like this 'author' (or actress? J.P.) Ah, I like her a lot. (D.A.)
> Even though I'm looking at the text, it isn't clear (J.P.)
> I'll clarify it (D.A.)
> Why not finish with "who finds it"? (J.P.)
> I very much wanted to come back to the idea of the inevitable success of O and in this discreet manner. But as you wish" (D.A.)

One day, the book was completely finished. Dominique Aury thought at once of Gallimard. The reading committee received copies of *Histoire d'O*. There were those for and those against. It was Jean Dutourd, they say, who got it refused. "You can't go publishing pornography," he said more or less to Gaston, who acquiesced. (Gallimard at the time was publishing Genet, whose texts could hardly be said to be respectable.) Then Paulhan, in a roundabout way, having first promised me the book, got Pauline Réage to sign a contract with Éditions des Deux Rives. Before getting me involved again.

What incited Paulhan's passion (and how easy it is to understand) is explained by Dominique Aury in *Une fille amoureuse* :

> What excited him, the man for whom I was writing the story, she said again, is the relationship the story has with my own life. Could it be that for him she was the inverted, deformed image of the heroine, that she was the shadow figure, unrecognizable, drawn tight, like a person walking in the sun in the Midi, or, still unrecognizable, diabolically stretched out in front of someone returning from the sea, the Atlantic, on an empty beach, when the sun dies in flames behind him?

And Dominique – one absolutely must read *Une fille amoureuse*, also signed Pauline Réage – plays with the possible memories of real facts or of dreams which arise, conscious or unconscious, but transformed, in *Histoire d'O*.

Histoire d'O will show up often in my personal history. To close this chapter, I'll note one other thing: Jean Paulhan, as well as Dominique Aury, were the main characters in the book. She said, "Books were their only freedom, their common country, their real journey; they lived together with the books that they loved, as others lived surrounded by family..."

And in an interview at the end of her life, Dominique Aury answered a question by Hector Bianciotti: "And when did your revelation that literature was something else besides everyday language, happen?" "I must have noticed the difference one day, between language and literary language, but I have no memory of that moment. [...] Literature, as it relates to language, is what is left."

Saint-Germain-Des-Prés In 1954 –
The New Palimugre

S aint-Germain-des-Prés in 1954 was still like a village. There was the Tabou, rue Dauphine, and two or three other nightclubs. It was both a place for locals, and local entertainment for the rare tourist. We pretty much lived among ourselves. On the rue des Ciseaux, there were three bookstores (today there are four restaurants and not one bookstore), including ours, and two on rue Gozlin, around the corner, without counting the art gallery of Marcel Zerbib. We would run into Max Ernst, sixty-five and still not famous; Sartre, of course, too famous, from whom I had distanced myself a little (without his having noticed, however) following his unforgiveable act before the National Committee of Writers (his ferocious attack on "collaborationist writers") and his blind attachment to Stalinism.

In 1954, the public had yet to notice the flamboyant existence of surrealism in the Thirties. Bearing witness to this long blindness, José Corti writes in his *Souvenirs désordonnées* (1983):

> Young people come to me [...] They envy my having known the great days of a past era which appear fabulous to them [...] Youth regrets not having had the privilege to live at the time of the great flowering of surrealism. Youth identifies with it and whoever gives lectures about surrealist texts today, and they imagine how wonderful it would have been to discover the texts as they came out [...] I astound them all by revealing that it took ten years to come to the end of the thousand copies of *Comme deux gouttes d'eau* by Eluard, of *Derrière les fagots* by Benjamin Péret, and as many years to finish *L'Immaculée Conception* (2,000 copies): the Eluard books came off the Guy Levis Mano presses before the war and were still in boxes in 1945…

In 1954, you could still find copies of leftover surrealist books from the Thirties in the good bookstores and stalls. They were almost as difficult to sell then as in 1945. There were two explanations for this: the heavy hand of the communists on the majority of presses, with their moralistic attitudes; and the hostility of Sartre and the "existentialists" from *Temps Modernes* towards Breton. There were those who couldn't forgive Breton his independent spirit since his definitive rupture with the Communist Party around 1935, his denunciations of the Moscow trials, and this rejection touched the whole surrealist movement. Only Eluard, René Char and Aragon still sold, selling as "resisters," and as sympathizers, or more, with the Communist Party. They had moved away from the Surrealist movement a long time before.

Here's just one example. I found Bellmer again, with whom I had corresponded (he was living in the provinces then) in 1947. Christiane and I had the crazy idea of organizing a Bellmer gallery show, rue des Ciseaux, in the spring of 1954, I think. We worked like crazy to cover the bookshelves with black paper. Bellmer brought us everything he had: engravings, original drawings. This had the desired effect. The tiny Palimugre was full of treasures. Bellmer for once set aside his neurotic, suspicious ways, and his sudden bursts of contrariness. Like us, he was counting on this effort a lot.

We kept the show on for two or three weeks. A few people dropped by out of curiosity. The net result: no sales. Not one, even though Bellmer had lowered his prices to a sacrifice, even though they hadn't been high in the first place. The three of us were horrified. The four of us really, since Ünica Zürn, Bellmer's companion, graced us several times with her phantasmagorical presence. Christiane and I liked her a lot.

Our little shop at the beginning of 1954 saw a lot of people come and go: Klossowski, Mandiargues, and Bataille often came by. I'd gotten to know Robert Chatté, the mysterious bookseller from Montmartre. He was thin, tall, very well brought up, with ears that stuck out amazingly; and he was fanatical about his apartment, extremely cautious about whom he let in. He only opened the door if you used a certain code. Specializing in eroticism, he had had printed the first edition of *Madame Edwarda* by Bataille in 1941 (signed Pierre Angélique), illustrated by Fautrier, whose wife later wrote some excellent books under the name Janine Aeply *(Éros zéro, Une fille à marier)*.

Chatté, who was under police surveillance, was often forced to leave France. I still have a letter from this period from Paulhan asking me if I had a way to send money to London. Emmanuel Pierrat, a great lawyer and book collector, on the other hand, had a letter from Paulhan to Chatté asking him to procure a "cat of nine tails." Surprising. Unless he wanted to try an experiment using it on the intern from the NRF who one day opened the door to his office entirely nude, exclaiming, "I'm Justine!" I remember her name very well, but I'll keep it to myself.

It was the spring of 1954 and I was still doing two things at once: some clandestine publishing, and, in the open, Sade; and soon the *Histoire d'O*, while I'd already published *Melmoth, ou l'homme errant*. "Melmoth, the admirable icon" (Baudelaire). The latter was published as a co-edition with the Club Français du Livre, which had acquired a preface from André Breton; Breton, who attracted me more and more; Breton, whom I still did not dare talk to directly.

Yes, there were some clandestine publications. And not just any old ones: *L'Anglais décrit dans le château fermé*, which Mandiargues brought me, *Le Con d'Irène*, by Aragon, and *L'histoire de l'œil*, which led me to meet Georges Bataille.

Gheerbrandt, in La Hune bookstore, or rather the Éditions K, had brought out a clandestine edition of *l'Histoire de l'œil* several years earlier, signed by Lord Auch, as was the original edition in 1929, and illustrated by Bellmer. I jumped at the chance: as soon as I could get hold of a copy, I published a new edition on *Hollande* paper without asking anybody. After all, these were clandestine publications.

A few days later, a very distinguished middle-aged man walked into Palimugre and introduced himself: Georges Bataille. He wasn't against my publishing his book, not at all, but could I give him some royalties?

A discussion followed, or rather a most courteous conversation. I was immediately taken by Bataille. Both Christiane and I were taken by him: Bataille, with his charming looks, his white hair, his voice as unctuous as a priest.

Royalties? Why not? But I was aware even so that this author had not acknowledged his work, which put it in the public domain and at the same time did not protect me from the competition. However, I wanted to please Georges Bataille, and we compromised on a flat fee. A friendship was born. I still have a copy of my little publication, "To Christiane and Jean-Jacques Pauvert, who make me think of my youth, and whom I like very much."

The case of André Pieyre by Mandiargues was simpler: an official publication was out of the question for him, too. He signed his book Pierre Morion, and we came to a compromise about the royalties. Hans Bellmer would do some copper engravings, and the book would be rather expensive. Mandiargues was also someone we liked a lot, tall, extremely polite, with a refined voice for expressing horrible things.

As for Aragon, I was short a printer for the moment, and I made use of a stratagem: I had the book published, officially, by a printer on rue de Buci who hemmed and hawed a bit about the text, but gave in because the publisher was mentioned and there was a copyright on the first page. This page also mentioned the number of copies. I signed "Joseph Rousseaux-Mauriac." Rousseaux because of André Rousseaux, editor-in-chief at *Figaro*, whom I particularly disliked, and as for Mauriac, one can guess why.

In short, when the copies were delivered, Christiane and I spent several days cutting out the page in question with a razor before delivering the books to businesses, then to some bookstores, and some individuals. I've been told since that we forgot to cut some of the copies; they are very rare.

There were about a hundred copies published on deluxe paper with an engraving by Hans Bellmer.[5]

But for *L'Anglais décrit dans le château fermé*, Bellmer took longer than was reasonable for engravings. He revealed an impossible side of his character: suspicious, mean, petty, sly. For my part, I wasn't very patient. In short, he wanted more money than had been agreed on, but he didn't want to say so. I kept to our agreement.

Towards summer, I'd had enough, and I had the book printed without Bellmer's illustrations. He delivered the engravings to me awhile later; he needed money. I paid him and kept the engravings. I had to sell them a few years later to Visat, the bookseller-publisher, who published them in a separate edition.

Pierre Klossowski also became a regular. We very much liked the caustic wit of this little grinning gnome, whose eyes sparkled with intelligence. We especially remember an unforgettable dinner at his place with Bataille. A kind of controversy started up between them, and they exchanged untranslated Latin quotes, like arcane invectives before the profane.

Klossowski gave me a manuscript which charmed both Christiane and me: *Roberte ce soir*. Sadly, he had already signed a contract with Lindon, who had just taken over the Éditions de Minuit from Vercors. Lindon kept to this contract, and, given the good relationship I had just established with him, all I could do was to resign myself.

Just before summer, in June, I published, very officially, *Histoire d'O*.

———

5   These deluxe copies have the title *Le Con d'Irène* spelled out in full, whereas on the "trade" edition the title is given more modestly as *Irène*. – Editor's note.

The (Discreet) Appearance Of *Histoire d'O*

Publication: a big word for the Éditions Jean-Jacques Pauvert. I still didn't have an official distributor. I simply had, as I said, a little network of bookstores and salesmen in bookstores, in Paris and in the provinces. When *Melmoth* came out in May, I got some press: *France-Soir* especially played it up by headlining it. The market was moving a little, I made some sales (not enough, never enough).

But for *Histoire d'O*, there was a deafening silence, one without precedent. There was only one article in 1954, which was good, but short, by Claude Elsen in *Dimanche-matin*, August 29, 1954. Elsent compared the book "to certain legends, to certain poems which glorified 'mad love', to the *Song of Songs*, or *Tristan and Iseult*." *Dimanche-matin* was already losing readers and few people, to my knowledge, apart from Paulhan and myself, read the article – at least no one mentioned it to me.

Paulhan, however, fussed over the book for years. I got a request every other day from him for copies: "Can I have ten copies of *O*? They will be put in good places...." "I need six or seven copies of *O* for the reviews; they'll be well placed." "Could you send a copy of *Histoire d'O* to Emmanuel Berl?" In 1958, once again: "Can I ask you for five or six copies of *Histoire d'O*. Many thanks for your trouble." But not much came out of it all. The press stayed mute with stupefaction. *L'Express*, which had just started up (May 1953), launched a big survey on recent books which had defined our era. Paulhan was approached, and cited above all *Histoire d'O*. The interview came out. Paulhan wrote to me: "*L'Express* deleted the part where I mentioned *Histoire d'O*. Strange behavior." Françoise Giroud, from what I'm told, was behind this. The times were austere.

Everybody was expecting a total ban. At the same time, reporters didn't hesitate to cultivate the colorful with little rumors, or openly to twist reality. They talked about a clandestine publication when, in fact, my name and my address were clearly written on it.

There were only two notable articles, but really notable ones, in May and June of 1955: one in *Critique* by André Pieyre de Mandiargues, "Les fers, le feu, la nuit de l'âme," the other by Georges Bataille in *La Nouvelle Nouvelle Revue française*. You can find this article in Bataille's *Oeuvres complètes* published by Gallimard, and the Mandiargues in the admirable *Belvédère*.

Mandiargues immediately got busy in support of the book. I still have in my files a letter from August 10, 1954: "I don't need to tell you how much I am enchanted by *Histoire d'O*. It is certainly the most beautiful novel which has appeared in French since the war (and even before), the newest also. This careful, precise prose, which is so chaste even when describing the most horrible things is admirable, intelligent, and perfidious. I like it, too, that the book is a fantasy but so simply done. Let's talk about this again soon." He then talked about a bookstore in Monte Carlo which would like some Sade, and which had never received its copies of *L'Anglais*. "Tell him I highly recommend Pauline Réage, who greatly deserves it."

Commercially, in the first year, the book was a disaster. I had brought out *La Nouvelle Justine*; I had just reissued *Histoire de Juliette;* I had *Les Cent Vingt Journées de Sodome*; and in spite of the difficulties with the police, there were a few (just a few!) Sade sales, which helped a little. On the other hand, for *Histoire d'O*, it was abysmal. Nothing at all. From time to time, some customers came by rue des Ciseaux furtively, "recommended by" Paulhan, Mandiargues, or Jacques Lemarchand, above all, in fact, from the NRF. Booksellers who always came on somebody's recommendation, too, passed through our store like a hurricane, always looking over their shoulders, never buying more than one copy at a time. They came from farther and farther away.

It took me a long time to understand the behavior of some of them. For example, on rue du Four, there was a bookseller I knew who came to buy one copy. When I stopped by his place, which was very near, he would always say with a perturbed air, "Still hasn't sold; customers are suspicious." I was ready to sympathize with him, and take back the copy.

It was only years later that I learned, after he had died, that he used to rent out the copy at a high price, like in a reading room, whispering that the book was banned, but he could, for a price, get hold of it. And, if someone gave him a big security deposit, he could RENT the book for forty-eight hours.

In literary circles, some copies got passed around, too, and a polemic started up, word of mouth, which promulgated opinions and was, for me, a touchstone about various feelings and ideas concerning *Histoire d'O*. Was Pauline Réage really a woman? I wrote: "From June 19, I looked upon as suspect and as someone I didn't want to know, as a citizen from another planet and missing an essential nerve, any person who asserted to me the conviction that *Histoire d'O* was written by a man. With time, and given that some of these people had qualities which, though not compensatory, were at least pleasant, it happened that I continued to see a few of them, but no longer without a certain reserve."

First of all, I think the idea that it was a woman was a big part of the rejection of the book. The novelty was surprising and shocking: that the most scandalous book that ever existed could have been written by a woman, played a primordial role.

There was also the "in" crowd: of course it was a joke. We all knew that. The author is Paulhan, or one of his friends. What an abject idea to attribute the text to a woman. How could anyone do that! Shameful! Among these "in" people was Francois Mauriac who consequently quarreled with Paulhan.

As late as 1975, poor old Michel Droit wrote in *La Coupe est pleine*, without blushing:

"How could a woman have been the author of such a well-written book, but one stinking of disdain for women, so overwhelmingly boring, so obviously the work of an old libidinous man of letters?"

There were those who sincerely admired the book, but whose macho nature did not allow them to believe a woman was capable of thinking of such turpitude. For instance, Albert Camus, who was ready to come to the defense of the book in a court of law (as we shall see) but who told me in his best Mediterranean way, "See here, Jean-Jacques, a woman could never have imagined such things! Never!"

Another reason helped the press keep silent about the book, perhaps a good reason: almost at the same time as *Histoire d'O*, a novel by a young girl had been published which caused a scandal but which could be talked about without too much audacity. They didn't hold back. *Bonjour tristesse*, by Françoise Sagan, had a million-copy run. I'd sold about a thousand *Histoire d'O* by the end of the year.

I put a little card in each copy, which read: "We predict that L'*HISTOIRE D'O* is a book which will make literary history everywhere."

A matter of time? I'd wait and see.

Setting Up And Settling In

Meanwhile, rue des Ciseaux had become too small. Girodias and I found a space to rent on the first floor at 8, rue de Nesle. Neither of us could afford to rent it alone, so we shared it. We each had two or three rooms, plus a common storeroom for stock. We moved in during the summer and autumn, with time to arrange the space, which had been a furrier's: there was black fur debris everywhere. I was to turn thirty-five on rue de Nesle. By the end of 1979, I owned a floor and a half of it.

We soon had another partner: Fred Loliée, a bit of a black sheep – at least a rebel sheep – of the great Loliée bookstore dynasty. And then someone else: Jean Castelli, about my age. Fred was the oldest of us all, by three or four years. There were four of us in the original group.

I also now had an official printer: Jules Rossi, boss of the SIP in Montreuil, who became a friend right up until his premature death in January 1969.

And I had an accountant. The Jean-Jacques Pauvert Publishing Company was taking shape.

And I had the law at my back, in spades. The Sade case was supposed to be settled by trial, they told me, because of four books I had published which they were focusing on: *Les Cent Vingt Journées de Sodome, La Philosophie dans le boudoir, La Nouvelle Justine* and *Histoire de Juliette*. Really, they could have found more serious issues to deal with. This had only taken seven years, soon eight. The police had stopped seizing books except the ones I gave them. About these books, I was fairly calm, up until the hearing in front of the judge.

What was more serious, it seems, was *Histoire d'O*.

Histoire d'O secretly had raised tempests in the judicial teapot. First, there were the orders from on high: find the author.

Jean Paulhan and I were summoned, separately, to appear before the vice squad. We were each confronted with two different mentalities. I had to deal with some inspectors and a commissioner (I no longer remember who, perhaps Fernet, by now an old acquaintance.) Everything went swimmingly. I had going for me, or at least I thought so, my professional word of honor. Yes, I had a contract. No, the police could not see it. Yes, I thought I knew the author: a charming woman. Of course, I wouldn't tell them her name, her age, or what she looked like, because she had chosen a pseudonym. I was sworn to keep her secret. No, Jean Paulhan was not the author of the book, only of the preface. He had in fact signed the preface and acknowledged the fact.

As for Paulhan, he played, as usual, a terribly convoluted game and with great hypocrisy. Yes, he said, I believe I know the author. Actually, not well. I can't affirm anything because I could be wrong. Names have been rumored, of course, well-known names. People have talked about Mme. Lucie Faure (Edgar Faure was a man of considerable political renown at the time). It's obviously a literary woman. But there are others, Louis de Vilmorin, for instance. You see the danger I would run into, and among respectable people, if I furnished even one name, just on hearsay.

The vice squad used great caution in carrying out their investigation.

August 5, Jean Paulhan made another, more truthful statement, and thus one that would increase the confusion. He said:

> August 5, 1955. We FRIEDRICH…have before us M. PAULHAN, Jean, man of letters living at 5, rue des Arènes, Paris.
>
> WHO DECLARES: about three years ago (NB: this is the only indication of the composition date of *Histoire d'O*), Mme Pauline Réage (a pseudonym) came to see me at the *Nouvelle Revue Française*, which I direct and gave me a large manuscript which was entitled *Histoire d'O*. Every day I receive around eight or ten manuscripts, but this one struck me immediately, first of all by its quality and then by its perfectly scandalous subject matter, so to speak, and by its restraint and its decency.
>
> I had the feeling I was in the presence of a very important work, as much by the style as by its tone, revealing a mystical thread much more than an erotic one, and which could be seen in our times in the same light as the *Lettres de la religieuse portugaise* or *Les Liaisons dangereuses*. This is what I told Madame Réage when she came to see me again. I added that I would quite happily talk to Gaston Gallimard about her manuscript, and that if Madame Réage managed to publish it, I would write the preface.
>
> Gaston Gallimard, after two years of hesitation, refused the book. M. René Defez, director of Deux Rives publishing, at first accepted it

and then, following a political affair in which he was involved (the affaire Despuech), he asked Madame Réage to take back the work.

It was then that M. Jean-Jacques Pauvert accepted it quite gladly and published it at once. In the meantime, I had written the promised preface which appeared at the beginning of the novel. This preface, which emphasized the philosophical and mystical side of the work came to appear untrue, in a certain way. M. Pauvert, with the agreement of Madame Réage, excised from the book without telling me in time the entire third part, in which the heroine is confronted with her fall.

(This is a point that has always remained the object of a little controversy between Paulhan, Pauline Réage and myself. I have a very strong memory – and Pauline Réage also – that it was Jean Paulhan, in agreement with me, who cut out this third part, a long chapter entitled "Retour à Roissy," which was later to be reinstated).

I was not privy to what happened to the book during the printing.

And I add that Madame Réage, being from a university family whom she did not want to scandalize, has always refused to give her real name. It was the first novel she had written.

I also add that I am not the author of the manuscript, and that I never made any corrections to the book. All one has to do is compare my style with that of Pauline de Réage.

I don't think this is a book that should be read by everyone, no more than should *Les Liaisons dangereuse* or *Les Lettres d'une religieuse portugaise*, but one only has to read it carefully, I think, to see that it is in no way pornographic. If it is dangerous, this is more from the violence of the passion described in the continual dream world in which it seems to be immersed.

I have nothing to say about the material condition of the publication, nor about its diffusion.

Therefore, as I have said, Madame Réage does not want her name known. I agreed to keep her name secret, just as I have done with other authors.

Nonetheless, given that I see her fairly regularly, I will tell her about the declaration that I have made here, and if she does decide to reveal her identity, I will ask her to contact you.

Dominique Aury, twenty-five years later (still under the name Pauline Réage), gave an account of our dealings in a short declaration which I cannot reread without the perfume of a friendship from long ago coming back to me.

> Jean-Jacques Pauvert is a modest man, who doesn't mince words, but tells you at once, after having read your manuscript (which up until then everybody had refused): "I like it, I'll publish it. Perhaps we'll go to prison; we'll see." Because he liked taking risks? No, because he liked the book. And he doesn't think there is such a thing as forbidden literature; he believes that anything can be written, that everybody, if they want, has the right to be part of everybody else's dream. Also, he published my book because he's not afraid of anything. It is because of him, and him alone, that *Histoire d'O* was published twenty-five years ago. Insults, threats, lawsuits, all lasted for years. He never flinched, neither from his conviction nor his courage: he was loyalty itself. How could I ever stop thanking him or telling people about him.

At that time, I also had a lawyer, a real one, for whom I will until my death have the greatest esteem and affection. When the Sade trial began, I started to wonder who was going to defend me. Without a second thought, I chose the lawyer best known for defending writers, a defender of free expression, and what's more a member of the Académie Française. Maurice Garçon. I wrote to him, I think. He answered right away. Come see me (he lived nearby, rue de l'Éperon). My situation interested him.

We got along well right from the start. At our first meeting, he offered me a valuable piece of information. Contrary to what people said, and something I had always heard, there were no banned books in France, not like in a number of other countries. In France, there were only books which had had lawsuits brought against them. Every time a condemned book was reissued, in principle it had to be retried. It was just a matter of luck, or the courts' whims. This was an enormous discovery.

Starting from there, Maurice Garçon developed a simple defense for Sade: yes or no, does the work of Sade interest the intellectual community? Yes, apparently. Thus, Jean-Jacques Pauvert did a good thing by publishing this work, as complete works, with no cuts, no illustrations, as an honest piece of publishing, in fact. Is the work of Sade "immoral"? Yes, without a doubt. But today, we have learned to look immorality in the face.

There were other elements that Maurice Garçon wanted to deal with. In fact, he wanted to make the trial about censorship as it was being practiced at the time, in the most hypocritical way possible. Later, I will draw a little portrait of it, which will bore those who have no interest in the subject.

Concerning *Histoire d'O* : it was a veritable legal battle between two magisterial camps and persons high up in the administration. There still were at that time (as we'll soon see) some magistrates and educated bureaucrats with open minds. Across from them were moralizing, doctrinal communists and members of the MRP (Popular Republican Movement – Christians as far as I remember), violently hostile to anything of an audacious nature, for different reasons, but all unified in the same violent reprobation of what they called the "demoralization" of society. Like the socialists, they had been puritans for the past hundred years.

As soon as it was published, and despite its meager distribution, *Histoire d'O* was referred to the Book Commission; the report which came out is worth reproducing. It's short but heavily weighted in moralism:

> The Commission, having listened to Monsieur X and his report and having deliberated.
>
> Judging that the book, published by Jean-Jacques Pauvert, means to follow the adventures of a young woman who, to please her lover, submits herself to every erotic caprice and abuse.
>
> Judging that the book, consciously and violently immoral, in which scenes of debauchery with three or more characters alternate with scenes of sexual cruelty, contains a detestable and reprehensible excitement, is in this way an outrage to common decency.
>
> Is of the opinion that there is enough here for prosecution.

An Affront To Public Decency In France
Through Books, 1954

L et's go back to censorship. It had then been perfected. I have mentioned the
three parties that shared power in France after the departure of De Gaulle
in 1947, and which were in agreement only on one particular point: France,
in order to be well thought of by other countries, had to present its MORAL
side (because it had been hopelessly made fun of and in every way classified
as a country of immorality). The Daladier system of 1939 (the July 1939 decree
destined for "the protection of RACE and the French birth rate," don't forget),
had empowered the advisory Commission on Family and the French Birth
Rate, and was certainly satisfactory, but more could be done. This turned out
to be the decree of January 15, 1948. I quote Maurice Garçon:

> Although the decree meant that the opinion of the commission
> had to come prior to any prosecution, the decree of 1948 no longer
> insisted on this opinion except when a case was sent back before the
> police commission, which thus allowed for an attack on freedom
> by seizure, without any prior deliberation by the commission. For
> several months there were arbitrary abuses...
>
> *(Plea against censorship*, 1963)

In fact, this sporadic abuse went on for several years, up until October 1955
when the appeals court shot down the decree by annulling all condemnations
which had been made according to this text.

I was not concerned, however. Procedures for the Sade case kept up with
the rhythm of my publications. The next juridical offensive against authors
and publishers took place in 1958.

The case of Maurice Girodias was special. Publishing texts in English in
France, he could come under the May 6, 1939 decree, which stated:

> Art.14 – The circulation, distribution or sale in France of news-
> papers or publications of a periodical nature, or other-wise, written

in a foreign language, can be forbidden by a decision of the Minister of the Interior...

Now, if one closely examines the report preceding the decree, it appears that the decree had only been written out of the "pressing urgency to remedy, with the goal of restoring public order and national defense," because of the entrance into France of "subversive publications, most notably foreign, whose direction and editorship were situated outside French borders.

It was obviously a manifest abuse of power to extend this decree to literary publications.

Nonetheless, in spite of action undertaken against the application of this decree to publications by Olympia Press, the Minister of the Interior held to his position and vindictively seized Girodias' books.

Madame Françoise

The world of clandestine books was sometimes peopled by engaging creatures. In the Fifties, I was well acquainted with a woman whose name was simply Madame Françoise. She was a large gossipy woman of about 40, very talkative, yet rather intelligent, and full of common sense above all. She was the wife of one of the waiters in a large café on the boulevards. She was more a pornography activist than a merchant. Watched by the police, she led a rather dangerous life, punctuated by frequent trips to Belgium. My activities threw her sometimes, above all my official publications, but she shared my refusal of censorship. Over and above the market harassments, she had a strong antipathy for the vice squad, with whom she did daily battle.

She pushed me to "produce" clandestinely. She even went so far as to give me a book to reprint. I no longer have even one copy of the books I printed on rue de Nesle. And I'd pretty much forgotten all about that time until Olivier Corpet, at the IMEC (Institut de la Mémoire de l'Édition Contemporaine) where I gave a little talk towards the end of the 1990s, handed me a copy of a book I'd printed. More precisely, it was called *Aventures lubriques* (I'd even forgotten its title).

Around 1954, the Madame Françoise adventure ended abruptly. The vice squad had done the necessary. When I saw her again, she told me of outrageous episodes of police stalking. For example, she often took the bus, but always stood at the open rear, sometimes with customers or suppliers. The vice squad decided to have her followed by an inspector on a Vespa, which drove just inches from the bus, trying to overhear snatches of conversation. They told her this after she was arrested.

There had been lots of other means used to get rid of Madame Françoise. The final operation took a long time. Simultaneous searches in several of her hideaways, and the arrest of her husband. The whole works. I wasn't worried, the police and judges had enough to do with the Sade case. As for the clandestine books, Madame Françoise knew enough to keep her mouth closed. What became of the *Aventures lubriques* stock? I no longer know. It must have been reissued, because the book was condemned several times around 1957. But at that time, I had other concerns.

I only saw Madame Françoise two or three times after that. It seems to me that she withdrew to the provinces. She was very nice. Perhaps she's still alive. Perhaps she will read this memoir. I would like her to know that I still feel great friendship for her.

———————

Les Bonnes –
The André Breton Approach

In July 1954, I also published *Les Bonnes*, by Jean Genet, in both of the versions he had written. I had never ceased to see Genet, except for my dark years of 1951–52. As soon as I was moved into rue des Ciseaux, I began seeing him again. From time to time, they had indicted him for "outrage against moral decency through books," but by now he was untouchable.

In the preceding years Gallimard had published the three first volumes of his *Œuvres complètes* (Volume I was made up entirely of Sartre's preface: *Saint Genet, comédien et martyr*), and Gaston Gallimard took him under his care and protection, a protection that was enlarged by that of the powerful society of Paris homosexuals. Genet didn't run any risks; *Histoire d'O* did. In this case, one saw clearly the invisible but terribly efficient barrier which separated female "pornography," with its single, unwilling representative, from its masculine homosexual counterpart, with its flag-bearer very much on display.

But we were always good together, Genet and I. He regarded Christiane with curiosity, as he had considered Marie-Claude. We talked about everything. I remember a long conversation in front of the Diderot statue across from Saint-Germain-des-Prés. Of course, he said, you're going to have children. Yes, of course, we think about it a lot. Genet was pensive. He launched into a long monologue about homosexuality and, according to him, his only regret: sterility. That year, in any case, he felt regret in his flesh, very strongly. Sterility. I don't think he ever wrote a lot on the subject, although it was terribly present, deep inside him.

He granted me the rights (without having them himself, naturally; they belonged in principle to Barbezat, at Arbalète, but that didn't matter to him) to publish two thousand copies of *Les Bonnes*. In spite of his renown, I would have copies of it left for years.

The two versions of *Les Bonnes* were not new; they had been published in Barbezat's luxurious review *L'Arbalète*. But when I asked him, Genet wrote a preface, which prefigured the new elements he was bringing to the theater (this preface was reprinted in the Gallimard edition. My name, of course, was deleted):

> My dear Pauvert,
>
> So you need a preface. But what is there to say about a play which I distanced myself from before it was even finished. To talk about its composition would be to evoke a world and a climate that has no greatness... Instead, it is theater in general about which I'd like to say a few words. I don't like theater. It's easy to see when you read the play. And from what I'm told about Japanese ceremonies and those of China and Bali, and given the magnified idea of theater in these countries which I have in my head I see occidental theater as too primitive. We can only dream about a theatrical art form which would be a deep tangle of living symbols, capable of speaking to the public in a language where nothing would be said, but everything presented.

****

(Genet here develops very interesting ideas. I'll quote only the beginning and the end of this preface. The whole preface can be read in the Gallimard edition.)

> Only shadow play theater interests me anymore. A young writer told me about seeing five or six children playing war in a public garden. They were divided into two groups and were getting ready to attack. We're going to come at night, they said. But it was noon in the sky. They decided that one of them would be the Night. The youngest and the most frail, having become a symbol, was master of the Battle. 'He' was the Hour, the Moment, the Inescapable. It seemed that he came from far away, as calm as a bicycle but weighed down by sadness and twilight pomp. As he approached, the Men grew nervous, worried... But the child, to their mind, came too soon. He was ahead of himself: both troops and the heads of the troops decided to do away with Night, who once more became a soldier... Only theater using this formula can delight me.

I printed deluxe editions of these two books: *Histoire d'O* and *Les Bonnes*. Copies printed on *Arches* paper, twenty copies of *Histoire d'O*, only eight of *Les Bonnes*. One of the first customers to buy both titles printed on elegant paper was M. Edmond Bomsel, a business lawyer, who came into the bookstore one day, and who followed my progress with interest. He was middle aged and had played a role in the Resistance, although I don't know what it was. He had been opposed to Hachette in the difficult founding of the Nouvelles NMPP after the Liberation.[6] Very intelligent, extremely clever, he had built up a beautiful collection of rare books. In particular, he had kept his eye on all the good deals that came with each disaster before 1939 – and afterwards.

He was rich in anecdotes about the great business deals in the press and in publishing. I remember enough of them to solidify my ideas about the backroom of real power: money. It was knowledge that sadly would do me very little good. I was not made for big economic ideas.

Bomsel was also a close friend of André Breton.

Certainly, an encounter with André Breton was inevitable. It was going to happen one day or another, I was sure. But such an encounter made me fearful for different reasons. First, beyond fearing that he would intimidate me (is that the right word?), I was vaguely afraid that he might disappoint me, that he would not live up to the person I had so long been expecting. I followed his activities, all his writing. A new publisher, Eric Losfeld, was now publishing a surrealist review, *La Brèche*. I was surprised (no, not exactly) to read a strongly laudatory article about my preface for the Sade, which I'd written for the Club Français du Livre: "The Marquis de Sade, the History and Literature," an article, they told me, inspired by Breton. Breton had also mentioned the *Histoire d'O* among the *Ephémerides surréalists*.

For this meeting with Breton, I was, in fact, waiting for the stars – or fates – to manifest themselves. It seemed to me that nothing ordinary could arrange our encounter. It had to be an extraordinary occasion. I would have been horribly disappointed if someone had introduced me to Breton at an art opening or in the street. Or any place else... In fact, more or less consciously, I did not want an intercessor.

---

6   NMPP : Nouvelles Méssageries de la Presse Parisienne, a French media distribution corporation. – Editor's note.

Allais, Jarry, Léon Blum And The Others...
And Darien... André Breton, At Last

The most essential aspect of publishing is the encounter; it is the essential one – or else it wouldn't mean much. An encounter with living people, of course; but also with the dead, the forgotten, and with stillborn authors whose unknown books we meet on unprinted paper. Phantom authors, the specters of manuscripts that never appear or the volumes of work erased, they are like memories and libraries. One lovely day they are there, given form by chance, eager to quickly create from this one encounter a network of other encounters, discoveries, coherent extensions or unexpected ones. Fifty years ago, at the end of 1954, a book by Georges Darien entitled *Le Voleur* fell into my hands (published by Stock, Paris, 1897); it had been missing from bookstores for a half century, and unknown to literary history. The following spring I reissued it.

I had been looking for it for a long time. Looking isn't the word, however. One only really looks for practical books, the possession of which is useful for a certain period or for the precise purpose it is needed for. It's important in itself and there is no real value placed on the desired book, whatever its interest might be. One can usually find these books in libraries. I didn't want to read *Le Voleur* in the National Library, for instance.

Why *Le Voleur*? I am certain that it was in Jarry that I first saw that book title and the name Darien. It's impossible to read *Faustroll* (which I did rather early) without pondering over the doctor's "paired books": Baudelaire, Bergerac, Desbordes-Valmores, *Les Mille et Une Nuits*, Lautréamont, Péladan, Rabelais, Mallarmé, etc. These I knew. Darien was a mystery. However, he was there, page ten of the Fasquelle edition, sixth on the list: "Darien, *Le Voleur*" with no other information. His presence on the list was justified eight pages later in the evocations "towards the third dimension." "From Darien, the crown of cut diamonds from Saint-Gothard." Not far from Kahn, Péladan and Mendès, these diamonds seemed full of tales and symbolist stories. I was wrong, obviously.

Around me, no one knew anything. On Wednesdays at Paulhan's, there was great perplexity when I pronounced the name of Darien. Only a few old book-sellers from the quays evoked the antimilitarist author of a *Biribi* book signed Darien, which rang a bell with me. This *Biribi* had been in my grandfather's collection in Berneval. Was this the same one? (Yes) And *Le Voleur*?

Luckily, there was also Alphonse Allais, who dedicated his *Conte de Noël*, at the end of 1897, to the author of *Voleur*, "that admirable book," reputed to place itself "naturally in the hands of those worthy of its name." And then there had been intriguing mentions by Rachilde, and by the young Léon Blum (at the time, still only the estimable author of *Du mariage*). Finally Paul-Victor Stock, not really aware of having put into circulation a master work, reported in his memoirs the remarkable epistolary exchange with its author: "Monsieur Stock [...] I will wait until October; if my novel" (another novel) "is not published by you, I will execute you [...] I will talk about it at the trial – Mr. Darien" [...] Or else: "To the letter that you just sent me, I say shit, and have one, too."

I found an inexpensive copy of the book at the Marc Loliée store, rue des Saints-Pères. Three days later, it was being typeset. I still have the copy, all ragged but whole, put back together by Jules Rossi at my request.

My edition went on sale in April 1955, around my 29th birthday. May 11, on the first page of the review *Arts*, an article by André Breton led off: "Darien the Cursed."

I would only concede to the illusion of being someone, socially speaking, a publisher, as it turned out, for a certain number of years (a good thirty, though), and this really started just a little after the article by André Breton – it was a lot because of him. "Jean-Jacques Pauvert publisher" did not figure on any calling card yet. Paulhan, Bataille, Klossowski, Mandiargues, each one in his own way, had pointed out the road. It is André Breton who gave me the strongest push. For a time.

> It's inexcusable and surprising, [*he wrote*] that Jarry's praise, for those who know what an infallible detector he was of 'modern' values, did not long ago bring Darien's *Le Voleur* from out of the shadows, and insist on its being re-issued. [...] Our era is incomparably better prepared to accept *Le Voleur* than the Belle Époque. [...] The work is charming enough that those who most object to novelistic intrigue as objectionable and boring (me among them) will quite enjoy read-ing it without being annoyed. From beginning to end, one is carried along by the extraordinary articulation of ideas and facts, which,

creating the impression of a natural flow, integrate organically with the language. [...] Let us seek in Darien a secret device, which is so well forged, that I am sure that we shall find in it the exceptional qualities of the heart.

This justified my choice. I also played a little part in the publication. It was very personal because I had picked from among the meager resources of the decorative type case at Rossi's place the ornamentation for the cover; I chose a strong red color to appease my color blindness, and the engraving of an elegant figure in the style of 1900, which would serve me for a long time, one whose posture, hand on the hip and carrying a cane, said clearly that there was no going back:

> Published today with great care by Jean-Jacques Pauvert, this volume touts a cover made with a remarkable economy of means, laying down a challenge by its very existence.

Well, that was it. The door was unlocked, even though the preface Breton had written for *Melmoth* two years earlier had not broken the dividing wall that stopped me from responding to the signals that I thought he had addressed to me. He had not waited for me in order to read *Melmoth* or Sade. But this time, I had helped him discover something. Now we could talk.

Strangely enough, *Le Voleur*, through which I discovered Darien and which at last brought me André Breton, also brought back to me from my youth somebody of very great importance: Georges Salmon, brother of André Salmon, who remains for me the great mediator, and who died far too young, along with so much else from the material world. He was my maternal grandfather who had died before I was twelve. It was in the library of this welcoming non-conformist, but very fretful about his territory (over the shelves was a large sculpted banner which read: "Non hic piscis omnium,")[7] that I first read Kropotkin and Bakunin; *Ceux du trimard*, the book about vagabonds; Arsène Lupin, as I said, the son of the *Voleur*; and long before I knew about Darien, *Biribi* (inexplicably, it seemed to me, he did not have *Le Voleur*). Georges Salmon, unbowed since birth, had experienced the penal battalions during the "War of Tonkin," before the word Indochina had been invented. And the first of the rare portraits of Darien that I ever saw struck me because of its resemblance to

---

7   "This fish is not for everyone." – Translator's note.

certain old photos of this grandfather of mine, so out of the ordinary. These two Georges returned to me together.

Le Voleur brought about other encounters and "revivals" of less importance. As a footnote to publishing and literary history, I note that I had to buy the publication rights to Darien (he had died in 1921, and was not yet in the public domain) from some scrap-metal workers in the suburbs, who were nevertheless highly urbane, and who had absolutely no relationship to Darien. But just before his death, Darien had married the woman who devoted herself to his care during his last years, Julie Delpech. She naturally inherited his goods and assets, including all the authorship rights. Now it turned out that although the books by Georges Darien were no longer being sold, his plays (he had written a few small works) mysteriously continued to be performed by little theater groups here and there. The Société des auteurs dramatiques used to give a few francs to Madame Delpech, Darien's widow, who had decided to sell her house a few years later to the iron metal workers in question. Since she felt she was not getting enough for the house, she had added the literary rights of Darien to the run-down place, just to make it worth more.

Although incredulous at the time about the value of these rights, the buyers must have changed their minds after 1955, when we signed the contract, and especially when Louis Malle acquired the rights to *Le Voleur* to make his best film, as well as that of Jean-Paul Belmondo, and his whole marvelous cast of actors.

Following all this, but I'm not sure under what circumstances, I naturally found myself one day at André Breton's, 42 rue Fontaine. If I remember clearly the large Chirico on the wall, *Le Cerveau de l'enfant*, a Max Ernst and Eskimo masks or perhaps ones from Oceania, some of which made me uneasy, it is because I returned several times to his place. This first time, I was in a bit of a fog. He showed me a certain warmth generated by curiosity. No matter how the conversation went – I was someplace else – I realized afterwards that something very strong had bonded us together.

Stories Of O

However, the first part of 1955 had not gone particularly well. *Histoire d'O* had won the Deux-Magots prize. Dominique Aury, Paulhan, and myself were tempted to refuse it, but there would have been a scandal, gossip... And besides, it was thanks to the efforts of Henri Philippon, kind and devoted, that the jury had decided the way it did. It wasn't the Goncourt, but it was a rather prestigious prize even so, which had first been given to Queneau, among others, before the war.

Unluckily, we couldn't avoid making some waves. Winter was dreary, marked by catastrophic flooding and continual rains. A howl of laughter broke out among the journalists when Philippon announced that the Deux-Magots prize had been awarded to *Histoire d'O*. Histoire d'O? D'eau (water)? D'eaux (waters)? It was too funny!

And then there were the prize photos, grotesque things. There was no question of showing or naming Dominique Aury. The jury decided it was all right, in spite of Philippon, to have a young lady, her head covered with a napkin, pose with the jury, supposedly Pauline Réage. This was clearly a game for mass consumption.

To offset the bad effect, I thought I'd have a cocktail party on rue de Nesle. We were at the height of the police investigations. Among the guests were two or three suspect figures, who, one after the other, tried to pull me aside to explain that they had mistresses – or spouses – a little capricious, or at least demanding, who were never content. Didn't I have somewhere in my store some dildos, or else some whips, to calm them. Gross police provocations. I laughed in their face, outright. They seemed irritated.

My relationship with Girodias was tense. To make foreign publications appetizing, beginning with an English translation, I had given him the manuscript of the book before the publication of my edition. Then I sold the English rights to him, warily, just for a translation of three thousand copies, and for a very small sum, with the agreement of Dominique and Paulhan.

It was then I realized that the translation had been finished in two months, and Girodias was bringing it out at the same time as my publication. I had refined my edition, going so far as to print some copies on *Arches* along with some ordinary copies and a small engraving by Bellmer, left over from our failed gallery show. All of this, including the extremely careful corrections of Paulhan for his preface, had taken a lot of time.

So I had a certain responsibility towards Dominique Aury, an "anglophile," as she would later say, perfectly bilingual because of her education in two languages, and a remarkable translator herself. She just fell apart. The text, which was already difficult to translate because of the poverty, or primitiveness, of the English vocabulary, had been translated word for word by the Olympia Press. One example: a character named Madeleine had been translated as the vague equivalent in English of the cake that we call a madeleine.[8]

I decided to ask Dominique Aury to write a harsh letter, which I gave to Girodias, with a warning that I would pull his edition. Here is a copy of the letter, never before published, to make things clear. For, at the same time, though I didn't know it for years, Girodias was trying to get a copyright in his name for the book in the U.S., which is why he was in such a hurry. He failed in that, I think.

Dominique Aury (or rather, of course, Pauline Réage) to Jean-Jacques Pauvert:

---

8   The first translation of *Histoire d'O* for Girodias was undertaken by Baird Bryant. Girodias subsequently commissioned a second, and far better, translation by Austryn Wainhouse. – Editor's note.

My dear friend,

You know as well as I that we were in agreement for the publication by Olympia Press for 3,000 copies (no more) of the translation of *Histoire d'O* in English, as planned by Girodias, but this was before seeing the translation. The translation horrified me. It is especially vulgar and has totally deformed the character of the book. There is no way that publication of this translation can go ahead, and I authorize you to put a stop to it at once.

I will see you soon, and most cordially.

Girodias realized he had a big problem, said he was sorry, and immediately began a much better translation (and it was), aimed of course at a very limited edition. This was the easiest way out, in the end.

Histoire d'O hung over our heads for some time. I have numerous letters from Jean Paulhan about it. This one, for example, without a date, but which obviously refers to the debate around the subject:

Friday
Dear friend,

I have some news today, which is not so good. I've been told that pitfalls are still possible – and that the first thing they do is pull your right to be a publisher. So take care that no copy of the book gets out [...]

Not many books were circulating, to tell the truth, but I wouldn't have stopped the distribution for anything.

The threat of searches went on for a long time. As late as 1957, there was an investigating judge committed to a search for the author so that a trial could take place, as is shown in these two letters from Paulhan, the first one dated by me at the time, May 27, 1957, and the second without a date but obviously from about the same period:

Dear Friend,

It was my turn to be given a summons today by M. Monzein, who announced that he found me guilty of complicity in moral indecency, counseled me to get a lawyer, and then went on to other things. He is a person who is abrupt and unpleasant. But I wanted to talk to you about all this (and ask if Garçon might defend me at the same time he is defending you? [...]

In a post-script to the second letter, Paulhan wrote:

> Witnesses: I have promises from
> Albert Camus
> Henri Mondor
> Jean Dutourd
> Guillaume de Tarde

à vous
Jean P.
Témoins : j'ai la pro-
messe de
  Albert Camus
  Henri Mondor
  Jean Dutourd
  Guill. de Tarde.

C'est suffisant, je
pense. Mais j'aurais
besoin de vous voir
au plus tôt. Et nous
allons être à deux pas
l'un de l'autre.

The presence of Jean Dutourd among the possible witnesses for the defense is remarkable. In the end, the trial never happened. The Commission had to be satisfied with pronouncing three bans on the book: the sale to minors, the display of the book and advertising, which, although very serious, did not go so far as a total ban, but it did constrain the distribution. Actually, for several years, the book only circulated in secret, as though it were illegal.

But a hidden movement irresistibly means that the circulation of a book becomes more and more widespread, through loans, or even thefts, or else copies sold at exorbitant prices.

Why did *Histoire d'O* never end up in the law courts? There are two different versions: that of Maurice Garçon who said he avoided trial thanks to his connections in the justice system, and that of Dominique Aury, who had it from her Chevasson friends that they were the ones who had some highly placed person intervene in the affair.

I will add a third reason, which, I think, has some weight: the existence at the time, as I said, of judges with an open mind, who were sensitive to ridicule. With what could one actually reproach *Histoire d'O*? Obscenity? Vulgarity? Paulhan was right in his preface to praise the "extraordinary decency" of Pauline Réage's prose. The content itself, the evocation of immoral scenes? This was the negation of literature.

We'll see these antagonistic forces in action in the Sade affair, with the surprising result of a trial, which took eight years to prepare, and which again stirred up debate about censorship in France, for a long time.

VI

TRIALS

Memory, that retriever dog of the mind, is also a circle.
Searching the whole length of the curve of circumvolutions limited
by the sphericity of the skull, it runs over and over again
past the same places... and brings back the goods.

— Alfred Jarry

Sade On Trial

I t was December 15, 1956, when the Sade trial began, in the 17th criminal court, under the judgeship of M. Pérony. The first afternoon, M. Garçon devoted his entire plea (a very long one) to laying out his conclusion: to summarize, after reminding the court that a constant of French liberal law was that books, to be judged fairly, had to be sent to a court of judicial inquest and not to the criminal courts; and that one of the most knee-jerk reactions of the law courts, when they moved away from liberal principles, was to criminalize misdemeanors committed through books. Maurice Garçon here gave the real reason for his conclusions, that the opinion of the Commission concerning *Histoire de Juliette* should be made null and void, given that two members of the Commission, M. Bertrand and M. Descaves (representing the Société des Gens de lettres) were not present at the discussion. An important point, as we will see.

But let's go to the hearing itself, which took place a bit later.

We won't spend too long on the statements of the witnesses. There were four: Jean Cocteau, who in a few words stated the general considerations: "Sade is a philosopher, and in one way a moralizer [...] He's boring, his style is weak, and these are the only things we can reproach him with..." André Breton, whose very important letter got lost and could not be read at the first hearing (but it carried a lot of weight later); Georges Bataille and Jean Paulhan, who gave long depositions (they will be available soon when *L'Affaire Sade*, a report of the trial, is reissued). These depositions are of great interest, because the whole issue of literary censorship is evoked, and because of this, they are of the utmost importance. I'll quote the essential parts.

Jean Paulhan chose to deal with the danger of reading in general, and the Bible in particular:

> The Judge: [...] If you had a little girl, would you prefer she be given the Marquis de Sade to read rather than the Bible?
>
> J. Paulhan: I did not say that; but I would take great precautions in allowing her to read the Bible.

(At this point, I saw the Judge blush suddenly and clear his throat. Dominique Aury, who was in the room, was also struck by this, as she would recount later.)

The Judge: Let's drop the Bible, which is not at issue here, or rather you're the one who made it an issue. I will focus my question on the Marquis de Sade. You don't see any drawbacks to letting these works be read by a young girl or a young man?

J. Paulhan: I think the works are dangerous for the reasons that I gave earlier. The despair, the disgust that the works of Sade inspire could lead someone who reads them to find refuge in a convent. I think that is the danger, but it's an imminently moral one.

The Judge: It's an imminently moral danger: but if it leads to or risks leading to corruption?

J. Paulhan: All books can lead to corruption. Baudelaire risks leading to all possible kinds of corruption.

The Judge: There's a nuance here: the poems of Baudelaire...

J. Paulhan: I don't think so, monsieur le President. Baudelaire seems much more insinuating, much cleverer.

The Judge: You don't think that the dots on the i in Sade are more dangerous than insinuations?

J. Paulhan: There is something repellant...

The Judge: We're in agreement...

The Judge was losing his grip. Georges Bataille oriented the debate towards the importance of Sade in the history of thought:

G. Bataille: [...] the Marquis de Sade was innovative because before him no one had said that human beings found satisfaction in contemplating death and pain. This could be considered reprehensible and I am of this opinion. I consider totally reprehensible the contemplation of death and pain: but if we take into consideration reality, we note that no matter how reprehensible the contemplation, it has always played a considerable role in history. I esteem that from a moral point of view it is extremely important to know, given that morality demands that we obey reason, what the possible causes of breaking the rules are. Sade presented us with a most valuable document, in the sense that he knew how to develop and sensitize the most profound cause that we have for disobeying reason...

The Judge: [...] To circulate a work like this one in public, with its constant apology for vice, leaving no basis for morality, you don't think this could constitute a danger?

G. Bataille: I don't think so, no. I must say that I have a rather large confidence in human nature.

The Judge: I congratulate you, monsieur. You have an optimism which does you honor. Thank you.

The letter from André Breton, which he wrote to me in very careful handwriting on rare and old paper, is worthy of being reproduced here in its entirety. Although it was not quoted during the hearing, it figures in *L'Affaire Sade* and played a role in the appeals process:

The Marquis de Sade was careful to say (and it's a sentence which is often quoted): 'I am only speaking to those people who are capable of hearing me; only those people will read me without danger." I hope that we can take this sentence literally. The idea that he is not speaking to certain people, means not only is he addressing certain people – but also that he will only be capable of moving qualified people to the point of influencing their way of thinking and acting because they can understand what is implied in what he says. We know that this is the case with poets like Lamartine, for example, or Petrus Borel, Baudelaire, Swinburne, Lautréamont, Apollinaire – those writers who have most deeply investigated the human soul, such as Stendhal, Nietzsche, Barbey d'Aurevilly. It is also significant that the interpreters of Sade's work (which cannot be abstracted from his life) are for the most part men of science. Doctors, like Eugen Düehren, like Maurice Heine, accorded Sade such an importance that they were the ones who took the initiative in publishing and republishing that which had been lost for so long or which one couldn't find. Under their guidance, the works that were put back into circulation are the ones in which the implied content, seen from the current moral perspective, for higher reasons, which they had to go beyond, rightly persuaded them that the manifest content, for those who followed him, would be of such a nature as to provoke repulsion, not attraction, at any rate – by these excesses – and would repel those who dabble in licentious publications, and there are a lot of them. The so-called 'poison' carries an inherent antidote:

Those charms found in that which is horrifying will intoxicate only those who are strong.

The work of Sade therefore places itself in its true light, which proceeds from that of certain Gnostics, from the Carpocrates of the second century in our era and, to a lesser degree, from the Cathars, but who extend far ahead of us.

One can, I believe, hold with the opinion of Charles Henry, who eventually became director of the Laboratory of Physiology of the Senses at the Sorbonne. In his brochure, *La Vérité* sur le marquis de Sade, published in 1887, Charles Henry quoted the epigraph that Sade stood behind:

One is not a criminal because one paints a picture of the bizarre penchants that inspire human nature

And he adds this: 'Those who have great experience with morality cannot conclude otherwise.' There are thus already seventy years for a mind such as this, Sade the representative, to evolve, not just a monster of subversion the very trace of which must be wiped out at any cost, but also the moralist whose lessons must not be lost, no matter what it takes.

I know – from knowing him personally – that Jean-Jacques Pauvert, by publishing works for which he is under criminal investigation, was not acting out of any other motivation than to be the executor of this judgment, brought as much to the 19th as to the 20th century through minds very differently oriented but who have one particular characteristic in common: they are as enlightened as they are enlightening. I don't doubt that the tribunal is aware that it is the hundredth anniversary of *Madame Bovary* and *Les Fleurs du Mal*. Culture, like freedom, being to my mind one and indivisible, I swear, with my soul and my conscience, that, like no other, Jean-Jacques Pauvert is fulfilling his role today and greatly contributes to the intellectual level of this country, when he re-issues Sade just as when he re-issues Littré.

For me personally, Breton added after his signature,

"For Jean-Jacques Pauvert, affectionately."

Sade Judged At Last –
For The First Time

In his closing, the judge was infinitely prudent. He insisted on contesting the conclusions of Maurice Garçon concerning the Commission, and he deplored the outrageous literature produced by Sade:

> I think I very much understate the truth if I say that reading the different works that you have submitted reveals interminable descriptions of scenes of lubricity or sexual cruelty alternating with long philosophical treatises (moral, they tell us); for me, all this is just a monotonous nightmare, a succession of sordid exhaustions. [...] Like me, I think, you will conclude that in reality whether he meant to or not, de Sade has become the leader of a school and the true inspiration for all this literature which, to use the word of Counselor M. Escholier, 'reveals only the sad, insatiable avidity of desire...'

He continued by stating that, "the writings that have been given to you [...] have not, according to the language of a high magistrate of our supreme court, garnered 'the esteem of the good people of France,' and therefore are in opposition to good morals." And he ended by emphasizing that M. Galtier-Boissière, in his magazine *Petit Crapouillot*, publicized the works of Sade and that elsewhere one found the work in "certain official sites which specialized in erotic literature and the licentious." He concluded that "for all these reasons, members of the jury, you will find that the lawsuit is justified and you will decide against the publisher Pauvert and will adjudge the sentence demanded by the law."

Maurice Garçon displayed (taking a little too long, in my opinion) his erudition by drawing a picture of the life of Donatien Aldonze François de Sade (at least what we knew about him at the time) and his prescient views about sexuality and lauding him (with reason) by saying that:

...this important author is, given the effect of a general conspiracy, kept from the public. We can only know him through someone who intercedes. We are reduced to reading the works of Lely, Klossowski, Dr. Dühren, Breton, Paulhan, Simone de Beauvoir. [...] We publish bibliographies but forbid reading of the books. We have to submit to these commentators without the permission to form a personal opinion, which is contrary to all scientific principles...

Moreover, Pauvert, the publisher, was "not out to cause a scandal." He had "avoided sending into the commercial world enticing volumes accompanied by equivocal drawings." My "edition, 'bound in black,'" (he was talking about *Cent Vingt Journées*) "was as sober as if it were meant to be part of a Jansenist library."

And last of all, "we have seen other cases," and Maurice Garçon launched into long quotes from Gide (Nobel Prize winner) and Proust. He ended by saying that he:

...could not believe a publisher guilty who had published, for a handful of readers [*it was true*] a work which, if it were licentious, was a literary document, psychological in the first degree, and indispensable for certain scholars.

The following January 10, I was condemned, unsurprisingly, to pay two hundred thousand francs in fines (eighty thousand for *Histoire de Juliette*, a hundred and twenty thousand for *Les Cent Vingt Journées de Sodome* and *La Philosophie dans le boudoir*) plus expenses. Beyond that, the court ordered the confiscation and destruction of all the incriminating works. The standard sentence.

The harshness of this condemnation didn't surprise me, however. Maurice Garçon was disappointed. The press remained reserved, keeping to the tone, "Who looks for trouble finds it." One newspaper, which might have been expected to be favorable, *Combat*, used a rather tendentious air when publishing the news: "It was a risk to defend M. de Sade in court. Especially when the jury such as the one yesterday in the 17th chamber, under the presidency of M. Pérony, felt a much greater grudge against the current publisher than against the 'divine marquis' [...] M. Garçon did not make much of a case for the imprudent publisher [...] The court, smiling a little... sadistic, responded that by launching this edition, M. J.-J. Pauvert simply wanted to sell books. [...] the final judgment recalled in particular that the work of the Marquis de Sade, in spite of all its philosophical aspects, constituted a systematic negation of morality..."

Three weeks later, I put *L'Affaire Sade* on sale, reproducing in their entirety all the pleas, the witness statements and the judgment, followed by juridical "Observations" which ended with the following paragraph:

> In the end, we can announce that the legal process going on has had no influence at all on the market for our work, and that the last two volumes of Sade's writings will be published in February. We do not intend to print Sade clandestinely.
> Of course we appealed immediately.

I'm not really sure, in fact I've never really known, what logic I obeyed in acting this way. It was not a matter of careful reasoning. I think instinct was stronger than anything. In fact, logic, if it had been at work, would have inclined me towards prudence. But to what end?

To the contrary, I felt that I was moving towards truth with Sade, and that I had to go there without delay. What truth? I didn't know! It was just a wild sentiment. I was holding on to something I was not going to let go of, like a bone, something that belonged to me through some sense of ownership that I couldn't define, which I had no desire to define. It was my business, that's all.

Jerome Lindon,
A Van And Us

At the same time, I was publishing other things. I was heading down a road which wasn't taking me any particular place (but I didn't care); but it was slowly revealing itself. All the better. Did I know where I was going? I didn't have the least idea.

I put together a little group of friends. Apart from the team on rue de Nesle (still very few of us), there was no one of my generation. In my little intellectual world, I had never yet met anyone near my age who really seemed to count for something. André Breton, Pierre Klossowski, André Pieyre de Mandiargues, Georges Bataille, Jean Genet, Jean Paulhan and Dominique Aury, sometimes Jean Cocteau (cautiously), all of them decidedly older, acted as my entourage, so to speak. Christiane, of course, was a case apart. She was a woman, luckily, in the fullest sense of the term. And a woman who held her own without any problem.

Among the rue de Nesle team and me, there had always been an attachment, guffaws and laughter, and then long moments when I felt all alone. Sometimes I needed some support, an older counselor, someone with experience, experience that I would often be tempted to reject, of course, but an experience I felt obliged to invent to some extent.

Rue de Nesle found itself the center of what could be called elements of a publishing house. For example, in 1955 I took over the review *Bizarre* from Losfeld, the editors of which no longer got along with him after only two editions. I was very much interested in *Bizarre*, which had an editor-in-chief, Michel Laclos, who was very resourceful. But I immediately took over the directorship, under my own authority, and the production: I was the one who put the mock-ups together. In the ensuing years, we very quickly published ten or twelve issues.

A little later, in the middle of a thousand financial difficulties, I began to publish another review, *Le Surréalisme, même*, edited by André Breton. It was a deluxe review, the whole collection of which is today worth a great deal, but which sold for nothing at the time.

To tell the truth, aside from a few brilliant pieces, and the espousing of positions on issues it was almost the only one to support, *Le Surréalisme, même* did not inspire me with a lot of enthusiasm; I found it a little repetitive about the *Révolution surréaliste*, with a touch of madness, but less so of genius. Only Breton really stood out.

I was learning a lot from the new book designers. Massin, Faucheux, Jacques Darche (the most gifted in the beginning) all worked for me. The surrealist group who put together *Le Surrealisme, même* conceived its design, with all sorts of ingenious discoveries (sometimes at an elevated cost).

Still, I distrusted these new book designers who tended to move toward free-floating extravagance, whereas my taste leant towards sobriety. Faucheux above all distinguished himself by either ingenious discoveries, or complete failures.

For example, in 1955, I issued the first openly published edition of *Madame Edwarda*. There was no way that Bataille, a government bureaucrat, could sign the book, which simply carried the name "Pierre Angelique," as on the original edition in 1941 (published clandestinely by Chatté, with a small print run, and illustrated by Fautrier, as I said). I had simply obtained from Bataille a preface signed by him. As a precaution, the book, a rather short one, came out as a hardback, with a double rhodoid slipcase (much in style at the time).

First of all, there were problems with the slipcase: measurements wrong, so you had a hard time getting the volume out of the case.

Then, Faucheux absolutely insisted on experimenting with new paper for the hardback cover: moleskin, about which he praised its extraordinary qualities. *Madame Edwarda* was, I believe, the only book with a moleskin cover to be put on the market. It turned out that moleskin, although pretty to look at, was totally incompatible with cardboard glue. So mold occurred right away, with discoloration, peeling, etc. Was it all these setbacks that made it possible for *Madame Edwarda* to escape the censors? The only ban was on selling the book to minors; Bataille had started to become a respectable author. At any rate, we couldn't look at a copy of the book without bursting into laughter.

And yet none of this stopped *Madame Edwarda* from also being the first crack in the wall of censorship, and about which Bernard Noël later wrote: "This thinnest of books belies its profundity."

I was, in fact, the main publisher of Bataille, along with Jérôme Lindon, who had become the owner of the Editions de Minuit, and Gallimard. Lindon was my age, with apparent financial difficulties (much better managed on his side: he belonged to a milieu which taught its inheritors the meaning of money). Tall and thin like me, he was in a sense my antithesis. He was meticulously prudent, with a concern for money that bordered on avarice, which all prefigured what he would become: an almost perfect publisher – in his way.

We had at any rate several points in common; in particular, we published books that had little to do with the broader public. We came up with the idea to create an association in order to study the provincial bookstore market, to wake them up a little, and praise the charms of our productions.

So we pooled our resources and bought a little Citroën van, nicknamed "Tube." We arranged bookshelves in it to house our stock. Fred Loliée was named chauffeur, salesman and corporate vendor. Then he took off on the road, in the direction of Brittany.

Why Brittany? It's rather vague in my memory. It wasn't the best idea as a starting point. It seems to me that it was Fred who suggested it; he must have had business over there, or a sweetheart. Would he have had a better chance elsewhere? Not necessarily.

Fred was supposed to telephone us every day with a report. After a while, the situation worsened. The bookstores were indifferent to our books. Anyway, they mixed up the titles: Minuit had *Le Voyeur* by Robbe-Grillet, which had no success at all (I think Lindon had sold a hundred or a hundred and fifty the first year). I had *Le Voleur* by Darien, which sold a little better, which is not a lot. The Sades were rejected with horror almost everywhere in those places where Fred dared to talk about them. *Bizarre* created some curiosity, but nothing more. *Madame Edwarda* raised suspicion (the cover was already beginning to get moldy).

I had published a beautiful book (and which has remained so) by Pierre Klossowski, *Le Bain de Diane*, with a book design (by me) as I like them: very simple, but – in my opinion – very lovely. No response from the public, evidently.

In short, it was a total failure. Lindon decided to cut his losses. Always stubborn, I reimbursed him for his half of the van and continued on a bit more – but not for very long.

1956 was a year of discoveries and advances. First of all, Christiane gave birth to a girl whom we baptized Corinne Isabelle Émilie (you will see why).

It was also a year of publications: in September and December, the first two volumes of my edition of the *Dictionnaire de la langue française by Littré* (Émile!); it was also the year given over to the Sade trial. We would wait for the verdict of the appeal court until the beginning of 1958.

The Extravagant Adventure Of Littré

It's difficult today to realize how important our publication of the *Dictionnaire de la langue française*, by Émile (thus one of the names of our daughter) Littré, was at that time. It was a sort of bomb in the world of French books at the end of the Fifties. It seems worth reporting the facts in detail.

To reissue the "Littré" had been one of my latent obsessions for some time. Why? I don't know why really. There was, of course, the fact that it had not been reissued in a very long time. There had never been an edition incorporating the supplementary volume into the volumes of the *Dictionnaire*, and these five fat volumes were incredibly hard to deal with to the point of being discouraging.

Above all, there was the notion that the "Littré" was considered by most good writers and grammarians as an instrument for classical work, the great classic of the French language, which could be outdated, certainly, in the sense that one can always add to a dictionary ("A dictionary is never finished," Littré himself had said at the beginning of his dictionary), but whose content always remained a guide to the French language. And one only found the Littré then (and at great expense) in used bookstalls and the second-hand bookstores.

I recounted how, beyond consulting it frequently, I had, at thirteen or fourteen years old, undertaken to read the Littré completely, beginning with the first page.

As I remember, the project ripened in the first months of 1955. I talked about it with friends. It seemed to me that the two decisive elements were the book designer Jacques Darche, and Maurice Garçon. With Jacques Darche from the start, and Maurice Garçon only becoming a very active supporter of the book after the business had gotten started.

I remember having passionate discussions with Darche, an extraordinary book designer, but lazy and alcoholic (he would die young a little later, falling out his window in Montparnasse and landing on the glass roof of the café-restaurant La Coupole).

As soon as he knew about the project, his imagination went to work. He had apparently found his favorite terrain, by which I mean a complete project: to create a new dictionary from A, so to speak, to Z. He had ideas about everything.

Very quickly he showed me the perfectly revolutionary results of his ideas: he had conceived the dictionary in ONE column. All other dictionaries had been printed in two columns – at least. He saw the Littré in one column, in a long, narrow format.

Reticent at first, I began to make calculations: wouldn't we considerably augment the number of volumes if we used just one column? Darche worked at his end on the fonts. The composition of a dictionary required several different fonts that had to be chosen carefully – in order to be readable.

Finally, he brought me a one-page specimen, dazzlingly organized, clear, efficient, a masterwork of typography. The fonts were perfect, while the differentiated subdivisions stood out like never before.

I redid my calculations: printed on thin paper, the Littré-Pauvert could be done in seven volumes using a 13 × 26 page, 45cm long and 15cm wide – thus, reducing by two thirds the size of this edition as compared with the old one. Rumors ran through the publishing world: a "scandalous" little publisher ("Ah, yes, Sade, *Histoire d'O...*") wanted to bring out a new edition of the Littré. Chez Hachette, they gasped. I checked the copyright once again: the Littré was indeed in the public domain. So, literary directors paid attention, and the sales department reassured them. Everyone was closely following the Littré situation. The latest news included a serious market study with sales figures at fifty-seven or seventy-eight copies a year, I don't remember the numbers exactly: less than a hundred, though.

Who would print it? Rossi wasn't big enough. Who would bind it? The binders who could bind relatively thick volumes were not numerous. I remember investigating the big firms. For example, one day I found myself in front of the huge printer Firmin-Didot, at the offices of the parent company, on rue de l'Université. A dozen people sat around a huge table covered with a green cloth. The big question was, for a job of this size, what guarantees can you show us? Well, uh... Real guarantees, not just rumors... Come back and see us when you've found a banker, an associate... And once again, Monsieur, bravo for your enterprising spirit, your courage; you do honor to the profession.

How did I come to meet Louis de Hauteclocque? It's a mystery. It was he, I believe, who introduced himself, a cousin, they said, of the famous Marshal Hauteclocque. He had somewhere in Courbevoie an old, dilapidated print shop, but with a certain number of monotype typesetting cases. I would need double that. He agreed to get them.

The paper? I knew a broker. He got a Bellegarde papermaker to make a thin, cream-tinted paper, with a beautiful effect. I wanted it tinted for the beauty of the thing, and also so that it wouldn't be so transparent.

The binding? The firm of Desmoulières, who had done the hardback covers for Stendhal, *Memoires d'un touriste*, *Promenades dans Rome*, was contracted to bind a first printing of ten thousand copies, volumes I and II.

All of this meant putting together an enormous budget, way beyond the size of my yearly income. The fact is that a lot of people were convinced by the project (at least I suppose they were) and agreed with me, or at least they said they did.

For the copyediting, which had to be impeccable, I put together an unusual but very competent team: Denise Klossowski, my old teachers Paul Schricke and José Lupin... plus some others, whose names I've forgotten.

I was given a loan, sure enough, but I still had to guarantee a part of the financing. I had taken over half of the first floor on rue de Nesle from Girodias. My general expenses were increasing. I had to pay the editors, the new collaborators, the paper broker, who was a very important part of the team. An essential one, as will be seen.

Several months after issuing the first two volumes, the sale of the Littré-Pauvert passed ten thousand copies. We had to do an emergency reprinting of the first two volumes.

As I was still learning every day, it was then that I discovered the world of brokering – for the better and for the worse.

But in the meantime, or rather at the same time as the end of the Littré adventure, there was, on March 12, 1958, the appeals verdict in the Sade case.

Sade Judged At Last –
For The Last Time?

I n a new edition of *L'Affaire Sade*, augmented with the text of this appeals verdict and quickly published soon after, I wrote:

> This remarkable judgment, the text of which is presented here, was handed down by the Court of Appeals on March 12, 1958. The judges declared that the philosophy of a writer worthy of the name does not cause the courts to get involved, but when the means of expression of the writer 'causes a conflict with the exigencies of public morals,' the publisher must limit the distribution. For the first time, the existence of 'adult literature' was officially recognized by the courts.

Will anyone believe me today, in March 2004, when I say that the full importance of this judgment came to me slowly, little by little, and that its total significance has only just revealed itself?

At the time, I admit that I was gripped, above all, by a feeling of victory. Eleven years of struggling in obscurity, in virtual solitude, hand-to-hand combat, with great periods of discouragement. And then, victory.

My victory, given so many reservations, was rather relative. But even so!

First of all, the judges (whose names, regretfully, I cannot recall) thought that Maurice Garçon was right on the essential point: the Commission, which was not unanimous concerning *Histoire de Juliette*, and above all acted in the absence of men of letters, had failed in its mission, and its condemnation of the work should be considered null and void. Since the publication of the names of the members of the Commission, some of them had become much more prudent.

Then (and this was a confirmation of the first judgment), the printer was absolutely not held to be responsible.

But, above all, if you will permit me the necessary liberty to quote extensively from the verdict, I will reveal the essence of the judgment; here, every word counts:

> Given that the first judges, at the beginning of the appeals decision, had examined the conditions under which the three works of the Marquis de Sade had been edited, published and sold by Pauvert.
>
> Then, answering defense arguments, the judgment contained an analysis of the works that were on trial and reproduced certain passages extracted from these works illustrating the doctrine of Sade, one of the most characteristic of which is the negation of the fundamental principles of morality, and because in the end it was concluded through the exposure of his doctrine that Sade broke all limits concerning the freedom of expression, and that one could not disassociate the principles of his philosophy from the abundant scenes of debauchery and violence which are the application of these principles.
>
> Whereas this assessment, based as it is in the philosophic and moral domain, does not, on the legal level, deal with the aspect of freedom of expression of thought that the law is meant to respect and protect, it appears necessary to bring certain modifications and precisions notably in recalling the principle that, in a free country, the most wrong-headed ideas must have the right to be heard when they remain notably in the domain of discussion, and when they are exempt from certain provocations and violence or offenses targeted by penal law; that such ideas can in effect be debated, criticized, and fought without the intervention of a penal judge who might use them to serve as a bases for a condemnation, which is not the result of an express rule of law;
>
> Whereas certain works by Sade included in the present investigation have, under the Restoration and the Monarchy of July, been condemned for outrage against public morals and religious law, these two incriminations were repealed by the Law of July 29, 1881, and are no longer applicable in any way; in effect, the penal law is not there to sanction the moral law but to reprimand insults to morality to the extent that these insults are capable of becoming a cause for disorder in Society;
>
> For example, incest, which Sade condones is not punishable except when it is committed between ascendant or descendant

minors or those who are not emancipated by marriage, and the same for homosexuality which is only repressed when it is practiced with minors;

Whereas, even if it were demonstrated that the works under investigation contain an expression of facts which could be qualified as provocative or the condoning of crimes or specific offenses in the law concerning the press, the said works could not be made an object of a lawsuit except on the basis of precise qualifications made specific by the said law and following the forms and procedures that they prescribe; and above all, it must be demonstrated that the publisher of these works published them intentionally with the design of provoking third parties to commit criminal acts or offenses which are described in the works or condoned therein;

It suffices to declare that this question is completely foreign to the lawsuit which the court is presently reviewing and that, following on this, the assessments about the philosophy or Sade are equally, from this point of view, without bearing on the current lawsuit and completely irrelevant to the issue;

Whereas [...] Pauvert argues in effect that the works under investigation constitute documents which are indispensable to the comprehension of philosophy of the 18th century, in as much as they contain an exposé of the materialism and the atheism in its most absolute aspects and that they embody above all the expression and the anguish of a tormented spirit in the face of evil [*a point of view that I do not agree with*]; that in the end the defense insists on the fact that Sade might possibly be the genial precursor of sexual pathology, in a way that his work, although clearly obscene, but precisely because it so candidly treats sexual perversions, it is as necessary to the study of these perversions as the works of Krafft-Ebing and Freud for example;

Whereas this thesis is founded on the fi ndings and the research of Düehren, Maurice Heine, Gilbert Lely, Klossowski, Ruff and Naville, whose objective character, knowledge, and high level of intellectuality is certain and that otherwise works of literature develop out of the works of Sade, of Restif de la Bretonne, and de Laclos...

Following then are the considerations, which, quite honestly, weighed the disadvantages of my publication in relationship to the aim of the lawsuit:

Considering that his good faith [*meaning mine*] could only be established if he could counter the accusation that he was fully aware of the pornographic and obscene nature of the books as determined by the original verdict...

Once again, considering the first court decision: sales sometimes escaped my control and publicity (there again, it had nothing to do with me) in *Le Petit Crapouillot*, etc.

Whereas, to pronounce in favor of Pauvert the acquittal that he wishes would result not only in permitting the free sale of Sade's most outrageous works, in light of moral standards, but also numerous other works which have already been condemned for infractions to the law of July 29, 1939, which would remain without effect at least in regard to books which, claiming a certain literary value, philosophical or historical, would with impunity set out in their pages stories or scenes for which the decency of the immense majority of readers..."
"...Whereas there exist extenuating circumstances in favor of Pauvert who has never previously been condemned and who is the object of good recommendations and who in this regard can be given a reprieve..."

In short, the verdict confirms in its provisions the judgment that had already been made, but it suppressed the fine and the destruction of the books.
How and why could this be considered a victory? Simply because at the end of this verdict, there was a stupefied silence from the police and from the judges, including from the Commission on Surveillance of Books. The members of the Commission hesitated to reformulate the bans on these works, which were, suddenly, culturally so important.
Thrilled by the considerations which, in short, left me basically in the right, and leaving to discussion only what I considered to be the details, I continued to reprint (when it was necessary) all the works of Sade as I had intended, and I never again expected to hear about lawsuits. Unbelievable as it seems, that's how it turned out.
Later, we'll return to the incalculable consequences, to my mind, at least, of this fact – the fact of the "silence of the law" about Sade, as he once put it himself.

A Little War – Brokers – A Fall

Had I made a wise decision in choosing this moment to undertake such an outsized project as the complete publication of the *Dictionnaire de la langue francaise* by Émile Littré?

To tell the truth, I hadn't chosen the moment at all. The adventure had been born out of an irrepressible inspiration. Besides, if I had thought about it, I would have had no reason to wait. In 1956–57, France's future was as backed up as ever.

The political world was in the dark. The "Algerian War," now an open conflict, was moving towards total disaster. Who remembers the government of Guy Mollet, the sinister socialist puppet (invested February 5, 1956), whose Minister of Justice was François Mitterrand? Or Robert Lacoste, named Minister in Residence for Algeria (February 9)? Or the independence of Morocco (March 7)? Or Tunisia (March 20)? Or the nationalization of the Suez Canal (July 26) and the aborted French-British expedition which followed (in November), everything framed by the insurrection in Budapest crushed by Stalin's tanks in October (approved by the French Communist Party)?

The Mollet government fell on May 21, 1957. Bourgès-Maunoury succeeded him for three months. Félix Gaillard was sworn in on November 5th (a little before, Camus had received the Nobel Prize). He fell on April 15, 1958. On May 15, de Gaulle spoke. On June 1, he was sworn in; on June 2, he was voted full power. In the meantime, the Littré adventure was born, developed and had grown dull for me.

How was the French economy doing in general (and mine in particular) during this rolling and pitching close to the limits of a national shipwreck? As well as could be expected, but still rather badly. "The whole history of the 4th Republic," to quote from the *Histoire de la France au XXe siècle* (S. Berstein and P. Milza, Complexe, 1991) "unfolded in a financial crisis."

At the end of the Fifties, the circumstances were hardly favorable for France to create an economy worthy of the name. Consumer credit, in particular, didn't exist. For example, there were Vélosolex (rare), but you couldn't buy one on credit. Everything had to be paid for in cash. Or some stores accepted credit certificates called *Bons de la Semeuse* which, in other words, let you borrow money from the *Semeuse*, which you had saved by using the *Semeuse* capitalization system.

There was some credit given for book sales of "weighty products," or expensive collections. Very large publishing houses with solid holdings (Larousse, Hachette, Quillet, etc.) agreed to time payments for those buying encyclopedias or complete works published by them. There was at the time, besides, only a tiny percentage of bills that weren't paid; to offer credit to French households was one of the safest operations in the world. However, this practice opened up only very slowly, without help from the banks, which rarely participated in this kind of thing.

The Littré-Pauvert was sold mostly through brokers who were finding a very interested market among young university teachers who'd never had the old Littré, and found the new format very useful.

There was no competition in the market. Among language dictionaries, the Littré stood alone. There had been a young competitor, the Robert, but it had received very bad press, and justly so. "Ah, it's a beautiful success, this Littré. The NRF will be in agreement. But you should think about a supplement. The Robert is not serious," Paulhan wrote me in 1957.

I had had a magnificent brochure printed in color which, thanks to Maurice Garçon, the principle writers from the Académie Française (Duhamel, Maurois, Mauriad...) with their photographs, praised the eternal merits of Littré. Sales on credit moved swiftly along.

The brokerage houses were obliged to pay commissions to the brokers, practically on the spot. This caused certain financial difficulties, which forced them into billing gymnastics that brought with them no end of promissory notes, which I was involved in, given the circumstances.

On the other hand, we had about five thousand individual customers, brought in by independent brokers we had to pay commissions to immediately, while our drawers were piling up with bank notes, because the banks weren't giving credit, in spite of everything I tried.

I was squeezed in a vise. I tried to fight with all the means I had. Besides the promissory notes signed by some little brokerage houses, and which I put together with a great deal of trouble, I ended up by creating a mechanism to make cash, through a process which I didn't invent, but simply perfected as best I could.

All the employees from the publishing houses (there were a half-dozen now), plus the authors and the teams from the reviews, opened bank accounts with my help. To make things faster, I had made a little machine, which imitated their signatures, in a wooden box, with a window and an electric light bulb. Through a process of transparency, I imitated a series of signatures on checkbooks, which I kept in stock.

Every morning (EVERY morning!) Jacques the broker took his motorbike and made a round of the banks (about a dozen) depositing checks. In certain banks, not always the same, he drew out cash to cover certain accounts. In principle, there was a delay of two or three days in order to cover each drawn check. But you had to be always on the lookout for the unexpected: for example, certain establishments sometimes presented their checks very fast. They had to be covered in two or three hours. Every day, we heaved a huge sigh of relief, Jean Castelli and I, the moment the banks closed. Castelli, who had a gift for numbers and who had joined the company in 1956, naturally handled competently everything having to do with the overseeing of the accounts and operations, which I sometimes had to deal with myself.

We were heading for a smash up, that much was obvious. I counted on some miracle: some associate falling from the sky, a customer insanely in love with books, a bank that would show itself to be different from the rest, one that would be interested in our clients' bank drafts which were multiplying in our drawers, like a pointless tidal wave. Or else a treasure, discovered in the garden of the little suburban home Christiane and I had just bought (on credit, obviously): a square house in the middle of a piece of land, without central drainage.

There was an unexpected reprieve at the beginning of summer 1957: a fabulous bank strike which has hardly left any historical traces (one wonders why), but which paralyzed French business for several weeks started on July 10. Businesses closed one after the other, and the whole financial circulation was blocked immediately. Our checks were lost in the void, and some remained so even after the new school year in September.

I think it was that year we decided to close the business for vacation, and rather early. The whole little group left in all directions, for a break. Me, too.

When the banks opened (one after the other), it was a mess – real or imagined. The telephone rang all day long. We got checks and more checks. What was happening?

We beat the pavement trying to salvage as many checks as possible. I remember at the Saint-Phalle bank, the clerk, when I had managed to get back my checks (knowing very well that our account was going to be closed right away), murmured without looking up, "Yes, but you will sleep better now."

True and false.

There was the inevitable episode with the Bank of France, where I was summoned as a formality. I found myself across from a courteous but very stern man, who tried to convince me of the danger I was running with my current practices ("Oh, you're not the only one, though!"). In the end, "[I was] throwing out the bank's daily balance sheet." I agreed (without being very convinced), but how could I be sorry for it? I brought up the millions represented by the clients' checks, which were impossible to cash. He threw up his arms in a sign of impotence. "I know, I know." But finally, hadn't I sinned out of pride, trying to play in a game that wasn't mine? He saw that he hadn't persuaded me, and insisted on warning me about the sanctions laid down by the law, which were, he said, horrendous. However, he could see, he said, that I wasn't a professional crook.

We left on fairly good terms. It's probably thanks to him that I wasn't credit black-listed.

Other, additional adventures were more secondary. I had started with the intention of associating myself with the Club Français du Livre in order to publish the Littré. Firstly, we had to wage a little war with Le Robert, the new but execrable dictionary (which has been considerably improved since) but which had marketing means. Then I noticed that the Club Français du Livre had begun to print its own edition without me, having expurgated the etymologies, but luckily without using my mock-up. I filed a complaint, diverse lawsuits, and won the trial very quickly. So that was that.

I was attracting a bit more attention from the French publishing world. Hachette agreed to sell the Littré in its bookstores (although the head of sales, the good Perset, had decided that these unusual volumes were "horrible"). Hachette kept a close eye on how things were moving.

So it was natural that I should turn to them during my greatest difficulties. A member of the Hachette family, whom I won't name, attended our discussions. It was my first close contact with a big publishing company, at the highest levels. I didn't understand that my counterpart was looking out, above all, for his own interests. To do this, he had to show his aptitude by twisting the neck of any victim who came forward, as quickly as possible. The negotiations rapidly turned into a strangulation without words.

I had begun acquiring good habits. I turned to Guy Schoeller, whom I knew well, and who at that time was an intermediary between Hachette and Gallimard. I will be talking more about Guy Schoeller, who died in 2002; he had an interesting life.

Guy immediately saw how things were going and reintroduced me to the Gallimard group. I met with Gaston again, then Claude, his son, and it went well. They directed me to a most charming financial director, Huguenin, who took me to good restaurants.

I'll skip over the negotiations, all the ins and outs, which are only interesting to those in the business and the history of publishing. Anyway, I was through with Hachette, which reappeared in the final days without saying anything in the discussions between myself and Gallimard. It was no longer my concern.

At the beginning, the result was an association with Gallimard-Hachette for the Littré operation. I was free of the affair in exchange for taking care of the subscriptions (subject naturally to the cashing of the bank drafts which I handed over to Gallimard). It was an outcome that left me no other benefit except to be free of a great burden.

However, there was a snag: five thousand bookstore subscriptions inexplicably disappeared from the final contract, and I was responsible for them. I didn't have any reason to hold this voluntary or involuntary slip-up against Gallimard. I was the one responsible for the publications, myself and my new attorney, Émile-Jean Bomsel, son of the elderly Bomsel, whom I had hired along with Maurice Garçon.

Each time I went to see them about this, Gallimard stood behind the contract: I was responsible for the five thousand subscriptions. I thought I saw the game: the advantage of this "error," voluntary or not, was that Gallimard thought they could squeeze me and then buy me out completely.

I remembered Reneé Bertelé and his Editions Point du jour, who were bought out by Gallimard for *Paroles* by Prévert (a huge success in 1946), and who whispered to me in the hallway of rue Sébastien-Bottin, "Don't ever let yourself be bought out: I'm horribly unhappy."

I was now in contact with René Juillard, thanks to Rolande and Jean Prétat, from the sales department, and I found his direct, straight talk very refreshing.

I soon signed a contract with him as an associate, with no pitfalls, similar to the one he already had with Robert Laffont and Pierre Horay.

I had one last interview – full of rancor – with the Gallimard family and team. Gaston reproached me suddenly and furiously (which shows to what extent he had felt disappointed – rather flattering) not to have been told about my negotiations with Julliard. Why? I think he meant he would have taken what was left of my capital. I could just as easily have reproached him for not letting me know of his intentions.

That would not be the last quarrel.

Or the last reconciliation.

René Juilliard

René Juilliard only had an average feel for literature. But he was a great publisher.

I need to quickly explain these seemingly contradictory qualities, because the public has no idea what publishing means exactly. And, after all, given that the mysterious aspects of this profession are often carefully guarded by those who exercise them, it's not a bad idea to put things right.

Publishing is above all a business, a special business, which borrows from many others (fashion design, cooking, high finance, the plastic arts...) and yet it remains unique.

"There are two ways of looking at publishing," Jean Prasteau wrote, rather summarily, after the death of René Juilliard, in July 1962: "Either one builds with an eye to eternity, or one lives in the present. Juilliard chose the second and made of publishing an industry oriented towards the topical, towards day-to-day life, every month or every week bringing in a new author. In order to obtain immediate success, Juilliard looked to the young. That's why he remained for so many years the publisher whose door every budding novelist came knocking at. If a manuscript pleased him, he published it three weeks after reading it and gave it all possible publicity."

"The printings of *Bonjour tristesse* and *Un certain sourire* compensated for the bad sales of those books they tried unsuccessfully to launch. Out of this came the tendency of the Julliard company to publish side-by-side with unknown first works by personalities with imposing names: journalists, political figures, Parisian celebrities, etc." (Jacqueline Piatier, in *Le Monde*, at that time).

"Of course, among these 'first works,' many could have remained, without harm to anyone, in the sad, anonymous shadows of rejected manuscripts. At least, both the reader and the critic were of this opinion sometimes. But never René Juilliard, who, even if didn't always believe totally in such and such a novel, he believed in the person behind it." (Michel Droit, in *Le Figaro litteraire*).

It's true. The old-timers from the company still remember a little scandal which occurred on rue de l'Université with the publication of an irritating novel by Francis Lopez, king of operettas at the time (*La Belle de Cadix*, etc.). Juilliard, alone his opinion, had pushed Lopez's novel, with this unique reasoning: "He has always been a success at whatever he undertakes. Why shouldn't his novel, no matter how bad it is, also be successful?" (Sometimes justice prevails: the novel was either panned dreadfully or not remarked upon at all; it was a resounding flop.)

Julliard, like all fine publishers, created above all an excellent "welcoming structure," through which the good as well as the bad passed, but in this the company resembled two or three other big publishers. At Juillard the authors, good and bad (like everywhere), were welcomed in any case, but the response was faster. It was a good company, as I said. And that could be seen right away.

In fact, it was an honorable company and held together by the humane qualities of René.

It was also held together by René's sense of financial assemblage, to call it what it was. Thanks to the relationships he knew how to build (Baumgartner, head of the Banque de France, among others, often had dinner at his place), René managed a rather sensational deal: he generated cash by writing bank drafts in the name of his distributing company, Sequana. Although this was ethically questionable, it made Éditions René Julliard unsinkable, and immune to a serious catastrophe, which he always knew how to avoid.

He also had a radiant authority, which he got in great part from his calm, which seldom left him. I remember very well a telephone conversation with Claude Gallimard in his office when I was there. Malraux, then Minister of Culture under De Gaulle, was very sensitive about the least reminder of his youth, which had been oriented towards the commercial exploitation of eroticism. Lo Duca had quoted too much of a preface written by Malraux for *Lady Chatterley's Lover* in one of the works in the collection entitled *Bibliothèque international d'érotologie*, which I had published. Claude Gallimard asked for an injunction against the work and telephoned Julliard to warn him. René Julliard (well aware of the situation) listened a long time to the story, saying briefly now and then, "I understand…," "Of course…," "You're absolutely right…" After a long time, he said, "So, my friend, I see that I will now be tried in court as a distributor. Good-bye, my friend." Nothing further happened, of course.

I got along rather well with René Julliard, during the two or three years that our partnership lasted. He ruled the association of Laffont-Julliard with an iron fist and no doubt thought that he could boss everyone that way. After several clashes, I found before the end of a year an unbeatable escape hatch from any disagreements. At the least sign of a dispute about the merits of one of my projects, I would say, "I see that you're not thrilled with this, René. I don't want to force you. I'll take full responsibility for the book: here are the conditions under which you will distribute it." Sometimes he would change his mind (often with amazing intuition); sometimes, he let me go my own way.

(I'll soon recount a book story where he was both right and wrong. Right because, in all honesty, given the conditions under which bookstores usually did business, no one would have bet a penny on the undertaking I'm going to tell you about. Wrong because of a series of unexpected circumstances – having to do with me, to be honest – which upset all the normal givens of the situation and in the end meant that I was right – when I shouldn't have been).

Robert Laffont found it very hard to put up with Julliard's authoritarian ways, which drove him crazy. Today he's eighty-seven years old and we lunch together from time to time. We often talk about Julliard and recognize that in the long run he had great qualities, certainly compared with those working in the profession today.

A Tightrope

At the end of the Fifties, I was over thirty and had twelve years behind me, following an uncertain career start. Finally, and for the first time, I was in the position of a small, full-time publisher with everything this implies. In particular, I had my own exclusive distributor. Girodias, carried away by the swelling sales of his erotic English-language books, had just left rue de Nesle and set up shop on rue Saint-Séverin in a building he immediately started remodeling, a crazy project. Was the remodel for office space? Not entirely. He put the offices on the top floor and began the transformation of the three remaining floors (plus the basement that he had to excavate at night). The whole project came to be called the Grande Séverine. Work lasted two or three years.

I was still reeling from the recent vagaries of what I now called my publishing house. The Littré affair had left some scars. Gallimard refused to deliver subscriptions subject to the conditions in the contract, and booksellers were threatening us with lawsuits – which they indeed embarked upon.

It was imperative that another company be created in case we lost the lawsuits, thus saving the SARL Librairie Jean-Jacques Pauvert from going under and taking with it all its capital and assets. It was the SCDL, Societé pour la Création et la Diffusion du Livre, which took over (in a questionable way, but oh well) the assets of the Librairie JJP.

In October of 1957, just before associating with Julliard, I accomplished something, through great insistence, that was dear to my heart. With Gallimard and Lindon I celebrated Georges Bataille's sixtieth birthday by seeing that three of his books were published at the same time: *La Littérature et le Mal* published by Gallimard, *L'Érotisme* published by Minuit, and *Le Bleu du ciel*, my publication, a new novel for which I had created a rather lovely cover, as always on a shoestring. I think it was about *Bleu du ciel* that Maximilien Vox, a great authority on design matters, said something that went straight to my heart: that I was a remarkable typographer. Yes, sometimes.

There are only one or two photographs of this cocktail party in the Pont-Royal bar, one of Bataille with Gaston Gallimard, myself, Christiane and my father. Obviously, Gaston Gallimard and I weren't quarreling at the time. I had a little eight-page brochure printed praising the glory of Georges Bataille.

At any rate, this cocktail party, successful over all, made our friendship with Bataille even stronger. I have found a note that he wrote me on September 30, 1957, a few days before the party:

> My dear Jean-Jacques,
>
> Thank you so much for your kindness and competency in putting together this celebration in spite of your troubles.
>
> This cocktail party frightens me in a way, but you know how much I appreciate the effort that you have gone to, an effort, in fact, that was not made by any of my other publishers before now.
>
> With much affection and I'll see you Friday.

Le Bleu du ciel did not sell, even when the Éditions Jean-Jacques Pauvert benefitted a little later from Sequana distribution. *La Litterature et le Mal* didn't sell either (and *Madame Edwarda* even less so). Only the sales of *L'Érotisme* were brisk. Bataille remained for the moment a cursed author.

The capital that I invested in the Sequana distribution company was also cursed. *Le Surréalisme, même?* It simply did not sell, as was the case with the little literary collection of surrealist texts (*Airia*, by Radovan Ivsic, *Agence générale du suicide* by Jacques Rigaut, etc.).

All of 1958 was spent working with Jacques Darche to bring out the first art book devoted to Max Ernst. It would be published at the beginning of 1959, with an excellent text by Patrick Waldberg, which was a mitigated success because there was no foreign edition. We still had copies of *Les Bonnes* in stock in 1960, as well as of my reissues of *Gobineau*, of Stendhal, and of the first critical edition of *Écrits politiques* by Benjamin Constant. It was very difficult to get these into the bookstores.

In April 1957, I put on sale a remarkable novel by an unknown writer, Henri Raynal, which Breton had brought me: *Aux pieds d'Omphale*. A critical success, as they say. We had the same result with a facsimile edition of *Fleurs du mal*, prepared by Marcel A. Ruff for the centenary celebration of the book, printed by Poulet-Malassis in Alençon.

In April 1958, I brought out a little book of drawings, very nicely formatted by its young author, with a preface by Marcel Aymé and an afterword by Jacques Prévert:

Innocent drawings by Siné
Nice murderous faces
Each night
An identical dream unites them

Each night
The tender desire to live without each other
Lights up their separate insomnias

Charming little blue flowers
The far-away birds of paradise
Blades with handles made from bed-frames.

Complaintes sans paroles by Siné was somewhat inspired by the famous American review *Mad*. But Siné's book (with its expensive gate-fold pages) went a lot further in its derision, its ferocity, its blasphemy and its cynicism. Marcel Aymé was right: "One could say it was humor right to the bone."

220   Sade's Publisher

But in 1958, the humor hadn't yet gone that far with the public.

As for Sade and the *Histoire d'O*, there had been talk that Julliard wouldn't distribute them. I made their distribution a condition of our agreement, above all for *Histoire d'O*. In my last discussion with René Julliard, I pointed out to him that *Histoire d'O* was a much better book than *Gretchen en uniforme*, a saucy translation without any literary merit but which sold well.[9] Ah, but nonetheless, said Juilliard, it's not the same thing! Exactly, I said. In the end, everything was distributed through Sequana. But *Histoire d'O* continued to sell in dribbles. Even so, it was the book which was most requested by the press service for its team of salesmen – and even by the editorial services of Julliard. How strange it was.

Just two titles had real success, to the joy of the young team representing Sequana, which strongly supported us. These were *L'Érotisme au cinéma* by Lo Duca, which I had brought out in January 1957, and *Portée de chats* by Siné ("Chat-pitre, chat-banais, entre-chat...") which saved the year 1958 and mitigated the relative failure of *Complaintes sans paroles*.

Oh, yes, *Bizarre* also sold a little, especially with the special numbers *Hétéroclites et fous littéraires* and *La Joconde*.

All of this, as I said, was with a serious political crisis in the background. Old France was cracking open everywhere; De Gaulle's hour had struck once again. I was astonished by the indignation of the Left-wing intellectuals, their march on Orly (with the participation of Émile-Jean Bomsel) to stop the soldiers coming from Algiers – who never arrived, as it turned out.

How lucky they were, in fact – and me, too. We were going to be in the opposition, a real opposition to something concrete.

Death intervened abruptly in the first part of 1960: Albert Camus and Michel Gallimard were killed in a car accident; while Lucienne B., my associate at the Bookstore Palais-Royal, committed suicide.

These three deaths were inextricably linked in my mind, but in different ways. I had remained rather close to Camus, and had just given him a short text. I was waiting for him to talk to me about it. Camus had introduced Michel Gallimard to me a short while before. Michel's death noticeably affected the Gallimard company. Gaston saw himself much more in Michel, his nephew (son of Raymond) than his own son Claude, whom he treated with severity and who stayed stuck in administrative tasks. The life of books and their authors, the very heart of the company, was Michel's domain. I remember one day when I was in a long private conversation with Gaston, and Claude entered

---

9   *Gretchen en uniforme : roman* (Paris : Julliard, 1954). A translation of a 1947 German work by Karl Heinz Helms-Liesenhoff. – Editor's note.

the head office without knocking. He was shown the door immediately, not being allowed to say a word: I'm with Jean-Jacques, leave us alone.

Lucienne B. was another matter. She had a little perfume shop on the corner of Palais-Royal, and I can't remember exactly how she got to know us towards the end of 1958. I was looking for a way to diversify my companies. I thought I could transform her shop into a bookstore and house some collections there, in particular the surrealist works, and the complete first edition ever printed of *Monsieur Nicolas* by Restif de la Bretonne, of which I was rather proud.

Jean Paulhan wrote to me about this on September 11, 1959:

> Dear friend, Thank you for *Monsieur Nicolas*. Yes, it's an admirable book, enough to pardon Restif his stupid and repugnant *Anti-Justine*. No one has written about the common people in villages like he does. It seems to me he encompasses and clarifies the entire 18th century. Rousseau is dull compared to him.

Tall, elegant Lucienne attracted attention by the refinement of her look, down to the last detail. Her apartment above the shop resembled her, furnished with a thousand little dainty things, which revealed a feminine delicateness – which was a little excessive, in fact. Breton and Siné, when they came to visit her, though, were fascinated, Siné remarking that it was paradise and Breton showing his interest in a thousand different ways.

Sadly, Lucienne was psychologically fragile. Divorced early from a talentless painter, she was a young mother with a little boy, living in a boarding house near Paris. Her moods went from deep depression to short spurts of euphoria (which were more worrisome than her depressions). She attracted a crowd of single – and not so single – men who disturbed her by always buzzing around her.

I was interested in her, as well, too much so, to tell the truth. I introduced her to my friend Jean-Francois, a psychiatrist, who also took an interest in her, and in the end was obliged to have her committed to stays in specialized clinics. She had just come out of one in early 1960.

She often told me in moments of depression that she would not live to be thirty. She used gas to kill herself – I was away – at the age of 29.

Books Move A Little – Éric Losfeld – Still Bound By Rogue Laws

There had been a sort of simmering going on in the profession for several years. The agitation was founded in general on the new format for books, a movement towards freedom and away from the moral conformity that had been imposed on us for the last dozen years, and new forms of literary expression (actually, drawn from the great period of Surrealism, from 1925 to 1935): nonsense (the beginning of Ionesco's theater); the "nouveau roman"; and eroticism, at last, for those who dared call it what it was in spite of the prudery of the major newspapers.

It would have been surprising if these leanings had not led to the creation of new publishing companies. In fact, there were only two new notable companies in the profession: Claude Tchou's Cercle du Livre Précieux and Eric Losfeld's Éditions du Terrain Vague.

Created by a former salesman for Halluin (Scorpion), the Éditions du Terrain Vague followed a first attempt by Eric Losfeld which had ended in insolvency. Les Éditions Arcanes had published rather pretty books nicely printed by the Arrault company from Tours: Alphonse Allais, Jarry, the first plays of Ionesco. It had been succeeded by Les Éditions de l'Hippogriphe, Les Éditions des Chimères, and lastly, Les Éditions du Terrain Vague in 1955, named by André Breton.

I had had a few dealings with Éric Losfeld when he was starting out, which had ended badly. I understood nothing about his personality: bipolar, a liar, capable of being charming one day, odious the next, subject to unexpected rages.

Over and above market issues, his relations with the vice squad and the judges seemed shady to me. While being capable of furnishing the vice squad with information he hadn't been asked for, he exasperated the inspectors by making indignant and ostentatious protests against the police, against censorship in general, etc., right after leaving police headquarters.

I had several things to reproach him for, some rather serious – and besides, at that time I wasn't very patient. For example, he had made a copy of my edition of *L'Anglais décrit dans le chateau fermé* by Mandiargues and presented it to his customers as a creation by Terrain Vague. I wasn't going to file a complaint, naturally.

I had been present at one of his hearings in the 17th criminal court, where Losfeld conducted himself in a lamentable fashion, excusing his publication of such and such a work because he had to make a living, finishing up by crying and talking about his children. Later, he would do worse, by revealing to the vice squad, at the time of *Emmanuelle*, the identity of the authors and their address. As a diplomat, the husband of Emmanuelle had a lot to lose.

In short, we were at each other's throats, when in fact our similar activities should have brought us together. Like me, he published surrealist reviews and from time to time important texts, like the *Petite anatomie de l'image* by Bellmer. We were different in our plethora of clandestine publications. He published "erotica" which was more or less well written, badly printed, badly edited, as well as new editions of expurgated classics taken from bad editions. This wasn't my cup of tea.

He had asked André Breton to intervene in litigation that opposed us at the end of the Fifties. I explained the situation to André who wrote me, or telephoned, to apologize, saying that that my version of the whole affair had been completely correct; he didn't understand Losfeld's attitude, but asked me to forgive him.

This fluctuating period, to put it mildly, lasted for Losfeld until 1968. After having previously and ostensibly signed the Manifesto of the 121 (which I didn't sign), Eric suddenly refused to keep a copy of a violent surrealist tract at his place, for fear of the police. Jean Schuster asked me to keep the stock on rue de Nesle, which I immediately agreed to, as related elsewhere by Schuster, who was the first to be astonished by Losfeld's evasiveness.

So that's when my old, cranky self burst out. I was to see Eric Losfeld again later, in a more favorable light. He explained his erring ways from the past, and we cobbled together a kind of friendship. He died (about 1972?)[10] and his daughter Joëlle told me later that I was the only one from the publishing world who came to visit her and her mother.

Through a strange turn of events, I took over Terrain Vague for a few months. But that's another story.

Le Cercle du Livre Précieux wasn't actually a publishing house. It was a commercial enterprise, founded on very traditional principles: fine reprints of the erotic classics, with a limited print run, on beautiful paper, well bound, and protected by the fallacious – or semi-fallacious – notice: "Not for commercial use," "Reserved for subscribers," etc. Claude Tchou, a genuine Chinese man from

---

10   Eric Losfeld actually died November 18, 1979. – Editor's note.

Belgium, was in no way a fighter for free expression, as would be proven. But his business had the merit of producing excellent publications.

Le Cercle du Livre Précieux, Le Terrain Vague and I were admittedly persecuted systematically by those in power under the 5th Republic, as under the 4th. The laws continued to crack down on publishers, given the silence, if not complicity, of the major news outlets.

In December 1958, a new act modified the law of July 16, 1949, thus introducing intolerable arbitrariness. I'll quote here at length the plea that Maurice Garçon made in 1963 in defense of François Maspero, manager of the Joie de Lire, a bookstore which had only recently opened. This store had committed the offense of displaying in a closed case, but with a glass panel, a copy of the *Dictionnaire de sexology*, which was not, by law, allowed to be displayed. Only the back cover of the book could be seen. Any readers who are weary of such old tales can skip the next few pages (the rest of this chapter, in fact). But I feel the need to tell it all.

Garçon used this example to defend Maspero, in order to point out that the law of 1958 extended to all publications. His reasoning was very clear (I printed it in detail in *Plaidoyer contre la censure*), and it needs to be read in detail to show the climate in which publishers at the time were forced to work. I have only excised comments and developments which could blur the clarity of the text:

> The hijacking of a law by way of an amendment inserted through a decree [of December 1958] has today re-established a censorship more arbitrary than we have seen since the 19th century. In the most arbitrary and dangerous manner a simple 'cease and desist' order from the minister of the interior can stop, without recourse, a book from being put on the market, while at the same time it is impossible to obtain a conviction against the book if one went to court. This whole business has been conducted in silence and as if by surprise, and the re-establishing of censorship in this indirect manner is matched for the offender by punishment which can go so far as to close the publishing house...

****

It is by deviation from the law of July 16, 1949, that this operation has occurred. This law is called 'About publications aimed at the young.' The first article clearly shows the object of the law:

> *Subject to the present law are all publications, periodicals or not, which by their character, their format, or their objective, appear principally aimed at children or adolescents.*

****

Article 2 in fact includes a general provision which can be criticized:

Publications included in the first article cannot include any illustrations, or texts, or stories, or rubrics, or insertions which present in a favorable light banditry, lies, theft, laziness, cowardice, hatred, debauchery or any act that could be qualified as a crime or offense, or be of a nature to corrupt children or adolescents.

Five copies of any publication destined for the young must be given to the minister of justice in order that it be subjected to an inspection com- mission. In case of an infraction to article 2, which means if the works do present in a favorable light banditry, lies, theft, laziness, cowardice, hatred, or debauchery the offender will be punished by one month to a year in prison and a fine of 1,500 to 15,000 francs.

The intentions of the legislation can be applauded. It is good that youth should not be presented with praise for capital sins. On the other hand, one must not, through an excess of prudery, create books which are, though permitted reading for children, so austere that they disgust the young by their virtue.

Thank heavens the courts appreciated and did not condemn booksellers for marketing the adventures of Arsène Lupin to teenag- ers, or those of Chéri-Bibi which, without pushing them into vice, amuse them by narrating the exploits of a gentleman thief and an escaped prisoner.

Up until then, nothing had been said about the law because judg- ments about the moral value of a work had been left to the courts, and no violation affected the rights of the defense.

However, this reasonable law, on condition of its wise application, did not satisfy the prudery of the paragons of virtue who thought that the courts had not shown themselves to be harsh enough to satisfy their suspicious intolerance. This is why, to the decree of December 23 1958, was added the law of July 16, 1949, along with article 14, which completely transformed the spirit of the law by re-establishing censorship in a form that the Restoration itself never dared to pro- mulgate. This is stated in the first paragraph:

It is forbidden to propose, to give or to sell to minors of eighteen years old, publications of any kind, which present a danger for the young by reason of their licentious or pornographic nature or by their focus on crime.

Thus, although the title of the law shows that it proposed to regulate only publications destined for youth and that article 1 decrees that the law only means to deal with publications, periodicals or otherwise, which by their nature or by their objective appeared principally to focus on children and adolescents, article 14 extended the law to publications of every kind, which meant to the whole of literature.

And paragraph 2 added:

It is forbidden, besides, ever to display these publications on public view in any public place and especially the exterior or interior of stores or kiosks or to publicize these works in any way.

Thus it is seen that publications of any nature can be the object of a ban: of course the decree states that the works cannot be proposed, given or sold to minors of eighteen years old, but in order to avoid these works being proposed, given or sold to minors, they must not be shown to adults inside stores either.

The measure could be understood if it were a matter of works condemned by a court of law, but books outlawed in this way have never been subjected to judgment by a civil court. They have been banned by the arbitrary will of the minister of the interior who has become a censor. Paragraph three made this decree:

Published works to which these sanctions apply are designated as such by a stop order issued by the minister of the interior. The commission charged with the overseeing of publications destined for children and adolescents is empowered to specify those publications, which appear to it to justify these interdictions.

This is an excessive, intolerable, and hypocritical measure, which under the pretext of protecting children, in reality allows the minister of the interior to create a black list of works of all kinds, which have nothing to do with literature for the young. These works, which would never be tried in court because a jury would refuse to condemn them, are kept from being sold even though the sale of the books is not actually forbidden.

In this way censorship has been re-established more severely than that found under the Empire which caused such an outcry and which, at least at the time of the Law of 1810, even then allowed the possibility of appealing a ban made by one blinkered censor, to another who might be more enlightened.

Today, if we look at the *Journal officiel*, where the stop orders made by the minister of the interior were published, it's easy to see that almost none of the condemned books had been written for children. They are novels, works of every kind, and the biggest publishers were hit by the most arbitrary measures.

****

Never had such an attack against freedom of thought and the written word been made so shamelessly.

The sanctions which accompanied any violations of such bans were exceptionally severe and the courts were expected to uphold them with no power to evaluate the sanctions but instead to rubber stamp them.

The infractions [...] are punished by imprisonment of one month to a year and a fine of 1,500 to 15,000 francs.

The officers of the court can, before any lawsuit, seize the publications which have been advertised; they can also seize and destroy all advertising material which accrues to these publications.

The court will make a pronouncement about the objects which have been confiscated.

And this is not all!

When three publications, periodicals or otherwise, published by the same publisher, have been sanctioned in the course of twelve months by bans relating to any of the various misdemeanors mentioned in the preceding three paragraphs, no publication or delivery of any publications coming from the same publisher can be put on sale without three copies having first been sent to the courts and after a waiting period of three months from the date of sending the material.

This article made eternal wards of publishers because, arbitrarily and without having to justify the motive, three stop orders could be made which would forbid all future publications without prior censorship, but with the aggravated factor that manuscripts should not be submitted, but only already printed works, with the risk of them being subsequently banned from circulation.

The sanction for non-submission, after three warnings, was of an unheard of gravity. The fact of not submitting or of marketing a publication before the end of the three-month period was punishable by...

...imprisonment of two months to two years. And besides, and as part of the same punishment, the courts can forbid, temporarily or definitively, the publication of the periodical...

It is incomprehensible why, unless it were to hide the exorbitant character of the measure, the word periodical was employed, because the article applied to publications of all kinds.

...and to order the total or partial shut-down, either temporary or definitive, of the publishing business. Every condemnation with more than ten days of imprisonment, for the misdemeanors described in the above paragraphs, will carry, over a period of five years, counting from the definitive judgment, a deprivation of rights, which are dealt with in article 42, § 1 and 2 of the penal code.

The rights focused on in these paragraphs are the right to vote, election and eligibility.

****

We are a long way from the protection of children in this overseeing of publications aimed at young people..."

Naturally, Maurice Garçon and I fought this law tooth and nail, pleading time after time against the "analogous" character of the targeted publications, and for the word "censorship" to be used regarding the targeted titles in our catalogs (there, we won), etc.

The net result was that I was deprived of my civil rights.

As for the press, it was much simpler. The minute we started to explain the law, reporters would put away their notebooks: you understand, it's much too complicated for our readers. Could you reduce it to a couple words? No, with the best will in the world, we could not explain it in a couple words. Well, okay. We're sorry, but maybe another time...

I thought about asking people to intervene. Who? Malraux, certainly. The Malraux who had written the preface for a clandestine erotic edition of *Lady Chatterley's Lover* in the Twenties, which had been translated by Gallimard in

1932, and who was currently the minister of culture under de Gaulle. I had published him in 1947.

I wrote him at the beginning of the Sixties a rather long letter (after all, we knew each other). I think I sent him a copy of M. Garçon's plea. He couldn't remain unmoved when confronted by these abuses of authority, such injustices as these.

At the end of several weeks, I received a rather incredibly silly letter, full of indescribable platitudes. I can no longer find it; a copy of it must be in the archives at the ministry.

It was signed Gaétan Picon (we had forgotten this "man of letters," assistant to the minister, and servile university man). The letter explained that Monsieur Le Ministre had read my letter, but really couldn't see any reason to interfere. It was simple: there were laws, which were well made, of course, in Général de Gaulle's 5th Republic; they only needed to be applied, and all would be fine.

This was not the only display of passive imbecility which Malraux would make. But it is good to recall this one in particular.

Eroticism In 1959

D ecember 15, 1959, the next-to-last surrealism exhibition in which André
Breton participated, opened in Paris at the Daniel Cordier gallery. He
shared direction of the exhibition with Marcel Duchamp. The show had
EROTICISM for its theme.

The way in which this theme belonged to Breton in particular was clearly
stated in his address to "the artists and visitors," which was the opening article
in the exhibition catalog:

> Surrealism at its most basic, must reaffirm that which specifically
> belongs to it, in an area which does not risk dividing those who
> practice surrealism, who are more and more numerous and of modest
> means today, who might otherwise be lost in the smoke of technical
> problems. If 'nature' today (in reference to the exterior world) has
> ceased to be dealt with in art for itself, and has been even completely
> revoked by some, there remains, in fact, a privileged area, a theater
> of incitation and prohibitions, where the most profound moments
> of life are played out. This area, into which surrealism has never
> ceased to make incursions, is the area of eroticism (which we know,
> far from necessitating the representation of scabrous scenes, draws
> primarily on ambiguity and lends itself to numerous transpositions).
> It has always been in this way – and really only in this way – that
> it has been necessary to establish between the exhibitor and the
> spectator, through perturbation, an organic link that is more and
> more lacking in art today.

The exhibition was a great success. For the opening, Meret Oppenheim
had the idea of a feast taking place around a table on which a young woman
was lying naked except for the *hors d'oeuvres* which were spread out on top of
her. Was I there? I have an incredible memory blank. I have no memory of

it, or only the memory of someone telling me this story so many times that I actually ended up seeing the scene.

A few days before, on December 2, 1959, the anniversary of Sade's death, Joyce Mansour hosted a production of *L'exécution du testament du marquis de Sade* by Jean Benoit, dressed in a costume that he had invented, with pieces of black wood more than six and half feet high. He entered with the guests, with an enormous penis moving in front of him, before writing out with a hot iron (real, not fake) the four letters of the word SADE on his naked chest. It was a great emotional moment, even if it made some idiots laugh.

The exhibition left behind it a mark, at any rate: its very special catalog, BOÎTE ALERT, stuffed with texts, ended with the *Lexique succinct de l'érotisme*, which included these definitions:

AMBROSIO – Hero of a novel by M.-G. Lewis, *The Monk* (1796). "How," he asks, "can she read the Bible and still be so innocent?"

ARDOR – Desire carried to its paroxysm. "Go on, lay your body on the snow white body of Ottavia and give free rein to your desires." (Nicolas Chorier).[11]

The year 1959 was also the year when *Emmanuelle* was first published (clandestinely, what a shame!). It was around June 1959, as Losfeld fails to point out in his rather approximate memoirs. In spite of the clandestine nature of the publication, it attracted several articles. André Pieyre de Mandiargues, as always, in the NRF, exquisitely made his point about what the novel brought to the literary world at the right moment, with its qualities and its defects.

> Like detective stories, or science fiction, erotic stories, we know, are generally prisoners of a frame, of a system of rules which keep them in a certain category. They also aim at a rather precise objective, for which reason we buy them. But there are those works which move out of the frame, which break the system or the rules and for which the objective is secondary. Carrying the spiritual mark of their author, they are original and become a part of literature. I think that *Emmanuelle* is one of these...
>
> ...The first chapter, which recounts the strange adventure of Emmanuelle who is seduced twice during a plane trip from London

11 Nicolas Chorier, the supposed author of Aloisiæ Sigeæ, Toletanæ, Satyra sotadica de arcanis Amoris et Veneris, a celebrated mid-17th century pornographicum first published in Latin, but later much translated into other languages. – Editor's note.

to Bangkok, is admirable. It echoes, both by its tension and its power to surprise, the best carnal episodes of Balzac and the heights of narrative reached in the novels of Lawrence Durrell. What follows, obviously, is not of the same quality, even though it manages to give us a glimpse of the underworld in the Siamese capital, which is no less feverish and beguiling than that of Alexandria. In the last part, the interest shifts. The author, a young Asian woman, it seems, has made it the duty of one of her characters, an Italian pederast named Mario, to express his own ideas on eroticism and on the role that is his, in terms of mankind and the future of the world. A little over-worked and infantile (and even charming because of this, perhaps), these conversations curiously open the window on vistas where nature is crushed by the triumph of the modern mind. Thus, the author of *Emmanuelle* is the counterpart of what we have read in Lawrence, for example, and in that she approaches certain attitudes of Baudelaire. She also moves away from those ideas often explored by Georges Bataille. Her idea of eroticism is optimistic, radiant, glowing, the image of an edifice affirming the glory of man freed from parochialism and ancient servitude. Not that I am in agreement with her on all of this. But her youth and fine spirit are very appealing, and her education (she even cites Hobbes, which few people have read and who it is pleasant to encounter on the threshold of an orgy) assuredly merits that she be distinguished among other authors who are supposed to be bad company.

Losfeld did not dare bring out *Emmanuelle* with his name on it until 1967! It should be remembered that *Emmanuelle* was one of the underground upsurges coming from *Histoire d'O*, as Emmanuelle herself recalls several times, and as she told me in her inscription to me (we got acquainted rather quickly) in one of her best books, *L'Hypothèse d'Éros*, in 1974:

> Without *Histoire d'O* – that is without Jean-Jacques Pauvert – *Emmanuelle* would never have seen the light of day. [...] And I am forever grateful to him.

Although I had to abandon the too onerous publication of *Surrealisme, même* after number 5 in the spring of 1959, I did try to keep the publication and the distribution of my little surrealist collection going. And my relationship with Breton was always constant, closer than ever. He had written a long letter to me on June 23, 1959, which moved me: "There is no point in holding forth about the causes of this failure at a financial level. [...] Let me tell you that my friends and I are deeply saddened by your decision and have not yet given up hope that you will change your mind. [...] I pray you, dear Jean-Jacques, to excuse my insistence. Just at the moment when surrealism is once again gaining great newsworthiness and with new sensational contributions assuring it resounding publicity, you understand that the disappearance of S.M. in my eyes now seems like a disaster."

But I was financially choked. I could only say that I had been moved by his letter. "Let me think about it a little. [...] I'll give you a definitive response on July 15." But it was over. I was hovering on the edge of bankruptcy. I would be saved by Julliard, but only just.

The miracle was that our relationship, mine and Breton's, hardly suffered at all. It seems that it would have taken something much more for it to be seriously broken.

Besides, at the end of 1959, André Breton pulled out of his magician's hat a marvelous and incomparable discovery.

The First Performance Of Concile D'amour

I had the impression that I had always known him. Nothing about him surprised me, or else he always surprised me, as you wish. Let's say that each time I waited for a surprise, for something astounding and dazzling.

But when I heard someone talking about him or if I read certain authors about him, then I doubted that we were talking about the same man. An authoritarian pope, him? A dictator? He was completely the opposite of that. I had never known anyone to be more open and more welcoming. To put it another way, he was charming, in every sense of the word. Of course, the minute he sensed an imposter, or an exploitation of false values, or an intellectual con, he'd cut you dead, and grow angry. Superficial types never forgave him for this.

I greatly loved his enormous sense of humor, his way of calling counterfeit the common-place, the ready-made phrase, without seeming to do so, like this famous line from his finest best years: "Avez-vous des amis? – Aucun, cher ami."[12]

Towards the autumn of 1959, André Breton came close to making me die laughing. I wasn't the only one. André mysteriously organized a meeting at Robert Lebel's, an autioneer and rich collector. I understood at first that it was to be a dinner. But the dinner was to be followed by a surprise. What kind? That was the mystery.

There were just a few of us. Marcel Duchamp was there, Robert Lebel, of course, Christiane and I. There might have been someone else; I don't remember.

The dinner was very pleasant. The food was well chosen, the wines all appropriate. Duchamp didn't eat much, as was his habit. He spoke little and seemed to observe everyone from far away. Robert Lebel perfectly maintained his place as host of great men. André, at his best, held forth with a conversation full of profound, ingenious insights. Christiane and I stayed in the background a little, as seemed appropriate.

When dinner was over, we went into a little room where everything had been set up as if for a talk: across from a table and a chair, seats had been placed for an audience. André took his place in the speaker's chair, in front of

---

12 "Do you have friends? – No, dear friend." – Editor's note.

a manuscript, with a pitcher of water and a glass, and announced that he was going to read to us a play, which had not yet been published in French. It was by an almost unknown German from the 19th century, translated by Jean Bréjoux, a teacher in Bordeaux. Title: *Le Concile d'amour, tragédie céleste en cinq actes*. The author: Oscar Panizza. He had been banned in his day. André began.

I had heard praise of André's great gifts as a storyteller. But never until that night had I seen such a dazzling demonstration of these gifts. André read us the work in its entirety, masterfully changing voices with each character. Here I am addressing those who know the play, and have perhaps seen it performed. Let them imagine the best performance one could ever dream of, with the best actors in the world. André was, one after the other, God the Father (tired, very tired), Jesus Christ (coughing, forlorn looking, a little lost), the Virgin Mary (a fading socialite), the Devil ("his allure makes one think of a Jew from good society"). And the angels, the cherubim, the little girl killed while in a state of sin. And the Borgia Pope, Herodias, Salome, and a dozen other characters coming from the sardonic and sacrilegious imagination of Oscar Panizza.

Breton made everybody speak, men and women, playing them all, giving each one a palpable life, with extraordinary precision. And with just two or three little interruptions, if I remember correctly, to catch his breath, to drink a little water.

We had never heard anything like it at the time. Text and interpretation convulsed us with laughter while Andrè, imperturbably, kept on reading. In the preface he wrote for the book (because of course I published the work as quickly as possible, in January 1960), Andrè Breton wrote this about Panizza: "Let's admit that Panizza's seditious spirit was carried so quickly to such a point and confronted such taboos that even now in our day, one presumes that they would lower the curtain before the end of the first scene."

What followed from all this was to be seen a few years later. Moral standards started changing quickly just afterwards, but we'll come to that.

In the end, in a certain way, they were good times.

JJP In December 1960,
As Seen By L'express

To tell the truth, it's a strange thing to look into one's memory when one isn't used to it, as is my case. And it's an even stranger thing to organize those memories. There are memories which are indelibly marked in the convolutions of the mind, as Jarry said. And then there are diaries, newspapers, recollection of facts and dates, which are just as indelible. Which ones should be believed? It is impossible that certain endless joys, should have been mixed at the same moment with somber hours, and that a vital and lively energy should have coincided with stubborn realities. So, where lies the truth? Realities are actually multiple, as we know, but they are above all equal.

When I look back at the years 1960 to 1973, I experience a bizarre sensation of power as I group them into a single period of time – that moment when I existed in social life as a "publisher." Before that, it was a time of discovery, along with the unexpected, a time of wandering sometimes blindly in the unknown, which was tamed only little by little – more or less. Afterwards, it would be like the exploitation of a magic trick, learned – sometimes the hard way – on the job, with the growing acquisition of greater speed, and more and more details without much importance in the end, aside from a few exceptional experiences, even if the path had been marked out with important steps.

Considering this period historically, I am struck by the extent to which these major stages of my life are so closely linked with a period of accelerated expansion in France and, perhaps, if one digs to the bottom of things, throughout the world itself. I don't know. I only felt, vaguely, what was happening all around me.

In no particular order, the opening of the Tancarville bridge, the films *Hiroshima Mon Amour*, À bout de souffle, *Les Quatre Cents Coups, Zazie dans le metro* (the book, then the film), Castro in power, the first "happening" (in the United States), China in Tibet, *Le Guépard* (French translation) 1959. January 1, 1960, the new franc. "Economic recovery: the reserves from the Banque de

France went from 377 million dollars on January 1, 1959, to close to 2 billion dollars on December 31."

So much the better. For me, 1960 was the year when I continued to knock on every door trying to find support from the banks. I remember, that summer there was a tiny incident which has stayed with me, god knows why. It was an instant, a second that marked me. I was going from the Opera into a bank on the second floor, the Financière d'Orient, perhaps. A very well-dressed gentleman took me in to be introduced. We took the elevator. Suddenly he pushed the stop button between two floors and asked me for his tip. He stuck the envelope in his pocket and we continued on our way. Why do I have such a clear memory of this moment?

Then there was the independence of African states, the week of barricades in Algiers, the first French atomic bomb (which was set off in the Sahara), *La Route des Flandres* by Claude Simon, the Nobel prize given to Saint-John Perse, the break between the USSR and China. The year 1961 was the failure of the putsch of the Algerian generals, Kennedy becoming president, Gargarin in space, the deaths of Céline and Hemingway. In 1962, the deaths of Bachelard and Bataille, Vatican II, and the discovery of solar wind. In 1963, Fellini's *8½*, the assassination of Kennedy, the opening of the tunnel under Mont-Blanc, Pinter, *The Homecoming*, Beckett, *Happy Days* (gripping!). A lot of other things happened, but I'm picking out just those which have more or less stayed with me.

There are missing aspects of those years, of course. Things get lost. What was I doing there in Paris, France, in the 6th *arrondissement*?

The publishing house really existed. We received manuscripts, the number of which began to pose a problem, however. Nothing interesting. Innumerable erotic novels, more or less inspired by *Histoire d'O*. I would have had to find a major work among them in order to take the risk of becoming a "specialist" (which I was, even so, in the eyes of a lot of contemporaries). Eroticism for me was something much too essential to be sullied by hackneyed repetition.

There were other novels, of course. All mediocre.

We were also sent a lot of critical essays, literary history studies. The house was beginning to have a reputation in this regard. We were the publishers, for example, of the facsimile edition of the original *Fleurs du mal*, presented by Marcel A. Ruff. And also of the *Correspondance* of Madame de Staël, with a forward by Béatrice Jasinsky, the costly caprice of the publisher (I never asked for any grants, although they wouldn't have given me any if I had). In my library of complete correspondences, I had those of Sainte-Beuve, Mérimée and Stendhal. Some of them were not finished: I kept an eye out every year for more. Others were in the project stage: that of Chateaubriand, for example, was waiting to happen. I wanted to be the publisher of letters. To each his foibles.

I published *Casanova* by the American J. Rives-Childs. I also published cinema reviews (*Présence du cinéma*). I re-issued rare books: Rossel's *Mémoires* (introduced by Roger Stéphane), *L'Unique et sa propriété*, by Stirner. There was my (international!) *Bibliothèque d'Érotologie*, an unequal collection but including some successes, and of undeniable commercial interest. Because of this publication, we were a great attraction at the Frankfurt Book Fair each autumn.

In November 1960, I was given the Médicis for *Le Souffleur, ou le Théâtre de societé* by Pierre Klossowski. Then André Breton gratified me with a sumptuous preface: "The discovery of the Gustave Moreau Museum forever influenced my way of loving..." for *Gustave Moreau* by Regnar von Holten, which, of course, had no success.

In December 1960, a great commercial success came with the *Dictionnaire des trucs* by Jean-Louis Chardans. The same month, on the 15th, there was a miniscule event in the eyes of the press, but which made a huge noise in the world of publishing: *L'Express*, a broad-sheet newspaper, assigned two entire pages to me with a large photo. Signed by Madeleine Chapsal, the article was in the form of an interview entitled, "PORTRAIT OF JEAN-JACQUES PAUVERT, PUBLISHER: From Sade to Siné, by way of Littré and Gobineau, a unique publisher introduced by Madeleine Chapsal."

Although there were a few minor errors, the article was on the whole rather admirable with an impartial objectivity. The journalistic notations were not correct ("a little room, low and furnished in wood," whereas in fact our offices on rue de Nesle were fairly airy), but they added a certain mystery for readers. But the actual interview was well reported. The whole piece created a relatively good portrait of Jean-Jacques Pauvert in December 1960:

> "I don't believe you can publish Bataille and Klossowski using the same book jackets."
>
> Moreover, he has wonderful memories of the Frankfurt Book Fair, while he was standing behind his counter, his merchandise in front of him:
>
> "I was the only publisher they stole books from... Next to me was Claude Gallimard and the representative from Julliard, each one behind his stand. Well, I can assure you that their businesses were not thriving like mine."
>
> He often meditates on the history of art, because he thinks that art and culture, as we have known them, are coming to an end! There's

the 'radio,' the 'TV,' and soon we'll put little gadgets in our ears and we'll be able to directly 'think' a condensed version of *La Chartreuse d Parme* or *Guerre et Paix*! To read takes an individual effort which is becoming more and more repugnant. There will remain a few lingerers, a few underground books – with lawsuits hounding them of course, they can't leave these 'dusty little islands' free to subsist; it wouldn't be hygienic! And these few books will, in cramped spaces, continue to deliver forbidden pleasures, and the last true readers, Jean-Jacques Pauvert says beatifically, with a hint of megalomania "will still read my little books".

A (somewhat novelistic) reminder of the Littré affair followed, then an incursion into the erotic: "Why are you interested so much in erotic literature?"

As Sade said, it's part of human nature. At any rate, it's part of mine. [...] I like erotic literature because it explains things." J.-J. Pauvert knows that by saying these things and by publishing certain books he is revealing himself.

Can you imagine people writing to Gaston (Gallimard) and saying: 'You're a bastard.' Well, that happens to me; I am the only publisher that I know who regularly receives insulting letters.

He recalls certain titles he published: Sade, *L'Unique et sa propriété*, *Le Voleur*, the drawings of Siné, *Le Concile d'amour*, *L'Art fantastique*, *Les Larmes d'Éros*... Julliard? "Julliard and I don't agree on anything and we get along perfectly well." Gaston Gallimard?

Someone once asked Gaston, 'Why do you publish books?' He had this admirable response: 'To build a library.' But think about it: he said this, but with everything he's published since, his library isn't so wonderful! I mean it has not been carefully selected. Personally, I only publish what I love: with thirty books a year (I don't want to do more), in forty years, that makes twelve hundred volumes. A nice little library, and all mine!

It was the first time that a major weekly had devoted two actual pages, with few concessions, to a publisher, and a "hellish" publisher at that. There would be repercussions and a backlash. At any rate, it was excellent publicity. Thank you, Madeleine Chapsal.

Petty Mauriac Hypocrisies

François Mauriac, who at the time was publishing his "Bloc-notes" in *L'Express*, seriously thought about leaving the newspaper. Someone had probably made him a better offer at *Figaro*. He always needed a pretext. I gave him a wonderful one. The following Thursday, he wrote:

> I am turning inwards, at this year's end, towards my little personal history, towards the Christian that I am, both average and militant, and towards the contributor to *L'Express* that I am also: a dual membership which I could accept as long as it did not cause any scandal, as long as I believed in my very special vocation which is to make heard a certain word where it is almost never heard.
>
> This vocation which I have assigned to myself speaks to everything, except if certain of my brothers whisper in my ear: 'Do you see what your periodical covers and what is now so widespread thanks to you!' And sometimes I shrug my shoulders and protest that it's nothing, nothing at all really; but also once in a while I lower my head, as I did last Thursday, for example, as I read the thoughts of a publisher specialized in eroticism and blasphemy.
>
> Please understand: I'm not outraged that agnostics or atheists are interested in a publisher like this, one who is risqué. I recognize their right to want brilliant information, and to stick out their tongues at traditional family values; I don't judge them. But I judge myself. A declared Christian must not help to spread that which causes him horror; because, for him, it is not a matter here of immorality in the current meaning of the word, nor of immorality in the light of Faith, it is absolute Evil which is suddenly unveiled; I would almost be inclined to write, the Evil which is the mind, the Evil which is Someone.

****

I had decided to stop Bloc-notes the first of January, was no longer going to stay with the newspaper except through a looser collaboration which would permit me to step away from the paper on tip-toe and without slamming the door, when a certain offensive odor from certain cauldrons wafted by my nostrils. But in the end friendship won out. I will wait until the political situation is clearer before deciding anything...

He came back the following week expounding on the letters he had received begging him to leave *L'Express* because of "the anticlericalism of Siné," "an eroticism which flouted marriage, conjugal fidelity, all notions of virginity and chastity, a loss of all sense of what makes a man..."

But I was the publisher of Siné from the start. And I would redouble my sin by publishing several editions of his *Dessins de L'Express*.

Mauriac finally left *L'Express* for *Le Figaro*. I went around for a while taking a certain satisfaction in being called the Cursed Cauldron, the Evil which is Someone (but brilliant!)... Poor Mauriac!

The Arrival Of Christian Bourgois

A
h! 1959 was also the year when Christian Bourgois joined Julliard, in the month of May. Don't forget this; it's important.

In his book *René Julliard* (Julliard, 1992) Jean-Claude Lamy has told the story of the headstrong adventure of Christian Bourgois:

> René guessed right away that this young man who the widow of René Laporte had introduced him to in Antibes in August 1954 was a brilliant man inhabited by a passion: literature. He had devoured books since the age of seven or eight and knew already that his professional life would be in a publishing house or in the press.

Bourgois pleased Julliard and the liking was reciprocal. But Julliard played a waiting game with him: ..."Pass the ENA[13] entrance exam. Let's stay in touch, I will always be glad to see and to know what you're doing. I will present you to Simon Nora who you admire so much, and his ENA graduate students, and then in five years, maybe ten, once you have had some experience in the public sector, we'll see."

After his military service in 1958, Bourgois met with Julliard again. "You have no inheritance, no relations," Julliard said to Christian. "You can't start a publishing house." This time René Julliard was feeling a need to change his staff, and he offered Bourgois a job. But there would be setbacks until the spring of 1959.

In 1960–61, Christian Bourgois was gaining a lot of importance in the Julliard publishing house by supporting Jules Roy or Djamila Boupacha. He was very involved politically and signed the manifesto of 121, which Julliard, as well as I, had refused to do.

Our first meetings were not very happy. It was one day in 1960, I think, that I had a visit from this tall, thin young man (he was 27 but looked much

---

13   École national d'administration. – Translator's note.

younger) who came to "inspect" the list of our press services. I politely showed him the door and talked to René Julliard about him who put the affair down to the zealousness of a beginner (which was true).

I was thirty-four with almost twenty years of experience in books, in many areas. I was in a way the opposite of Christian, who had just been hatched. So there was a hint of suspicion, but this did not stop us, before long, from becoming accomplices, as we had two different ways (fortunately) of being passionate about books.

And then, we are still here, both of us, forty-five years later, in 2004. That matters, even if we don't see each other that often.

VII

OUR CRAZY GOLDEN YEARS?

… the true essence of life is not a fact at all, far less a fixed reality.
It is a point of view, an attitude, a mood, an atmosphere,
a mental and emotional process.

— John Cowper Powys

Miscellaneous – Bachelard –
I Publish André Breton At My Place

I always found myself faced by the eternal problem of publishing: you have to have a minimum number of publications to assure the overheads are paid. But I refused to publish any old thing, to look blindly for something that might please the public in the pile of manuscripts that we received but about which we were not particularly enthusiastic. And those we liked didn't seem to please the public.

After the great success of *Chats*, the drawings of Siné were found shocking. I tried to start a collection of hard-to-find books: "XIXe siècle." I expected a lot from the *Nouvelles Asiatiques* by Gobineau, and even more from *l'Ève future*, by Villiers de L'Isle-Adam, which I still think is one of the great unknowns of literature. It was a critical success, as they say, no more.

Not to mention Benjamin Constant's *Mémoires sur les cent jours*, with its enthusiastic introduction by O. Pozzo di Borgo. If the book had not been printed in Switzerland (where I'd begun to pick up some credit), it would have ruined the company. The revival of *Vercingentorixe* by the marquis de Bièvre (18th century puns), was hardly mentioned at all except by *Le Canard enchaîné*.

As for *Bizarre*, yes, it sold a little. Special issues attracted attention. The new cartoonists that we launched surprised people but caught their attention. I devoted special issues to such unknown artists as Topor and Wolinski. Commercially, it wasn't very profitable, but at least they got talked about a little. I corresponded with Bachelard, who wrote me several times about *Bizarre*, which interested him enormously:

> In these times of conformism when everything in daily life is standardized, your efforts create a sort of signal. You give life to men through signals, which are signs of the super-human. Wise men, too wise, would be wise to read. (January 22, 1959)

This time, it's the circus fairground and all its wonders that you bring into my room... When I was little, some circus freaks came who used to be part of the local holiday fairs in my area. I saw the limbless man, giants and midgets. But no one took me to see the tattooed lady, even though a tattooed lady is not a naked lady. (March 26, 1961)

But April 4, 1961, I had lunch with André Breton and I left with a new treasure held tightly against my heart: the contract which said from that moment on I was the publisher of five of André's titles: the complete *Manifestes du surréalisme*, *Arcane 17*, *Martinique Carmeuse de serpents*, *La Clef des champs*, and *Anthologie de l'humour noir*.

It was the culmination of several anxious months, having to do with the archives of Éditions du Sagittaire. Léon-Pierre Quint, who managed the publishing house, wanted to sell it at that time. We had met on several occasions, but the legal situation having to do with Breton's titles was not clear, and it was the essential aspect of the company's name. Gallimard was, of course, very interested, and he laid siege to Breton's apartment on rue Fontaine by sending there Robert Carlier, one of his henchmen. André Breton, who had reasons to hold a grudge against Gallimard, didn't want to discuss it and shut himself up in his apartment so that he didn't have to receive Carlier.

Then there was the decisive intervention of the attorney Bomsel, an old acquaintance, the father of one of my lawyers with whom I had always remained in contact. He untangled the legal situation in a few days, tied up the ends of the contract, and on April 4, 1961, everything was signed. In April 1962, the new edition of Breton's *Manifestes du surrealism* was put on sale (with a cover which, to repeat myself a little, I was once again very proud of), in a full version, complete for the first time. It was the beginning of an adventure in which certain episodes were decisive, at least to my existence.

In October of the same year, another publishing adventure happened which showed the kinds of imponderables that publishers face. Those who aren't interested in the inside workings of the profession (but after all, these are the memoirs of a man who was a publisher for most of his life) can skip the next few pages.

To cut a long story short, I was in contact with some Swiss printers, large companies in Geneva and Lausanne, and with a Parisian office managed by Jean-Pierre Rouzet. The Swiss needed work and were offering a good deal on credit, very unusual in France. Up until then, I had pretty much just given them erudite books: Benjamin Constant, Madame de Staël. I was loyal to Louis Rossi, but he couldn't give me enough credit for books whose sales were less than slow.

Now suddenly someone brought me something (the "someone" was dear Francis Bouvet, who died too young): a project that looked crazy enough to tempt me. It was an undertaking of such breadth that it was beyond the capabilities of French printers: all the poetry of Victor Hugo for the first time in one volume. It would be the realization of a failed project in Canada a few years before; supposedly complete, in reality, the volume was greatly reduced and had been a commercial failure.

This time would be a veritable first: not only would all the previously published poetry be in the volume, but various fugitive pieces, uncollected texts, drafts, etc.

In all, there were 153,837 verses (I will always remember this, I think), and 1,800 quarto pages. The introduction and chronology were by Francis Bouvet, the design by Jacques Darche. The typography was set in two columns. The binding was a deep gray, but brightened up by the signature of Victor Hugo, in gold. It weighed in at 3,800 kg. I believed in it as much as René Julliard didn't. But I believed in the project so much that I wanted to do it alone, with the support of Rouzet. The Swiss believed in it because of Rouzet and I believed in it especially because most of the typesetting, paper for the printing and the binding came to a tidy sum. We then agreed on a long-term credit plan for paying back this enormous bill.

Preparation of the text took most of 1960 and 1961. I'll skip over the details. In September, we had already printed with the Swiss René de Solier's *L'Art fantastique*, a beautiful volume, but which had a slow start in sales. I warmed up the sales people about the Victor Hugo project: an edition never done before, an enormous printing outlay, etc. I ordered a printing of ten thousand copies in order to have an acceptable price. In fact, once again the future of the publishing house rested on the sales of a book.

In November 1961, there was a meeting with the sales reps. I was introduced in total silence. There were a few coughs. One of the salesman, Jean Pretat, spoke up for the others. His sector was the Right Bank, where one might think that the bookstores were better prepared to welcome such a considerable piece of work.

The result: only one copy had been ordered, and two or three were taken on deposit. In all the other areas, it was pretty much the same situation. Victor Hugo, what a crazy idea! He doesn't sell anymore. And then it's too big, it's too this, it's too that.

I fought back: it was a new undertaking, a revolutionary concept, never done before.

I think it was on this occasion that René Julliard addressed the sales reps: You are here to help support new works. "Even if Jean-Jacques is wrong, he's right. He's right because it's always the publisher who is right in regards to such a novelty. He's simply ahead of his time. You must support him." A long silence. They couldn't say anything against those facts. Revolutionary perhaps, but the bookstores didn't want it.

When I left there, all my fight disappeared. I was deeply in debt, even if it was in the long term.

Something happened in Paris about this time which ended by being a great publicity boon for the publishing world – the literary advertisements of MM. Lecoq and Lemerle. They had the idea of adding to their business through direct sales to individuals by placing advertisement inserts in newspapers. I knew the owners a little. They telephoned me: we saw your Victor Hugo. It might be the ideal subject for launching our business. We discussed it. We came to an agreement.

A few days later, at a perfect moment for end-of-the-year gifts, the press covered one full page with inserts and a large photo of the text: "A revolution in publishing: 153,837 verses. A single volume. 1800 pages, 3,800 kg." They used the same arguments in its favor that I had used. Orders arrived *en masse* at the literary advertisement office. The bookstores came alive. Soon we began a second edition of the text with ten thousand copies. We had been saved.

Allow me to cite a few extracts from the press:

"An extraordinary publication," (*Jours de France*), "A prodigious collection" (*Les Œuvres Libres*), "A book of poetry without its equivalent anywhere else in the world" (*Le Parisien Libéré*), "A marvel of art and discipline" (*Journal des Instituteurs*). "The event of the year" (*Le Bulletin du Livre*), "A delight" (*Marie-Claire*). "A tour de force" (*L'Echo d'Oran*), "An admirable experiment" (*Combat*). "One of the most appealing books of the year" (*Libération*). "An inexhaustible collection" (*Le Figaro*). "The most marvelous of marvels" (*L'Express*). "A success" (*Les Lettres Françaises*). "The event of the literary year" (*Arts*)…

This was just like the Littré adventure – maybe more so. If this episode in my publishing adventures proves anything, it's the impossibility of calculating through market studies what the outcome of a book will be. If there is a lesson to draw from this, it is that no one adventure resembles any other; that, in fact, no one particular adventure can serve as a lesson for any other.

Luckily.

The Frankfurt Book Fair,
Chapter I

Soon after the war I attended the Frankfurt Book Fair, the oldest of book fairs, going back to the 15th century. The fair that was the best (at a time when there were book fairs which were worthy of the name), and the only one of its kind in the world, and never equaled despite multiple attempts to replicate it.

Those first years, anyway MY first years in Frankfurt around 1957–58, the Fair was still in its infancy; and it was open an entire week, a mess, as only the Germans know how to create when they get involved in organizing such a thing. The fair was held in a single building (big, admittedly) which held all the publishers of the world – grouped by country. The telephone desks were handled by large, fleshy women who spoke only in German; the messages arrived haphazardly, and requests made to the organizational office were complied with three days afterwards – when they were complied with at all. It would take several years "to put some order into all this," as Sade said.

But it was Frankfurt. Publishers from around the world were there, and the publishers were there in the stands, unlike today when the managers of the publishing houses are there instead. One even saw, in the Sixties, Claude Gallimard at the Gallimard stand. In a space hidden from the public, it's true, but he was still obliged to come out from time to time.

The first year, I stayed with one of the people from the town; the hotels were too expensive. But the whole day I ran from stand to stand. A lot of the foreign publishers spoke French, luckily. A lot of them knew a great deal about the French publishing world, and I was surprised to see that almost all of them knew who I was and looked on me as a great eccentric.

We drank a lot in Frankfurt. I remember being mildly anxious when it was time to pay the bills in bars. One night, for example, I was with Feltrinelli (the great Italian publisher, for those who may not know), Rowholt, Jr., (German, same thing) and some others. Everybody, except me, kept having one drink after another. The night went on and the group thinned out. I was with

Rowholt, who never left my side, and it looked like soon there would be just the two of us to whom the barman would present the bill. And what would happen if Rowholt suddenly left under some pretext?

I was saved by the barman, who came to tell us he was closing. A little moment of angst. But one of the men who had drunk with us and who was staying in the hotel said, "Put it on my bill." I was able to leave with my head held high.

In 1961, I arrived in Frankfurt very proud of myself. I was going to be King of the Fair. André Breton confirmed it for me: the *Manifestes* had never been translated into English. Only a Czechoslovakian translation, then the war, then complications with Sagittaire. Now things had been cleared up. I was looking to every country in the world, but especially the United States, where surrealism, I thought, had been accepted, even though it was mostly accepted for its sensationalism (in great part it must be said because of Salvador Dali's publicity stunts). Publishers would be different, I told myself. They would not be able pass up this amazing novelty.

A resounding slap! Up until that moment, I had not truly measured the lack of culture in the American publishing world. I had usually dealt with "publishers" or courteous managers, who often spoke a little French (or a lot) and who were acquainted with my catalog.

I quickly learned about all this, starting with a tour of the principle American publishing houses. I came in as a conqueror and ended with my back bent lower and lower. I quickly understood my mistake.

In general, there were two levels of discourse. At the first level, I was warmly congratulated: "And so you're the one who now owns the publishing rights to the *Manifestes*? Ah, congratulations, Jean-Jacques! I knew André before the war. Magnificent personality. Montparnasse, Crevel, Man Ray, the first early Aragon, Eluard... You're the new torchbearer. Magnificent, magnificent, Jean-Jacques!"

Translate them? The American rights? Don't even think about it. My reading committee would laugh in my face. When were they first published? 1924? Ancient history for America! You don't have anything new? The life of André Breton, with stories about women would do. No, I didn't.

I very quickly abandoned my little speech: great publishers exist to conserve major works. There is no American edition of the *Manifestes*. It's a scandal! What scandal? They really didn't see it. It wasn't important.

So much for the first level of discourse, which was a minority one. For the second level, it was a matter of younger and more numerous publishers, all of them very nice. Not all of them spoke French: Hello! Jean-Jacques! What news?

surrealism? Of course. We're with you. André Breton? Ah! Maybe so. Although, is he still alive? Is he still writing? No, you see, in the States, it has to be new, preferably with pictures. Lots of pictures. Modern. In color, of course.

I already knew that Americans read very little outside of prefabricated best sellers (sometimes very good, however; one mustn't deny them their know-how). They were world-class consumers of printed paper because of the magazine market, with enormous American magazines stuffed with ads.

But otherwise, first novels were less widespread. Many fewer than in France, which had five times more potential readers. The classics? Very few. They often came from England. History, social science? Outside of large popularized works, nothing but small print runs. Of course there were the booksellers in New York, for example. And big used bookstores, superb, in perhaps three or four other big cities

But in the rest of the country? What? Old books? They got thrown away.

Finally, years later, it was an American university which bought the rights to the *Manifestes*, from us, for a thousand copies if I remember rightly. They had a section focused on the study of surrealism and their budget allowed (I'm not exaggerating) the outrageous expense of five hundred dollars, I think.

The Death Of Georges Bataille –
Siné-Massacre

I have talked about the death of René Julliard. July 1962 was to be the month of deaths and births. Georges Bataille died on July 9. Mathias Pauvert, my son, was born on July 15.

The last months for Georges Bataille were painful. His intelligence was fading slowly. Sometimes he showed up at rue de Nesle without calling first and he would ask for me. Even if I was busy, I agreed to see him. He sat down painfully in my office and stayed there, in silence. And then, speaking slowly, with difficulty, he said, "I don't know... I don't know anymore... I left my house... I had something to ask you, I think... Forgive me... I can't remember." I assured him that it was all right, that he had done the right thing by coming to see me. We exchanged a few words. He seemed to think about it, his brow furrowed. He stood up and made a gesture to indicate his impotence. Then he went away, walking with difficulty. It was really pretty awful.

A year before, we had published in the Bibliothèque International d'Érotologie *Les Larmes d' Éros*, his last book, in a way his erotic testament. I was not always in agreement with Lo Duca, the director of the collection, but I must thank him on this particular occasion. He absolutely took charge of the book – a complicated one, in which illustrations and text answer each other – for two years, starting in 1959, doing his very best to interpret the instructions given by Bataille, or guess at them when they weren't precise enough. "About the colored plates, I can't see very clearly the number of pages; I'm confused and very tired." (Bataille, letter of May 22, 1961).

And then Bataille would come back to life again, his ideas took form, he put his finger on a particular mistake that needed correcting: "I'm sorry to have to make such a particular request and I only do it, believe me, because it is absolutely necessary" (same letter). The market for books was taking off again. The book came out in June 1961.

In December 1961, Jérôme Lindon was summoned to the criminal court for the publication of *Le Déserteur*, by Maurienne. René Julliard and Claude Gallimard, among others, showed up to testify in his favor. The era was politically agitated, with the war in Algeria, but the growing prosperity enveloped the period in a protective fog.

A few months later, taking advantage of a (slightly) more stable financial situation, I started *Siné-Massacre*, the violent anti-Gaullist review by Siné of which, as usual, I was the official publisher. I was questioned several times by the police. *Siné-Massacre* was to play an important role in the withdrawal of my civil rights.

It wasn't that I was wildly anti-Gaullist; it just seemed to me that one simply had to balance the public voice which had become, frankly, a majority in favor of the General, despite the communist rancor, the importance of which had diminished a good deal. It was a balance that was equally sought after by de Gaulle himself, regretting greatly, for example, the absence of Mendès-France in the National Assembly, after the elections.

There was also *Les Temps modernes*, which would last much longer. Apparently, Sartre still had a certain readership, but he was so enmeshed in the USSR philosophy that it was only through his plays that he kept his audience.

Siné was much more straightforward, more frank – and much funnier, even when in bad faith. I stayed faithful to Siné for a very long time.

The Period Begins To Suit Me Better

In 1961 I had the strange impression that I had joined my epoch, little by little, and that I was starting to be a bit more at ease. At ease? Not really: there were so many things I didn't agree with. But, in the end, I was there to have my say about such disagreements.

My era was something for which I had been a precursor – more or less consciously. Signs began to appear.

In the month of April, for example, I finally agreed to meet Régine Spengler, a young bookseller from the drugstore on the Champs-Elysées. It was Jean Decamps, a salesman from Sequana, who had talked about her for some time. I was very reticent. The memory of Lucienne B. did not encourage me to want to meet women.

As Régine Spengler, the young bookseller (twenty-six at the time), put it later:

> My heart beating, I headed to the Deux-Magots café where I finally had an appointment – it had taken more than a year of asking a salesman in his publishing house to set up a meeting with Jean-Jacques Pauvert. Having been a bookseller for two years, I was full of admiration for the publications of this publisher who cut through the conformity found so often in the profession. Everything about him spelled out a profound love of books: his choice of texts, of course, but also the typography, the page layout, the quality of paper. The 'banned' side of his work also played a role in my infatuation with him. Sade, Bataille, the Library of Erotology, the *Dictionnaire de Sexologie*, *Histoire d'O*, all set me dreaming. I wondered what this man who had published the books that I loved would be like: an old man, probably, abominably cultivated, short-sighted, a bit sententious, full of humor, black humor obviously: the drawings of Siné, Cheval, Ylipe, Maurice Henry, and many others testified to this. All of this made up the portrait of an intimidating personality, but one I absolutely wanted to know.

(It's hardly reasonable to think that Jean Decamps, during this time, hadn't given the young Régine a more precise description of me, but I must say that a rather curious phenomenon occurred regularly: I would meet more and more people who thought that I was certainly the son of this publisher who had started in 1947. Well, I was called Jean-Jacques, like him! Strange.)

When I pushed open the door of the Deux-Magots, I was on the verge of turning around and walking out. But Jean Decamps came towards me. The café was half empty. I looked around. No one matched to my image of this publisher. I thought: 'He's backed out.' I followed Jean Decamps. He stopped in front of a table where a young, auburn-haired man was sitting, with very short hair, a large moustache and glasses, in a beige suit. Aghast, I glanced at Decamps. 'Let me introduce Jean-Jacques Pauvert,' he said. My astonishment must have been painted on my face. I must have blushed, too, feeling like a fool. I sat across from him, very stiff. How different he was from what I had imagined. So here was the publisher that I admired so much, this man whose courage was so extolled, and who was so young and so shy?

What did we talk about? About books, of course. Then we left to go have lunch. I almost burst out laughing: not only did Jean-Jacques Pauvert look nothing like I expected, he was wearing 'Pataugas' boots, which, for a respectable publisher in 1961, seemed to me completely incongruous!

(I need to correct a little something here. In fact, I had no desire to meet this young bookseller. Rather than shy, I was suspicious. And I had put on my hiking boots expressly to show that any idea of seduction was very far from my mind. A bit childish, when I think about it. And maybe not that convincing.)

The Glory Years

The year 1962 was really the beginning of my glory years. I completely remodeled the little house in Sceaux. Bigger and more comfortable, it would shelter us for another twenty-three years. I needed a garden. We had one. I would plant it, change it, make it bigger.

I then had extra space once or twice a year, in summer or at Christmas, at Le Rayol. I would soon turn in my car for an enormous Studebaker station wagon. Christiane had her own car. We started to be invited everywhere. I was asked for articles (about censorship, mostly). I would soon be the symbol for the era's fight for more freedom – with lots of misunderstandings, as usual.

It was the period when I began to express myself a lot, because I was often invited now for talks or debates. I had opinions, not only about censorship, but also about publishing, the evolution of which did not please me. All of this would soon give me (but let's not get ahead of ourselves), somewhat by chance, a forum for a much larger audience.

The Eternal Palimugre

A nd the Palimugre bookstore was still operating. At the end of the Fifties, we moved to rue Visconti (still in the 6th), in a former woodworking shop. Rue Visconti is a narrow street where you can hardly park a car; it's calm, a little too calm.

Dear rue Visconti, where we had two or three years to create some memories: a César exhibition, a Topor exhibition...

And then suddenly there was an explosion: in the heart of Saint-Germain-des-Prés, the old Loize bookstore, now the new Palimugre, were shining stars in a quarter which had become in just a few years the heart of chic Paris, bursting with activity, with life and creativity.

During the summer of 1962, we were expanding both commercially and also as a family, if I can put it that way, because another child was on the way.

I had known Jean Loize and his black goatee for a long time. He was the kind of educated bookseller (he wrote a long study of Alain-Fournier) who did not separate his knowledge of literature from his profession. A little earlier, in 1960 or 1961, he put together an excellent Jarry exhibition (the "ExpoJarrySition" as it was called in the catalog), with animations, a sound show, rare documents – that attracted all of intellectual Paris.

Un catalogue du Palimugre.

It was Loize's swan song. He retired. He sold me his bookstore on rue Bonaparte – so I could of course turn it into the Palimugre. There were lovely paintings on the walls that he could not take with him. Christiane and I lived there for several days.

It was lucky that we had the new bookstore, first of all because we had more and more potential customers who sent us back the cards which we put in our books, with the an engraving from *Le Voleur* on the back, and because the rue Visconti had become too small.

And then also because Christiane, on the verge of giving birth, Corinne and I had nowhere to stay for the moment. The work on the house in Sceaux had begun. It was very hot. We needed to be closer to the clinic than we were in Sceaux while the work dragged on. We put Corinne up with friends for several days.

So, we found ourselves living in the Loize bookstore, which was closed for remodeling. Luckily, that year I had my enormous American car, which could be used to transport anything we needed.

I seem to remember one day when I was in the midst of moving, around noon, when Régine Spengler came by (someone told her I was on rue Bonaparte). I cut the conversation short. I was very busy. Besides, she irritated me a bit. We had seen each other two or three times. She seemed shy, fearful, not clear on what she wanted. Okay, she had met me. So what then? She attracted me. I didn't really trust her.

And then Mathias was born, in front of my eyes. Christiane very much wanted a boy – I did too, without really knowing it... yes, I was busy.

The Death Of René Julliard –
The Discouragement Of Gaston Gallimard

"Certainly, there are a lot of these books which did not merit being published," said René Julliard in his catalog a few weeks before his death. He died July 1, 1961, probably from a chill following an esophagus operation, a weakness he'd had for a long time.

Awhile before that, he had thought about leaving his publishing house to Christian Bourgois and devoting himself to great undertakings, such as putting together co-publication groups, as Robert Laffont had just done with the *Dictionnaire des Œuvres et des Auteurs* by Laffont-Bompiani (or as I was doing with my ongoing complete Victor Hugo – but by myself – in four volumes).

"What remains from his era?" wrote Jean Prasteau about Julliard. "A few books and a few authors because – and here is the reverse side of this kind of publishing – he whipped up a lot of froth. One thing is sure, he certainly turned publishing mores on their head. The author got down off his pedestal, and came out of the chapel to become a hero of current events."

The lesson was not lost on the industry. From the Fifties on, the Gallimard company also undertook to whip up a lot of froth, as it had done before 1939. *Les Vraies Jeunes Filles*, by Poucette, one of the little characters of Saint-Germain-des-Prés, the gossip of Paris high society collected for *France Soir* by Carmen Teissier, *Le Soulèvement de la jeunesse* by Isidore Isou. The Gallimard catalog of the Fifties and Sixties, aside from Sartre and Simone de Beauvoir (a lot of froth there, too, in fact), Michaux and others, would shine because of such displays of froth.

But there was the matter of the prestigious back catalog from before 1914–1918, which overshadowed the lost years of the war of 1939, when Gallimard multiplied its collection of stories from Marseille or about Jews, etc., as well as weeklies such as *Voilà* and *Détective*, and very discreet vanity publishing. "The only time I was financially secure was when I published

Détective," Gaston told Madeleine Chapsal, one day. "The success was staggering. That was my outstanding commercial success."

One day, when we were getting along, in the Fifties, I think, and we were alone in his office, Gaston Gallimard had his say. In short, he no longer believed very much in his company, in publishing. "It's over," he said. "It's been over for a long time."

To my surprise, he pointed to the beginning of the end of NRF having to do with a single author, whose name he repeated several times, and the title of the work which brought about the end: "*L'Équipage*," he repeated dejectedly. "*L'Équipage* and Kessel." "My authors have been leaving," he said. "Gide went to Plon." (Indeed, Gide's *Dostoïevski* came out with Plon in 1923). "Then Valéry and Claudel left."

It was partly a way of getting out of this kind of impasse that Gaston Gallimard created in 1919 the Librairie Gallimard company. Robert Aaron recounts in his book *Fragments d'une vie* (he was at that time secretary to Gaston Gallimard) a stormy meeting between Jacques Rivière and Gaston Gallimard about a new collection, "*Les chefs-d'œuvre du roman d'aventures*," which published in the Twenties authors such as Gaston Leroux and Gustave Toudouze. Gaston is said to have responded:

> When you bring me a good manuscript but one which, obviously, will be a commercial failure, you are happy when I agree to publish it. But each time, it hurts the company. Do you, yes or no, want the company to continue to survive and to do its duty? I know as well as you do that Gaston Leroux or Toudouze are not worth Valéry, nor Claudel, nor yourself. The unhappy truth is that they sell better, at least for the moment. So, please Jacques, understand me; don't fulminate against what is necessary and inevitable. Let me, without compromising the "*Collection Blanche*" nor the acronym of NRF, nor the review that I am head of – play the whore if need be with publications for which I accept the entire responsibility [Indeed!] and which bear the imprint of 'Librairie Gallimard' and not that of the NRF. Let me do my duty by compromising and sacrificing myself.

Oh! Robert Aaron is being too kind. The *Collection Blanche* and the NRF insignia imprint had already been compromised. But that's how it is in the business. I was to pay later, so to speak, for such knowledge.

Don't forget that the publication of *L'Équipage* (a great success at the time, in fact) went back to 1923, and that Gaston Gallimard, who was already forty-two, was rightly measuring the bitterness that had grown in his publishing house over a period of thirty years, and not only towards Kessel. "Who remembers that during the Twenties, he praised to the skies and imposed on literary circles, on juries and on newspapers books by Henry Deberly – *Prosper et Broudifagne*, *Pancloche*, *Un homme et un autre* – or Lucien Fabre – *Rabevel*, *La Tarramognou*, *Le Rire et les rieurs* – of which absolutely nothing remains a few decades later." (Pierre Assouline, *Gaston Gallimard*, Balland, 1984).

In truth, rather than looking for a lack of taste in Gaston, as in Assouline's criticism of him, it should be asked whether or not the money that *Rabevel* earned, for example, didn't play a role.

And that didn't stop Gaston, a few years later, from sharing a table at the *Boeuf sur le toit* with Joseph Kessel. Publishing has its rules, which, however, are made to be transgressed.

At any rate, I had now been confided in.

I have wandered a bit from the topic. I have – ever so slightly – got ahead of myself. I must say that I was also recovering from some bad luck at the time. I would have preferred to emphasize the success, actually – and the good luck – that I had in the Sixties. Success, in contrast to the "big publishers," who publish a lot and, to tell the truth, sometimes any old thing, was different for me because I was not being led on by the sales figures. I had managed to avoid that trap up until then.

I will soon make this statement openly, and it will scandalize the majority of those in my profession.

All of this before succumbing to "necessity." But that's another story.

The *Gros Chiens* And The New Vice Squad

I passed a little too quickly over the beginning of 1962. In February, we brought out five new books that I think are remarkable, for different reasons: *La Terreur noire*, a book by André Salmon about anarchy; the *Dictionnaire de sexology*, a first of its kind; *Les Plumes du corbeau*, lovely fantastic short stories by Jehanne Jean-Charles; and the first edition of the *Album zutique* introduced by Pascal Pia, as a co-publication with the Cercle du Livre Précieux.

And also *Les Gros Chiens*, some texts by Chaval that I still see as a major work of very personal humor. It is the humor of the writer Chaval, as opposed to that of his drawings. While using the title, which René Julliard had used when first publishing it, I pulled all the drawings that he had insisted on putting in. They were unnecessary for understanding the text, to my mind.

"A constant pleasure," wrote Pascal Pia about *Gros Chiens*. Claude Roy published a fine article in *Libérartion*: he had understood what Chaval the writer had to say that was new:

> It's the funniest book of the year, and reveals an extraordinary
> writer of humor... In a hundred pages, Chaval becomes the true
> living prince of humor: a kingdom for this Chaval.

Very few sales, as usual. A tempered success. Christiane, Castelli and I also had a lot of affection for Chaval. A real friendship. I remember an astounding evening with Chaval at Bernadette Laffont's, when he was in fine shape.

In April, we published the État et empire de la Lune et du Soleil by Cyrano de Bergerac, introduced by Claude Mettra and Jean Suyeux. In May, the *Manifestes du surréalisme*, complete for the first time, and the *Journal secret de Napoléon Bonaparte*, by Lo Duca.

In June, a large volume was published, the *Romans et nouvelles* by Boris Vian, which had been of out of print for a long time (I'll get back to that).

At the same time, I began my publication of the Erckmann-Chatrian, complete with period engravings. A publishing folly.

At the same time, I was still dealing with the vice squad concerning the legal deposition of copies at the B.I.E (Bureau Internationale des Expositions). Times had changed. There was a friendlier feeling. Commissioners and inspectors "understood" better, although they still loathed Losfeld, because of his inconsistent attitudes.

They didn't like Girodias much either, since, thanks to him, they had to deal with Anglo-American diplomacy. Especially the British. In America, things were beginning to move, thanks in part to Barney Rosset, the Grove Press publisher, whom I would meet in Frankfurt. He had just managed to get the Supreme Court to allow *Fanny Hill* to be officially admitted into bookstores in the United States, banned since its publication in the 18th century.

For the first time, the USA was coming close to the freedoms allowed in France. They would soon overtake them. In France, many magistrates worked hard to keep the barriers up. "M. Pauvert thinks he's above the law," one of them said. The police knew which way the wind was blowing. But there was still a lot to do in terms of public officials.

In the end, I was leading a fight which the police came to realize was a good one, especially since I was making no concessions, and publishers like Gallimard were basically fighting the same fight. Once a vice squad commissioner told me, "Publishers like Gallimard and you aren't the same..." The Littré, Maurice Garçon, and *Histoire d'O*, too, about which I had revealed nothing despite urgings from the highest authorities, inspired in them a sort of precautionary respect. In reality, they were used to encountering my tenacious opposition. One day an inspector on the Quai des Orfèvres went so far as to say to me, "You're a friend, aren't you." I gently corrected him. He didn't take it badly.

These little stories were just part of everyday life. But from time to time they could provoke a rush of adrenaline when the stupidity of the administration went too far. But this struggle was just commonplace now. We often entered pleas, with Maurice Garçon, against public authorities, and sometimes we won: for example, when the Minister of Justice accused us of talking about censorship in our catalogs. Well, yes, there was censorship. That had now been recognized officially.

I then headed in another direction. Why, I have no idea. A current was carrying me along. I didn't know towards what.

A Missed Meeting

Let's take Boris Vian for example. I knew Boris Vian's various reputations. At the time of Le Tabou, I could not have been his friend; I didn't go to Le Tabou. I was in another world.

I sometimes read about Boris Vian in *Jazz-Hot*, because of the music. I was a collector – in my little way – of jazz records. During the Occupation I bought them from Christian Viénot, the trombone player for Claude Luter.

Then there was also science fiction, for which Boris was a fervent proponent. He praised Bradbury, who had won me over with his *Martian Chronicles*, and Van Vogt (*The World of Null-A*), which he had translated. For me, Boris Vian was interesting above all because of that. I also admired his efforts on behalf of Korzybski and his general semantics (*"The Map is not the Territory"*), which occupied a certain corner of my mind. I have lost, or rather François Erval, the director of essays at Gallimard (he is now dead) stole from me, the Korzybski volumes, which I had acquired after a great deal of trouble. I am still not sure exactly what the general semantics are about, but I know that it is because of Boris Vian that I knew about it at all.

And then there was his handyman side. Seriously. I don't know how some readers will take this, but the handyman side of Boris Vian was one of his particularities which intrigued and interested me. Having graduated from Centrale, the engineering school, it was said that he'd built by himself a good part of his apartment in La Cité Véron, where he lived with his wife Ursula. I had tried the same sort of thing myself. I think we could have had educational conversations about do-it-yourself work; I'm pretty good with my hands, too.

We ran across each other two or three times, no more. I didn't know about the more important things that Boris Vian had written. Gallimard, publisher of *L'Écume des jours* in 1947, had preferred Jean Grosjean over him for the *Pléiade* prize (a hundred thousand francs at the time) that Gaston had just established. Boris was outraged. He broke his contract with Gallimard, who had already published *Vercoquin et le planckton* in 1946, but had just refused to publish *L'Arrache-Cœur*. I knew he was secretly hurt by this for a long time. *L'Arrache-Cœur* and his other books, published by small, occasional publishers, had been out of print for a long time.

At the end of the Fifties, things between us had grown clearer. Boris had nominated me (or strongly participated in my nomination) as "Exquisite Commander" of the College of Pataphysics, for being the "Publisher of the Count de Sade and Others." Although I only had a mild curiosity about the College of Pataphysics, which was at its highest vogue at the time, I had been flattered, a little childishly so.

And then in 1958, I think, my friend Lucas (where is he today?), from Saint-Germain-des-Prés, who had been pushing me for a long time, introduced me to Boris, on the terrace of a café in Saint-Tropez. We cautiously approached each other, and did not talk about his books.

At the end of 1958, or the beginning of 1959, I received an invitation for one of those parties that Boris Vian organized. I wasn't available that day. I regretted it.

In June 1959, a new invitation arrived at rue de Nesle. There was to be a big party at Boris' place in honor of the "Baron" Mollet (a picturesque character and former secretary for Apollinaire; his memoirs can be got from Gallimard, if they are still in print). I was about to write this date in my notebook, circled so I wouldn't forget it, when I noticed that the party had already taken place, the day before, at the beginning of June, I think; the post office had taken its time delivering the card.

This time I felt it was an injustice on the part of fate. I thought about telephoning. I was very busy at that time, but the idea of calling never left my mind. Several days passed, however.

And then on June 4, 1959, I find out in the newspapers that Boris Vian had suddenly died from a heart attack in the movie theater where he had gone for the showing of the film taken from his book *J'irai cracher sur vos tombes*.

For a long time I had the feeling that I had missed a rendezvous. That's life, I told myself. I tried to forget it and I managed to. I was busy with so many other things.

It was in 1961, I think, when Pierre Kast, Jean Ferry and Noël Arnaud suggested that I reprint Boris' main novels. For the first time, I read *L'Ecume des jours*, *L'Arrache-Coeur*, *L'Herbe rouge* and *Les Lurettes fourrées*, some unpublished short stories. I had an idea which appealed to Kast, Ferry, Noël Arnaud and Ursula Vian, whose acquaintance I then made: I would bring out together the two novels and the short stories in a rather large volume, as a sort of commemorative monument, in three thousand copies, I think.

With their help, I had already published in May a slender volume of new poems by Vian, *Je voudrais pas crever.*

Surprise: during the summer and autumn of 1962, there had been some press reports. A bit too much of, "We really liked him," (that wasn't the point), but there at least was some press which was, on the whole, complimentary.

Second surprise: at the beginning of 1963, the print run of the large volume had sold out. I thought about republishing the separate novels, then I talked to Gallimard, suggesting that they take back *L'Ecume des jours* (it was a period when we were getting along again, or we had copyrights to exchange, I'm not sure). Gallimard accepted, so long as I sold off the back stock for a ridiculously low price. They didn't care at all about *L'Écume des jours*. So I took back almost the whole sadly unsold print run of the book.

I was to bring out my edition of *L'Écume des jours* in 1963. I was now the publisher of the main works by Boris Vian. Another publishing adventure was beginning. I didn't know it yet.

Liquidations

The sudden death of René Julliard plunged his group into chaos. There were conclaves with two or more people, total or partial meetings, coming one after the other. Robert Laffont spontaneously proposed becoming head of the group. There was lively opposition from the heart of the Julliard group. Gisèle d'Assailly, René's widow, as heiress, was against it. I was too, for that matter, but for other reasons. I had meetings and lunches with Gisèle Julliard during which we didn't get along that well. She seemed to me to be (to put it mildly) of rather limited intelligence, incapable of really understanding publishing, and really not someone who should play any role in the future organization. It seemed to me also that she viewed me with mistrust. I probably did not correspond to her idea of a publisher.

In the company, clans formed and broke apart, without me. I had been hurt that the Julliard Company had very quickly put out a little volume in homage to René without asking me to contribute in any way. I saw the volume once it was finished. I would have liked to have written something for it. We had liked each other, it seemed to me.

For the rest, I wasn't really concerned by the negotiations, which didn't seem to affect me directly, because my companies were independent from Julliard. Hachette made me some interesting propositions.

It was Christian Bourgois who convinced me to stay. We were becoming closer and closer.

I don't know in what way Gisèle d'Assailly-Julliard was put into contact with a limited liability general partnership company called the Union Financière de Paris. But however it happened, in February 1963, Gisèle handed over most of the capital in the Les Éditions Julliard to these financiers. In April, Robert Laffont left the group and in July set up Interforum, a distribution company, with Albin Michel and Stock (a subsidiary of Hachette). On September 1, we finally created with Julliard, i.e., the Union Financière de Paris, Pierre Horay and Christian Bourgois, the Société Nouvelle Sequana, of which I was a (small) stockholder.

Thus, I made my entrance into capitalism – for a few years.

In October 1964, the Union Financière de Paris acquired the last Julliard stock. It also controlled Éditions Plon and L'UGE (Union Générale d'Éditions), which published the paperback collection 10/18, which had been newly created.

The Union Financière de Paris was a curious entity. It was composed principally, it seemed to me, of two stockholders: Thierry de Clermont-Tonnerre and Jacques du Clozel. What role did Sacha Guéronik play, who rarely participated in our meetings and seemed to look down on our activities from on high? He was very intelligent and very nice; I ran into Sacha Guéronik and his wife in Le Rayol. We got along well, and were almost friends.

Let's be frank, the financial activities of the UFP seemed, from afar and to my beginner's eyes, fairly amateurish. In publishing, at any rate, its directors often showed themselves to have very little experience, which was normal after all. They relied heavily on Christian Bourgois, and for reason.

Apart from Sacha Guérionik, whom we didn't see much of, I was close to Thierry de Clermont-Tonnerre, who was intelligent, open and had a wonderful sense of humor. I remember the three of us, Thierry, Christian and me, bursting out into crazy laughter for no real reason. Often it was about the way the business was going, which wasn't, perhaps, a particularly good sign.

Ramblings

Looking ahead again, towards 1975, one day, when we were discussing some publishing projects with Chantal Pelletier (a young woman playwright), she proposed an "historical work" about the Sixties. "Basically," she said, "it would be your glory years." For me, it was like yesterday, and I even still felt like I was there. I hadn't yet developed the habit of framing my activities in a sort of continuity, with a beginning, but for which I didn't see the end. I wasn't in the habit of looking back at a road I'd taken (I still don't really do that).

As we talked, I suddenly realized that the Sixties were a sort of existential unity and formed, generally, a whole; and even if they had a beginning and a continuation like all eras, they were essentially over. I remember talking about this with others on rue de Nesle, and recognizing to what point, but sometimes in different ways, everybody was as struck by this as I was.

Our glory years. It was true. Financial wellbeing, the wild consumption which was taking place. The return of cheap credit, and thus the ability to buy equipment, houses, secondary residences, at interest rates sometimes lower than inflation. Vacations were organized in different countries. At the Club Méditerranée, with its bungalows under the coconut palm trees and its pleasant organizers (Paul Morihien left publishing and his bookstore to take a position as director of Club Méd; he sold me all his stock of Genet's *Querelle de Brest*, in the original edition, illustrated by Cocteau). People were leaving for faraway places on planes. Magazines were full of ads and beauty tricks. Then there were the products themselves.

I, too, was carried away by the wave – without realizing it, of course. The future was bright. I reprinted little by little all the titles Breton had published with Le Sagittaire – oh, but without huge print runs. We moved back into Sceaux in October. We set Mathias and Corinne up in a garden tent, in order to oblige the workers to finish the new house faster. I reprinted *Les Mystères de Paris*, by Eugène Sue, with an introduction by Jean-Louis Bory, but without noticing that there was an anniversary which was going to shift the book.

Bizarre was selling better and better. The review was a way for the company to broach unusual, strange, and often hair-raising subjects. It was really the magazine of the moment, along with *Planète* (aimed more at the general public, of course, but even so). The special issues particularly drew attention. We did *Les Fous littéraires* (n° 4), *La Joconde* (11/12), *Dessins inavouables* (13/14), *Les Mystères de Rembrandt* (10), *Les Monstres* (17/18). The cartoonists whom we introduced, starting with Siné, were renewing the genre.

At the beginning of 1960 we had already published two issues, one after the other (13–14): *Dessins inavouables*, and *Supplément aux dessins inavouables*, both with fi ne prefaces by Michel Laclos. They brought together the drawings which had been refused by the still very conventional French press: Folon, Chaval, Gébé, Topor, Cardon, Le Foll, and Siné of course, Maurice Henry, Trez, Mose, André François (I can't name them all). They introduced modern humorist cartoons. It was the beginning of an era.

At the end of 1961, we came out with a sort of special edition that was a big hit, and we came up against a curious literary phenomenon (more than literary, you might say). The title was *A-t-on lu Rimbaud?*, and it was signed, simply, with the initials R.F. He was a teacher from Vichy who didn't want to risk any trouble from his university. Why would there be trouble? It had to do with a sort of thesis, a new interpretation, at least in the beginning, of the famous sonnet *Voyelles*. It began this way:

> During my biographical research, I came to discover that the life of Rimbaud unveiled little by little its mysteries, while his writings kept everything hidden away. Even today, half the poems which make up his complete works remain frankly impenetrable.
>
> It is thus amazing that so many Rimbaud scholars attempt to explain to the reader the profound sense of a work, while its literal sense escapes them. This way of getting at the spirit, without dealing with the letter, seems to lack common sense. It does allow, it's true, for philosophic discussions – which are always easy – and it saves having to understand and to make understood poems as enigmatic as the forty-two *Illuminations*."

There followed a literal interpretation of the sonnet *Voyelles*, and then an analysis of several other texts by Rimbaud.

Although a little too systematic, the study appealed to me by its lack of conformity and its insistence on following the texts literally instead of getting lost in ramblings.

This 21/22 issue of *Bizarre* really set the cat among the intellectual pigeons. With approvals, indignations, etc. A polemic filled the columns of various papers, from *Le Figaro* to *France-Observateur* and attracted prestigious names. I then published issue n° 23 of *Bizarre*, entitled "L'Affaire Rimbaud," which was almost entirely devoted to the debate, giving voice to: Antoine Adam, André Breton, Henri Casals, Jean-Francois Devay, René Etiemble (particularly targeted by the thesis), Robert Kanters, René Lacôte, André Pieyre de Mandiargues, O. Mannoni, Pascal Pia, Robert Poulet, Robert Sabatier, and Anne-Marie de Vilaine. During this time, the author became known: Robert Faurisson, who was indeed a literature teacher from Vichy.

> Aside from a few really bizarre ideas, one discovers in these pages some excellent interpretations... the patient work of Monsieur R.F. is serious and documented (*R. Sabatier*). – Alas! Why did the author of this marvelous and perspicacious thesis believe that the same key would penetrate the secrets of *Illuminations? (Antoine Adam).* – The thesis of Monsieur R.F. is not just as vibrant as can be. It also moves as far away as possible from that jumble of interpretations, some of them left low on the ground, the others high up in the clouds, to which we have been subjected for a long time and which, in their utter irrelevance, aim at elucidating the work of Rimbaud, and extracting the secrets of his life. I roundly applaud Monsieur R.F. for having, through the quality of his mind, rejected from the outset these smooth and facile interpretations... I approve, globally, the thesis of Monsieur R. F. although I cannot always agree with the details of his demonstrations (*André Breton*). – I have read with great interest the very lively essay by Monsieur R.F. about Rimbaud. He has entirely persuaded me, even though this essay is one of the most eccentric and brilliant pieces on this subject I have ever read. One can only applaud the courage with which he has justly treated with disdain so many famous interpretations (*A. Pieyre de Mandiargues*).

I won't go into the details of this polemic. I simply wanted to point out the birth of the intellectual method of "shaking things up," as Breton put it, and the dangers there could be in being attached to any method too closely, either as an author or a reader, or even, perhaps, as a publisher.

Robert Faurisson was happy with the attention he attracted. Having produced fifty pages on Rimbaud, he devoted an entire volume to Gérard de

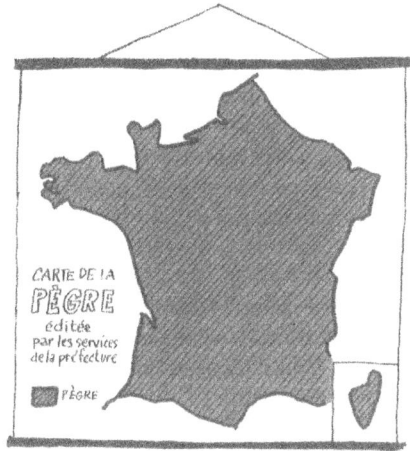

Nerval. He brought it to me. I did find in it the same qualities that were in *A-t-on lu Rimbaud*. But at the same time it had been developed in too much detail, which was the real weakness in his systemization.[14]

But Faurisson came back later. He had found, he said, something much better, but at an historical level this time: the Germans had not exterminated the Jews during the last war. The gas chambers, in particular, had never existed. He didn't want to discuss it and was happy just to leave with me on rue de Nesle a huge file which took me several weeks to plow through.

---

14   Robert Faurisson, La clé des Chimères et autres chimères de Nerval (Paris : J.-J. Pauvert, 1977). – Editor's note.

It was astonishing. Apart from mentioning several figures, which were of course contestable (and which had not yet been precisely established), nothing in his thesis went beyond the hypothetical. Unlike his literary studies, his political thesis rested on nothing concrete, absolutely nothing. In this enormous file, he had done exactly what he reproached other teachers for doing in their literary studies: he had based things on legends and anti-Semitic old-wives' tales. He had absolutely ignored the facts, or interpreted them falsely.

I met with him for a long discussion. This man, whom I imagined to be more intelligent than most of the members of his profession, lost all his critical sense and ceased to apply his method when it came to Jews. To my surprise, he became a simple fanatic.

I am recounting this anecdote because everyone probably knows what happened afterwards: Holocaust Denial and its excesses, to which I will immediately add the attempts to ban this same Denial and their hair-raising legal excesses, which have been condemned, of course, by all the intelligent Jews I know.

I was approached several times by Faurisson. He wanted to convince me. My obstinate refusal meant that I was attacked as a "homosexual Jew" by Faurisson's followers in their periodicals. What class!

Raymond Roussel,
Act One

How did I become Raymond Roussel's publisher? Who put me in contact with the Duke of Elchingen, Roussel's nephew? I cannot remember at all. Maybe someone will tell me before I finish this memoir. It's not, however, of great importance, after all, in relationship to the enormous event which occurred as a result, an event of first-class importance to my mind, but which made almost no waves at all at the time. The usual story.

The Duke of Elchingen was a charming, superficial man who spoke very warmly of his uncle. I think that Roussel loved him very much. The Duke had a room at the Jockey Club. It was there that I went to meet with him. At the Jockey Club, but not in his room.

We hit it off right away. He needed money. I offered him quite a bit, probably too much given the market value of Raymond Roussel, who was priceless in my eyes, but who hardly counted in the business of publishing. He had only had up until then (it barely seems credible) just a few partial propositions. For example, the book club Rencontre, in Switzerland, had reprinted *Locus Solus*, and Gallimard, quite illegally, was on the point of doing so, also.

No one was really interested in the literary estate of Raymond Roussel. But since his work had been notoriously self-published by Alphonse Lemerre, the copyright belonged to Roussel's heirs, and thus to the Duke of Elchingen.

Obviously, the Lemerre publishing house put up a defense. It should be remembered that in 1938 they had refused to let André Breton publish an excerpt from Roussel in the *Anthologie de l'humour noir*, leading to a furious declaration by André Breton: "But certain fragments that we had chosen to reproduce here are missing... fragments which the publishing house of Alphonse Lemerre has arbitrarily stopped us from using..."

But no one at the time realized that the Lemerre publishing house had no rights whatsoever over Roussel's texts, and all that was necessary for Le

Sagittaire, the publisher of *L'Anthologie de l'humour noir*, to do was to look up Roussel's heir, who wasn't that hard to find.

But since then no one had done anything, and so I thought that the rights must have been transferred.

As it turned out, I worked quite easily with the Duke of Elchingen, who openly admitted that his uncle's texts had never meant much to him (he wasn't the only one to think this), but he was very happy that someone should take an interest in them.

I took more than an interest. For a long time, I had been fascinated by Raymond Roussel, and I had collected his books one by one, following up on the *Locus Solus* in my father's library. Inexplicably, absurdly, and despite everything, I was attached to the "greatest mesmerist of modern times" (André Breton).

Then I took Gallimard Publishers, who had just published *Locus Solus*, to court.

Gaston Gallimard himself responded to the question put simply by the judges: "What right did you have to publish *Locus Solus*?" He answered just as simply: "But, Your Honor, I'd thought about it since 1933." That was the year when Raymond Roussel had died in the Grand Hotel des Palmes in Palermo, Sicily.

If the argument wasn't strong enough to convince the courts, it touched me. I had the idea of a co-edition of *Locus Solus*, with Gallimard on one side and Jean-Jacques Pauvert on the other. But I kept the rights to publish *Locus Solus* as my sole property. That year, Gaston and I had a number of issues to untangle: I had bought back *L'Écume des jours* which had gone under, while there was a (partial) Gallimard paperback edition of the *Manifestes* in the collection *Idées*; and I don't remember what else.

Then I returned to the Lemerre Publishing house, which was even simpler. In a curious coincidence, Éditions Alphonse Lemerre had announced that they were going out of business that year. It wasn't because of bankruptcy or a voluntary liquidation. No, it was quite simply the end. The company had been founded in 1864 by Alphonse Lemerre and had lasted for eighty-nine years; and, since the death of Alphonse, it had been run by his two sons, at the same address, 23/33 passage Choiseul. It had published Parnassian poets (self-published or not), then the little Lemerre classics (well printed, sewn or bound). Time for retirement had come. They were closing.

I was met by the two brothers, on the mezzanine floor that was built over the bookstore. They occupied two offices facing each other, like Bouvard and Pécuchet at the end of the novel. There were several boxes scattered about.

Everything went very well. A courteous conversation. As the surrogate inheritor, in sum, of Raymond Roussel, I was entitled to the few copies of his work which remained in stock. I signed a release and took my leave. In August, I published the first three books of my reprint of Raymond Roussel: *Impressions d'Afrique, Comment j'ai écrit certains de mes livres,* and *La Doublure.*

I created a very simple red cover, with shadowed fonts, black with white outlines – simple as always, but to my mind rather beautiful, and very appropriate.

We sent complementary copies to a few writers, among whom I could not forget Jean Cocteau, who had had a privileged relationship with Roussel (I didn't know to what extent). People can say what they like about Cocteau, but I always had a good relationship with him. He had a right to Roussel.

The day after (or thereabouts) we had sent out the copies, I received in the mail one of those cards that we used to put in our books, across which, in Cocteau's handwriting, were traced these words, above his signature:

> Thank you for at last giving us a Raymond Roussel worthy of our love. Your Jean Cocteau.

That same day, the newspapers told of the death of Jean Cocteau the night before. This card is one of the last pieces of mail he ever wrote, if not the last.

Within a year, I had reprinted the entire work of Raymond Roussel, in print runs of five thousand copies, printings which were watched over with great care by Jean Ferry, the author of two masterful studies of Roussel. Then came a special issue of *Bizarre,* introduced by Jean Ferry, with new texts by John Ashbery, François Caradec, and many others, and an interview with the Duke of Elchingen by Jean Chatard and Robert Momeux, plus a horoscope. Then a little later *L'Afrique des impressions,* a fascinating book by Jean Ferry, and later still, the volume of Épaves, uncollected texts, introduced by "Conception et réalité in chez Raymond Roussel," by Michel Leiris.

Needless to say, twenty years later there were still unsold volumes from this first print run. But they remain among the volumes which I am happiest to have placed my mark on.

However, contrary to appearances, my Roussel adventure was not over. We will come back to it much later. It is still following me and fascinating me even now, in 2004. And it will probably not end with me.

The Angelus Mysteries

It was at the end of the same year that I published *Le Mythe tragique de l'Angélus de Millet* by Salvador Dali, after a series of notable events that I will never forget. I have told about them several times in interviews.

In the spring of 1963, I was in a meeting, on rue de Nesle, when Gisèle, my secretary, knocked timidly on the door of my office (we were not to be disturbed) to tell me that someone wanted me on the phone. "A man who says he is Salvador Dalí wants to speak to you personally." I sent her away. She came back: "Listen, I think I recognize his voice; I've heard him on the radio." I left the office, picked up the phone and I, too recognized his voice. It was hard to imitate Dalí: "I have to see you URRRGENTLY. It's very important. I have just found a text that I believed had been lost since 1930. I am at the Meurice, rue de Rivoli. Godspeed, come. You are the only possible publisher. Come AT ONCE, I beg you."

I was there within the hour. Dalí rented an apartment by the year at the Meurice, for when he came to Paris. It was a very large suite, as always full of visitors: journalists, models, salesmen, cinema people. In a corner, silent but taking in everything with sharp eye, was Gala. I'll say more about her later.

Dalí took me aside and explained that he had just found ("MIRRRACULOUSLY") a text from the Thirties which had been the result of an epiphany he'd had while standing in front of Millet's *L'Angélus* in the Louvre: *L'Angélus* had been repainted by Millet. The real subject of the painting was death. The peasant couple were not praying while listening to the Angelus at the end of a day's work, but rather praying over someone who had died. Conclusion, *L'Angélus* should be X-rayed to get to the bottom of the mystery.

I might seem to be joking in presenting Dalí like this, but I have an enormous respect for him, and his painting, of course. I have also read many of his texts. All of them are very interesting. I'm not talking about the first texts from the great Surrealist period, but rather his later texts in which he gives his very sharp and pertinent opinions about the state of modern painting and about Picasso. I accepted his manuscript.

It was a thin bundle of typed pages, with a few corrections made on them using a fine ink pen. The paper had yellowed, and the typing, obviously, dated back several years.

But to X-ray *L'Angélus*, one of the Louvre's two most precious paintings, alongside the Mona Lisa!

Luckily, it so happened that I knew Madame Hours a little, who was one of the museum's principal curators. I called her and arranged a meeting for Dalí and myself. She listened to us, very interested. There could be a way to do it. By chance *L'Angélus*, which usually could not be moved, would in a short while have to undergo some kind of test (I can't remember what it was). Perhaps we could use that opportunity to X-ray it. She couldn't say when, but Dalí should be in Paris when it happened.

Dalí then left Paris for Port-Lligat. In the meantime, I read the manuscript. There was an immediate sense of visionary genius. "In June, 1932, [...] *L'Angélus* by Millet suddenly became for me the most troubling picture in the world, the most enigmatic, the richest in layers of unconsciousness that has ever existed."

What followed was the deepest and most rigorous analysis imaginable made by Dalí about the primordial structure of Millet's painting, including a subtle analysis of peasant life, the clear breakdown of the ulterior motivations of the entomologist Fabre, and a perfect reconstitution of the "atavistic forms of twilight." The incredible richness of the text thrilled me.

I have no intention of summarizing the text here. The legal situation surrounding texts by Dalí has become so complex that it doesn't seem to me that the Pauvert company, which remains in the hands of Hachette, wants to re-issue the book, which today is difficult to find, in spite of a second augmented and more affordable edition done in 1978 (the first edition appeared in November 1963).

I will simply quote the conclusion of Dalí's investigation in *Le Mythe tragique:*

> Some weeks ago, and for the first time, the painting *L'Angélus* was examined by X-ray in the laboratories of the Louvre. When I arrived at the museum, a little late, I found my friend and publisher of this book, M. Pauvert, showing Madame Hours, the laboratory head, a dark mass which appeared on the plate in the exact place that I had indicated. It was a mass with a geometrical form, quite like a sort of parallelepiped, whose perspective ended at the horizon line of *L'Angélus*. [*Meaning, according to Dalí, that it had been a sketch for a child's coffin.*]

Until further explanations come to light, even though mine may appear tentative, there does not seem to be another possibility.

At the end of this event, Gala said to me: "If this result proves your thesis, this will be marvelous; but if the whole book is just a pure construction of the mind, well, it will be sublime!" As for me, I think this is certain: this book is the proof that the human brain, in this case the brain of Salvador Dalí, is capable, thanks to a para-noiac-critical activity (paranoiac: soft; critical: hard) of functioning as a highly artistic, viscous cybernetic machine.

I continued to see Dalí for a long time, either in Paris or in Port-Lligat.

He had a fabulous mind, open to everything that was new and alive. One simple example: he had a date with me one day at his place, in Port-Lligat, at noon precisely. I waited in the village reading a science review that I'd bought the night before in Paris, *La Recherche*, I think. One of the first articles was about a new invention, the hologram. Without going into technical details (which I didn't understand very well, anyway), let's just say it had to do with a crystal prism, which projected into space a three-dimensional image that you could walk around. It was fascinating. Right at noon, I showed up at Dalí's house. There was the ritual embrace, then a non-ritual question. What's up? Still full of the hologram, I said: The hologram! And I started to explain it to him. Dalí interrupted me at once. He knew everything about holograms. He had already met one of the inventors.

I have often regretted the lost relationship between Dalí and Breton.

I must add this: André Breton was very interested in the *L'Angélus* adventure. After I went to see Dalí, he questioned me when I got back and took a great interest in everything I told him. As much as he displayed, at the least occasion, in short, caustic terms, his definitive mistrust of Aragon (amply justified practically every day by the articles Aragon published in the Communist press), he spoke with great respect about Dalí. There was no question that he would ever again see "Avida Dollars." True. But he stayed undeniably loyal, and I insist on this, to a mind possessed by genius.

A Good Use For Higher Science

My catalog of books was growing while remaining, to my mind, very respectable. On looking at the illustrated catalogs of the time (with photographic covers by Roger-Jean Ségalat), Jean Castelli, who was my collaborator for seventeen years from 1956 to 1973, told me that he was struck by the "rigor" they showed. And it's true, up until practically 1965. Or, when you think about it, my first twenty years of publishing.

At the end of 1963 or the beginning of 1964, a new section was added: alchemy, leading to astrology, and esoteric subjects in general. I owe this novelty first of all to personal taste; I also found myself in perfect agreement with André Breton in this area.

I would like to show, in passing, André Breton's constant attachment to the esoteric in general, as well as alchemy and astrology. Few people, in my opinion, are capable of understanding this attachment and in what way it differs from an affirmed or rejected "belief" in such "practices."

Let's look at what André Breton had to say. First of all, about astrology, in an interview with Jean Carteret and Roger Knabe (*Astrologie moderne*, n° 12, Oct., Nov., Dec. 1954).) To the question: "Taking astrology as a lyrical game, would you accept it as an element in the architectural relationship of the universe?" André Breton answered:

> Not being grounded in geometry, even less so in the earlier meaning of the term, I am not qualified to discuss this issue. What I have always appreciated to the highest degree in astrology is not the lyrical game which it provides, but instead the multi-dialectical game that it requires and on which it is founded. Independently from the very subtle means of appreciation that it supplies and the forecasts it authorizes, I see its methods as the most fecund way to make the mind more supple. To untangle a destiny from the relationship of the planets and their mutual interactions in the various signs and houses in relationship to the focal points of their ascendants and

the mid-heaven should suffice to hold in derision and see as childish the habitual modes of synthetic reasoning.

Speaking with Robert Amadou about the conclusion of a letter from him on December 1, 1953 (about a painting by Chirico, *Le Cerveau de l'enfant*, which Breton kept with him almost to the end of his life), André Breton states:

> As you were so right to say: 'Magic is a practice which furnishes a way of acting on an element in the universe by using the analogic correspondences which this element has with every other element in the universe'. For me, with *Le Cerveau de l'enfant*, we are at the heart of this system.

On May 21, 1956, responding to Jean Chevallier and Claude Gallocher's question about "surrealism and tradition," in terms of René Guénon, André Breton began by recalling, that in the beginning, "Surrealism [...] was intended to be the complete liberation of poetry and, through it, of life [...] The principle obstacle which had to be attacked was the rational logic which was all the rage during the twenties." Then he went on:

> It was impossible from that time on not to be struck by the analogies of texture which existed between what we were considering at the time and what had been expressed by occult philosophy. For my part, this was to convince me very quickly that those poets who are, almost without exception in the ascendancy today, are those who were most sensitive to estoteric thought, such as, in France, Hugo, Nerval, Baudelaire, Rimbaud, Lautréamont, Jarry, or Apollinaire. It would thus seem as though the most elevated poetry and what we call "higher science" take parallel roads and give each other mutual support. I even said in *Arcane 17* that, consciously or not, the process of artistic discovery is subservient to the form and the means of progression in transcendental magic.

And Breton added, as if it were necessary, that this process of artistic discovery "remains foreign, most often, to the entirety of its metaphysic (or religious) ambitions."

Without feeling the need to make my positions on the esoteric more explicit, it was instinctively almost fully in agreement with his. This is why he didn't need to convince me to extend my catalog to include two major titles of "higher science": *Les Demeures philosophales* and *Le Mystère des cathédrales*, by

Fulcanelli. And I would soon add a previously unpublished work, *Alchimie* by Eugène Canseliet, who held the rights to the Fulcanelli texts.

The first two titles had been stuck for many years, or rather filtered on speculative prices, by a shop on the Champs-Elysées that belonged to the Librairie des Champs-Elysées. It was child's play for Émile-Jean Bomsel, one of my lawyers, to obtain the rights after a mock legal struggle.

Eugène Canseliet, an alchemist, was a curious little man, wrinkled like an old apple, and with a precious way of speaking. He claimed to have produced the philosopher's stone in 1939. So why hadn't he made the most of it at the time? The war, of course. He then continued with all sorts of hints about the surveillance which he was under from the CIA and the KGB. Intelligence services seemed to be performing an infernal dance around him.

Was he the author of the works signed by Fulcanelli? He denied it. Who was Fulcanelli? He said he had known him well. According to him, Fulcanelli was not one of the French alchemists whose names had been mentioned. He died without revealing anything.

At the beginning of 1964, *Alchimie* was published by me. *Le Mystère des cathedrals* came out at the end of 1965, and *Les Demeures philosophales* a little later.

I took great pains over the design of these three books and I am still happy with the results today. They were well adapted to each book's subject matter.

These three important titles, after a difficult start, found an unexpectedly large clientele, and were reprinted numerous times. They were followed by several others, either texts by Eugène Canseliet, or alchemical classics. Sales increased. Alchemy and the occult were finding their way, mysteriously, obscurely, and rather blindly, one might say.

The success of the *Matin des magiciens* (1960) by Louis Pauwels and Jacques Bergier, and then the review *Planète* (and the publishers of the same name), had undeniably prepared the ground. These publications were violently attacked by André Breton, who was probably right, in principle.

I had read with interest *Le Matin des magiciens*; and twice each quarter, starting in the autumn of 1961, and for a long time afterwards, I bought the new issue of *Planète*. Yes, there was a certain amount of absurd "revelations" in both cases. Even so, I found it healthy to not leave everything in the media to the narrow form of rationalism, which dominated.

The Birth Of "Mass Culture"

Towards the end of 1963, the Cercle de la Librairie published its first catalog of paperbacks. Publishing and bookselling had begun a revolution.

Let's be clear: the French book trade had, since the 19th century, offered numerous collections of cheap books, some cheaper than those of the Sixties paperback. But only people on a very small budget dared to build a collection of such products. The BOOK, the classic format and price, continued to maintain its prestige in middle-class libraries, and poor students moved heaven and earth to procure the books that they needed. They loaned them to each other like real treasures.

After the Sixties, culture descended toward the masses, as they say, all in one go from on high. Not only did several collections offer texts, but university collections made it a point to make knowledge available to the young by putting in their catalogs texts which up until then had been reserved for people with a lot of money, or for libraries (also, photocopying began to be widespread at this period).

I would see a demonstration of this when, with François Caradec and some others, I participated later in a Roussel seminar at the University of Nice. There was a fine performance of *L'Étoile au front* (or *La Poussière de soleils*, I don't remember which anymore). And there were a lot of students at the different sessions of the seminar.

But when I said to the librarians, "You will probably have requests for these Roussel books now; they are all in print," one shook her head and answered that she'd had NO demands for them. What do they read, then? Books ABOUT Roussel, if they're cheap.

This broader cultural circulation seemed to be accompanied by a distancing, or depersonalization of culture.

When Roussel, thanks to Guy Schoeller, the best director that the paperback publishers Le Livre de Poche has ever had, became part of this circulation, it would be because of a mistake. His work *Impressions d'Afrique*, as a paperback, was bought above all in Africa, on the off chance by curious, unwary officials.

It's a shame that we never got any information about how Raymond Roussel's books were received in African libraries, by everyday readers from Dakar or Brazzaville; they seemed to be cut off from any critical commentary (perhaps for the best), and delivered straight from the factory to the black descendants by proxy of our Gallic ancestors.

This was the other side of the coin, as was the sale of the paperback edition of *L'Écume des jours* in the 10/18 collection, in May 1963, thanks to Christian Bourgois, who had asked me to bring out the cheap edition at the same time as my trade version. From that time on, about a hundred thousand copies of *L'Écume des jours* were printed annually, as well as many copies of *L'Arrache-Coeur*, *Herbe rouge*, and the rest.

It was a great posthumous adventure for Boris Vian, although in normal bookstore trade editions our print runs remained only at the level of "critical successes."

This was a curious phenomenon which deserves a more detailed analysis. They say that it is the young who buy Boris Vian. Maybe. If so, then these generations of young people have renewed themselves regularly over the past forty years.

Perhaps this should be related to a recent opinion poll (2003), I can't remember where, which placed "Saint-Germain-des-Prés in the Sixties" as the place the young of today would most like to have lived if they had a choice.

As far as I know, no one has ever really studied this question. Wouldn't it be interesting?

Since I'm digressing, let's talk again about André Breton in regards to Boris Vian, and the absurd legend that states that André "didn't like novels"!

It's enough to remember that Breton wrote a preface for *Melmoth*, and that he greatly admired Lewis' *The Monk*. But some will retort that these novels are from the 18th or first half of the 19th century. So let's add *Le Voleur* from the end of the 19th, and *Le Surmâle* by Jarry, from the beginning of the 20th. And finally, for contemporary 20th century works, we might mention the novels of Julien Gracq, *Le Seuil du jardin*, by André Hardellet, and several titles by André Peiyre de Mandiargues (in particular *Soleil des loups*). Among so many others.

But we were talking about Boris Vian. I used to send all my books to Breton. I've found a letter from him dated July 30, 1963:

> [...] Concerning Boris Vian, *L'Écume des jours*, as opposed to the two works by him that you previously published, is a perfect piece of writing. A masterpiece of playfulness and poetry but, to my great surprise, also of ingenuity, in the most perfectly innocent and fresh sense of the term.

Mac Orlan also called *L'Écume des jours*, "one of the rare few books about youth today."

Metamorphoses

Today I have been looking at the catalog for the 1979 exhibition dedicated to "The Universe of Jean-Jacques Pauvert," by the Maison de la Culture in Rennes. It's strange, probably significant. But of what, exactly?

Chérif Khaznadar (at the time head of the Maison de la culture in Rennes) wrote in his preface:

> The exhibition that we present today was not easy to put together. The team in charge of creating it experienced in its own ways with the joys and vagaries of the X-ray examinations made of the man in question. Multiple facets were discovered which will manifest themselves like watermarks in this exhibition. The personality of Jean-Jacques Pauvert is fascinating because it is both that which his friends recognize and that which his detractors accuse him of. The only incontestable fact is the role he's played in mid-20th century publishing and thought in France.

Yes, but what role precisely? The catalog of the exhibition contains several texts written by people I have known, and still do. Annie Le Brun, for example (who was to play an important role at the time and during the current period):

> We also owe to Jean-Jacques Pauvert the invention of the Sixties, as to others we do the discovery of the aberration of fixed starlights. It is a capital invention, which emerged from the passionate and underground contemplation of a half-century, which was supposed to be spectacular in every way. As a tight-rope walker, magician, explorer, it doesn't matter, Jean-Jacques Pauvert has been able to reveal what was going on behind the scenes. And underneath the folly of certitude, there appears the certainty of folly: Sade, Breton, Bataille, but also Maturin, Darien, Apollinaire, and Wilde, for the first time all together, could give to the French and to others their

eleven thousand reasons to run as far away as possible from everyday life. And if we ever need to find the origin of the delightful disarray we are now in then it was here that the first blow was struck against ideology, and its thinkers in livery...

We'll talk a lot about Annie Le Brun, later. On this occasion her particular enemies are ideologies and thinkers in livery. The discussion is not over yet...

But the invention of the Sixties? Perhaps. Well, let's just say that it had been a long time in the making.

I have once again skipped over some years. I was in the middle of the Sixties.

So let's make a real jump. Between 1959 and 1968, or more precisely between 1962 and 1966, the complete metamorphosis of the Éditions Jean-Jacques Pauvert took place. There were five or six of us, now there are thirty-two, without counting temporary help. We successively bought out our next-door neighbor, the venerable Journal des Communes, then the print shop on the ground floor, Imprimerie de Nesle, which was in great trouble because of the glass roof, which was leaking. We now occupy half of the building.

The buying out of the *Journal des Communes* deserves a little attention. As its title indicates, it was a journal of legal information about the elected officials in the twenty-two thousand *communes* or municipalities in France. It had existed for over a hundred years (a hundred and twenty or thirty), and it still had some subscribers, but fewer and fewer of them. A worthy old man watched over its workings, meaning that he cut out of the *Journal officiel* anything which might relate to the *communes*. An aging secretary helped him out, took care of the subscriptions, and met with the rare visitors. A complete collection of the *Journal*, since 1830, covered the walls, which were in their turn covered with dust.

Earlier, that is when Balzac was just starting out, the space was occupied by a bank. There were still two counters with grills at the entrance. To the side of one of them, a little ivory sign was attached which read, "The First Commissioner's pen." No one had thought it was a good idea to take down the sign or to get rid of the grills. A makeshift electrical installation, with an electric wire running through the room, had fed the few meager light bulbs, since about the time of the 1914–1918 war, I'd guess. Commercial premises like these still existed in the Sixties, even in the 6th *arrondissement*.

The transference of ownership was the simplest thing in the world. The worthy old man wanted to retire, and when the space was sold, he got a little sum of money. We simply bought the title to the space and notified the owner by registered letter. I gave him a choice: either I would continue the publication with very infrequent issues, which would assure us of a legal right to the space, or he could make a new lease for us. Logically, he chose the second option.

For Imprimerie de Nesle, the sale was even more conventional. Since it was in liquidation, the lease and the commercial property had to be sold at a special "candle" auction. The owner didn't seem used to such procedures. I wasn't, either, but the workings of the deal weren't, in the end, very complicated. Before the owner had figured out the essentials, we had taken over the lease for a paltry sum.

During the Sixties, I had rather turned myself into a bit of a traveling salesman for Éditions Jean-Jacques Pauvert. There were some bookstores, which organized exhibitions of our books, plus some universities and various groups which asked me to give talks. I went, motivated by more or less mixed reasons.

Once, I gave a talk/debate at the University of Montpellier, at the invitation of Marc Soriano, a brilliant professor of literature and a writer specialized in fairy tales and children's literature. I introduced him to a text by the Countesse of Ségur, which is to my mind quite astonishing: *La Fortune de Gaspard*. Soriano later wrote a preface for it at my request. It was Soriano who had invited me for the talk and the debate. He was a brilliant partner. Opposite him, I sounded particularly good. I prolonged the debates by giving a ragbag of an interview to the *Journal des Étudiants de Montpellier*. To the question: How do you see the future of books? I remember responding with a futurist prediction: With brains attached one to the other, they would think together…We would get there, but without the book disappearing.

I had been back in Paris for a few days, when a letter arrived for to me at work: "Monsieur, Being one, I think, of 'those people who have a certain common curiosity of spirit'" (an allusion to a passage in my interview), "I'm interested in your publications. Among the older ones, I would like you to send me…"

There followed a long list of volumes, all interesting, with the proposition to pay the bill by check, and the signature: Georges Pompidou, 24 quai de Béthune, Paris.

Although I was rather touched by the apparent spontaneity of this approach, I resolved, after a little reflection, to send M. Pompidou a bill without a single penny discounted. We received the check by return mail. At least, among politicians, there were some who were interested in books. He would go even further in the coming years.

Business

The metamorphosis of Éditions Jean-Jacques Pauvert, which I lived through as something very natural, was, in fact, I see now (not surprisingly), the obligatory consequence of something in the air. That I'd had, or seemed to have had, an influence of some kind on this state of affairs didn't change anything. I was only one element in the general climate.

As an indication of the collective spirit, which was pushing businesses that were relatively close, or which could be from one point of view, towards parallel growth, I might mention our Palimugre Bookstore, for example, or the Cercle du Livre Précieux, and the Planète group.

The Palimugre, as I said, had records, which, thanks to the cards we sent the readers of our books, ended up by including more than a hundred thousand customers, and bookstore activity by mail was growing every day.

The *Planète* review served us as advertising support. Its readers and ours had interests in common. In *Planète* we published large adverts for the Palimugre bookstore. They helped us sell various products, including the publications of the Cercle du Livre Précieux. In a short while, having enlarged our publishing group, we, in turn, started selling what have to be termed "products."

The Cercle du Livre Précieux was the creation of Claude Tchou, a Chinese-Belgian, in 1959. In its catalog of 1962, the Cercle du Livre Précieux (CLP) introduced its program: it offered to "make available to enlightened *amateurs* the masterpieces of literature dedicated to love." But beware: although the notice was addressed to enlightened *amateurs*:

> We do not intend to participate in the business of 'illicit literature' whose vulgarity is equaled only to by its bad presentation and its bad style. We have chosen only major works that a cultivated man must not ignore. This is a gallant effort, certainly, in which libertinism is pushed sometimes just to the limit, but capable of maintaining qualities of good taste, of refined preciousness and of perfect elegance.

In spite of this rather hypocritical, old-school escape clause, the CLP was to reprint and sell through the mail the greater part of classic French erotica, and some foreign ones too, often in attractive editions, augmented by notes and prefaces by specialists, some of whom used pseudonyms. These well-printed volumes, sometimes dressed up in flashy bindings, were characteristic of the period during which "consumer civilization" was spreading itself a bit too thin. But the contribution of the CLP to the enrichment of French libraries in the Sixties is a certainty.

There were to be exchanges about good procedures between CLP, Palimugre and even Éditions Jean-Jacques Pauvert. The CLP was to buy a thousand copies from Éditions JJP of its complete edition of *Monsieur Nicolas*, by Restif de La Bretonne in 1959, in order to dress it up with a flamboyant binding (in my opinion, greatly inferior to the refined cover that Massin had created for me). We were to work together on the co-publication in 1962 of the *Album Zutique* introduced by Pia. Then the CLP published a sumptuously bound edition of the *Dictionnaire de Sexologie* as well as a large edition of *Histoire d'O*, illustrated by Léonor Fini.

Palimugre was certainly the principle client for the CLP, in 1962, for the *Œuvres complètes* of Sade, in the new, so-called "definitive" edition, (definitive was humbug, of course, since the edition was incomplete, lacking the theater works, which I would publish in 1970, and important unpublished works such as the *Voyage d'Italie*, that Fayard would publish in 1995). It was published in octavo volumes, bound in plain cloth and leather, and with an elaborate precautionary notice: it was a "limited" and numbered edition, naturally, which was "reserved exclusively for subscribers" and "not sold on the open market."

These notices were destined above all to bait the reader, because my edition was not to be continued, and Sade would soon be in paperback from Christian Bourgois at 10/18. So what? The works had been edited and was established (controversially, it must be said), by Gilbert Lely, who was also working for me at the time.

I knew Gilbert Lely for many years. He wasn't very tall, but when standing in his heels and with his chin held high, he gave the impression – why not? – of someone from the *Ancien Régime*, both ceremonial and noble. He had hung around with the surrealists. André Breton, who had nicknamed him "the scabrous lamp," told me how he would carry on in public, never hesitating to throw himself down on his knees, in the middle of the street, in front of some unknown woman, to declare his love in flowery terms. Sometimes he was successful, it seems. The color red, in particular, women's red clothes, would throw him immediately into an ecstasy. He had taken up the mantle of Sade from Maurice Heine, whom he had known a little.

His *Vie du Marquis de Sade*, sometimes messy, and cut up arbitrarily, in my opinion, was still, even so, interesting and contributed much that was new. It never had any success from Gallimard, and I reprinted it several times (up until 1982), but it never reached very many readers. It had to be defended against such general indifference, of course. However, I wasn't very satisfied with it. Lely had a way about him, giving the appearance of loyalty, but sneakily denigrating certain aspects of Sade, which seemed to me misplaced. For example, his way of "regretting" in *Les Cent Vingt Journées de Sodome* everything that had to do with fæces, showed that he did not accept Sade as a total unit, as he should... oh well.

As of 1961, I found an audience for his poems, in prose and in verse, with their very personal form of eroticism. *Ma civilization* and *L'Épouse infidèle* were later united in his *Œuvres poétiques*, the pages set by a printer with excellent taste who designed it himself; it would not make us rich, but it fit well in my catalog.

There were even a few business dealings between the CLP and Girodias, which we followed from afar with interest. In a match between Claude Tchou, whose reputation had grown very quickly, and Girodias, who was now the rich owner of the Grande Séverine, a multi-use night club, including two restaurants which were very successful, and a far older and uncontested reputation as a corrupt businessman, who would carry the day?

We didn't have to wait long: Girodias sold the rights to Miller's *Sexus* to CLP (at a high price, I think), for an unabridged and magnificently bound octavo edition. Then the Hoffman agency, representing Miller, showed up in a fury because, naturally, Girodias had sold rights which no longer belonged to him. Tchou had to pay a second time. And, of course, Girodias didn't refund him; he simply opened an account for Tchou in the Grande Séverine restaurant, which meant that we once had a magnificent lunch for twenty people, with Tchou encouraging us to stuff ourselves with enormous quantities of caviar, partridges, oysters and other extremely expensive delicacies, which we washed down with champagne. I forget the end of the story, and whether Claude Tchou ever ate up all of his reimbursement.

For several years, the CLP mysteriously avoided lawsuits, then just as mysteriously they rained down on it. It had to close its doors because of the bans which arbitrarily hit both new books and dangerous reprints of works that had been in bookstores for years, such as Wilhelm Stekel's *Frigidity in Women* (published by Gallimard) or Havelock Ellis' *Psychology of Sex* (published by the Mercure de France).

This all took place in France, in about 1965.

Françoise Giroud (Half) Discovers Censorship

During these same years – a sign of the times? – the wind of freedom began to reach the major periodicals (in a haphazard kind of way, of course). *L'Express,* for instance, finally picked up on the moralizing censorship implied in the phrase "outrage against morality by way of books," following one of this reactionary court's worst excesses, arrived at through the splitting of hairs. At this period, the reactionaries not only wanted to ban books, but to suppress them outright. With Maurice Garçon, we pleaded against the judges who claimed that a banned book should not even be mentioned in a publisher's catalog on the pretext that a book that was forbidden to be advertised should not be mentioned at all. And they wanted to keep newspapers from mentioning banned books, too. *Le Figaro* and *L'Observateur* were dragged into court for having allowed in their columns publicity inserts where certain banned books were advertised. They published articles that condemned the practice and let me speak in wide-ranging interviews.

L'Express had published an article critical of a volume in the *Bibliothèque d'Érotologie* series, *Éros Modern'style,* by Patrick Waldberg, an old friend of Georges Bataille. It was an excellent text, well illustrated, like all the volumes in the collection. So it was that *L'Express* had published a piece about a book that was prohbited from being advertised.

Françoise Giroud, head of the magazine at the time, was officially summoned before the vice squad, where they explained to her that the critical article could be considered advertising and thus was against the law.

Jean-François Revel told me several times that Françoise Giroud, as a member of editorial committees, was always very prudish. She was the one who carefully watched out for libertine tendencies in certain critical articles and intervened to suppress such and such a review, or such and such a suspect sentence, as she had done in 1955 for Jean Paulhan and *Histoire d'O.* At any rate, the least allusion to censorship whatever was banished from any article in the columns of the magazine. The origins of Françoise Giroud (Sephardic Jew converted to

Islam!) and the middle-class respectability which characterized her, hardly meant that she'd be interested in libertinism.

She was, therefore, astonished by the inspectors who blithely denied the objectivity of journalism, claiming instead that it was being used as advertising, while treating her (though, with a certain respect) like a crooked business woman. She took it very badly and, influenced a bit by J. F. Revel, I think, published on February 8, 1965, in *L'Express* a long article which was politically one-sided and not always well-informed, but with the best of intentions:

> Jean-Jacques Pauvert, Parisian publisher, was condemned on January 27 by the 17th criminal court to a fine of six thousand francs. The motive: he had published in his general catalogue the titles of works which had been banned from being advertised... The reasoning is clear: if books disappear from the catalogs and are by consequence not advertised by the publishers, the existence of these books cannot be revealed and thus they will not sell, and thus they will no longer be published.

> Given that they will be taking a risk, bookstores will no longer carry these books. One of them has recently even been made a victim of a police set up: a client came in and asked for a book banned from being advertised. The bookstore clerk got the book out of his stock. The client took the book, placed it casually on the counter and pretended to be interested in some other book. A policeman then came in and saw the forbidden book in plain sight: the bookstore was then charged. [*This is an allusion to François Maspero who had been victimized in his bookstore, La Joie de lire, by this method of entrapment.*]

> As for advertising... Newspapers, themselves being hounded by lawsuits for inserting such and such an agreement, are no longer content to just be vigilant. Legal services for the *Figaro* have cautiously inquired to the Minister of the Interior to check that the *Histoire de l'art* by Élie Faure is not on the list of forbidden books, since the publisher is this 'pornographer', J.-J. Pauvert.

> If Gallimard has not yet been dragged before the courts, it's because the company has prudently abstained from noting in the last supplement to their general catalog such books as *Naked Lunch* by William Burroughs or *Mano l'archange* by Jacques Serguine, both banned from being advertised. And what would you do in M. Gallimard's place? If, out of the three hundred and fifty books that he publishes each year, only one were banned, he would still be obliged to submit,

before publication, his entire production to the Minister of Justice, who might take two or three months, before rendering a verdict.

No company could withstand such a restriction of its production. Censorship? Ah! Such a villainous word. Nobody censors French publications. It is the publishers themselves who, except those who are suicidal, will no longer dare publish a book which might displease in any way. Displease who? Mystery. These bans against advertisement are signed by M. Maurice Grimaud, director general of National Security, delegated to act by the Minister of the Interior. M. Grimaud proposes the ban and signs it in the name of M. Frey. Who suggests it to him? Other bureaucrats who read, when they have the time, and whose prudery can be alarmed by no matter what book."

And so forth. Very good. But why did Francoise Giroud, wanting again to go over the history of repression since the last war, skip so quickly over the scandalous laws issued by the coalition of the MRP, communists, and socialists, mentioning only, without emphasizing, the law of September 16, 1949, before noting coolly:

> The years went by without the law being abused. [*Let me pause to underline the absurdity of this; one must remember, I think, the ban of Miller, the trial of* J'irai cracher sur vos tombes *or Sade, etc. and hundreds of bans against the advertising and posting of banned books.*] But in 1958, nothing was simpler than applying the law to the whole publishing world and adding to it by a decree promulgated by the council of ministers and signed December 23...

Politics decidedly confuses thinking. If the difference between the political Left/Right means anything in the matter of censorship, it's more to the disadvantage of the "Left," which, since the invention of systematic censorship under Robespierre, has made "the outrage against morals by way of books" official. Her analysis is quite simply astonishing. Where was Françoise Giroud thirty years ago, when she was a journalist (though admittedly only as a Parisian gossip columnist) and while the censors were going crazy between 1944 and 1958?

Revel explained to me that, in fact, Françoise Giroud had never been interested in books, and only focused on political fights. I thought as much. I still had a few illusions. But we'll see that she was completely wrong, as were all good minds which were persuaded without having thought things through, that there is an automatic relationship between Left, Right and censorship. In fact, there are moralists – and fanatics – in both camps.

The Art Of Honoring The French Language

Françoise Giroud was a bad journalist on this point, in the sense that she wanted to see a political problem where, in fact, there was a real social one. She was late on getting sucked into a wave that had already been growing for several years. It was the wave in which public opinion, as usual, also identified various physical or moral discomforts. It was the period when *L'Express*, in fact, published a cartoon by Sempé showing a man about 40 who is sentenciously confiding in a friend of the same age: "I was a communist, I did Zen, now I practice eroticism."

As early as 1961, in *Les Mythes de l'amour*, Denis de Rougemont tried to address this evolution:

> Traditional Christians, lay moralists, nationalists and orthodox communists are united in deploring the invasion into our lives of "obsessive" sexuality. Posters in the streets, in offices, in metros and all along the freeways, illustrated magazines and films, detective novels and reviews of naked women, mass newspapers and comic books, popular songs, dances and stripteases: all you have to do is look at the surroundings, night and day, of citizens to verify the omnipresence of this call to sexual desire. This phenomenon has been described a thousand times and still remains astonishing by its suddenness and its enormity. It goes back to the first third of the 20th century, and even if we find parallels with other times its means of expression are without precedent. Commercialized culture, which is its principle vehicle, makes it no doubt irreversible, and totalitarian cultures (or those that are controlled), which are normally puritanical, will soon be overwhelmed. Furthermore, quantitative growth and, even more, qualitative leisure time are also increasing... the opportunities to practice eroticism. It's useless to deplore the problem. It's a matter now of understanding its causes and above all what it means.

And first of all, one must give it its real name. It is eroticism which is at work in occidental societies, from the West to the East, and not sexuality, strictly speaking, which is instinctive and procreative. And the means for eroticism lie in literature, in "movie houses", in the plastic arts (photography), popular music and dance, and even in certain philosophies that are more poetic than systematic: these are the places where the myths of the soul act out most often.

As an ivory tower view by an intellectual far from practical realities, this statement, on the whole, stands up well. *La Dolce Vita* by Fellini (scandalous, especially in Italy) was in 1959. It was also the time when Brigitte Bardot reigned. Marilyn Monroe was playing her most sexual roles, from *Gentlemen Prefer Blondes* (1953), still a bit timid, to *Some Like it Hot* (1959). *Playboy* conquered America, then the rest of the western world. England, in turn, allowed *Lady Chatterley's Lover* into bookstores (end of 1960). The mini-skirt was invented in London in 1964.

France hesitated, running on the spot. The administrative powers, the courts, all thought they could still get around all this by leaning on the old rules which had worked before. They could be summarized as follows:

1. In moral matters, the book, as a noble vehicle of thought, must be particularly monitored.
2. But there are books and there are books, just as there are publishers and publishers, writers and writers.
3. Publishers and writers "worthy of that name" when they commit an "outrage against morality with a book" merit having their motives examined with care, and should be considered respectable, while on the other hand those writers and publishers not worthy of that name should have their motives considered as basely lucrative.
4. All writers and publishers, who are known to be honorable and have been in the profession for a long time, should be, *a priori*, considered "worthy of that name."
5. After about twenty years in the profession, Jean-Jacques Pauvert can be considered to be at least halfway a publisher "worthy of that name." Thus, apart from of his struggle over questions of legal procedure, the books he publishes, other than the *Bibliothèque d'Érotologie*, can be considered with indulgence.

Basically, this is the logic used by Maurice Garçon in the Sade affair. Generally, he didn't discuss the literary and philosophical merits of the Marquis. He said,

"He died in 1814, and now he's a classic." He knew what would impress the judges most, at least on appeal. To be a classic in France is to accede to a sort of Olympian status, which is never to be doubted.

All this led me one day to a public hearing against Eric Losfeld; I wanted to see how it compared with mine. Losfeld said he was sorry and cried (this is on record): he needed money to take care of his family, which is why he published so many clandestine books. However, the book, which was being tried that day, wasn't totally without "literary merit." Couldn't one find a "little lyricism" in it in places?

The answer from the alternate deputy prosecutor judge was acerbic: there were other, more honest ways than pornography to earn a living. As for "lyricism," let's be serious. Couldn't Losfeld do like Jean-Jacques Pauvert who, at least with the texts of Georges Bataille, has been publishing books which "honor French letters" (verbatim).

I couldn't believe my ears. I was sorry that Losfeld hadn't called me as a witness. I would have read to the jury passages from the *Le Mort* and *Histoire de l'oeil*, which I had just delivered in great numbers to the public through the distributor Hachette (I'll tell this story in due time). And, of course, Sade.

Eroticism In The Sixties

Now I see much more clearly that I was, personally, in a particularly strange position. I was well past 30, the head of a publishing house that had become quite big, and on the point of getting out of the category of "common law publishers." At the same time, for some, I still remained someone who symbolized, if not the forbidden, at least everything that was looked down upon by a certain class of people. I was a "young and courageous publisher" for a certain group; elsewhere, pejorative labels stuck to me (and would stick for a long time, in spite of my age), such as "diabolical," or libertine.

Naturally, like a magnet, I attracted a little group who gathered around a particular point at that period: EROTICISM, considered as a recipe for a mysterious and attractive life, or a sort of private cult, like Freemasonry. Through eroticism, one could accede to a privileged existence in which conventional rules had been abolished, and where unknown liberty existed. I was seen, wrongly, as one of the high priests of this new religion. In reality, I was watching the emergence of this new fad with a rather critical eye.

Francois Mauriac seemed to have changed tack. Or at least from an awareness of what was happening around him, he agreed to think about the issue. Perhaps he had been influenced by his grandchildren, who were growing up, one of whom at least, his favorite (Anne Wiazemsky), would soon turn to the cinema. So it was that Mauriac wrote in *Le Figaro littéraire*, on February 9, 1963:

> Is the clinical study of eroticism worse in the eyes of God than the use that we put it to, we novelists? *Histoire d'O* is atrocious, certainly, and for a reader like myself, intolerable; but this horror perhaps might keep us from giving in to a confusion which awoke in me when I was 16 and read this passage in *Cruelle énigme* by Paul Bourget: "'Ah!' she said, pressing her perfumed hand over the eyelids of Hubert, 'how I would like to lie on your breast!'" Who's to say that this isn't worse than the *Histoire d'O*?

Yes, who indeed?

What seems certain to me is that I had reached a point where, if the Bibliothèque international d'Erotologie (B.I.E.) had not existed, I would at long last have been out of the clutches of the Commission du Livre. But there was this collection, which even included an abundance of illustrated volumes. This was the height of horror and danger for good morals!

The B.I.E. was directed (under my close surveillance) by Jean-Marie Lo Duca, a person who was hard to understand, but useful; he was Italian from Sicily (as he never stopped telling you), short, plump and lively. I can say that, during the dozen years that we worked together, Lo Duca hardly ever stopped being, if not a problem, then at least a preoccupation.

He boasted of his former contacts with Paul Valéry, for example. But we didn't see any clear signs of intellectual activity in his work. Though he was very good at looking for illustrations, which were often valuable (but sometimes much less so, alas) for the collection.

On the other hand, he was a very interesting literary case. He was personally responsible mainly for verbose texts which were – to my mind – somewhat confused, but he was also the author of a charmingly clear and mysterious volume, of a surprising literary interest, the *Journal secret de Napoléon Bonaparte*. Already published before we met, the *Journal secret* benefitted from a surprising welcome from minds as diverse as Cocteau and André Breton. Breton, in particular, wrote him a wonderful letter, addressed to me when he had received our publication, stating his astonishment at the quality of this text, although he never ceased from being disappointed by the rest of the Lo Duca's works.

There was a great mystery surrounding this literary production! We waited years – in constant disappointment – for another unexplained miracle.

Régine Spengler Becomes Deforges

I saw Régine Spengler again several times in 1963. We had begun going out together from time to time, then she would get back in her car, a little Fiat 500, and take the Marly-le-Roi road back to her home, where she lived with her husband in a residential building for well-off managers. She attracted me more and more, but left me perplexed. She had sudden enthusiasms, particularly concerning books, about which she was learning fast. I introduced her to Chateaubriand (the *Mémoires*, of course, but also the *Vie de Rancé*) and the little known aspects of his life. For example, Hortense Allart, with whom, at 70, he went to dance halls, had supper, and then afterwards "did what he wanted," as she puts it in her autobiography. There had been outside life, brilliant, but often very conventional, and the private life, which was far more engaging. The other side of the curtain.

M. Spengler appeared to be a banal executive, keen on fashionable parties; at Castel's he had a bottle of whiskey with his name on it. All three of us went out one night. He thought it was a good time talk about "our good little Régine." I cut him short, having no taste for "conversations between men." And I soon forgot about it.

Régine told me about her marriage: she had thrown the dice because it seems she had a number of suitors. In 1963 she bragged about this, though I thought it childish. Later, she confessed: "This wasn't about being brave, it was on the contrary a proof of utter imbecility! My idiocy went that far. Everything I knew about life at that moment came from books and my idea of honor came from some concept of chivalry." (Interview with Madeleine Chapsal). I also think that unconsciously she wanted something to happen in her life and hardly had a choice at the time.

M. Spengler profited from the marriage by having a baby right away, a boy. Where was he?

She also told me about her childhood, her youth. She came from the provinces, from Poitou to be exact, from Montmorillon. When she was 15, something happened to her, which I must talk about because it happened several times – but in different ways.

Régine had a sexual affair with another girl (they were about the same age) and behaved in a provocative way, bathing naked in the Gartempe, for example.

One day, a boy who Chantal, Régine's little sister, had told about the affair, stole her notebook and began reading from it in public, out loud. There was a scandal. The other girl's father protected her from the situation. Régine had to take the brunt of it all by herself. She was thrown out of the religious school, insulted in the street, booed and insulted in diverse ways. The final upshot was that she had to burn the famous notebook, page by page, publicly. She later said:

> Not once during the succeeding days and months following did I encounter the slightest intelligence, indulgence or goodness. Kept at a distance like a criminal and abandoned morally, I had to survive, ... my father, my mother, my uncles, my aunts, my cousins, they all rejected me: not one tried to understand me, nor even talk to me: I was alone, ALONE. (*Le Cahier volé*, Fayard, 1978).

Ten years later, what one was struck by in Régine was above all her double personality, on the one hand her great hunger to know everything: books, life, famous people, sexuality pushed to its limits (which she seemed ignorant of). A crazy desire to LIVE, which gave the impression that her existence at the time hardly satisfied her.

On the other hand, a subtle holding back of her emotions. Her sudden timidity, her submission (spoken, at least), when she was in contact with men. I can remember her telephone conversations with her husband, when her murmuring voice seemed to verge on the most prostrate subordination. From shyness? Fearful, rather. For almost two years, I remember having at my side, when we went out, an almost frightened feminine presence. She always wore, I remember, under her short skirts, what we called at the time pantyhose, whose use seemed difficult to explain, unless it was a protection against rape. She risked nothing from me.

She had strange terrors – and at the same time she desired to be terrorized. She told me, for example, that once she had met the devil in Montmartre, in the shape of a dark man dressed in a sort of long cloak. She still shivered when she thought about it, but with a sort of joy. One day, as we were walking outside Paris, she was gripped by an irrational fear at the edge of the forest of Fontainebleau. She had to return immediately to Paris. She was close to having a breakdown.

I barely approached her. I didn't touch her. I was sure that something was happening to her, but it was up to her, I thought vaguely, to decide.

At the end of 1963, on November 22 exactly, the night we had just learned in the La Grande Séverine about the assassination of Kennedy, the president of the United States, she turned to me and said out loud, very clearly, "You haven't understood yet that I want to make love with you?"

I knew, in fact. But it was better when it was said out loud.

A little while later, she set about leaving her husband, and she visited the provinces, charged with the task of inspecting bookstores for the Éditions Jean-Jacques Pauvert.

Bookstores In The Sixties

An excerpt from the reports made by Régine Spengler, who had taken back, even before her divorce, her maiden name, Régine Deforges, shows better than any commentaries the state of French bookstores in the mid-Sixties.

The profession, in fact, was coming out of a long lethargy. I knew a time, during the Occupation, when certain booksellers showed me with nostalgia certain books on their shelves: "You see these books here, I received them from Michel Lévy, the publisher. Ah! Monsieur, all these young publishers, Gallimard, Grasset, they're only amateurs, nothing more!"

Or else, at the mere mention of *Liaisons dangereuses*: "Monsieur, I do not keep that kind of book in my store."

In the Sixties, in a general manner, a bookstore owner (I'm speaking of new ones), was too often a distrustful man, who would scornfully eye some lost soul in his store and utter this icy phrase: "Were you looking for something, Sir?"

Things were beginning to change, but slowly. A great effort was made to transform these intimidating bookstores, which were closed in on themselves, into brightly lit places, with open windows looking out on the street, which one wanted to enter. In Paris, there was the example of the book department in the Drugstore on the Champs-Elysées, or the Éxpress bookstore, on rue de Berri.

During those years, the inspection reports by Régine Deforges showed some progress: "Generally speaking, the bookstore owners know the name of Jean-Jacques Pauvert." Generally speaking... But there were quite a number of exceptions. For example, the bookstore F***: "When the four clerks were questioned together before the shelf with the latest Roussel publications, they thought for a long time about who the mystery publisher could be. When questioned about Roussel, they continued to stutter until I took the Roussel books off the shelf, to their general surprise." In Lille: "They didn't know Pauvert's publishing house." "I have a few Pauverts, but I don't know." Roubaix: "I don't want to sell 'frivolous' books. His position doesn't allow it. [...] Wants to preserve the 'freshness' of his employees and his young clients."

All the same, my catalog also offered a choice of very conventional books!

There were new publishers, to which the bookstores, for better or worse, had to get used to. I'll name three of them, whom I knew well, and who began modestly around 1963: Balland, Belfond, and Henri Veyrier, whose three careers, which began in great solidarity, quickly grew very different.

All three came out of bookstores. Henri Veryrier did not get into publishing until rather later, towards 1972. But André Balland and Pierre Belfond began their activities around 1963, at first modestly, then getting bigger and bigger. The two of them were so close, they were sometimes confused one for the other, and they had even thought of getting together at the outset under a brand name such as BABEL.

They had very different destinies. Looking ahead: Balland got into literature, had some success, then was bought out, lost his name, started again with novels, then died early. Belfond relied heavily on his wife Franca, a remarkable administrator, and competed with Laffont for the American best-seller market, setting up in a luxurious private building on the boulevard Saint-Germain, and ended by going public in the stock market (a great novelty in the profession) and was then bought out by the group Masson, also losing his name. Comfortably retired from publishing, he is currently reprinting some out-of-print books, on rue Guénégaud, in a gallery where he also organizes art exhibitions.

Henri Veyrier, with whom I soon had a habit of working when it came to my discounted books, started publishing books about the cinema in about 1972. Then, giving up publishing, he became the owner of the biggest second-hand bookstore in France, with its infinite treasures, at the flea market in Saint-Ouen. We still see each other and are good friends. He became a great expert in books. He owns a vast library and has remained continually interested in this inexhaustible universe.

Towards the end of the Sixties, Balland and Belfond, then Veyrier, were to have their places, in different ways, in French publishing.

Libertés

Among the majority of "conventional" texts (with very few exceptions) in my catalog, there was, for example, the collection *Libertés*. Those were the years when the JJP back catalog kept growing daily. The *Libertés* collection posed a financial risk for the company. But how could I resist the creation of this collection, directed by Jean-François Revel?

I'd met Revel at Julliard's, around the time of René's death. He was a young graduate in philosophy and had just come out of a four-year experience in Italy, which had inspired a book, *Pour l'Italie*, which made me die laughing. He painted in it with such delectably cruel irony the great intellectual and sexual misery of that country, which was still subjugated by the twofold dictatorship of the Vatican and the Communist Party.

With his massive face and body, Revel, who was about my age, was a valuable teammate, full of humor and a little choleric. We had a great time together for several years.

He was the head of an excellent *Littératures* collection at Julliard, which was doomed to a rapid end because there had not been enough readers for it.

His idea with *Libertés* was for a collection of the best pamphlets, some of them out-of-print classics, while most would be interesting new publications as yet unavailable in paperback. The idea went right along with the thinking of my company. It won me over.

I naturally came up with an unusual presentation for the collection, which would be quite clearly inexpensive. It would have labels on ordinary paper with fonts used in the posters on the cover, as though cast out onto the book market.

I talked about the project with Pierre Faucheux, who was immediately taken by it and understood that we didn't want some technical innovation but rather something provocatively simple. I think that it was his idea to have brown-paper covers. He also thought of the Didot font for the interior which immediately pleased me. And above all, a major idea, to my mind, was the black spine. Then he created a very fine cover, with poster fonts, as I wanted.

Now, we all three of us had a design which corresponded exactly to our shared idea of the collection. We found a printer in Holland (the paper, the cover and the interior, as the black spine caused a problem in France): the Bosch printing house, managed by the excellent Van den Bergh van Emstede. All we needed were the texts.

Well, we had a wide choice. To start with, Revel and I were immediately in agreement. The first pamphlet should be *Pourquoi des philosophes?* by Revel himself, an excellent cat let loose among the university pigeons, which had caused a sensation at the time of its publication with Julliard in 1957, but which partly missed its public because there had been no paperback edition, which would have spread the text among students.

Number 2 would be Voltaire's *Lettres anglaises*. Number 3, the Écrits philosophiques of Diderot (with an enormous mistake on the back wrapper: Écrits PHILOSOPHES, which very few people caught). Number 4, *Napoléon le petit*, by Victor Hugo. Number 5, *L'Église et la République*, by Anatole France. Number 6, *Les Provinciales*. And finally, number 7, *Flagrant délit* by André Breton, which we must talk about a bit.

When Maurice Nadeau heard that I was going to reprint *Flagrant délit*, and what's more as a paperback, he telephoned me to beg me not to. "I'm your friend; you can't do that to me." It was as though we were going to hang him. I'd like to make something clear: Maurice Nadeau was incredibly naïve. I don't at all think that he was a "little pervert," as Breton called him (after having been insulted by him in *Combat*). Nadeau had behaved very badly, but without weighing the consequences, at the moment of the *Chasse spirituelle* affair. And so he acted totally without thinking, by calling me twenty-five years later: how could he think that I would censor Breton in his own favor? Taken for a ride by Pascal Pia (as we found out later) at the time of *La Chasse spirituelle*, and without a word of regret (he dismissed the affair in three lying words in his memoir), it seemed perfectly natural to him, in spite of our relationship – which was all right, not more – that I should stop an excellent text from being printed simply because he wanted it stopped. That was Nadeau: traipsing through the publishing world without much trouble, while ignoring most of the realities of the business.

I remember running into him one day, maybe twenty-five years ago, on the Place du Luxembourg, looking very troubled; he had just discovered that bookstores could return books sent to them on consignment. "It's incredible," he said. "How can that be? They haven't really bought them?" At the same time he remained a fairly good director of collections, in his own haphazard way. But we never broke off our friendship, as will be seen.

Libertés – was it a success? Yes and no. There were titles with print runs of a hundred thousand copies, like Siné's *Dessins politiques*. Some sold very, very well, like *Pourquoi des philosophes?*, Panizza's *Le Concile d'amour*, or the drawings by Sempé (*En avant*, 1967). There were also sales of a thousand or fifteen hundred copies, such as *Gobineau polémiste* or *Constant polémiste*.

There were booksellers who disliked the design: stiff black fonts on a cover made of brown paper? What a horror! And the newsprint! And the black spine!

There was also a big error in fabrication: in our enthusiasm (if this could have been fixed, I might have fixed it), we didn't notice that our format, which was so refined, was slightly bigger than the presentation displays of other paperbacks, where we knew we would be obliged to place ours, given the fact that we could not afford our own. So the *Libertés* collection didn't fit in anywhere. Later, much later, when there were enough titles, we had our own cases made to hold our books.

The *Libertés* collection still makes an impression, and it has reached its fifty-ninth issue, not counting the volumes in the new *Libertés* collection, which I'll talk about later.

The History Of Art By Élie Faure

The year 1964 saw the culmination of our "major" publications, and thus our costly investments, when the three volumes of *Œuvres complètes* by Élie Faure came out, two of which were luxuriously illustrated: the *Histoire de l'art* and *L'Esprit des formes*.

The minute there was a difficult undertaking, or something out of the ordinary, people applied to us. And I must say that it usually wasn't in vain, if the project was worth it. This was the case with Élie Faure.

The last edition of *Histoire de l'art* by Élie Faure dated back to the Thirties, the period when the technique of reproduction was still in its infancy. And what's more, many of the illustrations that Élie Faure wanted in his book could not be printed in the previous editions, because of a lack of means.

I don't really remember how I made the acquaintance of Élie Faure's two sons, who were already grown up. We came from the same region, Élie Faure having been born in Sainte-Foy la-Grande, where my paternal family had had its Protestant origins for centuries. At the middle school of Guyenne, in Sainte-Foy, there were the Pauverts, the Faures, and the Reclus, together. In Paris, I knew Jean-Louis Faure as a member of my generation.

The *Histoire de l'art* by Élie Faure was a monument, and his sons for some time had wanted to revive it. But there were two obstacles: the size of the project – it was a monstrous undertaking – and the opposition of André Malraux, who had become the all powerful Minister of Culture under De Gaulle.

Under Malraux, volumes on art (often an obscure hotch-potch, barely legible, full of phrases that were more brilliant than sound) came pretty much straight out of the best parts of Élie Faure, who was famous world over, but rather unknown in France, as usual. Just read the passionate preface that Henry Miller wrote for my edition or, more particularly, the introduction by Jean-François Revel which was printed on the flyleaf, and ended thus:

> …The *Histoire de l'art* and *L'Esprit des formes* by Élie Faure will never be surpassed, although they might be temporarily and unjustly

forgotten, because they correspond, not to a momentary quest or fashionable need, but because they relate to the two or three fundamental attitudes that humans can adopt, and will always alternate, in order to understand art and its history.

The new edition of *Histoire de l'art* followed by *L'Esprit des formes* was to be made up of two quarto volumes of more than five hundred pages each, with numerous illustrations in both black and white and full color, followed by another volume, also illustrated, of twelve hundred pages comprising all the rest of Élie Faure's work (*Les Constructeurs, Découverte de l'Archipel*, etc.) and also some unpublished correspondence.

The undertaking was only possible with the help of two of our biggest printers in Switzerland: Héliographia, a rotogravure printer for the text and the black and white illustrations; and the Imprimeries Réunies from Lausanne, for the color illustrations, including inserts. Again they allowed us a long-term credit (three years! And after a simple phone call!). And they set to work with astounding zeal. For the color illustrations, they were chosen by a collaborator brought in by the Faure brothers, Yves Lévy (who also did the typesetting), and a specialist chosen by the Imprimeries Réunies who went around the world, verifying the colors of the photos in the museums. To make a success of such an undertaking today would be almost impossible.

The *Histoire de L'Art* came out in September 1964. It was almost at that same moment, as I said, that *L'Express* discovered French censorship. The *Nouvelle Vague* was everywhere. The book business was in high gear.

Sadly, business for the Société Nouvelle Sequana wasn't going so well. The Union Financière de Paris had crashed, as they say in the stock market language, because of a real estate affair, and it was soon going out of business. Bankruptcy? I never really knew. As it was a simple partnership, this meant that its members, in principle, were personally liable for their assets in case of insolvency. But Thierry de Clermont-Tonnerre was the financial inspector! Some deal was doubtlessly worked out. A short while later, Thierry was named administrator of the Eiffel Tower. Quite a brilliant turnaround. I sent him a telegram of congratulations which touched him, as he told me awhile later when we met quite by chance.

Those Years

In those years, I was approaching 40. Riding along with the economic situation, Éditions Jean-Jacques Pauvert didn't stop growing, even if it was a little anarchic, a little at the mercy of chance. There were thirty-three people working there, including the Palimugre bookstore, not counting various interns. I bought up the Éditions de la Jeune Parque, by taking over *Le Crapouillot* (I'll talk about this). The Palimugre was doing well.

The literary department was taken care of by a team, including Jean Castelli. Jean-Pierre Castenau had joined us. We were now receiving lots of manuscripts. We had external readers who undertook the first severe selection. Then, all four of us talked about what remained.

But the incontestable head of this activity was Christiane. I have never met in this profession a mind better suited for this kind of incessant delving, for which she was by far the most gifted. Not only could she place writing in a context of publishing in general, but she put herself immediately in the mind of the writer and guessed perfectly what he had wanted to achieve and what he'd actually done. In a way, both the exterior and interior. At 80 years old today, she has lost none of these qualities.

Supported by this formidable reading machine, I read – sometimes not completely – only the last manuscripts that remained. My publishing business, in fact, had entered a period which only half satisfied me.

It was now a routine, the "profession of publisher," hundreds of manuscripts, propositions for projects, which were almost as numerous: "I could write a book, given everything I've lived through... Of course I'd need some help... Do you know a writer who...". In the wastebasket.

These were the failures in the day-to-day running. I remember an enormous manuscript, which was sent to us from the provinces, I won't say from where, even though it was forty years ago. It came as registered mail with a letter included, very pretentious handwriting, very smug. He was the head of an important medical clinic, about 75, very rich (he underlined this), with a high position in his town, a big family, sons, daughters, sons-in-law, grandchildren.

This person had sent us a work which was, let's say, the sum of an exemplary existence, destined to be given to his children and grandchildren, but via them, to all of France. "A book of wisdom," a bedside book, a guide for one's whole life.

Only a very few days later, the reader handed in his report: a hatchet job. Enormous boastfulness, profound stupidity from a great family head and dignitary (he had been copiously decorated, of course), all spiced up with supporting quotations. The comments were succinct in a casual style (the reader was a good writer and one of our friends): "The poor bugger! – Oh, right! – And your sister, too! – Such a marvelous numbskull! – Sad idiot!" The analysis concluded in a few words: Send it back with an insulting letter.

The manuscript, with the report, was handed around the company for everyone's delight. I leafed through it. It was appalling. After a suitable time, it was sent back (exceptionally – usually the authors came to pick up their manuscripts at our office) with a banal letter: This text isn't right for us, but that's only our opinion; it might please other publishers.

Unluckily, the reader's report had stayed with the manuscript, without the secretary seeing it.

Three weeks later, in my personal mail, a letter of twelve or fifteen pages showed up. First of all the insults (I was astounded at the vocabulary used by this distinguished gentleman). Then: why couldn't you see what his book would bring to the public in general? Then, several pages repeating the central theme: it's my life's work... It's impossible not to feel this... How could you not feel it? Right? It was a sort of desperate supplication in the last pages.

We had sensed perfectly well what was going on. It was just a failed work about a failed life. It was clear enough, in certain passages, that most of his children and grandchildren had distanced themselves from this insufferable old man (and some very early). Those who remained were hoping for an inheritance – he almost stated this outright. In fact, he was going to die alone.

I spent several days composing a letter to him (whatever became of it?). Without reneging on any of the motives for refusal, which I took full responsibility for, I explained that a publishing house is a big machine which has certain obligatory cogs. We had certainly made a mistake in sending the report back with the manuscript; but in fact, the manuscript had been read by several people, including myself, and if one overlooked the exaggerated phrases, our judgments were perfectly coherent. I gave him one or two suggestions, the substance of which was: don't write for others, but for yourself. What did he have to say exactly? Perhaps if he gave up looking at what he thought his image was and, instead, looked inside himself, he might interest the reader…

Maybe this made him think, maybe not. I never heard another word from him. Once again, I realized the responsibility that a publisher has to take when overly brutal opinions are expressed.

And, then, I was more and more absorbed by material demands. Relationships with the bank, in particular, took more and more of my time.

And on top of everything else, I was leading what they call a double life.

A Double Life

The avowal in the form of a remark addressed to me by Régine Spengler, duly registered by me, didn't take long to find a response. To be frank, I felt the same way she did. I was irresistibly drawn to her.

What happened, happened during one of my numerous trips to Geneva.

It was quite natural. I was in an ascendant period. I had too much energy then, which was crying to break out of the growing constraints that were attempting to crush me.

I was, one could say, happy; my material preoccupations were in the background, like an inevitable flow of water. I had a daughter, and a son who had just made his first steps in the summer of 1963, and a wife with whom all was well... And isn't it just at these moments, when all is going well, that the self aspires to just a little bit more? I didn't ask myself the question, though; that came afterwards.

It seems to me, now that I am nearly eighty, that the weakness in my nature is this: the blind desire for a universe which is full – and sometimes beyond – the limits of what is reasonable. But that's just it, I was not being reasonable.

It seemed very simple to me, already living a full life, to enter a parallel life, one with Régine Spengler Deforges. Of course, I thought this would be completely secret.

If there were still some obscure aspects to the personality of Régine (and they remained obscure for a long time, to tell the truth), in other ways, we had the impression that we had always known each other, with this one caveat: I had the impression of sometimes standing in front of a magnificent piece of virgin land, which harbored some surprises. This was an added attraction.

We had used the formal *vous* form for the past two years and we continued using it instinctively. We still use it today, when we see each other. Maybe there are explanations for this, which I am not aware of, that neither of us are aware of.

Books were a big part of our relationship. When we were in the provinces, we visited bookstores together. I copied out for her the complete text of Valéry's *La Soirée avec Monsieur Teste*, into one of the notebooks of blank paper specially made for me by Louis Rossi. It was a text that had obsessed me since I was 15.

She said it was the most beautiful present that anyone had ever given her.

JJP and Régine Deforges

1965 – A Scandal In The Publishing World

In 1965, I had everything I needed to make me happy, in spite of the complications with my personal life – which are inherent to a certain kind of life style. But an uneasy feeling never left me. No, I was not particularly happy with the profession that I was part of, nor with the place that I now occupied in it. Without thinking a lot about it, I found it too ostentatious, too wrapped up in the idea of "success," which in fact was rather far away from my deepest desires. I was aware that I was sliding down a hill and it would be difficult to stop. Where was it heading?

I didn't want to think about it too much.

The great dance of publishing houses being bought, taken over and regrouped, in expected or unexpected ways, had begun. I had escaped being bought out by Plon and by Julliard and the Presses de la Cité. I was now being distributed by Hachette – with all the inconvenience that a change of distributors entails – but I was still independent.

The worst was that, as always, there was a general murmur of lamentations rising up in the profession: Oh my God, books are difficult to sell. What are we going to do? Too many books are being published, too many. The public is getting tired of books. There's a crisis. And everybody blamed his neighbor for this state of affairs.

At the beginning of the month of August 1965, on a beautiful summer day on Boulevard Saint-Germain, while strolling, I ran into Pierre Démeron, the editor-in-chief of *Nouveau Candide*, a weekly magazine launched at great expense by Hachette. I got along well with Pierre Démeron. How's it going? Well. And then he said no, nothing was happening in the literary world, what was I going to publish in the next issues?

Something got into me: obviously, you can't *really* talk about what is happening in publishing. But what was happening? he asked, worried. All the publishers are sick. And I opened up with some of my problems. Interested, he listened to me: could you say those things openly? – You wouldn't print them, would you? – Of course not! We then made a date for lunch the next day. He brought a tape recorder.

I had a lot of things to say. I let go, then we parted. I left the next day for Le Rayol, where I was thinking of buying a piece of property, after fifteen years of renting.

I went back towards the send of the month. On Monday, August 30, I was having lunch with Régine Deforges at Petits Pavés (*Le Nouveau Candide* was coming out on Thursdays). There were a few people from the business here and there. One of them said to me, "Oh, my! What's this you're saying about us in *Le Nouveau Candide*!" I went out and bought it, and we started to read. Robert Laffont came in, all smiles: "What are you reading so passionately?" I handed him the magazine. I have rarely seen anyone fall apart so quickly. He kept saying: "Oh, no. That's not good. Oh! How could you?" He gave me back the magazine and left, his face white.

How can you briefly summarize a scandal, which shook the whole of Paris for a long time? The details came out in four issues over four successive weeks in *Le Nouveau Candide*, right at the beginning of the school year, just before Frankfurt. I'll quote some of the text, because after all it's part of my story. And besides, isn't it still topical, almost forty years later?

A headline announced the story, an article in two full pages, under the rubric LETTERS, and the title: "On the eve of the literary new year, an interview with Jean-Jacques Pauvert: A PUBLISHING SICKNESS [...] *They say that books aren't selling anymore, but they publish any old thing* [...] Pierre Démeron went off to ask Jean-Jacques Pauvert about all this, one of the few publishers started at the Liberation and who has survived, while being also one of the youngest and most dynamic. What should one think about this famous 'crisis in publishing?' No doubt his response will surprise and scandalize many of our colleagues. They can answer him in their turn; our columns are open to them."

The following week, two more pages of the interview (because those publishers who were incriminated said they didn't believe that these were articles by JJP, even though the magazine made clear that it was an interview and that's why there had been some paraphrasing).

I'll summarize, if it's possible. The interview started with the buy-out of Plon and Julliard by the Presses de la Cité. My conversation began with these on-going takeovers:

> From a strictly literary point of view, the takeover by Presses de la Cité of Plon and Julliard – or the opposite, one doesn't really know – is of absolutely no interest. Why is it important, I wonder, to know

that now it is the Presses de la Cité or Juilliard who is publishing the *Les Mémoires* de Soraya [...]?

A literary event, to my mind, would be if Nielsen bought out Corti. [...] If Corti died, it would leave an empty place.

A publishing house is a publisher, a Grasset, a Julliard, a Gaston Gallimard [...] Note that I have the highest esteem for Sven Nielsen in the area of popular publishing and administration. You have to have books for people who aren't interested in literature...

Publishers have made extraordinary statements... "Yes, it's awful, if you haven't noticed; there's a crisis in publishing. Ninety-eight percent of the French only buy a book from time to time. People don't use the public libraries, the cultural level of the French is deplorable, etc."

And me, I say that the general publishing situation has never been better. Do any of you know any other profession where there is less competition, so few newcomers ready to overturn the market and break everything up?

[...] I'll give you some statistics. These are from the *Journal officiel* for the bookstores.

In 1960, there were fourteen publishing houses who had a turn-over of more than ten million new francs (a billion old francs), with nineteen more, from five to ten million, twenty-nine from two to five million, and fifty from one to two million.

In 1963, what do you have? Eleven houses who have a turnover of more than twenty million (two billion), twelve, more than ten million, twenty-one, from five to ten million, forty-one, from two to five million.

At the same period, the turnover for French publishing went from six hundred and sixty million to nine hundred and ninety-nine million francs [...] And these people who are moaning have doubled or tripled their turnover in three years, very quietly, without having to worry about competition from a newcomer! ...

"No, it isn't publishing that is sick, it's the publishers. Never have books sold so well, and they would sell twice as well if we didn't publish just any old thing.

For a literary publisher, meaning someone who is out to discover manuscripts, new authors, there are two policies.

The first, that of Gallimard, Julliard and Le Seuil, is: "The more books we publish the more chance we have to win the Goncourt, the Femina or to find a new Françoise Sagan." A publisher who applies this policy and who publishes in a year, say, twenty novels can hardly, the following year, publish fewer books, whether or not it's a good or bad year, or his turnover will suffer. Crazily, he is forced to practice a policy of volume, of probabilities. Of course, from time to time, in the mass of books, there will be a Le Clézio. But if a publisher, who, out of fifty mediocre novels, gives me one Le Clézio, I will congratulate him; I will not admire him. He made his bet, that's all one can say. A publisher who only publishes three novels and two are good, him I admire. Les Éditions de Minuit, this year, for example, published almost no novels.

****

I next gave some examples of good books, which hadn't sold sell well: Roussel, and Klossowski's *Le Bain de Diane*. "People who read Proust in 1920, who read Bataille ten years ago, when no one knew them, who today are discovering Klossowski, are in a tiny minority." Then:

> Ask booksellers, they will tell you the same thing I do: they are drowning. The job of the bookseller is becoming impossible. It consists of undoing packages. [...] A bookseller receives an average of three hundred new books a month! The publishing crisis is there, on the book shelves, and for the bookseller who says: "Who am I going to sell all these books to? What am I going to do with all these insipid books, who don't interest anyone?"
>
> If there is a crisis, it's not a crisis in sales, it's a crisis in overproduction. If we published two times fewer books, we would sell two times more.

This was followed by a conversation about the profound lack of culture in the United States, and then by praise for the level of French culture. The following week, there was a new headline and two more full pages: "THOSE WHO MISTAKE PUBLISHING FOR A FACTORY." And then there was a banner quote from me: "For me, the profession of publisher is a profession which consists of saying no."

I won't quote everything; that would be tedious. Here and there in this book there are passages, which explain my points of view about the profession, at different periods. They have changed very little.

Nor am I going to go on about reactions from other publishers. I said it was a scandal. They asked Robert Laffont to answer me in the third issue of the *Le Nouveau Candide*. Nothing new: "Fifty-eight percent of the French population never read a book. [...] If the general turnover is growing, its growth index is inferior to the combination of the price index and the growth of the population. It is grossly inferior to the index of everything concerned with leisure: television, travel, cars, as well as household articles, refrigerators, etc." Yes, etc. One can see that the preoccupations of Robert Laffont are the most basic, even if they aren't wrong in principle. Besides, he more or less says that Jean-Jacques Pauvert only publishes erotic novels. (False, as anyone who has read this book will know. But Robert doesn't read what I publish. This isn't a reproach: to each person his own particular area. Generally, publishers read very little.) How many young authors does one have to keep alive? (As Talleyrand said, I don't see the necessity.)

Yes, etc. I also had a telephone call, very solemn and imbecilic, from M. Arthaud, president of the Publisher's Union, a grocer with no culture who I thumbed my nose at. And from Claude Gallimard, no less a dolt, who came up with grotesque comparisons. In 1880, he said, more or less, they published as many titles as they do today. Right. What he didn't say was that three quarters of these titles were technical: religious, agricultural, military, with print runs of two hundred or a maximum of five hundred copies, and they didn't crowd the bookstores. They were solid sales, printed on demand, one or two copies at a time, through fifty or a hundred specialized booksellers.

Jérôme Lindon subtly enriched my statements in a short note to *Le Nouveau Candide*. Paul Angoulvent, president and director general of University the Presses Universitaires, wrote in the same vein:

> The controversy about French publishing which has developed in your columns since the interview with M. Jean-Jacques Pauvert seems to me like a new chapter, and a very savory one, in the Human Comedy.
>
> Because, in the end, if M. Pauvert is rarely considered an altar boy, what he says about our profession is not heretical either. Besides some manifest inexactitudes, due perhaps to a too impatient pen [*don't forget that this had been taped and that Pierre Démeron had then corrected some mistakes he had made in the same edition*], JJP mentions a lot of things that all soothsayers know, and which can't be read without laughing.
>
> Some people, obviously, want these truths to remain hidden; I prefer that they be talked about, because the fearful reverence which surrounds taboos does not fit well with a profession like ours." ...

The Hachette group pretended to believe that I was attacking the big houses.

"Big publishers have always created big publishing houses," said their spokesman. I took this to mean: "Enormous publishers are always made from enormous companies." But that isn't at all what I said. Big houses, okay, they have to exist. I remember a recent round-table discussion, I don't know on which radio station, with Christian Bourgois, at the time with Presses de la Cité, Paul Flamand from Le Seuil, and some other notable publishers. Everybody spoke passionately about this privileged profession: Oh, to go home at night with an unknown manuscript which has come by mail! You start to read, indifferent at first, then excitedly. Oh, the fever of discovery!

Then Paul Flamand intervened calmly: I don't see anyone around this table, he said, no other publisher except Jean-Jacques Pauvert, who can seriously use such language. I'm at the head of a big publishing house, with Maurice Bardet; I don't pretend to read everything that Le Seuil publishes. We receive thousands of manuscripts. I have collaborators, directors of collections whom I have confidence in. If they are wrong, I take the blame. It's up to me to carefully choose my team. He was right; I applauded him. It was a period when, every day, little companies were being created which had all the faults of the big ones, aggravated by a lack of funds. My idea of the profession wasn't at all to classify the merits of companies according to their size.

The discussion no longer interested me. Only one remark made me stop and think. Raymond Queneau, I don't know where (maybe in *Les Lettres françaises*?), observed that if publishers didn't publish just any old thing, some new little things couldn't be published.

It was true, basically. But even so, did so many forests have to be cut down for so little?

On The Skids

At the same time that the last issues of *Le Nouveau Candide* were being
dedicated to my "scandal," there appeared in *Vogue* a long article (five
pages) by Jean-François Revel entitled PAUVERT, DAREDEVIL PUBLISHER,
which, although it had been prepared well in advance, could have been a
good and appropriate response to the screams of certain professionals about
my statements. I have other reasons for quoting from it at length:

> One hears: "Pauvert's success is because of erotica. Take away
> the obscene books, and he would disappear." I suppose that, among
> those who buy Érotisme au cinema, by Lo Duca, there are some who
> are more interested in the erotic than in the cinema. This doesn't
> prevent the fact that these works are a gold mine of documentation
> about the cinema; do you have to ban sculpture on the pretext that
> those who are sexually obsessed color in the pudenda of the nymphs
> in the park? I suppose that *La Métaphysique du strip-tease* is, in part, a
> joyous hoax, as are the "Pauvert Classics," which imitate the Larousse
> classics, and *Vercingentorixe*, the unforgettable tragedy/pun by the
> Marquis de Bièvre (1770) – which at the same time incarnates the
> entire collection of "Pauvert Classics." Who could complain, or deplore
> the existence of the *Dictionnaire des farces, attrapes et mystifications*, at
> a time when there aren't a lot of publishers who like to joke?
>
> No, the secret of Pauvert is not in the erotica, nor in philology, nor
> in typography, although he excels in all three disciplines. Why not
> see the secret of his success in his taste for the critical publications of
> venerable authors: Saint-Simon, Benjamin Constant, the correspon-
> dence of Madame de Staël? Or in the art of resuscitating unjustly for-
> gotten texts: *Le Concile d'amour, Monsieur Nicolas, Le Voleur, Melmoth,
> L'Unique et sa propriété*? Or in his intuition for certain very rare authors:
> Bataille, Klossowski, Mandiargues, *Histoire d'O*? Or his attachment to

great popular literature: Erckmann-Chatrian, Eugène Sue? Or in his preferences for the Dadaïsts or Surrealists: the republication of the *Manifestes Dada,* of the *Manifestes du surréalisme,* which had been out of print for a long time, as well as *L'Anthologie de l'humour noir* for which he is now preparing a new augmented edition? Or even in his secret flair for cartoonists, such as Siné, Bose, Topor, Chaval, Ylipe and so many others? Or that he so diligently searched through the public domain to establish a complete critical edition of Charles Cros, or that he paid a high price for the rights to the works of Raymond Roussel, or that he has put on the market the lost work of Fulcanelli, the *Mystère des cathedrals,* or that he has published special editions of *Bizarre* about Tarzan, the Countesse of Ségur or Joyce Mansour, and the *Max Ernst* by Patrick Waldberg, the *Gustave Moreau* by Ragnar Von Holten or *L'Anti-France,* by the readers of the *Le Canard enchaîné,* whether or not he lost money or made some, whether the press paid attention to him or ignored him, his only secret, and main strength is that, when he publishes a book, he always knows why. Never is his judgment influenced by fashions, and never did he change his mind about a book and find it bad, after a failure, when he had first thought it good while hoping for a success.

I'm afraid I didn't thank Jean-François enough for his excellent article. Why? I was being excessively sensitive. I was jarred by two or three inexact-itudes. For example, when Revel explained that the failure of my Littré had been provoked by a miscalculation about the profit margin (where did he get this false information?); or when he said that Julliard had financed my Erckmann-Chatrian (!?). I was also jarred when he wrote: "He had just bought *Le Crapouillot.* He's flying with his own wings again, but there are times when his wings have a hard time opening; the minute they feel light, he gives them one or two million francs more to carry."

In this, sadly, Jean-François was right.

Rebirth And Fall Of *Le Crapouillot*

In the spring of 1965, I succeeded Jean Galtier-Boissière as the head of *Le Crapouillot*. At the same time, I was negotiating with Hachette for ownership of the Editions de la Jeune Parque, at the end of the rue des Saints-Pères.

The adventure of *Le Crapouillot* was, in the end, the first notable failure in a professional career that was marked for several years by an ascendant sign.

Jean Galtier-Boissière, whom I had known since 1953, was noticeably declining. One could say of him what he said on the last page of his *Journal pendant la grande pagaïe* to Curnonsky, another great connoisseur of fine foods and refined drinks, at that time in a senior center in Meulan: "J'ai trop d'urée et trop duré."[15]

A very tall man at 6'1" (an amazing height in 1914/18 at the beginning of the *Le Crapouillot*), weighing more than 220 pounds, with a big mouth in every sense of the term, Galtier-Boissière paid the price of many years of excellent meals and heavy drinking. His arteries finally won, and he took it badly. Even more so, when they had to amputate a leg. He was now retired in Barbizon with his wife Charlotte, and he more or less called me for help. Who would take over the *Le Crapouillot*? The only people he knew anymore were sharks, he told me, who weren't worthy of continuing his magazine (which was no longer very interesting, it must be admitted). They wanted the title, he said, but he wasn't dead yet.

Luckily – or unluckily – I was greatly tempted. I had always appreciated the nonconformity and the art of *Le Crapouillot* in attacking those more powerful than itself, and it gave me pleasure to think of possessing a forum of its ilk. The Don Quixote spirit of its venerable director had led to resounding trials against newspapers or against famous, supposedly untouchable personalities: I saw myself in this rôle.

Looking ahead, his last months were tragic: in his bed or on his sofa in Barbizon, he lay around, doing nothing, constantly swearing, cursing poor Charlotte whom he insulted horribly, until a coughing spell would interrupt him.

---

15 "I've too much urea and lasted too long." – Translator.

At that time, helped by his lawyer M. Delattre, he signed over the title of *Le Crapouillot* to me. He died in January 1965.[16]

Since Hachette had sold me La Jeune Parque, distributed by Galtier-Boissière, I became the owner of a small stock of old issues. I also inherited material from Jean Santoni, the only employee at the publishing company. Christiane became the director of La Jeune Parque at rue des Saints-Pères, along with Santoni, a nice Corsican, with all the faults and qualities that brings with it.

I sinned through too much optimism in hoping to continue *Le Crapouillot*. I had even thought I would change its direction a bit, giving it a more present-day touch. But I lacked an editing team. I had inherited what remained of the team from Galtier-Boissière, and they were still putting out the magazine, now a little worn and a little repetitive.

As for *Le Canard enchaîné*, there was a deal of bitterness, because several of its collaborators had also been eying the magazine. They gave Galtier-Boissière's death three columns by Yvan Audouard, but they didn't mention me even once. I wrote a furious letter to the director (I was too angry, as I remember), Robert Treno, whom I didn't get along with too badly. But as I said before, I was relatively quick to anger in the Sixties.

Paris-Press printed a spiteful little notice by Edgar Schneider, announcing the death of Galtier-Boissière and adding, "To say that he chose his successor would be going too far."

Nonetheless, I chose someone from the *Canard* to be the editor-in chief: Roland Bacri, who strongly insisted that he could do the job. He had no idea what an editor-in-chief was, and in spite of his good will, was hardly ever a help.

Looking ahead again, to finish with this sad story, we published a good issue with *Hommage au Crapouillot* in May 1965, and then *14 juillet inconnu*. We published another issue right in line with the magazine's history, *Les Pompes funèbres*, edited by Philippe Grumbach, a good journalist, recently fired from *L'Express* by Françoise Giroud. Then that was it: I handed on the magazine. There was one last issue, edited by Philippe Grumbach, on *"Les Suédois."*

Crushed underfoot by the business end of things, unhappy with myself, I signed over the ownership of the magazine to Grumbach before the end of 1966. He made a good start with some issues about the Ben Barka affair, whose kidnapping had scandalized the media. I no longer remember how the magazine ended before falling into the hands of *Minute*. A total failure.

---

16   Jean Galtier-Boissière actually died January 22, 1966. – Edtor's note.

The Arrival Of Albertine

L et's return to September 1965. I had a catalog of around two hundred and fifty titles, of which thirty were novels. In order to arrive at this number it was necessary to include in this list *Les Liaisons dangereuses*, *Melmoth* (I had just published the first complete translation), *L'Ève future* or *Les Pléiades* by Gobineau, and other "novelistic" titles by Sade, or *Les Mystères de Paris*.

In fact, in twenty years of publishing, I had published exactly seven contemporary novels: *Le Bleu du ciel* by Bataille, *Le Souffleur* by Klossowki, *Aux pieds d'Omphale* by Henri Raynal, *Histoire d'O*, and *L'Écume des jours*, *L'Arrache-Coeur* and *L'Herbe rouge* by Boris Vian, all three rescued from the void. Very few. Robert Laffont was right when he reproached me in *Le Nouveau Candide* for "not feeding enough writers." It's just that I didn't find around me enough writers worthy of being fed.

As I would say in the next catalog, in a year when one has only mediocre manuscripts, "It's better to publish a good collection of crossword puzzles than a bad novel."

But then, in fact, in September, for the literary New Year, as they say, I was going to publish immediately after the *Nouveau Candide* scandal two novels by an unknown author, a young woman of 28, Albertine Sarrazin. These were the only two contemporary novels I published in 1965, almost, one might think, to give weight to what I had already said.

In the spring, Albertine was introduced to me by Jean-Pierre Castelnau. A journalist from Montpellier, René Bastide, a friend of Jean-Pierre, knew Albertine, who had been an adopted child, an escapee from correction houses, rejected by her adoptive parents (the author of *Albertine Sarrazin, une vie*, Jacques Layani, later argued that her real father had been a career soldier), and an ex-prostitute. Albertine lived in Montpellier with a small-time thug called Julien. She said she had always dreamed of writing and had just finished two manuscripts, *L'Astragale* and *La Cavale*, which Bastide very much liked and which he sent to Jean-Pierre Castelnau. Jean-Pierre read them and sent them to the office of Castelli, saying: I think I've found a writer this time.

A woman, Madame Gogois-Miquel, a devoted protector of Albertine, had on her own sent the manuscripts to Gallimard, and to Simone de Beauvoir, who was interested in them, but wanted cuts made before giving them to the reading committee. Nevertheless, she wrote to Madame Gogois-Miquel, "It's the first time a woman has written about her prison experiences. She has, at times, a magnificent tone, an attractive style."

Albertine told me later that Gallimard sent her a questionnaire: Who are you? Do you know any journalists who can help you launch your books (perhaps)? On April 27, I sent her a catalog and a letter saying that I was taking her two manuscripts. On May 1, Jean-Pierre Castenau took her a contract for *L'Astragale* along with a check.

I didn't meet Albertine right away. She was not allowed to go to Paris, so she joined me in Lyon, during one of my sales trips (often along with Régine). Apparently, I said to Jacques Layani several years later:

> She was very appealing. The first time I met her, she was a little distrustful [*I think, above all, she was intimidated*], but we 'got on' very fast. She was rather pretty, but lame, which she hid very well. She was bright and immediately became part of the house.

In September, the public discovered Albertine Sarrazin. I'd had an idea of which there are but few examples in the profession. (Was it a good idea? It was at least a sensation.) *L'Astragale* and *La Cavale* were published at the same time, both books being sent out together in large quantities by our press departments – I even had them sent to several publishers.

As is well known, the success was great and the reviews excellent, give or take an exception or two from misogynistic puritans. It wasn't that the texts were smoldering. But in 1965, the fact that a woman writer had at one time been a prostitute didn't go down well with certain readers. A journalist from *Méridional* even wrote a violent article against Albertine. I responded to it in the same tone. The head of the magazine stepped in to mediate. I think Albertine was struck by this, because awhile later she told a journalist from a small provincial paper, "The only man who has astounded me is Jean-Jacques Pauvert."

The two of us had a few dinners in Paris (I managed to have her ban on going to in Paris lifted, not without some trouble, through Maurice Garçon). Everybody wanted to know her. I went along as a guard dog; if anyone tried to treat her like a freak, I reacted with vigor. She felt protected, and she needed protection.

We were photographed by Lucien Clergue, who had dazzling memories of her. He told Jacques Layani later:

> She was radiant. I have never known a woman writer who was more attractive. She had a beautiful look, very impressive, it penetrated you. She had an incredible presence.

Régine, who was terribly jealous, was extremely preoccupied, it seems, with Albertine (she has admitted this in interviews). I think there was some literary jealousy, too (Régine was no longer writing, aside from her private journal). She confided to someone later, according to her biography, that she never wanted to ask me the nature of our relationship, being afraid of knowing too much.

I would have answered that it was only slightly ambiguous. I think Albertine was attracted to me, and I found her pleasant, but with a certain hardness. At the same time, she was eager to know a lot of people, and she didn't know many. We kissed when saying hello and good-bye. Julien told me that she felt I was kissing her more and more on the lips. I think she was wrong, or else she was the one...

> In fact, her books did not correspond exactly to the main line of books that Pauvert had set for his publishing company," wrote Jacques Layani in his biography [*I hadn't set any particular sort of line at all; if there were any lines, they drew themselves*]. He only agreed to publish them on the insistence of Castelnau, Castelli, and Christiane Pauvert, his wife. At the beginning of the affair, he was not totally favorable about the publication.

The first time I read these lines, I was shocked. And then, thinking about it, this statement was not unfair. He made it because of impressions he'd gotten from conversations with others in the company. The quality of Albertine Sarrazin's books was good. She was among the leading group of living novelists; but I was aiming higher, in some vague way. *Melmoth, L'Ève future, Le Voleur* or for contemporary texts. *Histoire d'O* or even *L'Écume des jours*, were the books that I wanted, fundamentally, in the way of "novels." *L'Astragale* and *La Cavale* were just good texts, and Albertine was a gifted writer. However, with her, the writing had slipped down a notch.

I think up to this point I'd had a rather personal – or even megalomaniac – idea of publishing. I was even aware of it. But the adventure had to keep going. With thirty or forty people to feed, I had to try something else, given the position I was in. So why not literary publishing with new authors, why not like Julliard, Grasset, Gallimard, or Le Seuil? So I took a step on that slippery slope.

Besides, I was being pushed by circumstances. Éditions JJP had pretty much run out of exceptional discoveries. Wasn't it time to move to more ordinary books? Living writers had noticed that we existed. More and more manuscripts were coming in. One had to live in one's time. (Wasn't that a necessity? I didn't have time to ask myself questions.)

Again, I have to point out something about Albertine, one of those signs of the times to which I am sensitive. It was between the publication of *L'Astragale* and *La Cavale* and that of *La Traversière*, her last novel, at the beginning of the literary year, 1966, that I realized (someone no doubt told me) that Albertine had already been part of my published works. In 1955, in the first issue of *Surréalisme, même*, Jacques Sennelier reported:

> Two young women had, for six weeks in 1953, an exceptional adventure which was more than a banal petty crime. In order to get food, Anne-Marie B. (16) and Emilienne G. (17) [*only the initials of their last names are used in order to protect the families*] attacked and wounded the owner of a confectionary shop, on December 15. [*This is the petty crime that Claude Autant-Lara used to make the very good film En cas de Malheur, with Jean Gabin and Brigitte Bardot*]. As it turned out, the cash register was empty, so the only things the two took for booty was a suit and a coat. They were arrested three days later during a hold-up in Pigalle. After spending two years in prison in Fresnes, were tried and sentenced on November 22, by the court for minors, in a closed session. Anne-Marie and Émilienne were respectively condemned to seven and five years.
>
> Anne-Marie and Émilienne had met in a 'reform school,' the Bon Pasteur institute in Marseille, on November 21, 1952. They formed an intimate relationship and then decided to escape and live together. Anne-Marie said to her friend: "Come what may, we will meet on November 1, 1953, at midnight, in front of the obelisk on Place de la Concorde." Anne-Marie, who was preparing to take her high-school exams, managed to escape the night after her oral, and arrived in Paris on July 13, 1953. Since she had to eat, she quickly found the

neighborhood where she could win earn a living and lose her life. [...] At the time and date they had planned, Émilienne was arrived at the foot of the obelisk...

The major interest of this text by Sennelier – a bit grandiloquent at times – are the passages from the notebooks and letters of Albertine. Layani, having found her *"Carnet vert"* published this extract:

I only read Eastern Philosophy and surrealism, and these make my head spin... Salvador Dalí, André Breton, humor, marvelous things and the dreams in your doctrines seduce me.

To tell the truth, when Sennelier, whose memory seemed to be good, wrote to her at the time when *L'Astragale* and *La Cavale* came out, Albertine wrote to Julien about this letter: "As for surrealism, I will respond... one of these days. These cadavers don't do a thing for me."

Would these old loves (she also had a great passion for Rimbaud in 1953) have come back to her later? No one knows. But we can speculate about it all. Let's give her the benefit of the doubt. In 1965–1966, Albertine was focused on material success. This was understandable. A few years more, and she might have returned to her initial spontaneity, and her instinctive intelligence, now unconstrained by everyday life, could have begun again to develop. So many things might have happened.

Novels

As if on purpose, 1966 saw Editions JJP Publishing turn more and more towards novels. Or rather, the press accorded more importance to novels, which still weren't numerous. In February, we published *Schrummschrumm* by Fernand Combet, who, I still maintain, was one of the most interesting and promising contemporary novelists – a promise not kept, I will say immediately, with great regret. And, at the beginning of July, the first book by Georges Bataille to have any success: *Ma mère*, a posthumous novel which aroused great interest in the press and sold more than thirty thousand copies. In November, *La Traversière*, Albertine Sarrazin's last novel, came out.

I have not included (and why not, in the end) the second edition by JJP of *Le Seuil du jardin*, André Hardellet's best novel, which I had bought back from Julliard in 1966. When it appeared in 1958, André Breton, mesmerized, addressed a letter to André Hardellet, which is often reproduced, but which I here quote (if only to provide further proof of the interest that Breton had in novels "which were worth the effort"):

> Nothing so necessary, so convincing, so exalted, nor so perfect has come my way in a long time. [...] In this novel you deal to great effect with the only subject which remotely interests me.

(At the same time, and I remember because these are texts which are not read much, I brought out *Les Chasseurs*, poems in prose by Hardellet, which Julien Gracq was to comment on in 1987 concerning *Les Chasseurs* and the second part – which appeared in 1973 – *Les Chasseurs deux*):

> [...] I have read over and over again *Les Chasseurs* and *Les Chasseurs deux*, two little volumes by André Hardellet which are always to hand on my book shelves. [...] For me, these two volumes, with their fascinating Pauvert illustrations, are as necessary to me as the edition

of Jules Verne illustrated by Hetzel. They represent a complete poetic world, a coherency, an absolute autonomy, and one which I consider it a privilege to have had access to from the moment when they were published, and which has made me aware rather in the same way that *Sylvie* by Nerval did (though there is no writer more Parisian than Hardellet, precisely in the Nerval manner), of the circulation of sustaining images and of the enchanted movement that continually links Paris poetically to the Île-de-France."

Diverse Points Of View

A nd Régine Deforges? I would not like – for a number of reasons the reader will understand, I hope – to be the only one to talk about her here. So I've borrowed a few pages from the biographer who Régine chose in 1995. Marc-Émile Baronheid, an admirable Belgian poet, it seems, mixes up the dates a little, but I'm going to choose extracts which are correct. After all, Baronheid had hardly been born in the Sixties, had he?

> One cannot be all at the same time in Strasbourg, Lorient, Toulouse and Paris. But she had now had some richer experiences [...] What about Paris? Not yet. It will be Limoges, a city that Régine knows. [...] In 1965, she set up there with Pauvert, the Gartempe Bookstore, place de la République. Bernadette (her mother) has just moved there with Franck (her son) and Éric-Jean, the son of Chantal (her sister). This whole little world moved into 12, avenue du Midi, while Régine decided to go off and create a department of erotic books. All of a sudden the city was bristling, divided between the partisans of tolerance and the hard and fast defenders of morality.

> **

> Camille Deforges was born in Paris, on October 25, 1966. It was a joyful birth, the result of a strong sexual and loving relationship. Her father did not officially recognize her as his daughter at this time; it wasn't quite the thing to do at that period. "I couldn't say that I didn't know it," Régine recalls.

> Despite multiple obstacles inherent to the situation, and even though the two of them were independent, they remained solidly attached to each other, and far from having come to the end of their relationship. Is this why very few of Régine's women friends liked her lover? Probably. They reproached him for his egotism – his way of fleeing his responsibility [*No, not all of them!*] and his refusal to make

official his relationship with the mother of his daughter (he was already a father) – and his insufferable machismo, which might come as a surprise, in the sense that like all seducers, he showed a feline/feminine side. He was of that race of womanizers, Casanova more than Don Juan, for whom seduction and conquest are second nature. [*Seduction, yes. Conquest was much less habitual for me.*] Régine, confiding in Madeleine Chapsal, who was preparing a book of conversations about jealousy, said: "I don't want to experience again the jealousy that I experienced for years, no, not that! I don't want that; I've taken too much! Years of tortures, that's enough!"

And contrary to Dorian Gray, Pauvert comes out superbly victorious after his struggle with time. [*I hadn't noticed that I was struggling with time: it's possible, though.*] Indefatigable and present everywhere, he was a leader in gallantry and literary activities. Through him, Régine met some great contemporary personalities. (M.-E Baronheid, *Régine Deforges, l'Inconduite*, Stock, 1995).

This is one way of seeing things. Yes, we made a couple that was very bonded. Very solidly bound together. I will add nonetheless (and this is not said to diminish anything) that it must not be forgotten, that I was a part of two bonded couples.

But let's rectify this image a bit. First of all, the business in Limoges: I don't know how (maybe through Régine) I had been informed that the family of the treasurer-general was looking for an associate to create a new bookstore in a downtown area that was being built in the middle of Limoges. This was a chance for Régine to settle down. I then took on the bookstore 50/50 with my associates in Limoges, and we opened very fast. Of course, almost immediately there were frictions between Régine, who created a section of erotic books, and the associates. Then, rather than imposing herself, Régine backed down a bit.

It's true that there were a number of associates, united, powerful in their provinces, and more present than I was, as I only came down from time to time.

The birth of Camille was another thing. I already had two children (not counting my first daughter, who was 20 in 1965, and who married early a man I didn't like much). I had a daughter of 10 and a son who was just 4. One more child? The result of a loving and strong sexual relationship? Yes. But it still seemed impossible to me.

The one most responsible person (at least, the one who helped make the decision...) was René Diatkine, the psychiatrist I've already mentioned.

I saw him regularly, for what some thought were bizarre reasons. I made an appointment, sat across from him, and I asked him important questions, as they came up, about my private life, but also about my business: did I seem ready for such and such an association? Or was I going to continue in such and such a direction? He didn't always have an opinion, but just seeing him made me feel good. René Diatkine, older than me by quite a bit, was remarkably intelligent; I trusted him.

Now, Régine was posing a problem. She wanted a child. It was both natural and grotesque. Both feelings were strong in me. She promised that the child would be her affair alone (this wasn't at all certain), that the child would never learn the truth, and that I would be simply the godfather, if that's what I wanted.

I saw Diatkine several times; I always thought the situation was impossible, but I also felt at the same time that if I said no to Régine I would take away the fullness of our relationship. Was I ready for that?

Diatkine felt up to the task. He had me explain in detail not only my relationship with Régine, which he knew about (because I think she had already come to see him without telling me), but also her reasons, and the conditions for the project.

His conclusion was the following: yes, it was a logical conclusion to the important adventure that I was living. There would be difficulties, but all the people involved (my wife, Régine, myself) were "quality" people (it's the word he used). "You will be her godfather, and it's better to have a good godfather than a bad father."

So I went in the direction that he indicated, not without cold sweats, as they sometimes say. Another side of me found it all normal.

I don't want to go into the details here, but I need to say that, even so, I still got along perfectly well with my wife, who knew almost nothing (at least, nothing that wasn't transparent) of the existence of Régine. I had essentially two parallel lives which I avoided thinking about. My coming and going from one to the other seemed like travels between two totally separate universes in my mind (which obviously made certain of my close friends laugh).

On Régine's behalf, Baronheid wrote:

> He never promised me anything, Régine insisted, except his nights alone. [*Oh, not always.*] "It was hard, very hard." Her sunny nature did not go well with the underground world that Pauvert liked. Nights that were too solitary, she filled with presences of which she remembers nothing, neither their first names, nor perfume, nor faces.

I knew about this. Sometimes, she left her unbound diary open (on purpose?) which she wrote in from time to time. I didn't hesitate to read it. We hardly ever talked about it. But when we did, we joked about the contents.

As for me, I don't believe, as the poet claims, that I am a "great seducer," or a "womanizer." I like to please, that's certain, so I am often pleasing. In society, I occupied a place which would have made things easy for me, if I had so desired. But for the moment, things stopped there. I now had two women, fine. They were both very different, good. And they are both charming, yes, both desirable. I wanted them both. That's all. My family of three people had a great priority in my life. Régine does too. Is it impossible? Perhaps. Nonetheless, it was to last.

The jealousy that Régine grumbled about was aimed in reality at only one person, or rather at three people. And she knew it.

Rather Far From My Line Of Books

The publication, with everything that involves – choice of fonts, page formatting with illustrations, long discussions with Hardellet – of a small volume like *Les Chasseurs* would have been enough to make me very happy. It's just that I was now head of an ENTERPRISE, and always looking for financial balance. The slippery slope had sucked me down it.

In January 1966, Girodias published his last book with the Olympia Press imprint, and he left for the United States. I wouldn't see him again for many years, not until around 1970. For some time, we hadn't seen much of each other, except in one of his nightclubs.

On February 15, the first issue of *La Quinzaine littéraire* came out, with the aid of numerous shareholders, of which I was one. I didn't have any reason to hold a deep grudge against Nadeau who was just playing his role, a thousand notches below Breton, yes. But I was forced to roam around all the floors of this world of letters, which I was now a part of. So it was that, up until his death, I was closely associated with Pascal Pia.

The times were now leaning greatly towards the erotic, something that I had never wanted to exploit in terms of literature. But public demand was growing. I was going to see this in July with the astonishing success of *Ma mère*.

And in the same way, public demand grew in April 1966, with the publication of the first issue of *Plexus*, from the Planète group. *Plexus* was published in the *Planète* format, and was openly designed to appeal to the erotic sensibility of the times.

Owning a second imprint, even if it meant more management problems, did make things a little easier. I now had the possibility of selling "products" which it would have bothered me to publish under my own JJP imprint.

In January we published *L' Érotique de l'art* by Lo Duca the same way we did *La Jeune Parque*, in a luxury edition with lots of illustrations and bound in plain leather, a work that I had strong reservations about but which was part of the *Bibliothèque d'Érotologie*. We agreed immediately to go along with

Plexus, publishing through the company Planète in order to take advantage of publicity with them and to promote the sales of *L'Érotique de l'art* through the mail with help from Palimugre (causing a few problems with the bookseller's union). Enormous success.

We were soon going to bring out, in the style of La Jeune Parque also, an astonishing work that I would have gladly published through JJP, if it had not been so lavishly illustrated, and with such an abundance of real leather for the binding. In fact, its presentation had been conceived as part of a collection, along with *L'Érotique de l'art*: Dr. Gérard Zwang's *Le Sexe de la femme*. I would have been delighted to publish this new work through JJP, which placed the projector squarely on a subject, which had been bizarrely taboo for centuries, even anatomically, or medically speaking, as Dr. Zwang pointed out brilliantly.

In the manner of La Jeune Parque, I also published Boris Vian's minor works, such as *Trouble dans les Andains*, or *En avant la zizique*. Elsewhere, the major works by Vian made their way, but in paperback, with 10/18. At the head of the list *L'Écume des jours*, with about a hundred thousand copies printed every year. We also published in 1966 the special *Bizarre* 39-40 issue, edited by Noël Arnaud. A great success.

Paperbacks were taking off. Our successful books regularly appeared now in 10/18 editions or in Livre de Poche from Hachette. I couldn't help regretting a little, like a fateful inevitability, that readers who had bought the paperback editions of Roussel or Hardellet, or even Breton (the *Manifestes* were now in the collection called *Idées* at from Gallimard, and the *Anthologie de l'humour noir* was with Poche Hachette) would never know the books as they had originally appeared in bookstores.

What was also disappearing was curiosity. I saw that with Breton, whose reprints did not sell well. I had told myself that when *Manifestes* came out in the *Idées* collection it would bring more readers, especially since the *Idées* collection edition was not complete. But no; its publication did not affect the other titles at all. There were no more additional sales of the admirable *Clé des champs*.

How could one struggle against this? Gracq's idea had been to obstinately refuse to publish anything as a paperback. The only exception he made was for *Littérature à l'estomac*, which he had given to our collection called *Libertés*. Was it possible to say no to "mass culture"? I had given in to the idea. Forty years later, I am still not sure that I was right. But there were authors dying with the desire to have a bigger audience. And how else could that be done, other than by following the general movement?

Besides, that autumn there was a television special on Channel 2, called "The Paperback Library," with Michel Polac, who had just joined Desgraupes and Dumayet's excellent program, "Books for Everyone." It was on the second of the two television channels. Television was reaching into French homes.

The Death Of André Breton

André Breton fell ill during the summer of 1966 at his home in Saint-Cirq-la-Popie, in the Lot region. His condition worsened very fast. Radovan Ivsic was in the ambulance with him – I hope he writes about this one day – and helped his wife Élisa get him to Paris, before taking him to the hospital Lariboisière. Breton died the next day, on September 28.

One day, perhaps, I will be able to express all the ideas I've been mulling over ever since. Perhaps not. What I do know is that it was a terrible shock. I went over to rue Fontaine; Élisa let me in. I saw behind her, seated, head lowered, the young people from the group. My throat tightened. Incapable of saying even one word, I left.

In my diary of September–October 1966, there was is only one note: "André Breton, Batignolles cemetery, 10:45." Was I there? I just can't remember. André Breton was buried next to Benjamin Péret, whose tombstone was engraved with the words, "I don't eat this kind of bread." The tombstone of Breton, engraved in the same manner, read, "I seek the gold of time."

Breton's death was a signal. A death as important as this one could only mean a change of epic proportions. It was only vaguely that I realized this.

Politics And Censorship

I have found a note in my schedule book that mentions a lunch which, sadly, I cannot remember precisely. Surely, it must have been lovely, because I was dining with Béatriz de Moura, on October 7, 1966. Very young at the time, and already charming, she would become the finest publisher of Spanish language editions of our time (along with her companion Antonio Lopez Lamadrid). She was going around Europe at the time (Franco was still in power and would be until 1975), and had come from Barcelona in order to find the best publishing houses, or at least the most audacious. She would soon create the excellent and subversive Tusquets publishing company.

The year 1966 was a year of preparation for an event that I would qualify, without hesitation, as extremely important for French society. It went by unnoticed, except when it was officially recognized in January 1967. And then it was mentioned very little and in a misleading way.

During 1966, Georges Pompidou, then Prime Minister under De Gaulle, had indicated, off and on, his intention to modify the famous law of 1949, which had been changed several times to make it worse. Pompidou, almost alone among the parliamentarians, understood its absurdity and injustice. He began by obtaining from the Council of State an amnesty for those publishers who had been convicted. I thus got my civil rights back (I hesitated for a while before exercising my right to vote).

Following this, he was present at a dinner (in May, I think) with a small circle at Christian Bourgois' home (at the time, the husband of Jacqueline Guitaut). Pompidou and his wife Claude were there, Christian and his wife, and Christiane and I. Perhaps there were one or two other people; I don't remember.

Pompidou explained his project to us. He showed us that he understood the entire situation, down to the smallest detail. He simply wanted to get rid of the law of 1949. I told him my doubts about it, that his project would never pass because he would be hounded not only by the far Left, the communists above all, but also by a good part of the Gaullists. Nonetheless, he stood his ground.

His theory was simple: monitor images, and leave writing totally free. Images were not a problem for Christian and me; if he obtained a reasonable improvement in the laws concerning writing, that would really be something.

Pompidou was genuinely optimistic; I, a little less so. But it was a lovely dinner.

I was too busy at the time to follow things as they happened; they escaped me in great part.

The Swiss publishers, for example, came to Paris, as well as sometimes loud and boisterous boards of directors. They arrived right after André Breton died, which I have just mentioned, though not enough. His death was almost never out of my mind.

In November, we brought out the third novel by Albertine Sarrazin, *La Traversière*, scheduled for September, but which Albertine had dragged her feet about, in spite of help from Castelnau. In December, Régine opened a bookstore in Avoriaz (where I had an apartment).

On December 1, another revolution took place. The Neuwirth law was adopted, authorizing the sale and advertisement of contraceptives (still with a prescription, I think) as the Parliament booed and hissed. Traditional mores in France were already cracking, and now they had been shattered. A fully charged current spread throughout France, for good or for bad, which allowed for strong permissiveness, with profound consequences, which were not yet perceptible by everyone.

This event took us quickly to January 1967.

On January 4 the Pompidou law passed.

As I had foreseen, Georges Pompidou could not totally suppress the law of 1949. The new provisions, nonetheless, brought considerable advantages for publishers. For example, one very important provision meant that various administrations now had only one year after the publication of a book to ban it. I remind the reader that since 1949 books could be forbidden (or at least their advertising and posting) at the sole discretion of the administration, whereas they could have appeared without problem up until the Thirties, and even before.

A few days later, a young woman, whose name I forget, a spokesperson for the lawyer Georges Kiejman, published in *Le Monde* an article entitled (I'm quoting from memory): THE POMPIDOU GOVERNMENT WORSENS CENSORSHIP. Blindly (recently participating in a television program with Georges Kiejman, I was able to check that, for example, he did not know the precise implications of the March 1994 statute), or else in bad faith, the Left was always wrong or misleading on this score.

I insist on emphasizing this fact: Pompidou, Prime Minister under De Gaulle when he proposed the initiative, WAS THE ONLY POLITICIAN WHO INTERVENED IN FAVOR OF FREEDOM OF EXPRESSION FROM 1945 TO 2004.

Robert Badinter, who was Justice Minister under Mitterrand for several years, never dared to deal with these repressive laws. He even let pass (although he protested a little, it seems) the new penal code of March 1994, which was even more absurdly repressive. I bring this up with him on a television program. Very much at ease, he smiled without responding.

Christian Bourgois remembers that, during the Mitterrand years, he tried several times to talk to Robert Badinter and Georges Kiejman about modifying the law, but without success; it was clearly not part of their demagogic preoccupations.

An Incident:
Georges Bataille And I Confront The Courts

At the beginning of July 1967, there was an amusing interval, representative of French inconsistency. I was, as I have said, distributed by the
Hachette Company. My 1967 publishing agenda included two volumes by
Georges Bataille, *Le Mort* and *Histoire de l'œil*. I announced these two books to
the salesmen, and they were very alert to possibilities, given the success of *Ma
mère* the previous year. Perhaps I wasn't precise about the exact nature of the
texts, but after *Ma mère,* they knew that these texts were not Harlequin stuff.
Some readers today know what that's about. And besides, the salesmen were
there to sell books, for their satisfaction and ours.

We had even taken precautions: each volume was packaged in a box, rather
simply, admittedly, but elegantly. The design was done by Pierre Faucheux. *Le
Mort* was in a black hardback cover, which was appropriate, and *Histoire de l'œil*
in a pink cover, and why not? We printed (I was thinking big) ten thousand
copies for *l'œil* and six thousand for *Le Mort*. Both of them with the name Georges
Bataille as author; nothing prevented this now, since he had died in 1962.

Well, I must say that Hachette undertook a heavy distribution of these
books, with no problems. The texts were sent out to the four corners of France
and other French-speaking countries.

A few days later, the head director of sales for this estimable distribution
company, the much-missed Perset, called me urgently on the phone. I gladly
took the call.

I can still hear his strangled voice: "But have you read these books? Really
READ THEM?" I asked him nicely what he was talking about (knowing perfectly
well): "About these... these two volumes which... You know very well." I had
a difficult time getting him to tell me that he was talking about Bataille's two
books, which he never named. "Have you read them?" He kept coming back
to this question over and over again.

Finally, duly informed, I took great pleasure in answering him. Yes, of
course I had read the books, a long time ago, and even several times. And I

was absolutely of his opinion (although he had not yet expressed his opinion). Nothing so obscene, so shocking had ever been officially offered to French bookstores and by a firm as respectable as Hachette, as these twin bombshells.

He finally formulated an opinion: the texts had to be recalled, as soon as possible. I proffered the opposite opinion: isn't it too late? And on what pretext? Are the two books banned? No? Well then... there he was caught short. "But I don't know," he said, miserably, "I don't know – You see very well..." he said. And I wished him a good vacation.

There is justice (if one can call it that): nothing happened. The two books were simply forbidden from being sold to minors, and I thought that was fair, and it didn't bother anyone. Sales were good.

This was the period during which the judge from the seventeenth chamber crushed poor Losfeld by telling him to proceed in the same way as I was doing, remember?

Couldn't he do like M. Pauvert, who published books by Georges Bataille, "which honored the French language"?

But had the judge read READ them? In the end, everything rests on that. It's not certain. Or else...

One more little anecdote: a few days later I received a sad, strict phone call from Claude Tchou who had read the two volumes and who was worried about his daughter (ten or twelve?). Didn't I feel some responsibility with the idea that she might read them and then...? What might happen? Had I thought about that?

Yes, I'd thought about that. I also had a daughter of twelve and from whom I hid as much as possible these horrible books that I put on sale. Sadly, I couldn't hide from her all the daily newspapers. And a little while earlier, my daughter had been badly traumatized by a news item generously commented on in the press, with photos and precise details. A doctor from Versailles, aged about sixty, whose wife had divorced him, had an only daughter he brought up in a very dignified way, according to the neighbors. He was a model father. When she was fourteen or fifteen, he one day killed her and then killed himself.

Where had my daughter read this news item? It was after weeks of nightmares and waking up in tears for no reason, supposedly, that she finally admitted she had read the account and it had haunted her. Above all, the photo of the doctor father, so gentle, so dignified, with white hair. It took her a long time to forget it, if she ever did.

I explained succinctly to Claude Tchou that it was much more valuable to better prepare children for this type of inevitable shock, and better to talk about it, rather than avoid the subject at any price, leaving their education up to the minister of the interior and the book police. One could always try to instill in children the difference between the imagination in books and the reality found in news items.

I don't think I convinced Claude Tchou. This distinguished pornographer had principles, apparently. But which ones, precisely? I'm still asking myself. There is certainly a wide variety of pornographers.

The Frankfurt Book Fair, *Chapter II*

JP Publications had changed, and the Frankfurt Book Fair as well. There were not many "halls" to accommodate the thousands of international publishers who had followed the hundreds in the beginning. There were now telephone personnel who spoke English and some French. The parking lots covered dozens and dozens of square miles.

I was staying at the Schlosshotel, where my room was reserved from one year to the next, in the village of Kronberg-Taunus, a "typical" German town, with pretty ancient houses, in the area lying just outside of Frankfurt. Jean Castelli, now general director of our limited liability company, who was responsible, among other things, for foreign copyrights, also spent the entire week in Frankfurt during the book fair. We had a big stand, which attracted a lot of people. One year we put together an enclosed double stand, in which our new publications were exhibited on the outside, held in place with a chain. What a success!

We had memorable dinners in the Schlosshotel, to which we invited foreign publishers, especially the Spanish ones like Beatriz de Moura, who was with Lumen's at that time; or the French, like Christian Bourgois; or the Swiss, like the young Jean-François Gonthier. We spent time with John Calder, the Englishman, and Barney Rosset and Richard Seaver, the Americans. The caviar (still relatively inexpensive in Germany) was served in large tins, which were weighed in front of us when we arrived and when we left.

At night we went to the cabarets. Beatriz de Moura remembers the Europa Club, where the valiant stripteasers from the area went to a lot of trouble to entertain the French customers. We dragged Thierry de Clermont-Tonnerre and Jacques Du Clozel with us one night into a popular cabaret where an employee masturbated with various odd instruments, like the paw of a stuffed bear. She asked our forgiveness because she had nothing better to work with, "nothing like what you have in Paris!" If only she knew!

The Death Of Albertine

In July 1967, Albertine Sarrazin decided to have a second operation. It was a matter of removing an infected kidney. It is not clear why she chose a clinic in Montpellier for her operation, given that Jean-Pierre Castelnau had found for her none other than Doctor Merle d'Aubigné in Paris for her previous ankle operation. Perhaps so as to fit in better in this provincial town, where she had chosen to live. Possibly.

They operated, and one thing followed another: the anesthetist, for one thing, had not examined her, and prescribed rather haphazardly too strong a dose of anesthetic. The surgeon did not keep an eye on things and left very quickly. On July 10, Albertine died on the operating table. In 1970, Julien sued and won. The surgeon was acquitted on appeal. Six years later the Supreme Court condemned him again. These had been grave medical mistakes, especially those of the anesthetist, but the surgeon's error could be proven. In fact, everybody at the clinic was guilty.

Many of the important citizens of the city came to the trial to defend the assassins.

We went to the funeral on July 13, 1967, Castelli, Christiane and myself. Jean-Pierre Castelnau, badly shaken by seeing Albertine in her coffin, was not able to come. For me, it was just the opposite.

An Intense Phase?

L osfeld thought the moment had come to put *Emmanuelle* officially on sale, and then *L'Anti-vierge*.

And, after that, *Nouvelles de L'Érosphère*. Françoise Giroud (her again!) published an extraordinarily hypocritical article in *L'Express*, first and foremost about the bad influence of certain kinds of literature, which seemed to her "pernicious." "The better a book is," she continued, "the more dangerous it is." Then (I'm quoting from Losfeld's *Mémoires* since I don't have the article in front of me), "I just read a very good book by a person I take to be very cultivated. This book is exceptionally well written; the philosophy, of course, is debatable, but what intelligence! I won't tell you the name of the publisher, nor the author. I will simply tell you that the cover is blue."

Displaying *Emmanuelle* was immediately forbidden, as was its advertising, etc., and the same for the other two volumes, as well. There was a silent struggle among the public authorities; the recent relaxation brought about by the Pompidou law was opposed by various committees, by the minister of the interior, by the most reactionary parliamentarians, and by the communists – a picturesque team!

It was a rearguard action. Raymond Abellio, a lucid observer of the currents of feeling in the 20th century, noted in *Sol invictus* (JJP 1980) that the years 1964–1968 could qualify as the "second hinge of the 20th century." (The first hinge, as he saw it, were the years 1929–1935). He continued:

> Here, action and love still remain fundamentally related, but at *another level*. From 1964–1968 the second phase began, with intensity this time, with a heightening of the eroticism that had been developing for a third of the century and which subsisted besides in an adjacent and degraded form, in pornography among the growing masses.

It's utterly remarkable that this current of feeling was also developing throughout the entire western world. *Histoire d'O*, the rights of which I had sold to Barney Rosset at Grove Press, had just been published in New York under the title *The Story of O*, in a competent translation (in spite of the English-speaking people's lack of love vocabulary). The book was wildly successful throughout the States (along with numerous pirated editions). I got on very well with Barney Rosset, a very combative and a very good American publisher whom I saw in Frankfurt, and who did a lot to liberalize American publishing. He soon came to Paris.

The Nouveau Monde amoureux by Charles Fourier had just been released, introduced by Simone Debout, who also gave me, at the same time, a critical edition of the *Théorie des quatre mouvements*.

It was no coincidence that the publication of this fabulous text added to this general "modernizing," as announced by Raymond Abellio in *La Fin de l'ésotérisme*. The work of Charles Fourier is very good, as Breton put it, "the greatest constructive work that has ever been elaborated from constraint-free desire." Its time had come.

All areas of expression were affected by the movement. Cartoonists made more and more audacious drawings. The young Wolinski, who at the end of 1966, had given us an irresistible *Carnet de croquis* (*Bizarre* 42), and who was already a bit tendentious, brought me a little album, *Je ne pense qu'à ça*, which obviously courted a ban because of its joyous obscenity. I did a more or less "non-trade" print run, which made a lot of people happy on New Year's Eve 1967. It would later be published as a paperback in 1972.

And does anyone remember that in February 1967 the first issue of *Monde des livres* was published?

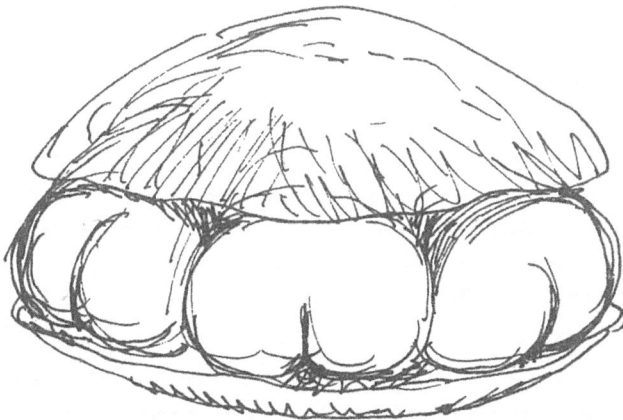

FEMME-BURGER

Régine Deforges felt more and more at ease in the current atmosphere. She appeared to have found her path. I realize now, much more clearly, something I only talked about obliquely before (Régine too, I think): she was destined to brandish sexual freedom like a flag-bearer flying a banner, which entirely masked her secret shyness.

This apparent metamorphosis was going to liberate her, by turning her from a facile conquest into a conqueror, a position that she would never give up. She was also supported by my presence, which began to be visible.

Little by little, I renounced the idea of the role that she might play in regards to me. She was not made to be a woman in the shadows. She was made for a leading role, but only in appearance, only for show. One time, I sent her to negotiate with a devious and tough old Swiss publisher. What a catastrophe! She came back crushed, defeated, and having accepted conditions that I could have imagined only in my worst nightmares. Obviously, it had all been my fault.

She had moved into mail order sales, and in 1967 she published a catalog entitled, without hypocrisy, LA CONQUÊTE DU SEXE, which, I think, we advertised in *Plexus*. That same year, I helped prepare her entry into the world of erotic publishing, starting with *Le Con d'Irène* (under the short title *Irène*) for which I wrote the preface: "One of the four or five most beautiful and poetic texts produced by surrealism now comes out of the closet, forty years after having been published without place, date, name of author, and under a slightly different title." I expressed my frustration: "...I can say that *Irène* is one of those titles which I felt, for a long time, I would one day publish. If in the end I didn't do it, it was because of this unknown author about whom we now need to talk."

I can only say this about this man, who is or is no longer alive: I think I know who he is – but I could be wrong. Up to the present, he has always refused to acknowledge this book, and to give his permission, even secretly, for an official second edition. This is an uncomfortable and absurd position, given that I had a conversation [*in truth, several during 1967*] with this phantom, and during which, as a publisher, I spoke to the author of a book that he had perhaps written. He said "the author" when talking (perhaps) about himself: "The author refuses... the author forbids... It is impossible for the author..." I answered, because the third person is contagious: "However, the publisher would be ready to..." For many things, extreme concessions can be made. There was nothing to be done:

he wanted no one to welcome this rejected child. It should be noted that this position is legally untenable. If a writer has the perfect right, as sometimes happens, after having published a text, to regret it and forbid a re-publication, he cannot at the same time deny having written it and then claim ownership in order to forbid its circulation. So, nothing could stop me from publishing *Irène*. But, a little crazily perhaps, I have felt bound ever since then by this illogical and stubborn refusal.

And I ended this way:

It is good, it is excellent, that a young publisher, for her first book, should place *Irène* in bookstores with no further ado, manifesting in this way various forms of daring. If publishing is a profession that is starting to become boring, this is because there is no fresh blood coming in and because the new generations seem afraid of taking risks of any kind. We must, however, without worrying about anything, try to make with ink and paper the most beautiful and the most surprising things before libraries disappear from our lives and the children of our children forget what a book is.

Since that time, we know more about *Irène* and the magic has disappeared. It was simply a fragment from a large manuscript by Aragon which he says he destroyed – but which he actually kept – *Défense de l'infini*, which today has been published in its entirety. As a whole, the text is extremely disappointing, and in 1927, Pascal Pia excised very cleverly from it the only piece worthy of Aragon, who, at the time, was already beginning to lose his form.

VIII

RUPTURES

Dear imagination, what I love in you is that you never forgive.

— André Breton

Was France Getting Bored?

*I*rène appeared in January 1968 under the imprint L'Or du temps, which had been created for Régine. The book took off. I had forgotten a detail: the cover of the book did not include the name of the author (understandably), and the law was very specific: without the name of the author, a book can could be seized. So, it was seized. All sales were stopped after lawsuits were announced, which gave us time to put out a second edition with the name of the author "Albert de Routisie" (one day I'll explain where I got this bizarre name).

It's rather remarkable that in January 1968, I could write that the publishing world was starting to get boring. Wasn't this about the same time that Pierre Viansson-Ponté wrote in *Le Monde* this phrase, which just a bit later became famous, "France is getting bored"?

I've found the exact date: the article by Viansson-Ponté was printed on March 15, 1968, and its title was, "When France gets bored." I'll quote a couple sentences: "In a smaller France, almost reduced to its European continental possessions, which is not really unhappy, nor really prosperous, at peace with everybody, without much to say about world events, passion and imagination are as necessary as well-being and growth."

There was something like a general waiting going on, though no one really know knew what for. I felt it, too. It was like a desire that this overly smooth Western world would change.

I struggled in my own way. At the beginning of 1968, for example, I managed a little revolution in my *Libertés* series, without really knowing why – away with the brown paper, black spines, and newsprint – we'd seen it all before. *Libertés* was four years old. I had asked Faucheux to come up with a new design, in lively colors. This was the new *Libertés*, which would not be long for this world. Like me, Faucheux also saw it as an attempt to renew the series, nothing more. Besides, he was involved in some ambitious architectural projects for the Shah of Iran (Dubuffet, for his part, created his first houses in 1967).

A bizarre period: "France is getting bored!" No one was very clear about what was rising up around us. In the USSR, the first *samizdats* started in 1966. Around the same time, the Americans got tangled up in the war in Vietnam. Dien Bien Phu was a long way off for us. The Evian accords had rid us – without glory – of the war in Algeria in 1962. Africa was rising up? Let them cope!

Once again, turned back in on itself, France abandoned wars of conquest and tried to move in new directions, with a new analysis of things – which wasn't so bad after all – whether or not the new direction was justified. In November 1966, the Situationists from in the University of Strasbourg published *De la misère en milieu étudiant considérée sous ses aspects économique, politique, psychologique, sexuel notamment, et de quelques moyens pour y remédier*. The formula "Live without wasted time and enjoy without hindrance" caused a scandal. The daily scenery changed: on October 1, 1967, color TV arrived (on channel 2). In November 1967, Guy Debord's *La Sociéte du spectacle* was published, and in 1968 *L'Homme unidimensionnel* by Herbert Marcuse.

So it was that was the color of the coming events was going to be incontestably EROTIC throughout the entire West and into Russia. Berkeley, in the U.S., had its first upheavals, with the war in Vietnam as the backdrop, but there was also sexual liberation. In Nanterre, on March 22, things were heated up confusedly. The Minister of Education at the time was booed when he told students about sex, "If you have sexual problems, just go for a swim."

Sartre himself felt the electricity that filled the air. Later (in *Le Nouvel Observateur*, on March 17, 1980) he presented what he felt, in his cerebral, convoluted manner, which still managed to be divorced from reality:

> In the course of the insurrectional work taking place, a shift has occurred: this was clearly seen in 1968; it was no longer an exit, or birth, which constituted the logic of the events, but a confrontation, a rupture in both the erotic and the social senses given to it by Georges Bataille.

(In my opinion, what was floating in the atmosphere was as far away from Georges Bataille and from his "transgression" as possible. But at least the philosopher must be given credit for vaguely sensing what the movement was all about.)

In April 1968, I think, I had lunch with Henri Flammarion. Student agitation was mounting, but it was still sporadic. The two of us had a peaceful lunch in a good restaurant. Chaos hadn't reached Paris, apart from the Sorbonne or the Beaux-Arts, which were occupied by students and which we visited like curious tourists.

Henri Flammarion told me he wanted to know me better. It seemed to me he had other things in mind, but he spoke very little about them, and just discreetly asked me about the situation of my publishing house.

I remember the thoughts he had about the evolution of publishing. He told me that in 1922 he had personally profited from the enormous success of *La Garçonne*. He bought a house, a diamond for his wife and, I think, a boat. "Today," he confided sadly, "I get a monthly salary from the company, which doesn't go up even if one of our books sells a million copies. We are no longer directly involved in company business. We've become administrators, above all. Publishing has changed." That was obvious.

May Conquests And Then Regressions

I would have had a lot of difficulty explaining what was happening at that time. I still have trouble today, although the events of thirty-five years ago have been researched in their depths by an enormous mass of pseudo-historic exegeses. Never mind. I'll just dive in.

JJP, Brigitte and Jules Rossi

A general strike was decided for May 14. Hachette was occupied. It was impossible to get our books. The banks were closed. The government declared a moratorium. Rossi found us a store which gave us bicycles, indispensable for those like Christiane and myself who lived outside of Paris. In the city, almost without cars, everybody walked or used a bike.

Groups of students went over to Renault to encourage the workers who were striking in the factories. In Flins, for example, numerous happy women students joyously made love to the workers in the fields adjoining the occupied buildings. A lot of the male students viewed these frolics with a disapproving eye.

What's more, tracts from certain universities demanded increased penalties for licentious publications, thus stigmatizing "bourgeois permissiveness."

Around May 25, we published the first issue of *L'Enragé*, founded by Siné, around which almost all the new cartoonists rallied: Gébé, Topor, Reiser, Cardon, Bovarini, Lagneau, Cabu, Malsen, and some foreign cartoonists as well... This was a new adventure which left all of us from the rue de Nesle with great memories – without knowing exactly about what.

We paraded in front of the ORTF public television and radio HQ. Our sign JEAN-JACQUES PAUVERT PUBLICATIONS had a certain success. Régine was in the crowd and could not stand seeing Christiane at the head of our little group. She wrote me a furious letter and took revenge by sleeping with a young publisher who was strongly involved politically (extreme Leftist, Marxist, orthodox – !? – thus, strongly opposed to *L'Enragé*). He fell madly in love with her, and she had a hard time getting rid of him in spite of (or because of) the "sexual decrepitude" of her lover, as she described him to me in a great rage. I thought it served her right, but I couldn't say so, of course.

As soon as when the first movements in the streets started, Siné joined the newspaper *Action*, the fiery rag owned by Jean Schalit. As early as May 19, he was no longer one of the contributors. In the sort of diary that he was keeping at that time for his future wife, Catherine, through letters he sent her in Rio, he noted on May 20:

"Monday morning, 10 a.m. Shit, I'm not even awake. Friends called me at 5 this morning – without news – they've put out the paper by themselves! They rejected three of my cartoons: I'm furious! They claimed that the workers would not have understood and that for them the CGT[17] is still what is best for them. Shit, it still goes on, the censorship is still happening...

Monday, 2 pm. I just went to the printers to check out the damage. Had lunch with the "owners." It was painful! Of course I like them a lot, especially Schalit, but they refuse to acknowledge their

17   CGT – Confédération générale du travail, the main French Labor organization. – Editor's note.

weaknesses. They are overwhelmed and don't think it's useful, right now, to attack the P.C.[18] Their notorious "strategy…"

Ten days pass and it's Thursday, May 30.

> I abandoned this letter on Monday, May 20 – ten days! Incredible, impossible to tell you unless I did it in person. I don't know if I told you about my projects and essays drafts for a new "Siné-massacre?"… well, it's done, it's out, 10,000 copies already sold and the second one comes out tomorrow. What a job! No end! I found a great title: "L'ENRAGÉ." […] It's wonderful! Of course, I put in my cartoons that had been refused by *Action*, the assholes! I asked Wolinski to work with me. […] Like always, it's Jean-Jacques Pauvert who is paying for it and who is publishing it. I didn't want to be the editor in name, but I am in reality. The first edition is smoking hot, the second one will be even better! It's enough to blow up all of Paris – publishing in secret print-shops and everything… threats, cops, Stalinists, etc. […] Friends have done the drawings: Topor, Malsen, Cabu, Gébé, Miot, Cardon and I included a poem by Jacques (Prévert)…
>
> (Siné *La Chienlit c'est moi*, Balland, 1978)

I was both publisher (which it said on the cover) and the editor, responsible to the authorities. The second issue after the Siné was with Wolinski. All day long at rue de Nesle there was a joyous work atmosphere among the whole team. We went out in the streets and sold *L'Enragé* ourselves.

One of the issues sold more than a hundred thousand copies. The historians of May '68 don't talk about it, but *L'Enragé* had a notable influence on events. No other publication was as ferocious or benefitted so much from this kind of talent.

Siné, in order to avoid going home (the police asked his concierge twice a day if they could talk to him), slept a couple times in the Nesle print shop, which had not been occupied. We piled up issues of *L'Enragé* in there, and we stored issues of *L'Archibras*, which had frightened Losfeld and which his editors had brought us. The police never tried to get in.

Since we had no money, we lived on the sale of the newspaper that we shared in order to eat.

An enormous crowd circulated around rue de Nesle. Our office might have been compared to a joyous beehive, if every minute had been devoted to work. It wasn't. Along with the cartoonists for *L'Enragé* there were their friends, and

18 P.C. – Shortened form of P.C.F., the Parti communiste français. – Editor's note.

above all, female friends. Flirting (let's be polite) was going on all over the place. In one corner there was a huge rifle, protected by a sign, which was even bigger: "Watch out! Loaded Rifle! It belongs to Siné!"

Reactionary newspapers asked: where's the money coming from? Yes, where could it have come from? We anxiously scrutinized the horizon, in vain.

Yes, there were threats. One night we guarded our printer, Louis Rossi's, place. But strangely, in spite of the menacing phone calls, and the address of rue de Nesle that was printed on *L'Enragé*, I wasn't very worried at the time. I was summoned a couple times, I think, by Commissioner Broussard. They were courteous conversations, discussions about principles, the usual kind: all the same, you're going too far, you may get into trouble... Be careful... I prefer to warn you... It wasn't clear what I supposed to be careful about.

Soon, I would know.

Cuba Sí

Nothing is more instructive about the mindset of people, I think, than their attitudes about the period in which they live. One shouldn't focus too much on their thinking about fateful circumstances, which everybody at one time or another is trapped in. For example, Cuba and Che Guevara, which a lot of people thought about for quite a while in 1968.

With the appearance of Fidel Castro in 1959, the situation, seen from the outside, appeared confused in Cuba. We only knew that the new regime was more and more supported by the USSR. Starting in 1967, at the same time that Castro's power hardened, a vast propaganda movement was aimed at Europe. From the 4th to the 12th of January 1968, an event was organized in Cuba: "The Havana Cultural Congress." Like many "Leftist intellectuals" (I wasn't really, but how to place myself otherwise?), I was invited. I had misgivings about the adopted resolution, published as early as October 1967 in *Opus International*:

> If one wants living culture, beyond accumulated knowledge, to manifest itself as a necessity, as generalized and as fundamental as being able to lead a free life, intellectuals from developed countries, as well as under-developed countries, must join with all revolutionaries who take up arms in revolt.

Blindly join with *all* revolutionaries in under-developed countries? No way was this acceptable; many of them seemed impregnated with a childish and doctrinaire Marxism, as dangerous and backwards as the twisted maneuvers of the CIA. I was still waiting to see about Cuba.

Anyway, it was impossible to go to Havana in January 1968. However, I did send a message of sympathy to the Cuban representative in Paris, M. Baudilio Castellanos Garcia. From afar, Cuba, for the moment, seemed able to offer some hope.

A second trip was organized for June 1968. But rumors were already spreading about the excessive personal power of Fidel Castro; a repressive police force had been put in place, with censorship, rigorous control of private behavior (homosexuals were banned…), excessive planning for the harvesting of sugar cane… I was waiting to see… What was happening in France seemed more interesting.

It was ultimately chaos, an anarchic upheaval, as the General said. And in every way, the great hope (for what, really?) we were carrying with us fell like a soufflé.

Everything came apart very quickly. There were the Grenelle accords starting on May 17th, the victory of the CGT, which had paraded bellicosely with a certain number of chance allies. And the group *Tel Quel*, led by Philippe Sollers who had organized a rearguard action to which he would now consecrate the rest of his existence. (Already in 1966, *Tel Quel* was for the "cultural revolution" in China; and he would stubbornly hold to that view until 1972–73 – with twenty million dead in the end.) As Bernard Brillant says (in his well-documented book *Les Clercs de 68*, PUF, 2003):

> Confusedly, the team of *Tel Quel* continues to multiply its dec-larations and its acts of allegiance in the spring of 1968 to a party, whose revolutionary function is now contested on its left by a fraction of the youth movement and the intelligentsia. The confusion stems from a lack of knowledge about the political field and the orthodoxy of the communists. *Tel Quel*, well anchored in the literary rear-guard, in the "trendy structuralist movement" [*another howler*], appears to be completely out of step in relationship to the political feelings of the youth movement of May–June 1968.

In 1993, Philippe Sollers, still anachronistic and decidedly unlucky, attempt-ing to play up to Guy Debord, who always refused to meet with him, was to be snubbed by Debord again in *La Mauvaise Réputation* (Gallimard, 1993): "In *L'Humanité*, Nov. 5, 1992, a disgusting newspaper, as full of blood and lies as the accounts of Doctor Garetta, there was even some praise accorded me [Debord], but this was insignificant because it was signed Philippe Sollers."

Union members chased down the streets anyone selling *L'Enragé*. We pub-lished a series of collections: the *Bibliothèque Enragée*, little tracts (*La Crise de l'ORTF*,[19] *Les Citations de la revolution de mai…*) on a shoestring. Hachette took up once again, more or less (more less than more), the distribution of our books.

---

19   ORTF – The Office de Radiodiffusion-Télévision Française, the national agency which, between 1964 and 1974, provided public radio and television in France. – Editor's note.

Enthusiasm fell by the end of the year. Everything returned to normal.

It was the vacation period, and most of the students returned home and forgot about the exaultation after all the danger, and thus the profound meaning of the movement got lost in old political theories. The elections on June 23 and 30 saw the triumph of the Gaullists, who got three hundred and fifty-eight seats out of four hundred and ninety-five in the General Assembly. Dissent drowned in doctrinal utopias. No one was dreaming any longer. In Czechoslovakia, during the night of August 20 and 21, three hundred thousand Russian soldiers put an end to the "Prague Spring." The communist myth had come to an end, except in little intellectual groups like *Tel Quel*, which would be behind the times for another fifty years, at least.

Fidel Casto was simply the current fashionable dictator – like all dictators in the beginning. Che Guevara was nothing more than a beautiful photo for poster collections (the poster vogue was at its highest).

It was the end of May 68. Repression by Raymond Marcellin, the new Minister of the Interior, would be hard.

What Was May '68?

What exactly happened in May '68? Luckily, there are still some traces. I have just found an issue of *L'Archibras*, which had so terrorized Losfeld, and everything comes into focus again. I couldn't describe more accurately what was in the air at that moment than by simply quoting at length a lead article from *L'Archibras* n°4, a "special edition" of sixteen octavo pages.

The article was titled LES AVENTURISQUES in response to the violent attack against the "troublemakers," or the "adventurers." The allusion at the beginning refers to an enormous march that was held on May 30 and 31 on the Champs-Elysées in support of the regime:

> May 30, 1968, all the old people, from 70 to 18, held hands, and it wasn't only ridiculous, as prophesied, but terrifying, with thousands of convents, military bases and prisons on the march, harboring in their limited respectability the violent scandal of a world of segregation, of "every man-for-himself" cunning and cowardice. This was the imbecilic response, fearful and peaceful, so they say, of a society which had just received the greatest slap in the face ever seen in these plast few years: that of a child slapping a sleeping father after he has had too much good food and wine.
>
> BEFORE IT'S TOO LATE, thousands of young people have left a world, slamming the door behind them, lighting the greatest number of fires possible, in order to answer at last to the merciless insults made to spontaneity, to the unique character of each individual, following the well-known saying, "strike while the iron is hot." You have forgotten, Sirs, the incandescence of red-hot fire in your great hurry to plunge the iron into the glacial waters of passing time, into the world as it is. So don't be surprised by the violence that happened recently, and don't be surprised by the apparent gap between cause and effect. The explosion of certain looks, the color of certain nights, have escaped you and will always escape you. It is

this fringe of indetermination in every daily life, that the necessary violence found its energy; it is thanks to this power of refusal which responds to all your interdictions that the force has been found to write the truth on the new pages of the streets, if it was only for an instant. In May, do as you will; a trail of gunpowder, which you have called in your worn-out vocabulary craziness, frenzy, delirium, will set fire to the anonymous masses. And the masses are coming alive, destroying, individual by individual, the myth of abstract inertia. Your guard-dogs, sociologists, psychiatrists, professors, politicians (while you unleash specialized hounds in a sinister hunt for adolescents), wonder feverishly about the difference in age and of class of those who take to the street: the greasers, the workers, the students, the outrageously made-up girls who come from the outskirts of the city, with around their waists chains that have nothing to do with security barriers, are all responding to an UNCONTROLLABLE (since the word is quite reasonably topical) URGE TO LIVE, with all the risks that that implies, with the extreme violence of a desire that has been muzzled by fifty million extremely French Frenchmen side-by-side, paralyzed by all their those hands joined in prayer, and then finally, skillfully repressed by pseudo-socialistic morals belonging to the same family.

The wind escaped from weekend meteorological speculation to serve as an immense collective breath of fresh air. I am not talking about a laughable, scout-like fraternization, which is always ready to do something for others, nor of the kind of humanistic solidarity that comes from base human fear. All this is absolutely not about being demonstrative, but instead about inviting people to live. For the first time in a long time in the streets, people were beautiful because they were passionate. There was talk of political organizations breaking their banks, because for the first time, people were not talking reason but passion. The poverty of the human relationships, which provide you with your pathetic security, was suddenly revealed.

A rumor got around that anything was possible, because thousands of human beings were no longer separated from each other, but most of all because the individual was no longer separated from himself. The ebbing and flowing of spontaneity, in a passionate game of the utmost seriousness, with the freest kind of humor at the risk of death, meant the repressive forces left everybody. The irrational escaped from its game reserves with poetry, painting, art... stripped by collective spontaneity of its rigorous disguise, as recognized by you here and there, from time to time, and without risk, as genius, then reduced to nothing the usually tariffed distance between the signified and the signifier, and sabotaged bourgeois individualism's network of counter-intelligence.

But the game isn't over yet, dear Sirs, nothing has been lost and all is to be created.

We have our supplies of dreams.

We are armed with our discoveries.

Desire is the only thing that doesn't die.

I looked for the author of this extremely lucid text; I found him. We will talk about this shortly. The author was one of the sharpest spirits of the time, in the flower of youth.

Nothing like the pitiful extrapolations made by student politicians.

The Public Usefulness Of JJP

Political threats hovered over JJP Publications on all sides, along with an already disastrous economic situation. The moratorium decreed by the government finished at the end of June. The banks once again functioned normally, which added to our troubles.

We were practically in a state of bankruptcy. We were very conscious that this could not last. What was going to happen?

The huge cloud that burst above us came from a place we were not expecting.

One could say that all of Europe had its eyes fixed on France, especially on Paris. Many countries thought that the capital was burning. The Swiss, especially, went crazy. What was going to happen to their investment in JJP Publications, which decidedly was not lined up on the side of order?

I never clearly knew by what circuitous routes our Swiss printers were put in touch with the Presses de la Cité, which we had already left. Which lawyer gave them this wild advice: there is a law which protects publicly useful businesses in economic peril, and a publisher as big as Jean-Jacques Pauvert would be just the kind to benefit from it.

Without telling us, the lawyer sent a request concerning our situation to the court of commerce. We learned this from telephone calls made to us by journalists. *Paris-Presse* ran this headline: IS PAUVERT PUBLICLY USEFUL?

The tribunal made its decision in a few days; it summoned me, put me in receivership, and named a trustee.

Apparently, I was not publicly useful.

The Butterfly Case

Aparenthesis. I was going to forget. We also had waiting in our pile of manuscripts a fat text sent in by someone named Henri Charrière, who had recently arrived from Caracas. Jean-Pierre Castelnau was greatly taken by the manuscript, and read it into a tape recorder with a certain verve, I must say. They were the memoirs (rather embellished, clearly) of a former escaped convict. The title: *Papillon*.

Like Christiane and Castelli, I recognized the commercial qualities of the text. But the author, who had already been to visit us, displeased me greatly: a phony tough guy, but naturally obsequious, sprinkling the adventures of "Papillon" with thank-you's to the police force and the authorities, and vain in the extreme. I had a hard time tolerating him the only time we met. He wanted to be published by us because of Albertine Sarrazin. "If a thieving little whore like that can sell a hundred thousand copies for you, I could sell a million," he never stopped claiming.

In fact, with a bit of retouching, the text had all that was needed to please a great many people. It could save us. Even our accounting commissioner (no doubt contacted by Castelnau), who was also working for the weekly *Noir et Blanc*, had talked to the owner of the newspaper, *Valdeyron*, about it. But he finally took fright (why?).

Everybody was in agreement. *Papillon* would be a huge success. But I definitely did not want to be the publisher of it. With Castelnau, we worked out a compromise (a little hypocritically, I must say). He could propose the manuscript to another publisher, on condition that I got a percentage of the sales. We exchanged letters of confirmation.

Then Castelnau asked advice from Jean-François Revel, who, in turn, was very enthusiastic about it and took the manuscript to Robert Laffont, who finally signed the contract, after a few incidents which Revel talks about in his memoirs (*Le Voleur dans la maison vide*, Plon, 1977). What happened next would be out of place here; the main threads are well known. So I deviously made a lot of money from *Papillon* without being the publisher. It isn't fair, I know. But what is fair in the world of publishing?

1968,
And Then What?

It's time to take a breather. The year 1968 lends itself to this, I think. It was one of those passages of time when, accidentally, everything that was more or less unconscious in the perceptible world externalizes itself in events, which affect the mind (although the effect is only "the froth of things," as Valery said). Around that year, the period continued to turn at its own rate, but it had visibly evolved this time, for those who were paying attention.

Next, since this is a memoir, the legal order that stopped me from going forward in the summer of '68 was a significant moment in this story.

What is more, I have now forced myself to retrace (more or less effectively) thirty years of my life. And not only my life. I have also discussed the progression of events in the publishing profession, and the general situation around me.

It was a big, complex job and a source of unexpected juxtapositions and endless discoveries. Up until now, I have not at all been used to this kind of introspection – nor in scrutinizing the actions of others. Important things change when one turns 79. It's worth a moment of rest.

Oh, yes, in '68, it wasn't over for me, far from it. I will now have to retrace my life from '68 to 2004, almost as many years as I have just evoked in this memoir. Three years later, in the middle of the legal and financial storm, I received the Goncourt prize, (the second best ever for the number of copies sold). Four years later I was to be part of the Hachette group. Ten years on, I became independent again, and I invented a – perfect – new way of publishing which was to lead me into more original adventures, while also allowing me to broaden my horizons. I distanced myself little by little.

I was to have more encounters – many of them – and experiences, more and more experiences. I was to continue down all the paths in the world of printing. I was to be part of numerous shake-ups at the heart of the profession which, strangely enough, hardly changed publishing's fundamental structure. This will be the material for a second volume, if all goes well.

In the meantime, we've moved from the 19th to the 21st century. About the 19th century, as Céline says, "I can talk about the 19th century; I saw it end." I recently found in a historical work, a little fact which seemed to me very enlightening: in Paris, the Paris as it appeared to me when I was little, when I visited the city – only rarely – as a cauldron of infernal modernity, the first traffic lights appeared only in 1932. I was six years old. One only has to remember the crowds of 1939, and even those of 1945: workers in caps, office clerks in derbies, then the privileged few, at their garden parties, in their top hats, as in 1910. A lot of deliveries were still being made in vans pulled by horses, up until the Fifties.

The 20th century, well, I was part of it.

I have tried to give a vague idea of this past era, this lost time. Perhaps I haven't succeeded. I have also, perhaps, ignored some events that touched me deeply. Oh well.

What I most regret is not being able to recall more precisely certain men and women who accompanied me through these long years. One has to realize that there were thirty-two or thirty-three collaborators at the busiest times; that represents, with departures and replacements, a good hundred people. I can see some of their faces only very indistinctly, with two exceptions: Gisèle, my secretary for many years, and Brigitte, whom we hired when she graduated from the L'École Estienne. She was very young, but she became in a short period of time a remarkable production head. Jean Castelli helped me find her trail again...

One last remark, for the record: through almost sixty years of good and bad fortune, I managed to save my imprint: JEAN-JACQUES PAUVERT. In 1979, it remained at Hachette as simply PAUVERT (there are a certain number of Pauverts in France, relations or not), which was used, in principle, only for books basically reprinted by Hachette. Since then, I've seen it used when they've published new books that I have had nothing to do with. That's their problem. As for me, from time to time, I issue a work in association with one publisher or another, always using the imprint JEAN-JACQUES PAUVERT AT [the name of a publisher]... I have even published two volumes with the imprint JEAN-JACQUES PAUVERT CHEZ PAUVERT, as an in-joke.

J.J. Pauvert and Mathias

But after I'm gone, the imprint Jean-Jacques Pauvert will not be continued. For better or worse (that is to be decided), I have been the only person to use it. Somehow or other, I managed to create it, and it will disappear with me, remaining only on a few dilapidated books owned by booksellers. It's better like that, it seems to me.

INDEX

Mondor, Henri : 189
Monnier, Adrienne : 114
Monroe, Marilyn : 297
Monsieur X : 132–3
Montandon, Georges : 85
Monteilhet, Hubert : 140
Montherlant, Henri de : 19, 28, 30–1, 52, 60, 93–4, 96, 99
Monzein (Mr) : 88
Morand, Paul : 95
Morgan, Claude : 128
Morihein, Paul : 114, 121, 170
Morion, Pierre : 165
Mose : 271
Mouloudji, Marcel : 137
Moura, Beatriz de : 342, 348
Mousset, Paul : 51–2

Nadeau, Maurice : 97, 114, 147, 149, 307, 338
Nagel : 96
Naville, Pierre : 207
Nerval, Gérard de : 1, 18, 273, 333
Neumann, Erika : 101
Nielsen, Sven : 318
Nietzsche, Friedrich : 194
Nissotti, Arys : 100
Noël, Bernard : 200
Noël-Noël : 100, 115, 200
Nordling, Raoul : 65
Nouveau, Germain : 147

O'Connell, Pierre : 100
Oppenheim, Meret : 230
Oudry, Jean-Baptiste : 62

Pacôme, Maria : 141
Panizza, Oscar : 235, 308
Parinaud, Anne : 146
Parker, Daniel : 113
"Patrick L" : 76, 78
Paulhan, Claire : 26
Paulhan, Jean : 28, 42, 46, 49, 96–7, 113–4, 144, 153, 156–9, 161–2, 164, 167–8, 170–2, 183, 186–9, 192–3, 197, 199, 210, 221, 293

Paulus, Friedrich : 47
Pauvert, Christiane (Sauviat, Christiane) : 135–8, 140–2, 145, 152, 159, 165, 179, 199, 201, 211, 218, 234, 257–9, 263, 311, 342, 349, 370
Pauvert, Corinne, Isabelle, Émilie : 201, 259, 270
Pauvert, Jacques : 10, 36, 75, 88, 93, 98, 101, 119, 121–2, 173, 187, 195, 207, 232, 256, 287, 297, 304, 317, 322
Pauvert, Marcel : 2
Pauvert, Marie-Claude : 56–60, 66–7, 76, 81–3, 99–100, 117, 134, 179
Pauvert, Mathias : 253, 259, 270, 374
Pauvert, Paul : 2
Pauwels, Louis : 283
Péguy, Charles : 52
Péladan, Joséphin : 182
Pelletier, Chantal : 270
Péret, Benjamin : 163
Pérony (Mr) : 192
Perset : 212, 345
Pétain, Philippe : 21, 63, 78
Philipe, Gérard : 138
Philippon, Henri : 185
Pia, Pascal : 148–9
Piatier, Jacqueline : 263, 272, 307, 338, 353
Picasso, Pablo : 13, 27, 127, 278
Picon, Gaétan : 229
Pierrat, Emmanuel : 164
"Pierre X" : 57, 66
Pinter, Harold : 237
Ploquin, Raoul : 100
Polac, Michel : 340
Pompidou, Claude : 342
Pompidou, Georges : 289, 342–4
Poucette : 260
Poulet, Robert : 219, 272
Pozner, Vladimir : 128
Pozzo di Borgo, Olivier : 246
Prassinos, Mario : 135
Prasteau, Jean : 214, 260
Prétat, Jean : 213
Prétat, Rolande : 213, 248
Prévert, Jacques : 213, 219

www.ingramcontent.com/pod-product-compliance
Lightning Source LLC
Chambersburg PA
CBHW031040110426
42740CB00047B/763